The Northern Way:

The words we speak and the visions .... our souls all spring from the roots of a great tree, in the depths of a well which holds all that shapes us still. Those roots are the roots of the Northern way, of the gods that our ancestors held holy and the heroes whose great deeds still show us the way to live with bravery and strength. The task set for us is to find out what we are by finding what we were—the wisdom of ages past, which has been suppressed or stolen by an alien church and ways foreign to our folk. The way of the North teaches bravery, pride, and strength; wholeness of body and soul; and the oneness of humanity, the earth, and the god/esses who shaped and still shape us—the true elders of the human clan. By worshiping Wodan, Frija, Thunar, the Frowe, Fro Ing, and the other gods and goddesses of the North, we bring ourselves closer to the ways of our ancestors and to the rediscovery of our own souls.

The way of the North is a way for all: contrary to the popular stereotype of the "macho" Viking, the Teutonic way is, and has always been, a way of power for both women and men. *Teutonic Religion* shows the true culture of the Germanic folk, in which women were chieftains, heroes, and wise counsellors, and always equal to their men. The path of the North is a path of balance, neither male-centered nor female-centered, but honoring both masculine and feminine in the cosmos and in the realm of humanity. The Teutonic way is one of integration: we who follow it do not set outselves above the earth, but strive to work with the natural world around us, protecting and tending field and forest for the good of all.

In this age of alienation, where the resources of the future are wasted even as the past is forgotten, the Teutonic pathway offers a new might of being—of life springing from the roots of our heritage to heal the present and renew the future. In a world of mediocrity, the god/esses of the North challenge their children to greatness; in a world of weakness, compromise, and corruption, the god/esses of the North challenge their children to strength and honor.

About the Author

Kveldulf Gundarsson was born in New York City in 1967 CE to a family of mixed Scandinavian and British Isles antecedents. He shares his birthday with Alexander the Great. He has known and loved the Teutonic god/esses since reading the large illustrated *Norse Gods and Giants* at the age of six.

Kveldulf is currently working on a doctorate in Ódhinnic studies in Britain. He regularly contributes to *Idunna* (the official newsletter of the Ring of Troth) and to the well-known Ásatrú publication, *Mountain Thunder*. Kveldulf's hobbies are jewelry-making, woodcarving, home brewing, and music. He travels frequently through Scandinavia, Germany, and Britain in his continual quest to reclaim the wisdom of his ancestors.

To Write to the Author

If you wish to contact the author or would like more information about this book, please write to the author in care of Llewellyn Worldwide and we will forward your request. Both the author and publisher appreciate hearing from you and learning of your enjoyment of this book and how it has helped you. Llewellyn Worldwide cannot guarantee that every letter written to the author can be answered, but all will be forwarded. Please write to:

Kveldulf Gundarsson
c/o Llewellyn Worldwide
P.O. Box 64383–260, St. Paul, MN 55164–0383, U.S.A.

Please enclose a self-addressed, stamped envelope for reply, or $1.00 to cover costs.
If overseas, please enclose international reply coupon.

Free Catalog from Llewellyn

For more than 90 years Llewellyn has brought its readers knowledge in the fields of metaphysics and human potential. Learn about the newest books in spiritual guidance, natural healing, astrology, occult philosophy and more. Enjoy book reviews, new age articles, a calendar of events, plus current advertised products and services. To get your free copy of *Llewellyn's New Worlds of Mind & Spirit*, send your name and address to:

Llewellyn's New Worlds of Mind & Spirit
P.O. Box 64383–260, St. Paul, MN 55164–0383, U.S.A.

Llewellyn's Teutonic Magic Series

Teutonic Religion

Folk Beliefs & Practices of the Northern Tradition

Kveldulf Gundarsson

1993
Llewellyn Publications
St. Paul, Minnesota 55164-0383, U.S.A.

FIRST EDITION
First Printing, 1993

Cover painting by Lisanne Lake
Drawings by Gunnora Hallakarva

Library of Congress Cataloging in Publication Data
Gundarsson, Kveldulf, 1967–
   Teutonic religion : folk beliefs & practices of the northern tradition /
Kveldulf Gundarsson
        p. cm. — (Llewellyn's teutonic magic series)
   Includes bibliographical references
        ISBN 0-87542-260-8 : $13.00
   1. Mythology, Germanic.   2. Mythology, Norse   3. Europe, Northern—
Religion.   I. Title.   II. Series.
BL860.G85   1993
293—dc20   92–40589
                                                                          CIP

Llewellyn Publications
A Division of Llewellyn Worldwide, Ltd.
P.O. Box 64383, St. Paul, MN 55164-0383

Llewellyn's Teutonic Magic Series

Teutonic magic is as vast as the northern sky and as deep as the shrouded northern mists.

Many of the most powerful forms of magic in the West were developed to an early perfection by Teutonic magicians: Albertus Magnus, Agrippa, Paracelsus. Some, such as Faustus, were elevated to legends.

Teutonic magic is multifaceted and it has its own innate traditions—those of the ancient Germanic peoples (Anglo-Saxons, Germans, Dutch, Scandinavians). In addition it has incorporated the general Western Tradition, which the Teutonic magicians received from southern Europe in the Middle Ages and proceeded to develop with characteristic scientific zeal.

The world of Teutonic magic is full of truly secret, and some sinister, corners as well. Many of these, like so much else that we believe to be sinister, are thus characterized simply because they are unknown and perhaps also misunderstood. There are whole realms of Teutonic magic that have largely been kept secret until the latter part of this century.

Llewellyn's Teutonic Magic Series is the first to explore this world in a systematic and authoritative way. It will reveal the secrets of German rune magic, the obscure mysteries of Gothic Kabbalah, the magic of Faustus, and the deepest mysteries of the German occult orders such as the Rosicrucians, the Illuminati, the Fraternitas Saturni, and the dreaded FOGC-Lodge.

The path of Teutonic magic is focused on the expansion of consciousness through a will to power and knowledge—the way opened for the Teutonic magician by the Archetype Woden and followed by Faustus and most modern magicians.

Also by Kveldulf Gundarsson:

Teutonic Magic

TABLE OF CONTENTS

Author's Note

Names and Word-Forms

In my previous book, *Teutonic Magic*, I used the Old Norse (ON) names for the god/esses and other wights, and a great deal of Old Norse terminology in general. In this book, I have chosen instead to revive Anglo-Saxon or generically Germanic names and terms, and to use English equivalents wherever possible. However, because of the great body of material existing in Old Norse, and no other language, I have had to retain Old Norse names in some instances. Further, when describing events spoken of in the Old Norse Eddas, I have used the Old Norse forms to avoid confusion for the student. When reading this book, you will need to keep in mind that these are not different names, but rather variant linguistic forms of the same name. Thus:

Deities:

WODAN: Old Norse Ódhinn (often Anglicized to Odin), German Wotan, Anglo-Saxon Woden.

FRIJA: ON Frigg (Anglicized to Frigga), Wagnerian Fricka.

THUNAR: ON Thórr (Thor), German Donar, Donner.

THE FROWE: ON Freyja (Freya), German Frau, Wagnerian Freia.

FRO ING: ON Freyr (Frey) or Ingvi-Freyr

NERTHUS/NJÖRDHR: This is actually the same name in Early Germanic and Old Norse, respectively. I use the form Nerthus for the goddess of the North Sea Germans, the form Njördhr for the god known by the Norse.

BERCHTA: also Perchta in Upper German dialects, where the "b" sound becomes a "p."

Other terms:

walkyrige: ON valkyrja; valkyrie

idis: ON dís (pl. dísir)

godman: ON gódhi; Ring of Troth goodman

godwoman: ON gydhja

harrow: ON hörgr (altar)

ix

Chapter 1

LIFE WITH THE GODS: THE GOAL OF THE WAY

HE GOAL OF RELIGION is to bring the human into a proper relationship with the godly, and by doing this to create a state of harmony between all the realms of being. You who are now beginning to call the gods and goddesses of the North into your lives and into the world around you have already taken the greatest step towards this state of wholeness; you have shown that you are willing to learn a sounder and truer way of living as a partner to the earth and the hidden worlds of spirit around you. May all the gods and goddesses bless and help your works!

The faith of the Germanic peoples is deeply rooted in prehistoric times. Germany and Scandinavia were originally settled by a non-Indo-European people, about whose religion we know very little. Although it has been suggested by some that these folk were matriarchal and/or worshipped a "Great Goddess" above all, there is no evidence for this. The forerunners of the Germanic folk, together with the ancestors of the Celts, Greeks, came across Europe from the area between the Carpathians and the Caucasus—the original Indo-European homeland. Such sparse evidence as we have suggests that the group who were to become the Germanic folk then went up to Scandinavia, mingling with the pre-Indo-

European natives and possibly absorbing some elements of the native religion into their own Indo-European faith. Many centuries later, perhaps driven by the stress of climactic changes or of expanding population, one group of tribes left the area which is now southern Sweden and went south and east, into the steppes of Eastern Europe, while other groups migrated into the area which is now modern Germany (previously ruled by the Celts), expanding south and west until they were temporarily halted by the Roman Empire and the Celts of Gaul. At last, through a long series of diplomatic negotiations and military conquest, Gaul fell to the Franks, Spain to the Visigoths, and Britain to the Angles and Saxons, while the Ostrogothic leader, Theoderic the Great, became Emperor in the West. The Germanic peoples had conquered; but as part of the price of their ascendancy, many of them were forced by political necessity to abandon their native faith and to maintain Roman administrative mechanisms and authority.

The Teutonic way as we know it now was born out of the stormy and turbulent times of these migrations. Although its most traceable roots are those stemming from the original Indo-European religion, it swiftly became something wholly unique, shaped by the harsh weather and mountains of the North, the fierce warrior spirit of the Migration Age, and the troth (unfailing loyalty and honor) to kin and folk without which the Germanic people could never have survived the rigors of their world. It is to regain that strength and that troth that we who follow the way of the North struggle each day; to reclaim the religion that grew from the souls of our ancestors and the heritage in which we can take rightful pride. We have come far from the rocky mountains of Scandanavia and the misty depths of the German forests, but our gods are still with us, hidden in our souls, in our hearts—in the very days of our week—Tiw's Day, Woden's Day, Thunar's Day, Frigg's Day—knowingly or not, we have honored them all our lives.

In the year 1000 of the Common Era[1], the Lawspeaker of Iceland declared an end to the old religion, decreeing that the land should be Christian thereafter. But . . .

> It was not in Wotan's nature to linger on and show signs of old age. He simply disappeared when the times turned against him, and remained invisible . . . working anonymously and indirectly. Archetypes are like riverbeds which dry up when

the water deserts them, but which it can find again at any time
. . . The longer it has flowed in this channel, the more likely it
is that sooner or later the water will return to its own bed . . .
The "German" god is the god of the Germans.[2]

Now that millenium is over, and it is time for the ancient river
to flow again as we stand to greet the gods of our ancestors.

Germanic heathenism is braided from three great strands: the
individual, his/her clan or social grouping, and the god/esses. All
three of these are equally important and equally dependent upon
each other. The path of the North begins at an individual level,
with personal study of the ways of your ancestors and what they
knew about the god/esses with whom they dwelt and worked.
Then, as you begin to take notice of the god/esses and to call upon
them and consider their power in your daily life, they will take
more and more notice of you. At the same time, you will come
closer to all your ancient kinsmen and kinswomen who have gone
before you, whose strength is reborn in your blood, and you will
learn to deal with your living kin and those around you according
to the ancient ways of troth and honor.

The greatest differences between the Teutonic way and that of
mainstream Christian culture stem from the relationship between
human beings and the god/esses. Most people are taught at a
young age that there is a single masculine God who is all-knowing,
all-powerful, and all-benevolent, and to whose will they must submit themselves if they are to find fulfillment. This teaching has
been used over the ages to justify the subjugation of women, the
maintenance of the most extreme sorts of social stratification up to
and including slavery, and the suppression of individual thought.
In contrast to this, the last thing the god/esses of the North expect
from humans is submission—our ancestors found few things more
contemptible than a willing slave! Wodan, Frowe Holda, Fro Ing,
Thunar, and the rest do not lay down commandments for those
who worship them. Instead they issue challenges to show courage
against adversity and strength through difficulty; to stand on your
own as a free man or woman, trusting in your own might and
main; to use the gifts of life, mind, and might which the god/esses
have given to you in order to carve out the path you choose.

Another great difference between Teutonic and Christian
beliefs and attitudes stems from the fact that the Northern folk had

no concept of "sin," only of honor and dishonor. "Original sin"— the idea that you are born with something innately wrong with your soul—is a concept that makes no sense at all in the context of Germanic heathenism, no more than the idea that the individual human is too weak to redeem his/her own honor and must have it done by another. On the one hand, the Northern god/esses do not niggle over the "sin" or "virtue" of petty actions; on the other, they do not offer the chance for dishonor or weakness to be washed away by a single act of grovelling before their majesty—in our tradition, every human being is fully responsible for his/her actions and their consequences, and every act of ill must be paid for in some way.

Mainstream Western/Christian culture is grounded on the Classical Greek belief in a stark separation between the worlds of spirit and of things physical. This has led to the dual concept that humans have and ought to have dominion over the natural world, and that the soul is in some way superior to the body, which is at best no help and at worst a thing of "evil." This separation has led to Western insensitivity to nature and continues to lead towards the destruction of the earth as we exploit and poison her—a thing which our ancestors would not have tolerated. To the peoples of the North, the earth was not only the mother of all, but a demanding goddess on whose kindness they depended for every bite they ate; as an agricultural society, they were able to see the need for honoring her in a way that most modern Americans do not, for one year of bad harvest meant one year of famine. A great deal of the Teutonic faith is based on this awareness of the need to live with the natural world in a balanced fashion—and on the intense love for the free woods and meadows of the world which is still part of modern German and Scandinavian culture, as the passionate writings of the German Romantic period show.

The Western belief in a separation of body and mind/soul has also taught us to be contemptuous of either our own bodies and our physical needs or of our intelligence, to the point where popular American culture hardly admits that the two can go together—our stereotypes are those of the physically strong/attractive but stupid football player or cheerleader, and the physically weak and unattractive "egghead." Our ancestors, in contrast, honored both aspects of the self equally. Nearly all the heroes whom they held highest were great poets as well as being mighty warriors. The boasting verse which the Earl Rognvaldr Kali made about himself in his teenage years expresses the Norse ideal of manhood: "I'm talented at tables [a chesslike game] / at nine skills I'm able / scarcely spoil I runes / I'm often at books and writing / swiftly glide on skis / I shoot and row well enough, / at each of these I'm able: / harp-playing and poem-making.[3]—In other words, Rognvaldr Kali was the equivalent of a high school athlete who was also in the orchestra and the chess club, while writing poetry for the school literary magazine and maintaining a high grade point average. To the Vikings, the most attractive women were those who could meet them as equals in both bravery and intellect, exchanging swift-witted words and poetic staves with their menfolk, risking and bearing wounds and death with the same steadfastness as any male warrior. Individuals who are true to the ancestral ways will develop their bodies, intellects, and artistic faculties to their highest peaks; to leave out one side of being is to be less than a whole human.

While much of modern culture seems to be rooted in the worship of the "norm" and the "average person," a standard which requires entertainment and society to maintain a level of mediocrity that excludes no one, the ways of the Germanic folk offer a continuous challenge of excellence. The average is worthy of nothing; the best is our goal, in every way. We come of a heroic folk; it is our duty to make ourselves worthy of our ancestors and our gods.

Because the Northern ways offer no comfort to the weak—no leaders or prophets whose voices can replace your own conscience; no set laws which you can point to and say, "That's against my religion"; no promise of absolute bliss or dammnation in the afterlife; no free absolution; and no god/esses who claim to be simultaneously all-knowing, all-powerful, and all-benevolent—they do not appeal to the masses who prefer comfort to struggle and certainty to risk. What the ways of the North offer is a guide to honor and troth; to a strength which is not only yours, but that of your entire clan; and to a way of life which harmoniously integrates your own being, your society, the world of nature, and the god/esses. These are your byrnie, shield, and sword in all the struggles of your life, if you have the bravery to take them up and step into the fight.

NOTES

1. Common Era. See Glossary. CE/BCE dates are identical to AD/BC dates, but have no religious connotations.

2. Jung, C. J. *Essays on Contemporary Events*, 20, 22.

3. *Orkneyinga saga*, ch. 58.

Chapter 2

THE SHAPING OF THE WORLDS AND WYRD

N THE FIRST POEM of the *Poetic Edda*, "Völuspá" ("Prophecy of the Völva"), the ancient etin-seeress, recalls her earliest memories of the time "when Ymir lived, when there was neither earth nor heavens over, and no green things anywhere." The *Prose Edda* tells us more of the creation of the first things. First there were the icy Niflheimr ("Mist-World," or Nibel-Home) and the fiery Muspellheimr (Muspell-Home). The venomous rivers which together are called Élivágar sprang from the well Hvergelmir ("Seething Cauldron"), flowing down the side of Nibel-Home where they froze into the layers of a growing glacier. The ice was melted again by the sparks and molten particles that flew from Muspell-Home; and where the rime thawed and dripped, the drops were quickened by the heat and became a manlike figure—Ymir, first of the giants. As the etin Vafthrúdhnir tells Wodan in "Vafthrúdhnismál," "From Élivágar frothed venomdrops / and waxed til there was an etin. / From his *ætt* are all (etins) come / thus are they terrible all" (st. 31). As Ymir slept, he sweated; male and female rime-thurses* came forth from under his arm, and one of his legs fathered a six-headed son on the other.

---

*See glossary.

From the dripping of the ice also came the *ur*-cow ("proto-cow") Audhumbla, on whose milk the ancient rime-thurse fed; but Audhumbla licked the rim of the ice-stones which were salty, and under the licking of her tongue came forth the shape of a man who was fair and mighty, the first of the race of gods. He was named Buri; he got a son named Bor, who married an etin-maid called Bestla, the daughter of the giant Bolthorn. Bolthorn also had a son from whom Wodan learned much wisdom; it is thought that this son, Wodan's uncle, is Mímir, keeper of the Well of Memory, because Mímir acts in the traditional role of mother's-brother to Wodan, teaching him the wisdom of his etin-forebears. It is said that Bor and Bestla had three sons, Wodan, Will, and Wih ("Holiness"); but Will and Holiness are clearly hypostases of Wodan himself, as Snorri Sturluson implies in the *Prose Edda* when he has the Wodanic triplicity "High, Just-as-High, and Third" tell Gylfi: "And that is my troth, that this Wodan and his brothers must be the rulers of heaven and earth; that is our opinion, that *he* should so be called."

Wodan, Will, and Wih slew Ymir; and all the giants were drowned in the icy blood that flowed from his veins except for one called Bergelmir, who escaped with his wife on a raft. Then the gods made the earth out of Ymir's body, and out of his bones and teeth they made rocks; from his hair they made the trees and from the maggots that crawled through his flesh they made the dwarves. They shaped his blood into a ring around the world, which is the sea; they also lifted up his skull and made the dome of the sky from it, setting the four dwarves East, West, North, and South under the four points. The melted particles and sparks from Muspell-Home they set into the sky and appointed courses for. Thus the earth "is ring-shaped around the edge, and around the outer edge lies the deep sea, and they gave the sea-strands to the kin of etins to settle; but on the inner side they made a fortification against the unfrith of the etins, and this they made with the brows of the etin Ymir, and they called that burg the Middle-Garth."[1]

This was the point at which the Nine Worlds reached their final shape, as shown in figures 1 and 2. The first shows the Teutonic cosmos on the horizontal plane. Outside are the four worlds *útangardhs*, "outside the garth"; they are separated from us by the sea, Jormungandr the Middle-Garth's Wyrm, and the spiritual walls of our world. Within is the Middle-Garth, and inside that, in

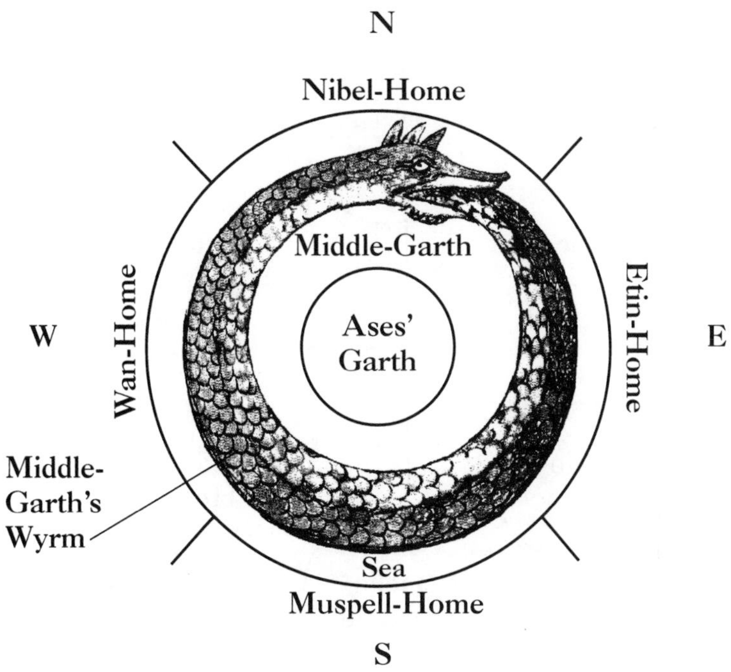

N

Nibel-Home

Figure 1—The horizontal world-pattern

a yet more holy ring, is the garth of the gods—the Ases' Garth (Old Norse *Ásgardhr*). The second drawing (page 10) shows the worlds on the vertical plane. The Ases' Garth is above; Light Alf-Home is in the upper reaches of the Middle-Garth's air. The four elemental worlds, Etin-Home (ON *Jötunheimr*—air), Muspell-Home (fire), Wan-Home (water), and Nibel-Home (ON *Niflheimr*—"World of Misty Darkness"; ice) should be understood to be on the same level as the Middle-Garth. Etin-Home is to the East, Muspell-Home to the South, Wan-Home to the West, and Nibel-Home to the North. Nibel-Home is, however, canted downward and should properly be seen as lying in the level of the Underworld; in some accounts, it is the lowest part of Hella's realm. Swart Alf-Home is in the depths of our earth, and Hella's realm is below. The heavenly god/esses (Ases; ON *Æsir*) dwell in the Ases' Garth, Light Alfs (elves) in Light Alf-Home; etins, rises, and thurses (types of giants; see chapter 6) dwell in Etin-Home; the god/esses of earth and water (Wans; ON *Vanir*) dwell in Wan-Home; Muspell-Home

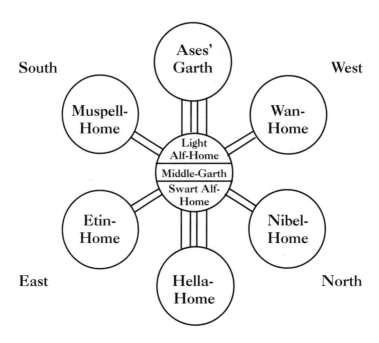

South

West

East

North

Figure 2—The vertical world-pattern

is inhabited by the Muspilli, who may be a sort of fire-giant; the dwarves or Swart Alfs dwell in Swart Alf-Home, and the dead in Hella's realm and Nibel-Home. Eastward in Etin-Home is a forest called the Iron-Wood: there dwell a number of giantesses and troll-wives. One in particular, the Hag of Iron-Wood, is the mother of the two wolves who chase the Sun and her brother the Moon; this thurse-frowe (giant woman) may be Angrboda, the concubine of Loki, who also bore the Wolf Fenrir and the Middle-Garth's Wyrm to him.

The Outgarth, the realm outside the Middle-Garth's bounds, is the realm of wild power—of magic, the supernatural, and the unknown. It is also the world of the dead—Hella's world and Swart Alf-Home, although they are shown below the Middle-Garth upon the straight vertical axis, are thought of as lying outside the garth. The realm within, which encompasses the Ases' Garth, the Middle-Garth, and Light Alf-Home, is the world of things social, stable, and ordered. Most of the time, the purpose of Teutonic religion is to strengthen the garth and to bring the three worlds within it closer to one another—to enhance, not necessarily the artificial (and sometimes arbitrary) laws of an existing society, but the natural laws by which humans, the earth, and the gods and wights work together in kinship and frith (fruitful peace and happiness).

The cosmos is held within the branches and roots of the World-Tree, Yggdrasill—the vertical axis of the universe, which both separates the underworld, the world of humans, and the overworld, and unites them within its structure. The language used to describe this tree in the Eddas is often difficult to understand; the *Prose Edda*, for instance, says that it has one root in Nibel-Home, one in Etin-Home, and one in the heavens, in the Ases' Garth; which presents a certain problem of visualization. What this means, however, is that these three realms—the world below, the middle world, and the world above—are the three sources of might from which the life of the Tree stems, which weave Wyrd together. The Tree is the living embodiment of all that is and is becoming. At its roots, deep in the Well of Wyrd, many serpents gnaw and the dragon Nith-Hewer (ON *Nidh-höggr*) coils. The four harts Dain, Dvalin, Duneyr, and Durathror run in its branches and feed on its bark and leaves. These stags may be the same as the four dwarves Northri, Suthri, Ostri, and Vestri ("North, South, East, and West") who hold up the corners of the world on the horizontal plane; Dáin and Dvalin are dwarf names, and the stag is a fetch-shape taken by dwarves during the day, since they themselves are turned to stone by the light of the sun. At Yggdrasill's crown sits a wise eagle, with the hawk called Vedrfolnir between his eyes, and the squirrel Ratatosk runs up and down the tree to carry insults between the eagle and Nith-Hewer.

The Well of Wyrd, in which the roots of Yggdrasill lie, is divided into three aspects, which encompass the three levels of the vertical plane. First, and eldest, is Hvergelmir ("Seething Cauldron") in which the serpents and the dragon lie. This well, as mentioned before, lies in the underworld, in Nibel-Home: the yeasty rivers of might first sprang forth from it. Second is the well of Mímir, which lies in Etin-Home, guarded by the wise etin Mímir; it is the Well of Memory, which holds the knowledge of all that *is*. Wodan's right eye lies in this well, as does Heimdallr's horn (or hearing; see the section on Heimdallr in chapter 4). Third is the Well of Wyrd (ON *Urdhr*), which lies in the Ases' Garth, and where the god/esses speak their laws and decisions. This triple well, when spoken of as a whole, is also spoken of as the "Well of Wyrd." From the level of Hvergelmir comes the essential force of being; the level of Mímir shapes it according to the *ørlög* (see below) of what *is*; Wyrd is the level at which the Norns cut staves, lay *ørlög*, and decide what *shall be*. All works of great might take place, literally or metaphorically, at the Well of Wyrd.

The Sun and Moon are drawn across the sky in their wains by horses. The Moon's horse is named Rimefax (Ice-Mane), the Sun's is named Shinefax (Shining-Mane); in other Norse sources, the Sun's steeds are called Arváki (Early-Awake) and Alsvith (All-Swift). Both are chased by etins in the form of wolves; the one who follows Sunna is called Skoll, and ahead of the Sun runs the wolf Hati Hrodvitnisson, who follows the Moon. You should know that in all Germanic languages and traditions, the Sun is always female, whereas the Moon is always male; a source which tells you otherwise is likely to be untrustworthy. While the warming and fertilizing light of the Sun may occasionally be personified in a masculine form or associated with a masculine god such as Fro Ing, she herself is always female. This is one of the more difficult things about the Northern tradition for folk raised in a culture that has been shaped by the Greco-Roman images of the sun-god Apollo and the moon-goddess Diana to accept; but this reversal of the Mediterranean tradition must be understood as a firm and unshakable truth of the Germanic cosmos.

The Ases' Garth is sometimes seen as sitting on the top of a mountain, sometimes in the upper branches of Yggdrasill. It can be reached only by crossing over Bifröst, the fiery Rainbow Bridge, which is warded by the god Heimdallr. Many rivers flow about Bifröst and are heated by its flames. The gate of the Ases' Garth is called Walgrind ("Gate of the Slain.") The Ases' Garth is divided into twelve realms, as described in the Eddic poem "Grímnismál." The greatest is Bilskírnir in the land of Thrúdh-Home ("Strength-Home") where Thunar dwells; Yew-Dales, where Wuldor's hall stands; Wal-Seat, a hall of Wodan's; Sunken-Bench or Fen-Hall, Frija's hall where Wodan comes to drink with her; Gladhome, the realm where Walhall stands with spears as its rafters and a shield-shingled roof; Thrymheimr, Skadhi's *udal* (ancestral) hall; Broad-Shining, where Balder dwells; Heaven-Berg, Heimdallr's hall; Folk-Meadow, Freyja's land, where her hall Seat-Roomy is built;

Gleaming, the home of Forseti, which is propped up with gold and shingled with silver; Ship-Stead, Njördhr's dwelling; and Wide-Land, the wooded stead where Vídharr dwells and rides out. Alf-Home, which Fro Ing rules, is also mentioned as part of the holy lands, but it is not numbered among the twelve, being a separate world. These halls are peopled by the ghosts of those humans who were the friends of each of the god/esses in life.

We know more about Walhall, where Wodan's adopted sons the *einherjar* stay, than about any of the other halls. The stag Eik-thyrnir and the goat Heidhrún stand on its roof, eating the leaves of the World-Tree; Eikthyrnir's antlers drip water into Hvergelmir, and Heidhrún's udders provide Wodan's warriors with mead. A *warg* (either a criminal or an actual wolf) hangs before its western gate, and an eagle hovers above it. The cook Andhrímnir boils the boar Sæhrímnir in a cauldron called Eldhrímnir every day; and each day the boar, like the warriors of Walhall, rises alive again. Before Walhall roars the river called Thund; those warriors who have not gained the aid of their *walkyriges* (valkyries, Choosers of the Slain) in passing over Bifröst must force their way through it, and only the strongest of soul can do this.

The horizontal plane of the world is divided by the four cardinal directions and by the *ætt* ("eight" or "family") of the sun-ring (fig. 3, next page). The winds are also divided according to the directional *ætt*, and the worlds can be ringed around the Middle-Garth likewise (fig. 4, p. 15). The winds of woe are those which blow from the northwest, north, northeast, and east; the winds of weal blow from the southeast, south, southwest, and west. However, the north and the east are also the directions of the greatest might. All might flows first from the well Hvergelmir in the north, and the north is where the roots of all being lie. The east, Etin-Home, is the direction from which this might rises up into the worlds; Fro Ing comes from the east in his wain, bearing life, and the east is the direction of the rising Sun. Nearly all rites are carried out either facing north or facing east.

After the gods had shaped and set the worlds, three mighty maids came out of the east, from Etin-Home. These maids are Wyrd (ON *Urdhr*—"that which is"), Werthende (ON *Verdhandi*—"that which is becoming"), and Should (ON *Skuld*—"that which should become"). They are the "weird sisters" of *Macbeth*, the three wise women who tell the warrior his future and that of his line. It

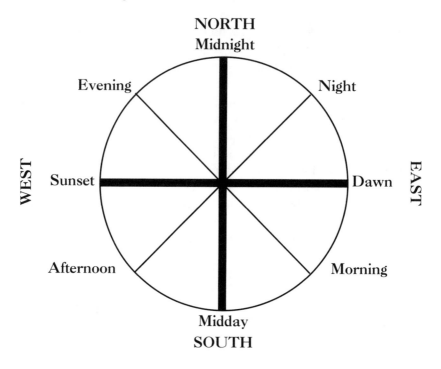

Figure 3—Division of the world by the ætt of the sun-ring

is they who sit at the Well of Wyrd, laying the layers of being which shape the ever-growing tree Yggdrasill; thus they shape what shall become of humans and god/esses alike. The term used in Old Norse to describe this fate is *ørlög*: the *ur*-("proto") law or the "primal layer." This is used because the first layer of being—the first actions, the first words spoken—shape all the following layers which grow out of it and are laid upon it; the first primal pattern is the pattern which names the terms of being, becoming, and ending. This idea appears in a number of legends throughout the Indo-European world; the hero/ine's life and death are described on the day of his/her birth or name-giving, and thereafter all must follow as it has been spoken—as it *should* become. This is the same for the Nine Worlds as for the individual life; all things, however great or small, have their *ørlög* which cannot be escaped, their own personal *wyrd*. *Wyrd* cannot be escaped; it is the act of a *nithling* ("despicable coward") to flee it, but the hero/ine, knowing his/her *wyrd* ahead of time, goes boldly and even joyfully forth to meet it. Wyrd may be written around—events arranged so that what should/must be

Figure 4—The worlds ringed around the Middle-Garth

will, in the due course of time, work out for the best—but it cannot be escaped.

Wyrd, Werthende, and Should are also the embodiments of time in the Germanic world. The Teutonic time-sense is not divided, like the Mediterranean, into a linear past, present and future. Rather, all that has ever become exists now—it *is*—as the living roots and the *ur*-layers which shape the sharp-edged moment of *becoming*, of the present. Without the use of modal verbs (should, will, might), it is impossible to speak of the future in any Germanic language, including English. Unlike Latin, we have no future tense; we see what *is* and what is *becoming*, with only a shadow of that which these *ur*-layers *should* shape.

As with the beginning of the worlds, so with the end; the *ørlög* of the cosmos was laid in ice and fire, and so shall its *wyrd* one day turn towards an end—Ragnarök, "Doom of the Gods."[2] The final battle shall be preceded by the Fimbulwinter—a lightless winter which lasts for three years without spring. During this time, all human social bonds shall be broken as all the order set up by the god/esses at the beginning of the worlds disintegrates. Neither kin nor troth shall hold anyone's hand from murder; the world shall become lawless. Finally the wolf Sköll shall swallow the sun, and the wolf Hati shall swallow the moon. Then all bonds shall break; the Wolf Fenrir shall run free, and Loki be freed from his bonds, and the sea shall rise onto the land because the Middle-Garth Wyrm, no longer confined to holding the boundary between the Middle-Garth and the Outgarth, will rise up and crawl onto the land. The earth will shake everywhere, and the ash Yggdrasill will tremble. The ship Naglfar, made of dead men's nails, will float, bearing a cargo of foul ghosts and steered by Loki; humans will tread the road to Hel. The Muspilli, led by their drighten Surtr, will come forth from Muspell-Home to burn the worlds.

In the last battle, which takes place on the field Vígrídr, Thunar will meet the Middle-Garth Wyrm again; he shall slay it, then stagger back nine paces and die from the venom it sprays. Loki and Heimdallr shall slay one another, as shall Tiw and Garm (the hound which guards the gates of Hel). The Wolf Fenrir shall swallow Wodan; Vídharr shall then set one foot on the Wolf's lower jaw, seize his upper jaw, and tear them asunder, and so shall Wodan be avenged. Then Surtr and Fro Ing shall battle; Fro Ing, armed only with the horn of a stag, shall fall before Surtr's sword and Surtr shall cast fire over the earth and burn everything.

After all has been destroyed, there will be left only the sea. Then a new earth shall be born, green and fair; before Skoll eats the Sun, she shall have given birth to a daughter, and a new Sun shall rise. Wodan's sons Vídharr and Váli shall live through the fire, as shall Thunar's sons Módi and Magni, who shall inherit Thunar's hammer Mjöllnir. Balder and Hödhr shall be loosed from Hel then, and sit in Wodan's seat, and they shall remember all of the *ur*-old lore of the gods; Wodan's brother Hönir shall handle the blood-twigs of the runes. In a shoot of the World-Tree, called "Treasure-Mímir's Holt," a woman named Líf ("Life") and a man named Lífthrasir ("The Stubborn Will to Live") shall hide through the fire, and they shall come forth, and people all the new earth with folk.

Like all true legends, Ragnarök can be understood on many levels. To the *vitki* (magician), it describes the initiatory process of destruction and recreation which the soul must pass through on a cyclic basis, reaching a higher level every time. For everyone, it is a description of the process of death and rebirth, in which mind, might, and life all fall before the forces of destruction and the body is eaten by the greedy flames of cremation; but all of these are reborn in time, as the gods are reborn in their children. As cosmic theology, Ragnarök is an integral part of the Germanic religion, no matter how literally or metaphorically you choose to interpret it. Most of Wodan's works, especially the dark and devious ones, are aimed at staving off Ragnarök while he gathers his might to ensure that a new world can be reborn afterwards. Ragnarök is always a possibility; eventually it must be a certainty, for it is laid in the *ørlög* of the god/esses, but the works of both humans and god/esses can hold it off. This work is worthwhile because, although the ultimate results may be for the better, the possibility of improvement in the next cycle depends on the strength the forces of the god/esses can gather before the final battle takes place. Thus Wodan gathers his *einherjar*, the slain heroes of Walhall, because no one, not even he, knows for sure when the battle will begin: "the gray wolf gapes ever / at the dwellings of the gods."[3] This is his work of writing around *wyrd*; knowing that he must be slain, he fathers Vídharr to avenge him and free his soul from the belly of the Wolf Fenrir; knowing that the world must come to an end, he strives ceaselessly to be sure that the rebirth can take place; and in this he leads both the god/esses and those humans who are true.

NOTES

1. *Snorra Edda*, ch. 6.

2. Sometimes this is called "Götterdämmerung," a phrase which, to English speakers (aided and abetted by the fiery finale of Wagner's opera of the same title), conjures up the same image of cosmic destruction. However, "Götterdämmerung" merely means "Twilight of the Gods," and does not actually refer to an all-encompassing final battle; it is not properly synonymous with Ragnarök, though the two terms are often used interchangeably.

3. "Eiríksmál."

Chapter 3

KNOWING THE
GOD/ESSES

HE FIRST STEP in practicing the ways of the North is to learn about the god/esses of our ancestors. Most of the knowledge which has been preserved is collected in two books: the *Elder* or *Poetic Edda,* and the *Younger* or *Prose Edda.* These are not precisely holy texts in the same way as fundamentalist Christians consider the Bible to be holy; that is to say, they are neither infallible nor "dictated" by the god/esses, although many of the poems in the *Elder Edda* may have been composed during states of high spiritual excitation and vision. There is reason to think that the literary accounts of the god/esses did not always correspond exactly with the worship actually carried out by the folk; for instance, there is very little evidence that an active cult of Baldr ever existed, in spite of the prominent place he plays in the myths.

Nevertheless, the Eddas are our best primary source for understanding the god/esses of the North. The most helpful editions are Anthony Faulkes' translation of Snorri Sturluson's *Prose Edda* and Patricia Terry's translation of the *Poetic Edda.* Lee Hollander's *Poetic Edda* is a good poetic translation, suitable for gaining an understanding of the basic stories; in many places, however, Hollander sacrificed accuracy to poetic effect.

Any of the poems of the *Poetic Edda* may have reached their present form at any time between about 700 CE ("Common Era"—see Glossary) and 1200-1300 CE; many of them deal with materials which may in some form go back to the earliest times of the Germanic peoples, but many also may show signs of Christian influence. Nevertheless, they are generally taken as the most reliable and authentic source for the myths, if not the daily religious practices, of the North.

The *Prose Edda* was written ca. 1220 by a well-educated Christian Icelander named Snorri Sturluson, some 220 years after the official conversion of Iceland to Christianity. Sturluson intended for it to preserve the lore and culture of his nation, if not the old heathen belief. Since the composition of Old Norse skaldic poetry—the poetry of the *skalds*, or bards, of the North—was largely dependent on knowledge of *kennings*—elaborate periphrases for everyday things which were almost wholly based on a thorough understanding of the god/esses and legends of the North—the *Prose Edda* was also meant to be an instructional text for the construction and understanding of skaldic verse. To authenticate the tales he told, Snorri often quoted the poems from the *Poetic Edda*, which were his primary authority, and the poetry of skalds from the ninth century onward. At times, Snorri attempted to synthesize and systematize the mass of chaotic material which he had inherited; in some places, such as his account of the death of the god Baldr, his Christian beliefs may have affected his rendition of the elder tradition. Nevertheless, his Edda explains clearly a great many things which are only mentioned in passing or taken for granted in the *Poetic Edda*; sometimes he has preserved non-Eddic folk tradition, and in a few places he quotes poems which are now lost to us.

The third major literary source for knowledge about the religion and ways of the Scandinavians is the genre of prose literature known as the saga. The Norse sagas were written in Iceland, between (roughly) 1200 CE and 1450 CE. One group—the "family sagas"—deals with the settlement of Iceland and the deeds of the settlers in the first two hundred years; one group—the "kings' sagas"—with the deeds of notable historical kings of Norway, Sweden, and Denmark; and one—the "ancient sagas"—tells the deeds of the great heroes of the distant past. The historical authenticity of all of these is always a matter for scholarly question; some preserve details hundreds of years old with remarkable authenticity, others can be proven to contain misinformation. They do not, by and large, deal much with the god/esses; nevertheless, they show a great deal about the most enduring ideals and beliefs of the Icelanders, particularly concerning matters such as troth and trueness to the clan. Most of the sagas are available in translation through Penguin Classics.

The best way to study any form of spirituality is to work slowly and steadily on a daily basis. This is particularly important in the Teutonic path for two reasons which may seem contradictory at first, but will become clearer with experience. The first is that the Germanic people, as farmers and herders, lived closely tied to the slow and regular rhythm of the seasons. If you think of the understanding of your soul as a field which you are tending as it ripens towards harvest and work on your studies every day, without either neglecting or trying to force too much growth, you will also personally undergo the experience of the natural processes which directly shaped every day of our ancestors' lives. The second reason for maintaining regulated, constant study habits is that the Teutonic god/esses are often prone to bring about swift and sudden changes in the lives and beings of their children. If you have not built yourself a firm and solid basis of understanding and knowledge which daily consideration has worked deep into your soul, these flashes of lightning are as likely to destroy as to transfigure.

Begin by setting aside a short time each day—perhaps no more than 15 or 20 minutes—in which you can study. Using this short time-frame, you ought to be able to read one story from the *Prose Edda*, the corresponding poem from the *Poetic Edda* and the section in this book on the appropriate god/ess (according to the Program of Study laid out in Appendix I), at least within three days. If you are a particularly slow reader or pushed for time, it might be better to do your readings during the day and to save your time for contemplating what you have read. Keep a journal in which you write down whatever ideas and thoughts you have, as well as dreams and other events in which it seems to you that the power of the god/esses is beginning to touch your life.

When you have gotten through all the tales and other readings, you will then have a sound understanding of the god/esses of the North, and you will be ready to start taking a more active part in your relationship with them. By this time, you are likely to have developed a certain feeling of kinship with one deity or another. This is not necessary for continuing your work in the Teutonic pathway—it is conceivable that someone could become a *godman* (priest; ON *godhi*) or *godwoman* (priestess; ON *gydhja*) and function thus all of his/her life without ever becoming attatched to any single god/ess. In my experience, however, it is very rare to find someone who does not feel some sort of preference. The sagas and other accounts of Teutonic religion also bear this out; it was normal for each person to put his/her trust primarily in a single deity while continuing to give worship to all the god/esses. This personal trust often seems to have been more meaningful than the attributes generally associated with a god/ess; in *Heidhreks saga*, for instance, the hero sacrifices to his patron Ódhinn (Wodan) to end a famine in the land, although Freyr (Fro Ing) and Thórr (Thunar) were more often considered gods of fertility among the Norse.

Your relationship with a particular god/ess is likely to have a great deal to do with who and what you already are—you will probably be drawn to the god whose gifts are strongest in your own being. I know very few runic magicians who are not Wodanists; women who are strongly aware of both their own sexuality and their personal power are most often drawn to the Frowe, while more maternal and quieter women tend to prefer Frija, and so forth. The most beloved of gods in Viking times was Thórr, the mighty protector of humankind, and he is still the most generally called upon among those who are Ásatrú ("true to the god/esses"—the name usually given to the Northern religion). If one of the god/esses has chosen you, be assured you will know about it!

In discussing the god/esses, it has become common in recent times to call upon the "tripartite Indo-European structure" put forth by Georges Dumézil. Dumézil insisted that both the societies and religions of Indo-European peoples could be understood through this model, which he interpreted roughly for the Germanic peoples as shown at the top of the next page.

Although the tripartite model is useful for discussion of the various attributes according to the function to which Dumézil assigned each, a literal reliance on this system is more likely to lead the seeker away from ancestral troth rather than towards it, since the social classes and the distinction of gods according to purely Dumézilian functions are not in any way supportable for the Ger-

Function	Title	Attribute	God	Social Class
First	Priest/ Judge	Rulership, wisdom	Wodan/ Tiw	Kings
Second	Warrior	Battle, strength	Thunar	Warriors
Third	Provider	Fertility	Ing, the Wans	Peasants

manic peoples. According to this model, Wodan and Tiw should be the gods followed by all leaders and thinkers, Thunar by all military personnel, whereas Ing and the other Wanic god/esses should be the deities of farmers and blue-collar workers alone. Historically, however, Ing/Freyr was more strongly associated with kingship than any god except Wodan, and, through his emblem the boar, was called on by mortal warriors far more often than Thunar, who never took part in the battles of men; while it was Wodan who trained young warriors and awarded battle-victory (and death) to his chosen heroes. Likewise, it was among farmers that Wodan continued to be honored in Germany through the nineteenth century—as a god of fruitful fields. Further, the king was personally responsible for the fertility of his lands, as mentioned in the Eddic poem "Helgakvidha Hundingsbana I": "The host thought to see a king to be / the warriors said together good harvest-years should come."(7) Also, all free Germanic folk, whether kings, members of a warband, or farmers, were expected to be warriors; and the notable poet, fighter, and Ódhinn's-man Egill Skallagrímsson was himself a farmer and the son of a smith. Although a certain sense of tripartite society survived down to Christian times, the three classes described in the Eddic poem "Rígsthula" bear little resemblance to Dumézil's three. The lowest is that of the thralls, or slaves, who carry wood, water, etc. but do not actually produce anything. The middle class is that of the carls, who are shown as farmer/producers in "Rígsthula" and who, as we know from Norse records and Anglo-Saxon law, were also not only expected, but required to be warriors at need. The highest class is that of the earls, who combine the first and second functions by being both rulers and full-time warriors.

Given these cautions, an awareness of the "functions" and their attributes is very useful as a tool for discussing the gods. A more appropriately modified chart, without absolute reference to social position or individual god/esses, follows thus:

Function	Attributes
First	Rulership, judgement, wisdom, magic, poetry/writing, etc.
Second	Battle, strength, protection
Third	Fertility, peace, productivity, material happiness

Nearly all the gods have aspects in all three functions, just as all levels of society could and can still take part in all three. Thus, Fro Ing acts in the first function as the holy king; in the second as the giant-slaying warrior and battle-boar; and in the third when he gives good harvest and riches. There is often a tendency for one function to be more significant than the others in the individual characters of the gods (or of humans); most of Wodan's distinctive traits, for instance, tend to fall into the realm of either first or second function, however, the sort of sharp distinctions and hierarchic exclusivity which mark general Western thinking are alien to Germanic thought; it is our way to synthesize and integrate rather than to hierarchize.

ASES AND WANS

The major division of the Germanic divinities is the distinction between the Ases (ON *Æsir*) and the Wans (ON *Vanir*). These are the two great tribes of divine beings, who differ both in origin and in character. The term "Æsir" was, however, used for all the gods and goddesses in general including the Wans, whereas "Vanir" was only applied to those who clearly fell into that specific category.

The Ases are clearly Indo-European, with relatively little admixture from other cultures. They are all descended from Wodan. The Ases include Thunar and his children, Vídharr, Váli, Balder, and so forth. In the natural world, they are largely associated with air, sky, and fire; in the social world, with battle; in the world of the mind and soul, with consciousness. The Ases embody the forces of creation, particularly of conscious creation; they are gods of activity, strife, and positive change.

The origins of the Wans are not known. Because cattle seem to have been such an important element in their cult, and because their nature as god/esses of fruitfulness and sources of basic life-energy seems to imply it, it is possible that they may be in some way descended from or related to the *ur*-cow Audhumbla, who was formed from primal fire and primal ice along with the first giant Ymir and whose milk provided the nourishment for Ymir and all his children. Nothing is recorded of this being's fate in any of the Norse creation stories; she vanishes into the unknown—and the Wans arise from the unknown.

The earthly pattern of the development of the Wanic cult is almost as cloudy; it is not certain whether they, like the Ases, are directly descended from Indo-European originals or whether the existing religion of the non-Indo-European peoples among whom the Germanic peoples settled had some part in determining the perception of these beings. The earliest Scandinavian rock-carvings show images which are associated with the Wans in later myth and art, such as the bare feet which appear in the tale of Skadhi and Njördhr and the ithyphallicism which characterizes Fro Ing (Freyr); however, continuity cannot be proven. The Wans seem to have occupied a much more powerful place in the overall religion and thought of the Germanic peoples than did the "third function" deities of the Indo-Europeans, and it may be that this perception of their significance had something to do with an earlier position as chief god/esses of a religion which was assimilated into that of the Indo-European settlers. However, certain aspects of the mythology also imply an Indo-European origin; for instance, the war between the Ases and the Wans which the Eddas record bears a strong similarity to the war between the "third function" fertility deities and the "first/second function" gods of rulership and battle in the *Rig Veda*.

In the natural world, the Wans are associated with earth and water; in the social world, with family, prosperity, and material sufficiency; in the world of the mind and soul, with deep wisdom, intuition, and prophecy. They are embodiments of the basic life force which nourishes and preserves.

The general symbolic roles played by the three great races of non-human wights can be expressed within the tripartite structure of becoming-being-passing away:

Wans—Preservation
natural power used for weal

Ases—Creation   Etins—Destruction
shapers of earth and power   unshaped or ill-used power

These three forces continuously interact as the cosmos evolves. Again, this model should not be taken as an absolute format; both the Ases and the Wans interbreed with the etins, constantly renewing their strength by the controlled assimilation of these wights' great energy. As with the Dumézilian three functions, nearly all the god/esses have aspects of creation, aspects of preservation, and aspects of destruction; while some of the etins also work weal and aid the god/esses.

GODDESSES AND WOMEN'S LORE

A study of Teutonic holy lore will reveal that much more is known about the masculine gods than about the goddesses. The overwhelming role which Wodan (Odin) and Thunar (Thor), in particular, play in the surviving tales has led to a popular view of the Germanic beliefs as being "a man's religion for manly men." This stereotype has, unfortunately, been aided by a long line of movies and books presenting the Vikings as bloody-minded raiders who respected nothing but physical strength and courage and viewed women as objects to rape and plunder. In actual fact, nothing could be further from the truth!

From the first accounts of the Germanic people, it was made very clear that "They think that there is something sacred and provident about women. They neither fail to consult them nor do they neglect to regard their replies. A woman named Veleda was regarded for a long time as a deity."[1] In heathen times, Germanic women enjoyed a higher legal and social status than women in any other culture—a status which was grossly degraded at the time of conversion by the combination of Christianity and Roman law. Germanic women had an especially powerful place in religious and mystical affairs, being expected to cast the runes and to prophesy in times of conflict. The vast majority of figures wielding spiritual influence over the Germanic people in Roman records were women. This state of affairs seemed to wane later; accounts from the Viking Age (roughly 792–1066 CE) show kings or local leaders performing most large-scale social ceremonies. However, women were still greatly revered for their ability to receive and interpret wisdom from the worlds beyond the Middle-Garth, particularly in dreams. A woman named Thórgerdhr, who became an *idis* (ancestral goddess of a family) of great power after her death, was given the nickname Hörgabrudhr ("bride of the altar") because of her devotion in making sacrifices and tending to her religious duties, and one of the sagas also tells of a priestess of Freyr who rode with the statue of the god in his wagon and was considered to be his wife. Most of the time, however, when women took a leading role in religious activity, it was within the context of their own households.

Beyond this, relatively little is known about women and the cults of the goddesses—surprisingly little, given the consistency of references to the high holiness in which the Germanic peoples held the feminine. The reasons for this are severalfold. First, women's mysteries tend to be orally passed down from elder women to younger women—sometimes as spinning chants or work-songs, which were deemed to be relatively unimportant until the nineteenth-century resurgence of interest in folklore. Although there were female skalds in the Viking Age, the majority of the poems from which Snorri Sturluson learned—and from which we today know—about the religion of the North were composed by and for men whose interests were not in the secrets of women—who were, in fact, usually personally devoted to Wodan, the patron of poets and giver of inspiration. Therefore, the myths are not always an accurate reflection of the religion; neither the goddesses nor the Wanic cult in general are particularly well documented in literature and myth.

Further, the collection of written materials on Germanic religion depended largely on Christian scholars, who were generally male and thus socially, as well as religiously, outside the sphere in which they might have heard about women's beliefs. This lack of information was probably combined with a strong tendency either to dismiss women's lore as unimportant or actively to suppress it, particularly wherever it dealt with the subject of sexuality. As a consequence, the process of reconstructing the feminine side of our ancestral beliefs is fraught with conjecture and difficulty, more dependent on folklore than on the specific Eddic sources. The fact that less may be written here about Frija and the Frowe than about Wodan, Thunar, and Fro Ing should not be taken to imply that the goddesses are or ever were in any way less mighty, less important, or less beloved than their husbands and brothers. Likewise, it does not mean that the Germanic way—in the days of our ancestors or now—has or will ever set women in any sort of subordinate or lesser position. Rather, women of today who are true to the goddesses of their fore-mothers should strive to rediscover this lost lore through accurate historical study and through spiritual experience so that the scales of our knowledge can be put back into a proper balance. Nor is the knowledge of goddess-lore limited to women; there were also men devoted to the goddesses, such as Óttarr of the Eddic poem "Hyndluljódh," who was the Frowe's lover and "ever trusted in the goddesses."(10) The reawakening of our ancestral soul is something which must be undertaken as a whole work by all of us, women and men alike!

Although there is no "tripartite goddess" in the Northern tradition—which is to say, no figure or group of figures which can be lumped into the invented/archetypal division of Maiden/Mother/Crone, a woman's personal focus on a goddess may shift as her condition changes through life in a way which the focus on a god does not. Thunar, for instance, appears in every form from that of a young and strong man to "Old Man Thórr"; while those given to Wodan follow him all through their lives; the followers of a god choose their deity more by their own character than their stage of development. In the case of the goddesses, however, virgins are specifically associated with Gefjon; women who are unmarried (or divorced) but sexually active with the Frowe; and married women, especially from childbirth onward, with Frija. There is no goddess who can be seen as a "crone" figure. Societies in which a Crone exists are societies which cast a woman out of the social structure as soon as she can no longer bear children and is thus no longer useful to men; the old witch makes dark magics partially because she is free of social strictures and male rule, partially because she has no other recourse or position of strength left to her. In the Teutonic tradition, on the other hand, whether a mother is bearing children or not, she remains a mother and the mistress of the home. Even where frightening witch-figures appear in the North, whether in sagas, Eddic poetry, or folklore, their first concern is always for their children, on whose behalf their most terrifying magics are worked; their fierceness is that of the protective mother, boding ill only for those who threaten their bairns.

Gunnora Hallakarva also points out that "the Crone is heavily associated with figures such as Hecate and exists only in cultures where sexually active women are feared and powerful (female) roles such as magician/witch suppressed by the male power structure—as in societies such as Greece where women are actually kept powerless; worship of Hecate was known, but was an underground activity and totally contrary to accepted feminine religious activity . . . We don't need a Crone-figure, because Norse/Teutonic women are not feared and are allowed (relatively) lots of social power via economy, marriage, social role, laws, sexual freedom, etc."

It may also be that part of the reason for this difference between Germanic religion and archetypal religions of modern invention is that archetypal religions draw the identification of the Moon as a goddess from Greco-Roman culture and have associated the phases of waxing, full, and waning/dark with the three phases of Maiden, Mother, and Crone; while in the Germanic languages and tradition, the Moon is always male and the Sun female. Thus attempts to make any sort of correlation between the phases of the Moon—or Maiden/Mother/Crone—and the goddesses or cycles of the Teutonic woman's life have no grounding whatsoever.

NOTES

1. Statius, Papinus; James Chisholm (tr.). *Germania*, excerpted in *Grove and Gallows*.

Chapter 4

THE ASES

WODANN (ÓDHINN, WODEN)

HIS GOD, whose name means "Master of Fury," appears in the Viking Age literature as the highest and most powerful of the gods. Of all the gods, he is the most mysterious and the most complex. As you will discover in your reading, he is often called by other names or *heiti*, over a hundred and fifty of which have survived in early literature. This habit may well have come from a fear of invoking him directly, as well as from his frequent wanderings through the worlds in various disguises. Among the major names which appear very often in the Old Norse sources are Yggr (the Terrible); Grímnir (The Masked One); Sigfadhir (Father of Victory); Valfadhir (Father of the Slain); Hár (the High One); Alfadhir (All-Father); Hárbardhr (Graybeard); and Hroptr (the Maligned). A fuller list of Wodan's *heiti* may be found in Appendix III: Names. These names are useful for understanding the various aspects of this god's character and for calling upon his aid or giving thanks to him in specific instances.

The origins of Wodan's cult are very uncertain. He is first known as a god of poetry, magic, and death, which were very closely related in the Germanic mind, as the religious/magical *wod* ("fury/inspiration") of poetry was understood to come from the world of the dead (even in late Icelandic tradition, for instance, one could become a poet by sitting out on a burial mound for a night, if one didn't go mad in the process). As the god leading the souls of the dead to the Otherworld, Wodan may have then been identified as the chooser of the dead and then specifically with the selecting of the slain in battle. This is also suggested by the name given to his handmaidens, the *valkyrjur*, or walkyriges—"Choosers of the Slain." From that, his role as chooser of victory and god of war in general would have been a natural development. At the same time—roughly the first couple of centuries before and after the beginning of the Common Era—the runes, with all their attendant magical might and wisdom were discovered and the knowledge of them spread through the various branches of the Germanic peoples. It is thought that the runes may have been transmitted by bands of initiates in the cult of Wodan. The combination of runic power and the growing identification of Wodan as the god of victory probably led to his usurpation of Tiw's (Týr's) position as the Sky-Father and ruler from the original Indo-European pantheon.

Above all, Wodan is a god of wisdom. His wisdom is not, however, that of peaceful serenity, but that of continuous, restless activity; his is the furious might of the storm wind, which is never stilled. The tales of Wodan show him on his endless search for knowledge, forever growing and forever seeking to become greater. He is the very prototype of Goethe's Faust, who in his moment of highest inspiration cries, "He alone earns his freedom / Who daily conquers it anew."[1] He is also the sacrificer of self to self, as it tells in the Eddas. He discovered the runes by hanging nine nights on the World-Tree, pierced by his own spear; he also gave up one eye for a drink from Mímir's Well, the Well of Memory. As Hár ("the High One") he sits on Hlidhskjálf, from which he can see everything that happens in the Nine Worlds, but he is never content merely to watch. Wodan often travels alone through the worlds, cloaked in any of a number of disguises, in order to seek out knowledge wherever it might be. He is a god of subtlety and deception—CIA personnel might do well to call on Wodan! The name "Wodan/Ódhinn" was either glossed or translated into Latin as "Mercurius" from the beginning of the Common Era through the eleventh century. This probably stems from his nature as a god of all verbal skills, including runic writing and poetry; it may also be connected with his aspect of *psychopomps,* or leader of souls. At some point Wodan was also associated with transport and commerce; this does not appear in the Scandinavian myths, but the *Óðhinsheiti* "Farmatýr" ("Cargo-God") survived through the Viking Era.

The central myth of Wodan is the description in the Eddic poem "Hávamál" of how he hung on the World-Tree as a sacrifice to himself.

> I wot that I hung on the windy tree
>   the nights all nine
> gored by spear given to Wodan
>   self by self to me,
> on that tree of which none knows
>   from what roots it rises.
>
> Not with loaf they comforted me nor with drinking horn,
>   I looked below.
> I took up the runes took them up screaming
>   fell I after from there.

The association of the gallows with the self-sacrifice of the god may have existed fairly early; when Christianity first came to the Germanic peoples, the word "gallows" was initially used to translate the Latin "crux," but that practice was swiftly abandoned in favor of taking "crux" as a loan-word—quite possibly because the "gallows" was still understood to be heathen and therefore dangerous. This potential for confusion between the sacrifices of Wodan and of Christ may have smoothed the transition from heathenism to Christianity; however, it also ensured that the folk did not entirely forget their ancient beliefs. As an example of the survival of Wodan under the guise of Christ, Turville-Petre quotes a Shetlandic folksong of the 19th century.

> Nine days he hang pa de rütless tree;
> for ill was da folk, in' güd wis he.
> a blüdy mael was in his side—
> made wi' a lance 'at wid na hide.
> Nine lang nichts, i' da nippin rime,
> hang he dare wi' his naeked limb.
>   Some, de leuch (laugh);
>   but idders gret (weep).

"The subject of these lines is Christ, but the nine days, and perhaps the nipping rime accord better with the myth of Ódhinn than with the legend of Calvary."[2]

In this account, Wodan appears as gallows-god, spear-god, the god with power over life and death, and the lord of wisdom, especially magical wisdom. Through the single act of his self-sacrifice, Wodan gained the might which makes him the greatest of the gods.

As the leader of souls from the world of the living to the worlds of the dead, it was also understood from an early time that Wodan was able to lead the dead back again to the world of the living. One of his most powerful aspects does not appear in the Eddas, but survives very strongly in the folklore of all the Germanic peoples: that of the leader of the Wild Hunt. From Winternights to Ostara—the autumn/winter half of the year— particularly during the twelve nights of Yule, Wodan leads the dead through the storm behind a pack of ghostly black hounds with red eyes. For the living to be out of doors when the Wild Hunt is riding is to risk madness or death; this is Wodan in his oldest and most terrible form, an aspect that few indeed are prepared to meet. The same nature, however, is also the source of one of his most weal-bringing aspects: the ancestor-god, the god who brings about rebirth and ensures the continuance of the family line by bringing the powers of the ancestral soul (*ættarfylgja*) forth from the worlds beyond into the Middle-Garth. This is described in *Völsunga saga*, which tells how Ódhinn fathers a heroic line and then intervenes again to bring fertility to a sterile descendant and his wife.

> Rerir won himself great booty, and likewise a wife who seemed well matched with him; but they were together a long time and yet they had no child or heir. This was a soreness to them, and they prayed often and earnestly to the gods that they might have a child. Now it is said that Frigg heard their prayer and told it to Ódhinn, and well could he give rede in this. He called a wish-maiden of his, the daughter of Hrimnir the giant, and put an apple into her hand, bidding her to take it to the drighten. She put on her mantle of feathers and flew till she found the drighten, who was sitting on a mound in search of rede in this matter. She let the apple fall down onto his knee; he took it up, and it seemed to him that he knew what end it would serve. He went back from the mound to his men, and there he met the queen, and he and she both ate some of that apple.[3]

The child who was born thereafter was Völsi, father of the line of the greatest heroes of the Northern tradition, Sigmundr (Siegmund), Signy (Sieglinde), and Sigurdhr (Siegfried). Through Ódhinn's intervention, Sigmundr is reborn as his own posthumous son Sigurdhr, the slayer of the dragon Fáfnir.

As the leader of souls from one realm to another, Wodan often appears as a ferryman. In *Völsunga saga*, he comes in a small boat to collect the body of the dead hero Sinfjotli the son of Sigmundr. He is also a ferryman in the Eddic poem "Hárbardzljódh," in which he meets Thunar at the river separating Etin-Home and the Ases' Garth.

Wodan the ancestor-god appears not only as the guide of the family-souls, but as the direct father of a number of clans of heroes and kings. One of the most notable of these still survives: the royal house of England can still trace its bloodlines back through Hengest and Horsa, the first Saxon kings on British soil, to Woden. Although in later times many of the genealogies of the Anglo-Saxon royal houses were imaginatively expanded to bring the symbolic power of Judeo-Christian figures such as Noah (!) into the royal lineages, general knowledge still held Woden to be the primary source, as even the Venerable Bede, who was himself no friend of the old gods, had to admit. "Hengest and Horsa . . . were the sons of Wihtgylse, whose father was called Witta, whose father was called Wihta, whose father was named Woden, from whose stock have sprung many tribes of the kin of kings."[4]

Although Wodan is the All-Father, neither Frija nor the Frowe is called the All-Mother; he is no faithful husband to either of his wives. He fathers various clans on mortal women; his son Vídharr is the child of a giantess, while Váli is the son of a human woman whom he enchanted. Likewise, when he and Thunar are telling of their deeds across a river, while Thunar talks of the many giants he has slain, Wodan boasts of the many women with whom he has slept.

Wodan is a god of binding and unbinding, of the fastening and loosening of fetters both physical and psychological. He claims mastery over fetters through magic in "Hávamál," having spells to bind and spells to release. In early times, sacrifices to Wodan were bound or hanged as well as being pierced through with spear or arrow. Tacitus records that the tribe of the Semnones had a holy grove which "no one is allowed to enter unless he has been tied with rope . . . all this superstition is concerned with the notion that this is the place where the god dwells, who reigns over everything."[5] Among the Chatti, the bravest of the young men also wore "a ring of iron, which among their folk is a sign of dishonour like chains," which they were allowed to take off after slaying their first foe in battle.[6] Among the walkyriges serving Wodan is one named Herfjötr, or War-Fetter. This name describes a psychological state of immobilizing terror; it was a fetter laid on the mind of one's foes in battle, which both Wodan and his walkyriges could set or break at will.

Wodan's sign is the *walknot* (ON *valknútr*—"knot of the slain"), an interwoven figure of three triangles. Used as an abstract religious symbol (as on a harrow, blessing-bowl, etc.), it symbolically binds the realms of being together; worn on your person, it symbolizes that you are bound to the god. The walknot appears on many of the Gotlandic picture stones (circa 750–850 CE), often together with the rider-and-horse design which is thought to represent the dead man riding to Walhall. It also forms a major part of the Hammar's Stone scene (see opposite page), which is evidently a picture of Wodenic sacrifice: one warrior stands by a tree with a rope around his neck, ready to be hanged; another man is held down, about to be sacrificed by a spear. Behind him the leader of a line of warriors holds out an eagle or hawk for sacrifice; another bird of prey flies above the walknot, which points downward at what appears to be a harrow-stone.

In the earlier, more violent times of the Migration and Viking Ages, Wodan was the particular patron of the *drighten* or leader of the warband; of berserks, those warriors who became possessed by their beast-fetches and went into a state of battle-madness; of warlike kings; of poets and of runic magicians. The sort of battles which our ancestors fought with sword and axe are rarer now. Nevertheless, Wodan Sigfadhir has his place in all conflicts where one struggles against another, whether with the sword, with gun and bomb, or with word and will.

The aspect of Wodan which is most often called upon today is that of the god of poetry and inspiration. It is told in both the *Poetic* and *Prose Eddas* how the god disguised himself as a serpent and beguiled the giant woman Gunnlodh, keeper of the three cauldrons holding the mead of poetry, Ódhroerir or, in English, Wod-Stirrer. Having won this mead, Wodan deals it out to his chosen heroes at his will. Thus he can be called upon for inspiration in any work of verbal creation—poetry, fiction, help in arguments or speechmaking, or even non-imaginative writing.

Hammar's Runestone, depicting sacrifice to Wodan

In many ways, Wodan is a dangerous god to follow; although his gifts are great, they demand a high price. Even in the early times of our folk, he was more feared and respected than loved. He is often thought to be untrustworthy; he is called both "Oath-God" and "Oath-Breaker." In "Hávamál," he says of himself, "A ring-oath Ódhinn I know to have sworn, / Who shall trust in his troth? / Suttung swindling he stole symbel-mead / and left Gunnlödhr to weep."(110) He is also the god who sets strife among kin, turning brother against brother and encouraging his favorites to bring about the death of their siblings for their own gain. He does not work towards reconciliation and compromise among humans, but rather stirs up strife on both sides, as in the saga of Heidhrekr in which he encourages both of Heidhrekr's sons, Angantýr and Humla, to do battle.

Wodan had, particularly in the Viking Age, a reputation for betraying his own chosen heroes to their deaths. This reputation was well-founded; however, he does not act capriciously, but rather according to his ultimate plan. The heroes Wodan chooses for his own gather in Walhall (ON *Valhöll*, often Anglicized to Valhalla) where they fight every day and feast every night until Ragnarök, the final battle in which the cosmos is to be destroyed. Although the gods will go under, their strength in the battle will make it possible for a new world to be reborn after the old is brought down. Wodan works so that this transformation will be one of growth, rather than of destruction.

Only two singular examples of an Ódhinn-compounded personal name exist, as opposed to literally thousands of names compounded with the elements Thórr and Freyr/Freyja, and those names, the masculine Ódhinkaur ("he with Ódhinn's hair") and the feminine Ódhindís ("goddess or woman of Ódhinn"), may possibly have been cultic titles rather than given names. Parents are likely to have been reluctant to name their children after this perilous patron. However, names containing the Wodenic elements "Wolf," "Raven," and "Eagle" are very common throughout all the Germanic peoples. In Continental German, we find Wolfram ("Wolf-Raven"), Wolfgang ("Wolf-Goer"—possibly a berserk-name); in Old Norse, Arnbjörn ("Eagle-Bear"); Ulfr ("Wolf"); Hrafn ("Raven"); Modern English preserves Arnold ("Eagle-Wood"), and so forth. Wodan himself is called "Eagle-Headed" because he was known to take that shape. All of these names were meant to bring fierceness and battle-victory to their bearers—the blessings of Wodan. The three most Wodenic creatures were also the "beasts of battle" in the conventions of Anglo-Saxon and Old Norse poetry, showing the extent to which this god, more than any other, was associated with the functions of war.

Wodan's great weapon is the spear Gungnir, made by the dwarfish sons of Ivaldi. Spear-holding male figures appear in the oldest Germanic rock-carvings; it cannot be proven that these are truly representations of Wodan (or Tiwaz, the other god associated with the spear), but the continuing might of the image is undeniable. One of the plates on the Torslunda helmet shows a one-eyed spear-carrier, who is almost certainly Wodan. The casting of the spear is, like the swinging of the hammer, an act of hallowing. However, rather than being blessed, those over whom the spear has flown are doomed to fall in battle, given to Wodan as sacrifices. Several spear-heads have been found with runes and holy signs engraved on them or even inlaid in silver. Though he is the giver of magical swords, Wodan does not himself wield a sword; when he comes against his chosen hero Sigmundr the Völsung, the sword which the god gave to the hero breaks on the shaft of the spear, and Sigmundr knows by this that "It is not Ódhinn's will that I draw sword again, since mine is broken. I have had my battles as long as it pleased him." Wodan may in certain cases lend his spear to a mortal who works his will, as in the Second Lay of Helgi Hunding's-Bane, where it is said that "Dagr, the son of Högni (whom Helgi had killed), sacrificed to Ódhinn to get revenge for his father. Ódhinn lent Dagr his spear. Dagr found Helgi, his kinsman, in the place which is called Fetter-Grove. He went against Helgi with the spear. There fell Helgi." When Dagr tells his sister of her husband's death, he says, "Ódhinn alone wishes all evil / therefore between sibs bore he runes of cause."(34)

Wodan most often appears as a one-eyed old man with a hoary beard, clad in a hooded cape of dark blue. He often shifts his shape, becoming eagle, wolf, or serpent at need. He is accompanied by the two ravens Huginn (Thought) and Muninn (Memory), who fly throughout the worlds and return to him each night with news. As he says himself, "Huginn and Muninn fly every day / over the great earth; / I fear me for Huginn that he come not back, / yet more I fear me for Muninn."[7] Wodan also has two wolves, Geri and Freki, both of which names mean "the Greedy." The day

Gold bracteate depicting Wodan and his raven

named after him is Wednesday. In addition to Walhall, Wodan also
has the hall Válaskjalf (Hall of Slain Warriors), and spends much
time in Frija's hall Sokkvabekk or Fensalir, drinking with her.

The runes of his name, ᚹ ᛟ ᛗ ᚨ ᚾ, reveal the various sides of his
being. The first two, wunjo, "joy," (ᚹ) and othala, "udal lands," (ᛟ),
are runes of clan and ancestry; these are the runes of Wodan the
All-Father, sire of the gods and of the greatest human lines of the
North. The rune dagaz, "day," (ᛗ) shows his highest and holiest
nature: the moment of dawn, the awakening of the full consciousness which is Wodan's best gift to those who reach up towards
him. Ansuz, "Ase," (ᚨ) is the rune of Wodan himself, as the Old Icelandic Rune Poem makes clear with its reference to "the ruler of
Walhall"; as god of poetry, of death and rebirth, of *wod* as both
inspiration of madness, of the winds that blow through all the
worlds, Wodan's true nature is shown in this stave. Lastly, nauthiz,
"need," (ᚾ) is the rune by which Wodan works to turn the wyrd of
the worlds so that new life can spring forth after Ragnarök.

Frija with spindle and distaff

FRIJA (FRIGG)

Frija is the first wife of Wodan, and the only goddess who appears
in what might be called a traditional domestic arrangement with
him. Her name comes from an Indo-European root meaning "pleasure" or "beloved." Although she shares the traits of fore-sight and
silent wisdom with the Wanic god/esses, there is nowhere any
implication that she is not one of the Ases. She gives her husband
counsel, as the Anglo-Saxon "Maxims" says the wife of a great man
ought to do:

> And wife / (shall) flourish / loved among her people be of
> bright mood / hold secret counsel (or "hold runes") be boun-
> tiful in heart / with horses and treasures at the mead-counsel
> / before the kin of the warband always everywhere. / The
> protector of athelings ("nobles") she shall greet first / the first

cup to the fro's ("lord's") hand / swiftly reaching and knowing rede for him / the land-owners both together.[8]

Very little is recorded about the cult of Frija, but there is reason to think that it was quite significant in Germanic cultural and
religious life. All that we know about Frija portrays her as a goddess of domestic affairs and one of the main supporters of social
and cultural norms. This side of her character appears strongly in
"The Flyting of Loki," where she counsels Loki and Ódhinn, "Your
ancient *ørlögs* you should hide / and stay far from saying / what
the two Ases in ancient days did / keep it ever from ken of men."
(25) She is, above all, the patroness of marriage and of childbirth—
a goddess for mature women, as Freyja and Gefjon are for younger
women. Frija also represents the figure of the "peace-weaver," the
woman who makes peace between men when their pride will not
allow them to compromise. This was a vastly important aspect of
the woman's social and political function among the Germanic
folk, as seen by the figure of Hrothgar's queen Wealtheow in
Beowulf: Wealtheow is both counselor to her husband and a diplo-
mat who keeps peace among her husband's warband and deals
with the foreign warriors who have entered the hall.

The constellation which is generally known as "Orion's Belt"
was called "Frigg's Distaff" by the Norse. The scarcity of references
to the practice of the cult of Frija makes it difficult to prove; however, given her position as a goddess of the household and of
women's affairs in particular, it is probable that the distaff was as
much a symbol of Frija's power as the hammer was of Thunar's, or
the spear of Wodan's. The significance of spinning and weaving to
the social organization of the Norse should not be underestimated;
Iceland's primary export and source of economic stability in the
Medieval period (and up until at least 1600) was the cloth produced by its women![9]

Her role as goddess of cloth-craft points the way to understanding another side of Frija's character: that of the silent seeress
who "*ørlögs* . . . all knows, / though she herself does not speak."[10]
The Norns are often said to weave or spin the fates of humans, as
in the First Lay of Helgi Hunding's-Bane where they come to the
newborn hero and "Spun there . . . *ørlög*-threads / that which was
kept in Bralund. They gathered together the golden threads / and
in moon-hall's (the sky's) middle made them fast."(3) In *Njala*

saga, walkyriges appear weaving the bloody web which is the fate of the battle to come. A mother, in particular, may also weave or sew some item for her son on which his *ørlög* depends, as the mother of the Jarl Sigurdhr does in *Orkneyinga saga* when her son comes to her to ask for counsel. "Sigurdhr's mother was a sorceress, so he went to consult her, telling her that the odds against him were heavy, at least seven to one. 'Had I thought you might live forever,' she said, 'I'd have reared you in my wool-basket. But lifetimes are shaped by what will be, rather than where you are. Now, take this banner. I've made it for you with all the skill that I have, and my belief is this: that it will bring victory to the man it's carried before, but death to the one who carries it.' It was a finely made banner, very cleverly embroidered with the figure of a raven, and when the banner fluttered in the breeze, the raven seemed to be flying ahead."[11]

The protective power of motherhood is also specifically associated with Frija. When her son Baldr tells his foreboding dreams, "the gods took counsel together, and it was decided to ask for protection from all kinds of danger for Baldr, and Frigg received solemn oaths to this: that Baldr should not be harmed by fire or water, iron and all kinds of metal, stones, the earth, trees, sicknesses, beasts, birds, poison, snakes."[12] Throughout this tale, she appears as the wielder of the only might which has even the possibility of altering her son's *ørlög*; it is the weaving of her foresighted actions in which Loki must find a hole which will enable him to bring about Baldr's death, because it is she who has gotten all things, except the young mistletoe, to swear to her son's safety. After Baldr has been slain, "Frigg spoke and asked if there was anyone among the Ases who wished to have for himself all her love and favor and was willing to ride on the Hel-way and try to find Baldr and offer a ransom to Hel, if she would let Baldr fare home to the Ases' Garth"; it is at this bidding of hers that Hermödhr rides down to Hel's realm, and only Loki's ill will prevents Baldr's return. It is also to her that prayers seem to be first offered for the conception of children, as in *Völsunga saga*; while her husband brings the heroic kin-soul to his chosen line, Frija makes wives fruitful.

Although she is Wodan's wife, and her role is often misconstrued to be solely that of the domestic, if sometimes shrewish, housewife, Frija never appears as submissive or subordinate to her husband in any way. He asks her for advice on matters of significance; at times, when their wills cross, her cunning proves to be greater than his, as the Eddic poem "Grímnismál" shows. In the prose version of this poem, it is told how Ódhinn and Frigg have fostered two brothers; his chosen one is Geirrodhr and hers Agnarr. At Ódhinn's advice, Geirrodhr betrays his brother and takes the rule of the kingdom for himself, but when Ódhinn boasts to Frigg about this, she arranges things so that he is forced to destroy his own fosterling and give the kingdom to Geirrodhr's son Agnarr, whose name implies that he is in some sense a rebirth of Frigg's fosterling.

A similar tale of Frija's wisdom appears in the seventh century *Origo gentis Langobardorum*:

> ... the Vandal leaders, Ambri and Assi, asked Godan (Wodan) whether he would grant them victory over the Winniles. To this Godan replied: 'I will give victory to those whom I see first before the sun rises.' At the same time, Gambala and her two sons requested of Frea (Frija), who is the wife of Godan, that she be well disposed towards the Winniles. Frea gave them a plan in which they would go out with their women when the sun was rising. The women were to loosen their hair and wrap it around their faces so that they would appear to have beards. Then the shining sun rose and Frea turned the bed upon which her husband was sleeping so that it was facing the East. Then she awoke him. Godan looked out and saw the Winniles with their hair on their faces and exclaimed, 'Who are those long-bearded ones?' Frea replied to Godan, 'Just as you have given them a name, so shall you grant them victory.' He gave them the victory, and when he appeared, they conquered and had the victory. From this time on, the Winniles have been called the Lombards.[13]

In this account, Frija appears in her full power as a goddess on whom women can call to further their own interests even in areas which were not normally considered her sphere of influence, such as battle. The turning of the bed so that the sleeper must awaken facing a certain direction and with a certain sight before his eyes symbolizes her control of the currents of spiritual force within the home—when within her domain, even Wodan is subject to her guidance. The belief in the importance of the direction of wakening survives in the saying that "So-and-so got up on the wrong side of the bed this morning"; the first influence of the day shapes the rest of the day's events (up through the seventeenth century, Icelanders carved spiritually upifting messages in runes on the headboards of their beds, probably also as a result of this belief!). In Scandinavian marriage tradition, the bed itself is also part of the wife's dowry, coming with the other household goods which she brings with her; it is part of Frija's domain. Finally, she works through the means of maintaining the rules of society; the giver of a name was obligated to give the recipient a "naming-gift" to go with it. Having gotten Wodan to name the Lombards, Frija is quick to step in to make sure he goes through with the social ritual.

Frija has a hide of hawk-feathers in which she can fare through the worlds. None of her ventures outside of the Ases' Garth are told of in the surviving legends of our folk, but the mention of her hawk-shape shows that her power and her person are in no way confined to her own home.

Frija is the daughter of the god Fjörgynn; she has a sister/ handmaid named Fulla, whose name, "full," shows her character as a goddess of prosperity and fruitfulness. Fulla may once have been a more important figure in Germanic religion than she had become by the time Snorri wrote his *Edda*, where she is only identified as a handmaid; the "Second Meresburg Charm," an Old High German spell, says "then chanted Frija and Fulla her sister." Fulla is also especially mentioned in Snorri's version of the Baldr-story: Nanna, Baldr's wife, sends gifts out of Hel, "to Frig a linen robe and many gifts, and finger-gold to Fulla."[14] Snorri also says of Fulla that "she . . . is a virgin and goes around with hair flowing free and has a gold band around her head. She carries Frigg's casket and looks after her and shares her jewels."[15]

The other goddesses named by Snorri generally seem to be either handmaidens or hypostases of Frija. Of them, he says:

> Frigg is the highest . . . The second is Saga . . . The third is Eir, who is the best of physicians. The fourth is Gefjon, who is a maiden, and attended by those who die maidens. A fifth is Fulla . . . The sixth is Freyja who is highest in rank together with Frigg; she is married to a man who is called Odhr (Wod) . . . Seventh is Sjofn; she is greatly concerned to direct the hugrs

(thoughts/feelings) of people to love, men and women, and from her name affection is called sjafni. Eighth is Lofn; she is so mild and good to pray to that she often gets leave from the All-father or Frigg for people to marry, women and men, although it had been banned before, and from her name it is called per-mission (lof), and so also is it praised (lofat) among people. The ninth is Vár; she listens to the oaths of people and private con-tracts which are made between women and men, and for this reason these contracts are called varar; and she takes vengeance on those who break them. Tenth is Vor; she is wise and enquir-ing, so that nothing may be hidden from her; therefore there is a saying that a woman becomes aware (vor) of something, when she comes to know of it. The eleventh is Syn; she keeps the doors of the hall and watches against those who should not go in; and she is set as a defence at the Thing in cases which she wishes to refute. For this reason there is a saying, that a denial (syn) is set before when someone wishes to say no. The twelfth is Hlín; she is set to protect those people, whom Frigg wishes to save from some danger; for that reason there is the saying that a person who saves himself finds refuge (hleinir). Thirteenth Snotra; she is wise and prudent of speech; from her name a wise woman or man is called snotr. Fourteenth Gná; Frigg sends her into various worlds on her errands. She has a horse which runs over air and water and is called Hofvarpnir ("Hoof-Tosser") . . . From Gná's name it is said of something that it towers (gnæfa) when it goes high up.[16]

There is also Gefjön, who is called upon by virgins and to whose hall chaste maids go after death.

Frija's own hall is called Sökkvabekkr, "Sunken Beach," which "cool waves glimmer over" ("Grímnismál" 7), or Fensalir, "Fen (Marsh) Hall." The character of this hall may point, again, to an early role as a goddess of earth and water. In this hall, she is also given the name Sága, or seeress, which is connected with (though not the same word as) the Old Norse word for story. This is where Wodan comes to drink with her from golden cups and get her wise rede.

Adam of Bremen reported a "highly ornamented" statue of Frija which the Christian Eginus cut to bits at the church of Scara-mensius, and Saxo also describes the adornment of her statues. It should not be surprising that the wife of the highest god should be hung with great quantities of gold and jewels, as befits her status.

Saxo also levels the accusation at her that she prostituted herself for a necklace. This story is recounted of the Frowe in a fuller form, and Loki also accuses Gefjön of the same fault. As will be discussed under the section on the Frowe, this is probably something associated with the earliest forms of the earth-goddess and thereafter attributed to whichever name her attributes, particularly fertility, seemed to belong to at any given time or in any given place.

Because of the apparent similarity of their names and their marital associations with Wodan, Frija is often confused with Freyja or thought to be the same goddess. This is highly improbable—their characters and their natures are almost complete opposites. Whereas Frija's handmaidens protect vows and uphold marriages, the Frowe is a goddess of sexual abandon, who often takes lovers among humans, alfs, and gods. Freyja's origins, as will be discussed later, are both relatively explicable and unquestionably part of the Wanic cult, whereas Frija is one of the Ases. In the Eddic and other Norse sources, Frija does not have any associations with death, and the accusations of non-marital sexuality leveled against her are highly dubious.

Although both Frija and Freyja are said to be wives of Wodan, this is easily understandable within the customs of Germanic marriage. In some branches of the Germanic folk, a man might have more than one legal wife; among the rest—even after the coming of Christianity, as in the laws of the Franks in Charlemagne's time— he could have concubines towards whom he still maintained certain legal and financial responsibilities. Frija is the only goddess who appears in a domestic relationship to Wodan, giving him advice and sharing Hlidhskjálf with him; she is clearly his first wife, while the Frowe is his "concubine"—which, among the Germanic people does not imply a relationship of ownership or female subservience. The relationship between Wodan and the Frowe, as the myths show, is merely rather less constrained and formalized than the relationship between Wodan and Frija.

FROWE HOLDA/FROWE BERCHTA

In Germany, a number of folk beliefs concerning a goddess called Frowe Holda (in the north) or Berchta/Perchta (in the south) survived into the last century. There is some question as to whether these names, meaning "kind, merciful" and "bright" might have been titles given to Frija or the Frowe as taboo-names or in an effort to escape Christian persecution. The connections between Holda/Bercha and Frija are stronger than those between this figure and the Frowe; however, both seem related in some ways. As the spinner and weaver within the home and the overseer of women's work, Holda/Berchta is very like Frija. On the other hand, the Frowe's name Hörn, "flax," ties her to the agricultural side of this activity, and it is also told how Holda gave the flax plant to humans. It may be that in considering these figures, we can see more about both Frija and the Frowe than survived in the relatively scanty accounts of the Eddas.

Grimm says of Holda that "In popular legends and nursery tales, *frau Holda* . . . appears as a superior being, who manifests a kind and helpful disposition towards men, and is never cross except when she notices disorder in household affairs."[17] Holda, or Berchta, is the goddess who is particularly responsible for making sure that spinners finish their spinning before the last day of the Yule celebrations and that the proper food, gruel or dumplings and herring, is eaten on that last day. It is said that the goddess punishes those who neglect to eat the proper food on her day by cutting their bellies open and filling them with a mixture of straw and sticks. Interestingly enough, one of the characters in *Laxdaela saga* also experiences a vision in which a woman comes to him, cuts him open, and replaces his innards with brushwood. In this case, however, the woman is his guardian idis and it is done as a protection; he is mortally wounded in a battle the next day and thought to be slain, but he is quite well the next morning, and says that the woman had come back to him and put his entrails back. Terror and help seem to be equally mixed in the character of Frowe Berchta, as indeed they are in most of the elder god/esses.

Holda, or Berchta, appears chiefly in the winter, around Yule-time. In some parts of Germany, it is said that the snow falls when Frau Holle shakes her feather bed (or feather pillows). As a weather-goddess, she can also bring fog. There are several mountains called Hölleberg (Holda's Mountain); one, the Aßmanhäuser Hölleberg, produces an excellent light red wine. The Hölleberg was also a center for witch hunts in the late Middle Ages.

In Waidhofen, milk is left out for Perchta and her host; the same milk is then given to poultry and cattle so that they will thrive. Her wild procession brings fertility to the lands over which she rides or walks; she is also said to have taught humans how to grow turnips. Some of the aspects of "Santa Claus" are originally aspects of Holda: she punishes naughty children, but in Göttingen she brings gifts to good ones.

The dark and wild aspect which is prominent in Frowe Holda/ Berchta does not appear in the Frija whom we see in the Eddas and the scanty Continental references; however, the descriptions given of this side of Frowe Holda may also reflect back upon Frija. Like Wodan, Frowe Holda is said to lead the Wild Hunt; the spirits in her train, however, are said to be unbaptized children, who belong to her realm. In this context, she is actually called "Frau Wodan," which is less likely to be a shift of gender such as may have occured in the case of Nerthus/Njördhr than an identification of her as Wodan's wife.

The wild procession which Holda/Berchta leads is not only a ride of spirits, but also takes place among humans during earthly festivals. The best known of these is the Perchtenjagd (Berchta's Hunt), in which young men dress in either traditional clothing or masks and costumes of black fur and run through the town ringing bells, cracking whips, and shouting. Manuscripts from the fifteenth century on describe groups of wild women running about behind Perchta during the Yule season.

The most significant and consistent attribute of Frowe Holda is her association with spinning and, from that, with fate. It is said that she is the giver of flax to humankind, and taught folk how to spin and weave linen. Her first duty is to make sure that the spinning is done properly; in some regions of Germany, women must have spun a certain amount of thread by Yule; in Franconia, Frau Holle soils the flax of lazy spinners; while near the Hörselberg girls fill their distaffs with flax at Christmastime "when Frau Holle starts her round, for she promises 'A good year for every thread,' but the material must be worked off by Epiphany, for on her return she threatens, 'A bad year for every thread.'"[18]

As well as gathering the souls of small children to her, Berchta also aids in their rebirth. In Tyrol, those who want a child go to the cave which she shares with unborn babies; women who bathe in Frau Hölle's well also become fruitful. This motif hearkens back to Frija's hall Fensalir and also to Nerthus' lake (see Njördhr/Nerthus in chapter 5).

Sometimes Holda/Berchta appears as a frightful hag, old and ugly, with a long nose and huge teeth; sometimes she is fair and gracious, clothed in white and crowned. She drives very swiftly in a wain; she always carries a whip, with which she scourges the lazy.

THUNAR (THÓRR, DONAR, DONNER)

Thunar was and remains the most beloved and most often called upon god of the Germanic peoples in general. His name means "Thunder," and it is through the might of his thunder and the lightning he wields that our ancestors first came to know him: the god of strength, of might and main; the warrior who fights ceaselessly against the thurses that menace the walls of our world, the Middle-Garth. A common picture of the earliest religions is of primitive humans cowering in terror before the thunder. For the peoples of the North, this is a false image; for us, Thunar has always been the protector and friend of humankind, flinging his hammer of lightning to ward us from all wights of ill.

The earliest images of Thunar may appear in Bronze Age rock carvings which show ithyphallic male figures wielding axes. Amber axe-head amulets have been found among the sacrificial goods unearthed from Danish bogs; as Norse technology moved into the Iron Age, the axe disappears and is replaced by the hammer. However, the axe has continued to play an important part in the thunder-lore of the Germanic people to the present day. It was believed that thunder hurled stones eight miles deep into the earth, from which they rose at the rate of one mile each year until they lay on the surface. Stone axes found after a thunderstorm were considered to be particularly mighty talismans, protecting the house in which they were kept from lightning, fire, and woe-working magic. In the excavation of one Bronze Age village, a general layer of charcoal was found which showed that the village had been burned down. Just above that—immediately after the burning—there was an oaken stump in which a bronze axe-head had been buried; the evidence of living folklore indicates that the village was probably burned down by a lightning strike and the axe put there afterwards to prevent a recurrence. Although stone axes were particularly notable, all stone weapons (arrowheads, etc.) were considered to be thunder-stones and thus mighty amulets of Thunar.

This belief also appears in the Eddic poem "Thrymskvidha," in which the giant Thrym steals Mjöllnir and buries it "eight rosts the earth beneath"(8), exactly as the thunder-stones were said to sink in the earth. Grimm suggests that the giant Thrym ("the Noisy") was an older and more terrifying personification of thunder temporarily reclaiming his own power of destruction, which Thunar had to retrieve from its buried hiding place in order to make the thunder-hammer into a weapon of warding again.[19]

Thunar is the son of Wodan and the Earth. From his father, he has inherited the powers of the air, of storm and wind; from his mother, he has gotten his matchless might both as an inherited part of his nature and through the gift of the belt Megingjardhr, the girdle of strength. In the natural realm of being, he brings earth and sky together through the lightning and rain which unite them; Thunar is called upon to bring the beneficial storms which make the fields fruitful and to ward off the hail which destroys the crops. He is married to Sif, whose golden hair represents the fields of grain which the lightning of late summer was supposed to ripen. By her, he has fathered his daughter Thrúdhr ("Strength"). Thunar also fathered two sons, Módhi ("Courage") and Magni ("Might"), with the giantess Iron-Sax. These three children can be seen as embodiments of the three special gifts of Thunar to his worshippers: the courage of the warrior who trusts in his own power; might in the sense of spiritual/psychic power—the might of the soul; and strength both physical and mental.

In the religion of the Teutonic peoples, Thunar is not only the warder of the garth's walls against the wights without, but also the god who holds up the pillars of the house and the hof. He is the guardian of social order; not the rigid, legalistic order embodied by Tiw, but the order maintained when everything is going along as it ought, free from the external disruption represented by the thurses and the internal disruption represented by Loki. Thunar represents the spirit of the law, in contrast to Tiw who represents its letter. He does not hesitate to slay giants whenever they pose a threat to god/esses and humans, even in cases when that involves going outside the normal codes of behavior, as can be seen in the story of the rebuilding of the walls of the Ases' Garth (Âsgardhr). The gods had hired a mason to rebuild the walls which were destroyed in the war between the Ases and the Wans; at Loki's advice, the contract was that if the walls were built within a year and a day, the gods

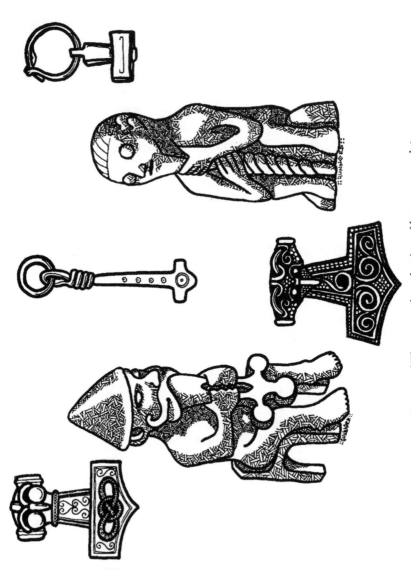

Statues of Thunar and a selection of hammer amulets

would give the mason the Sun, the Moon, and Freyja as his wife. The wall would have been completed within the given time, but Loki, forced by the other deities, transformed himself into a mare and lured the mason's horse away. The mason then revealed himself as a giant, and Thunar slew him, despite the oath of contract the god/esses had sworn.

When reading Germanic holy writings or studying folklore, it is easy to get the impression that Thunar is a relatively uncomplicated character; a "good ol' boy," always eating, drinking, or bashing the bad guys. It is true that Thunar is not a god of subtle wit, who often comes out second in contests where verbal and deceptive skill are the primary factors. He does not, like Wodan, seek wisdom for its own sake; when he fares to Etin-Home, it is to fight or else to bring back physical objects of power for specific ends. The wisdom Thunar displays is the wisdom of common sense; his intellect is not showy, but practical. This appears in the Eddic poem "Alvíssmál," where he questions the dwarf Alvíss ("All-Wise") about the names which the dwellers in the various worlds give to items such as the Sun, the sea, and so forth. He does not do this because he is interested so much in the information himself; as the poem reveals, it is a cunning trap. The dwarf has declared his intention to marry the Thunderer's daughter Thrúdhr, for which the gods have apparently given him permission in Thórr's absence. Thórr is reluctant, but finally says, "The love of the maid must go to thee / wise guest, as you wish, / if you of the worlds each can say / all that I wish to know."(8) He then makes Alvíss recite the kennings for various natural phenomena until the light of dawn turns the dwarf to stone.

Thunar's solutions to problems are generally simple, straightforward, and effective, as when Loki lured him to visit the giant Geirrodhr without his hammer:

> Then Thórr came to the river called Vimur, greatest of all rivers . . . And when Thórr got to the middle of the river, the river rose so greatly that it washed over his shoulders. Then Thórr spoke this: 'Rise not thou now, Vimur, since I desire to wade thee into the giants' courts. Know thou that if thou risest, then will rise the Ase-strength in me up as high as heaven.' Then Thórr saw up in a certain cleft that Geirrodhr's daughter Gialp was standing astride the river and she was causing it to

rise. Then Thórr took up out of the river a great stone and threw it at her and said, 'At its source must a river be stemmed.'[20]

Thunar is the mortal foe of the Middle-Garth's Wyrm, the great serpent Jörmungandr which wraps around the world. Without Thunar's might holding it down, the Wyrm would rise up to destroy the cosmos. The Thunderer meets the Wyrm three times: twice early, first in the hall of Utgardh-Loki where he attempts to lift it, the Wyrm having been disguised as a cat; secondly in the fishing expedition described in the *Prose Edda* (pp. 46-47) and in "Hymiskvidha." Lastly, he will fight it single-handed at Ragnarök, where he will slay it with his hammer and be slain by its poisonous breath. The battle between Thunar and the Middle-Garth Wyrm which takes place during the fishing expedition is important for understanding Thunar's role. This event has its parallels all through Indo-European history; it is the Northern expression of the truth behind all dragon-slayer legends. Thunar goes fishing and brings up the Middle-Garth Wyrm; he strikes it on the head with his hammer, causing the earth to shake; the serpent sinks back into the sea. The Middle-Garth Wyrm embodies the untamed, rampant, and frequently destructive energies of the earth. By striking it on the head, Thunar, who is himself an embodiment of the unification of sky and earth, pins it down; its power hereafter must hold the world together, until it frees itself from the effects of his blow at Ragnarök. As Nigel Pennick describes the archetypal dragon-slaying action, "The sword of St. Michael, the lance of St. George or the arrows of giants . . . all represent the peg or pole which pierced the dragon's head, immovably fixing it at the omphalos"[21]—the process by which the wild earth energies are forced to work weal towards humans.

The dragon or Wyrm was also a symbol of death to the Germanic peoples; as the foe of the darkest aspects of the Serpent, Thunar is the protector of the dead against all the devouring monsters of the other world. Hammer-amulets were buried with the dead for this reason; such amulets were also hung over the crib to protect children.

In places where tornados are a frequent danger, Thunar is called on to ward the true against the "sky-wyrm"—the coiling funnel of the tornado.

As god of storms, Thunar is called upon to still storms at sea and to bring seafarers out of danger. From this aspect, he has become the warder of all travelers, especially those who go into places outside the boundaries of society.

Thunar appears as a burly man with red hair and a red beard which bristles with sparks when he is angry. He is always shown with his great weapon, the short-handled hammer Mjöllnir, "the Crusher," which is also called "Thrúdh-hamarr," "Hammer of Strength." Sometimes he is described as a young man; sometimes he is described as "Thórr Karl" or "Old Man Thórr." He is also called "Father Thórr."

Images of Thunar were commonly put in hofs (temples); in the great hof at Old Uppsala, according to Adam of Bremen, Thunar's image stood in the middle place between those of Wodan and Fro Ing and was set above them. The house pillars were often either carved in his likeness or dedicated to him by the driving of a "gods' nail" into the posts. His statues might have a nail driven into the forehead as well, in memory of the fragment of whetstone which stuck in his head during his battle with the giant Hrungnir (as described in the *Prose Edda*). It has been suggested that these nails were used in ritual to strike sparks for kindling holy fires.

Oaks are particularly holy to Thunar, especially oaks which have been struck by lightning. The Continental Germans worshipped him at the great "Donar's Oak," which was finally destroyed by the Christian missionary Boniface. The rowan is also associated with Thunar; in the story told above of his visit to Geirrodhr, it is also said that after throwing the stone at the giantess he grasped a rowan to pull himself out of the river, and thus the Scandinavian proverb says that "the rowan is the salvation of Thórr." Because of its magical powers of protection against fire, lightning, and ill-meaning witchcraft, as well as its red berries, the rowan is naturally harmonious with the energies of Thunar.

The oath-ring, on which many of the most solemn vows were, and are, made was also very important in the cult of Thunar. Hammer amulets often appear with small rings soldered to the top; these rings are pointed in the wrong direction for hanging the hammer on a chain. It may be that Thunar was often called upon to hallow the ring-oath and to strike the nithling who broke it.

Though place-name evidence shows that many of the Ases were worshipped on specific mountains, the great number of mountains named after Thunar imply that this practice was especially strong in his cult. An Icelandic priest and famous Thórsman, Thórolfr Mostur-Beard, established a holy place on the headland which he named Thórsnes ("Thórr's Headland"), and held a mountain there so sacred "that no one was allowed even to look at it without having first washed himself, and no living creatures on this mountain, neither man or beasts, were to be harmed unless they left it of their own accord. Thórolf called that mountain Helga Fell ("Holy Mountain") and believed that he and his kinsmen would go into it when they died."[22]

A quarter of all recorded Norse names used "Thórr" as an element, showing how widely beloved this god was. Some of these names were given to children in hopes that they would gain blessing and strength from them; others were taken on by adults to show their particular dedication, as in the case of Thórolfr Mostur-Beard, whose name had originally been Hrólfr, but "He was a close friend of Thórr's, and he was in charge of Thórr's temple there on the island, so people called him Thórolfr."[23] Likewise, his son Thórsteinn fathers a son "who was sprinkled with water and given the name Grimr. Thórsteinn dedicated this boy to Thórr, calling him Thórgrimr, and said he should become a temple priest."[24]

Today Thunar is called upon for hallowing and for warding in all things. In her seminar on Thunar, Gunnora Hallakarva suggests that Thunar the giant-slayer and protector of the common man can be called upon for aid in the struggle against giant corporations such as the IRS and in breaking down the barriers of ice-locked bureaucracies. Turville-Petre states that "It was to (Thórr) that men turned, not only for protection against Christ and giants, but also against the landgrabbing, upstart kings of Norway," and he can still protect against the imbalances and injustice of government.

SIF

Sif is the wife of Thunar; little is known about her, except that she gave birth to Wuldor (Ullr) before wedding Thunar and she is the mother of his daughter Thrudhr. As mentioned above, her golden hair is thought to be a symbol of the ripening grain; the tale in which Loki crops it and then gets the dwarves to forge hair of real gold for her (together with Fro Ing's ship and boar, Wodan's spear, Thunar's hammer, and the ring Draupnir) is interpreted on the natural level as an account of slash-and-burn agriculture, with Sif embodying the field and Loki representing fire. In "Lokasenna," Loki claims to have slept with Sif, and no one can deny it; the cropping of a woman's hair is a traditional Northern European punishment for the breaking of the marriage-bond, so Loki's action may have been meant as a form of boasting. From this, however, came many of the mighty weapons and treasures of the gods—the "harvest" growing greater after a small destruction.

In his euhemeristic prologue to the *Prose Edda*, Snorri says, "In the northern part of the world (Thórr) found a spae-woman who was named Sibyl, whom we call Sif, and got her in marriage. No one can tell the kindred of Sif; she was fairest of all women; her hair was like gold." The description of Sif as a *spákona*, or prophetess, and Snorri's association of her with the classical Sibyl tell us that she is, like Frija, the Frowe, and Gefjon, a seeress.

The Lappish version of Thunar has a wife called "Ravdna," "Rowan." Turville-Petre suggests that "Probably the wife of Thórr was once conceived in the form of a rowan, to which the god clung."[25] In this connection, one can note that a rowan tree is first crowned with white—"fair"—flowers, then loses them and gains red berries; and the Germanic peoples perceived the metal gold as being, not yellow in color, but red, so that it is always described as "the red gold" or as "fire." Thus the rowan, as well as the golden grain at summer's end, may be a plant of Sif's nature. Its berries are also brightest at and just after harvest-time, when the golden wheat is cropped.

Sif is spoken of together with the Frowe as one of the most beautiful of the goddesses; the giant Hrungnir says that he will kill all the gods and take Freyja and Sif home with him. Her chief function is probably similar to that of the Frowe and Idunn, as the source of life-force and fruitfulness. Note that it is precisely these three goddesses against whom Loki offends in the myths; cropping Sif's hair—the very embodiment of her life-force—and offering the Frowe and Idunn to the etins are all actions which would, if fully successful, deprive the Ases' Garth of these goddesses' might. She, the mother of the winter-god Wuldor (Ullr), may be seen as the autumnal counterpoint to the Spring Bride Eostre.

TIW (TÝR, ZIO, *TIWAZ)

This god plays a relatively small role in the mythology as it survives in the Eddas; nevertheless, every description of him which survives points to a much larger significance in early Germanic religion overall. His name in Old Norse, "Týr," is one of the generic words for "god"; it is cognate to the Latin "deus" and the Greek "Zeus." It is generally thought that Tiw was the Germanic version of the Indo-European Sky-Father god, whose position as chief of the gods was then gradually usurped by Wodan. In understanding Tiw, however, it is necessary to consider his specific evolution among the Germanic peoples; neither the Romans who came into contact with his cult at the beginning of the Common Era nor the Germanic folk of later eras who tried to equate their own or their ancestors' gods with the gods of the Greeks and Romans considered him to be similar to Jupiter/Zeus. Rather, he was *Mars Thingsus*, "Mars of the Thing (Judgement-Assembly)"[26]; among the names of the days of the week, which were adapted by the Germanic folk before Christianization, Tiw's Day—modern Tuesday—was not the day of Jupiter, but *dies Martis*, the day of Mars. Tacitus reports that the Germans held "Mercury and Mars" highest of all the gods, and no successful argument for seeing this pair as anyone other than Wodan and Tiw has yet been advanced.

Although Tiw's most obvious character is that of a warlike god, he is also a god of contracts and of law, as the title Mars Thingsus would imply. The Old Icelandic Rune Poem calls him "the ruler of the temple" even as it glosses his name as "Mars." Dumézil presents Tiw as the Judge-King equivalent to the Vedic Mitra, the sovereign who rules by law, the meotod ("measurer")—an originally heathen title which remained current in Anglo-Saxon and was eventually co-opted by Christianity for their god. According to his model, the Judge-King ruled together with the furious and unpredictable Magician-King. "The cruel, magical Ódhinn is thus contrasted with Týr, as Varuna, god of night, is contrasted with Mitra, god of day."[27] In the Anglo-Saxon Rune Poem, the names of the gods—except for Ing, who was euhemerized to "the hero"—were deleted and replaced with hononyms which were also appropriate in context. Just as the "os" (Ase) Wodan became "oss," "(Mouth), the chieftain of all speech," so did Tiw become "tir," the star, which "holds troth well / with athelings ever fares on course, / over mists of night and never weakens."

Tiw is the first form of the god who separates heaven and earth; it is his might which "Caedmon's Hymn," despite its nominal Christianity, seems to be celebrating.

> Now you shall hear of heaven-realm's Ward;
> of the Measurer's might his mood and thought.
> Glory-Father worked as wonder of all,
> eternal drighten established first
> and first he shaped for bairns of earth
> heaven to roof, the holy Shaper,
> then Middle-Garth, Mankind's Warder.

It is likely that Tiw was the original "irmin-god," the greatest of the gods, to whom the Saxon Irminsul (Irmin-Pillar) was dedicated. On the daily human level, the Irminsul is embodied by the house-pillars; on the cosmic level, it is the World-Tree, which preserves the levels of being by holding them apart and at the same time, as the central axis of the universe, connects them; and this is shown in the shape of the rune tiwaz, which can be interpreted either as the spear or as the pillar holding up the heavens. In the Old High German "Hildebrantslied," the warrior Hildebrant calls upon "irmingot" ("the Irmin-god") and "waltant got" ("the ruling god") to witness the terrible fate which "Woe-Wyrd" has wrought for him. These titles, used as they are to invoke the laws of society and nature against the caprice of Wyrd which has brought him to a fatal conflict with his own son, are far more likely to be addressed to Tiw than to Wodan, who was blamed for setting strife between kinsmen, not called upon in the attempt to turn it away.

The association with the house pillars/Irminsul and the names "Heaven-Realm's Warder" and "Mankind's Warder" ought to sound familiar; these are all things which, in the Viking Age, had come to be associated with Thunar.

Tiw is wedded; in "Lokasenna," Loki boasts of having cuckolded him and not paid any reparations. The name of his wife has been lost; it is probably, however, safe to assume that she fits within the general character of the Earth-Mother, as the pairing of Earth-Mother and Sky-Father seems to be part of the basic Indo-European tradition.

As he appears in the Old Norse sources, Tiw is unquestionably a god of war, but his oldest aspects are still visible. Snorri says of him that "There is yet one Ase, who is called Týr; he is the bravest and best of thought (*hugadhr*), and he rules greatly over victory in battles; it is good for men of action to call upon him. He is also wise, so that it is also said that a man who is wisest is Týr-wise . . . he is one-handed and not called a maker of peace between people."[28]

The one significant myth which has survived about Tiw is the story of the binding of the Wolf Fenrir, the son of Loki and Angrboda, as told in the *Prose Edda*. This wolf grew so large that none except Týr dared to feed him. At last the gods began to be afraid and decided to bind him. They made a great iron chain and dared the Wolf to let them set it upon him and see if he could break it. He broke that one; they made a second, even heavier, and he broke it too. Finally Freyr's messenger Skírnir went to the dwarves and got a ribbon made of the roots of a rock, the breath of a fish, the beard of a woman, the sound of a cat's footfalls, a bear's sinews, and the spittle of a bird. The Wolf Fenrir was unwilling to have it laid on him, for he said he would get no glory from breaking a slender ribbon, but if it were made with magic he would not have it on his feet; he knew full well that if the gods had him bound it would be long before they would loose him. At last Fenrir agreed to allow it if one of the gods would lay his hand in his mouth as a pledge of troth. "And each of the Ases looked at the other, and none of them was willing to lose his hand, until Týr reached forward his right hand and lay it in the mouth of the Wolf." Then Fenrir was bound, and the harder he struggled the more firmly the band lay upon him, and "all laughed except Týr; he lost his hand." From this, the wrist is called the "wolf's joint."

The rune tiwaz is named after Tiw; its stave-shape shows the spear which may have been his particular weapon before it was Wodan's. The Old Norwegian Rune-Poem says of this stave that "(Týr) is the one-handed among the Ases"; the Old Icelandic Rune-Poem says, "(Týr) is the one-handed Ase / and the wolf's leavings, / and the temple's ruler." This last probably refers to his strong role in the religious life of the folk.

BALDER (BALDR)

Balder is one of the more perplexing gods of the Northern folk. Slain by Loki with an arrow of mistletoe despite his mother's attempts to ward him (as described above), Balder is given a great ship-funeral and fares to Hella's realm, only returning after the battle of Ragnarök is over. Many scholars have attempted to put him into the context of a fertility god who is slain and then revived seasonally, but his death and return are neither seasonal nor connected with the fruitfulness of the earth; that is part of the cult of Fro Ing.

In the *Prose Edda*, he becomes a rather Christian figure of Good martyred by Evil—a suffering god, whose death heralds the final battle and who returns to rule in a purified world. Because of this image, he has been seized upon as a point of transition by some who wish to return to the old ways, but cannot quite divest themselves of Christian beliefs.[29] Many modern Ásatrúar also see Balder as a sort of solar figure, who is particularly to be worshipped at Midsummer and whose death represents the decline of the Sun. Aside from the fact that the Sun is personified in her own right and is always feminine, there is not even the foggiest hint of any sort of seasonal or solar association for Balder.

Looking at other forms of Balder's tale, a clearer understanding of this god begins to emerge. Saxo Grammaticus relates the story in a rather different version which, though euhemerized and less valid from a religious point of view, seems to show older elements of the god's character. Saxo's Baldr is a warrior, the demigod son of Ódhinn, who contests with Hödhr for the hand of the woman Nanna. Hödhr is warned of his rival's intention by several walkyrige figures; gets a magic sword which can kill Baldr and an armring which will bring him wealth (clearly Ódhinn's ring Draupnir); and battles with Baldr several times. Finally he meets the forest-maidens/walkyriges again. They are preparing the magical food which gives Baldr his strength; Hödhr convinces them to let him taste it, and this enables him to defeat and mortally wound his rival. Baldr has a dream in which the goddess "Proserpine"[30] promises him her love. Ódhinn then, by trickery and magic, begets a son on the woman Rindr, who avenges Baldr on Hödhr. In Saxo, this son is named Bous; in the Eddic renditions of the tale, it is Ódhinn's son Váli who, when one night old, takes the revenge for Baldr.

In Saxo's version of the story, Balder appears as a fierce and mighty figure, a heroic warrior rather than a victim embodying innocence. The name "Balder," like the name "Freyr," means "lord"; its ultimate root implies virility and masculine potency. Before his Christianization as a peaceful and "pure" youth, Balder must originally have embodied the image of the heroic young warrior—his character and the circumstances of his death both recall the figure of Sigurdhr/Siegfried, the most beloved hero of the Germanic folk. Further, even the Eddic Balder is not a simple innocent, but rather a figure of wisdom—a spae-man whose dreams tell him of his own *ørlög*, as happens in both Saxo's account and the Eddic poem "Baldrs Draumr." In this mingling of wisdom and warlike character, he is the very mirror of his father Wodan. Saxo's version also associates Balder with the walkyriges, who, as is typical in tales of Wodan-heroes, both give him strength in battle and help in arranging his death.

The name Hödhr means "warlike," while "Vali" means "little warrior"; these names are not really appropriate for names of gods, but rather seem to be *heiti*—descriptive "use-names" taken by the gods (especially Wodan) for specific purposes. The figures of Hödhr and Loki also present a certain problem in the context of the Ases: they, especially Hödhr, are probably not meant to be understood as independent figures, but rather as aspects of Wodan. Hödhr's blindness closely recalls Wodan's impaired vision, especially when one considers that one of Wodan's names was Tvíblindi—"blind in both eyes." In the Eddic version, Hödhr's hand was guided by Loki, who himself often embodies many of the darker sides of Wodan. What appears here is not the simple triumph of destruction as Snorri shows it; rather it is that Wodan himself has planned, or at least found a way to arrange, Balder's death for his own reasons.

Polomé interprets this tale as a mythologizing of an Ódhinnic warrior-initiation, similar in aim to the wolfskin-initiation in *Völsunga saga* where Sigmundr slays and revives his son Sinfjötli. "Presumably the initiate stood in the middle of a circle of men; all kinds of weapons were thrown at him. Then 'Odin' appeared under the shape of Hödr—the 'warrior' par excellence; he cast the mistletoe. As struck by death, the initiate fell on the ground. This was probably enacted very realistically, so that the youth was really considered dead—hence the display of grief!"[31] The tale then appears, not as a presager of doom, but as an initiation in which the young warrior's death is symbolic; he is "slain," and is reborn into the company of adult men as his own avenger, "Váli," whose first task as a man is to seek out and slay his enemy. When it is interpreted in application to the human level, the account of Balder does indeed serve as a fitting model for the Wodanic initiation of a young man.

For the purpose of worship, however, the implications of the Balder-story are much wider. These are borne out by Balder's return from Hel, together with Hödhr, after Ragnarök, and their assumption of Wodan's place, as described in "Völuspá": "Shall unsown acres wax, / all ill shall grow better Baldr shall come: / Hödhr and Baldr dwell in Hropt's (Wodan's) sig-halls, / well, gods of the slain would you know more, or what?"(62) For this reason Balder is not meant to come back before Ragnarök. Thus, when Hel says that he may return if everything in the Nine Worlds weeps for him, Loki—the agent of transformation and of Wodan's hidden plans—refuses to shed a single tear, saying, "Let Hel keep what she has." Likewise, though Balder is stabbed through with a shaft and given a cremation-funeral, he cannot come to Walhall, because that would make it impossible for him to return after the final battle. This secret is kept from all but Wodan and his son—even from the other god/esses. In "Eiríksmál," it is told how the clamor was so great when Eiríkr Blood-Axe and his troop came to Walhall that the god Bragi said, "The benches all creak Baldr must be coming again to Ódhinn's hall," to which Ódhinn replied, "Witless words should wise Bragi speak not." This may well be the secret which Wodan whispered in Balder's ear as his body lay ready for the bale-fire: that Hella would hold him safe through the last battle and bring him forth into the new world.

Balder's death is not, as Snorri makes it, the beginning of a descent into hopelessness, but rather is needful if hope for the worlds is to be preserved. The pair Baldr and Hödhr, who die and are reborn, are matched by the avengers Vídharr (who slays the Wolf Fenrir after it has swallowed Wodan) and Váli, who, according to "Vafthrúdhnismál," "settle *wih-stead* (holy enclosure) of gods / when Surtr's flames are slaked" (51). Between them, these two pairs of brothers make the rebirth of the worlds possible. Vídharr and Váli, by taking revenge on the slayers of their father and brother respectively, make the honor of Wodan and Balder whole again by turning their defeats into eventual victory over their foes.

Balder and Hödhr together represent the hidden seed of Wodan's soul; their return from the land of the dead is his own return to life.

In Balder, we see the shining young warrior hero who embodies all children to come; he is the bold and beloved god of the worlds that shall be. He also represents that joy and hope of the soul which hides itself in times of woe and ill, but springs forth again when the battle is done—the promise of rebirth on every level. His hall lies in a land called Breidhablik, "Far-Shining": "there Baldr has / made for himself a hall, / in that land which I know to lie far / fast from all false staves" ("Grímnismál"). His wife is called Nanna; it is said that she dies of grief when he is slain and fares to Hel with him.

HEIMDALLR

> One was born   in eldest days
> of greatest strength   of godly kin.
> Nine bore him   the weapon-glorious man,
> etin-maids   at edge of the earth.
>
> Gjálp bore him   Greip bore him,
> Eistla bore him   and Eyrgjafa
> Úlfrún bore him   and Angeyja
> Imdhr and Atla   and Járnsaxa.
>
> He was made strong   with main of the earth,
> the ice-cold sea   and sacred boar's blood.
> ("Völuspá hin skamma")

Heimdallr is best known as the watcher of the rainbow bridge Bifröst, who wards it against the rock-giants. He needs less sleep than a bird; he can see a hundred leagues by night as well as by day, and hear the grass growing in the fields and wool on the sheep. As well as being a warder, he is also a giver of wise and cunning redes to the god/esses, as in the Eddic poem "Thrymskvidha" in which he suggests that Thórr be dressed in bridal linen and disguised as Freyja in order to regain the hammer Mjöllnir from the giant Thrym. He is also known as the highest-minded of the gods, and is able to see into the future as the Wans are. He owns the horn named Gjallarhorn, "The Resounding Horn," which he shall blow

to call the hosts of the gods together at the beginning of the Ragnarök battle.

Heimdallr is a fair and shining god, called the "white Ase";
his teeth are made of gold. His hall is called Himinbjörg, "Heaven-
Mountain," which reinforces the image of the eaglelike watcher
from the heights.

In the myths, Heimdallr is best known as the foe of Loki, against
whom he struggled in seal-shape to reclaim the Frowe's necklace
Brísingamen; the two of them will slay each other at Ragnarök.

Some of what we know about this god is mysterious. As
"Völuspá hin skamma" relates, he was born of nine mothers at the
edge of the world; he was slain at least once, with a man's head,
and for this reason, as Snorri says, "a sword is called Heimdallr's
head . . . " "Heimdalargaldr" speaks of this, and afterwards the
head is called "measurer (or 'bane') of Heimdallr." (Skáldskaparmál 16) Unfortunately, the poem "Heimdalargaldr," "The Magical Song of Heimdallr," where these things seem to have been
explained in detail, has been lost to us. According to Völuspá,
Heimdallr's "hljódh" is hidden at the roots of the World Tree, in
the depths of Mímir's Well. Snorri interprets this word as meaning
"horn," implying that the Gjallarhorn is concealed there. However,
"hljódh" is more normally used to mean "sound" or "hearing,"
which invites a comparison with Wodan, who sees all that happens
in the world from his high seat, Hlidhskjálf, and who left one eye
in the depths of Mímir's Well; it may be that, like Wodan, Heimdallr "sacrificed" half of his most important sense to the Well of
Mímir, thus gaining the same wisdom—the awareness of the great
realm of the "past," or "that-which-is," added to his awareness all
that takes place through the worlds.

Another aspect of Heimdallr's which points to a higher place
than most of the myths show for him is his role in shaping and
teaching the human race, as described in the Eddic "Rígsthula."
Heimdallr takes on the name Rígr (probably derived from the Irish
word for "king") and walks through the earth. First he stays with a
couple called Ái ("Great-Grandfather") and Edda ("Great-Grand-
mother"), begetting a son called Thrall, from whom the kindred of
servants springs. Secondly, he stays with Afi ("Grandfather") and
Amma ("Grandmother"), begetting a son called Karl, first of the
kindred of free farmers. Lastly, he stays with Fadhir and Modhir,
"Father" and "Mother," begetting a son called Jarl, "Earl." When

Jarl has grown to manhood, Rígr comes to him, teaching him runes and counseling him towards great deeds. Jarl's youngest son is named "Konr ungr," "Kon the Young," from which Norse folk etymology derived the title "Konungr," "King." This youth is able to strive magically against Rígr and win his grandfather's title for his own. Here, we see a process of successive evolution in which the god puts more might into the human race in each generation, till the youngest has become his own equal. The tale of the godly fathering of the tribes of humankind is one which goes back at least to Indo-European times; the identification of Heimdallr with this father was probably fairly well known among the Old Norse, because at the beginning of "Völuspá," the völva starts her prophecy by saying, "Hear me, all you hallowed beings / both high and low of Heimdallr's kin."

A similar tale was recorded among the Germanic tribes in the time of Tacitus, describing how the god Mannus fathered the three great tribes of Germania (the Ingvaeones, nearest the sea; the Hermiones, in the interior; and the Istavaeones, who made up all the rest). The name Mannus simply means "man" in the sense, not of "male," but of "human being, person"; it implies all the highest attributes of wisdom and intellect which Heimdallr brought (and brings!) to the human race. He can be seen as the embodiment of the Rainbow Bridge which he wards; the link between the Ases' Garth and the realm of humans both in a spiritual and a physical/genetic sense, a two-way link by which the might of the god/esses is brought down to the Middle-Garth while those humans who receive it can in turn rise upwards to the level of the god/esses.

Heimdallr's holy beast is the ram; although no stories survive concerning this, the form "Heimdali" survives both in reference to the god himself and to the ram, which implies that either he took the form of a ram or else that it was associated with him as the cat is associated with the Frowe or the wolf with Wodan. Likewise, his by-name Hallinskídhi is also given as a poetic word for "ram." The sheep was an important sacrificial beast among the Germanic peoples; its Old Norse name is related to the Gothic word for "sacrifice," and *Ljósvetninga saga* describes how a man, in claiming another man's share of the godhordh (priesthood), carried out the ritual of slaughtering a ram and reddening his hands in its blood as he spoke his claim.[32] Snorri specifically says of Heimdallr, as he does not of the other gods, that he is "holy"; this also implies a special position for Heimdallr in ritual and religion.

As mentioned above, Heimdallr also became a seal to fight with Loki, and has other ties with the water: he was nourished on "the ice-cold sea," and the nine etin-maids who bore him "at edge of the earth" may well be the nine waves, the daughters of Ægir and Ran. At the same time, he is the warder of the holy and cleansing fires of Bifröst; his by-name "Vindler" ("Turner") may also show that the need-fire[33] was associated with him. His horse is called Gulltoppr ("Gold-Forelock").

LOKI

Oh, the great Gods of Asgard are noble and free,
They are upright and forthright (as great Gods should be),
But there's one in their midst doesn't follow the rule—
That sly mischief-maker called Loki the Fool.
He lies and he pilfers, tells jokes that are crude,
He's raucous, he's ribald, he's rowdy, he's rude;
He tricks and he teases, though he's not really cruel—
(Just don't turn your back on that Loki the Fool).
—Alice Karlsdottir, "Loki the Fool"

Loki appears only in the Scandinavian sources. He is not, properly speaking, one of the gods, but rather an etin with whom Wodan swore the oath of blood-brotherhood. He is, however, one of the most vivid and unforgettable characters of Norse myth, though he presents certain problems to the practice of Ásatrú.

Traditionally, Loki is understood as a wight of fire[34]—the embodiment of that element, which, as Loki is, is an untrustworthy servant, a deadly master, and an indispensable companion. He has also been identified as Lódurr, who, together with Wodan and his brother Hoenir, gives life to humankind. The gifts of Lódurr are physical appearance and vital warmth; Loki himself is described as being handsome and fine to look at, and as a fire-being, he quite naturally would be the giver of bodily warmth. According to Snorri, the gifts given by Lódurr were "appearance, speech and hearing and sight"—the bodily senses.

In the myths, Loki is shown as tricky and untrustworthy. He gets the god/esses into trouble almost continually, playing a constant game of double-agentry between the god/esses and the giants in which he is always betraying one side to the other. He delights in malicious practical jokes and the giving of deceptive redes; yet when forced to make reparations, he has been the source of many of the best treasures possessed by the god/esses— Wodan's horse Sleipnir and the ring Draupnir, Thunar's hammer, Fro Ing's boar and ship. In all things, he embodies the force of change—sometimes for good, sometimes for ill. As Snorri says, "Time and again he has brought the gods into great trouble, but often rescued them by his wiles."

Loki is the son of the etin Fárbauti ("Cruel Striker") and a female named Laufey ("Leafy Island"). He is usually referred to as "Laufey's son," which may imply that he is a bastard, since the Norse "surnames" were normally derived from the father. He has a brother named Býleist, about whom nothing is known; the name given to Ódhinn in the list of Loki's kindred is Helblindi, "Death-Blind," which may reflect back upon the Balder episode (see above). He is often called "Loptr," "he who flies aloft," and in "Thrymskvidha" he borrows the Frowe's cloak of falcon-feathers to fly over Etin-Home and find Thunar's stolen hammer.

Loki also has a darker side: he is the father of the Wolf Fenrir, who will slay Wodan at Ragnarök, and of the Middle-Garth's Wyrm, Jormungandr, against whom Thunar will fall. He fathered these two wights on the giantess Angrbodha, "Distress-Bringer." Some of the Scandinavian sources, most notably Snorri, also identify Hella as Loki's daughter; but this is more likely to be a consequence of Christian contamination than a genuine tradition (see the chapter on Soul and Afterlife). In "Völuspá hin skamma," it is said that Loki ate an evil woman's half-burned heart and thus became pregnant, giving birth to every female monster in the world. He forged the sword Lævateinn, "Guileful Twig," with runes beneath the gates of Hel. As discussed above, he is the immediate cause of Balder's death. Eventually the gods bind him with the guts of his son Nari, while his son Narfi is turned into a wolf. Skadhi hangs a wyrm above him to drip venom into his face—a scene which appears on a Viking Age stone cross in Cumbria. His wife Sigyn stands by with a cup to catch it; but when she turns away to empty it, the venom falls upon him and then his struggles of agony cause great earthquakes. At the beginning of Ragnarök, he will break free and steer the ship Naglfar (a ship made from dead men's nails) from the east with a crew of dead men and Muspilli (the fire-etins of destruction).

The theme of *ergi* (passive homosexuality/cowardice) is strong in many of the portrayals of Loki. To get the god/esses out of the bargain they had made with the mason who was building the walls of the Ases' Garth, he turned into a mare and lured the mason's stallion away; from this union, Loki bore Wodan's horse Sleipnir. Since the worst insult that could be given to a Germanic man was to call him a mare, this can fairly be taken to show a certain defectiveness in Loki's person. The pregnancy mentioned above also falls into the category of *ergi*, as does Wodan's accusation (in "Lokasenna") that Loki had been a milkmaid beneath the earth for nine winters and had born children. He also borrows Freyja's falcon-skin at least twice so that he can fare to Etin-Home, which can be taken as metaphysical cross-dressing, since the falcon-hide is usually worn only by goddesses.

Despite this, Loki also appears as a figure of masculine potency; he boasts of having enjoyed the favors of many of the godesses of the Ases' Garth, including Sif, Skadhi, and Týr's wife. It is he who, by tying one end of a rope to his testicles and the other to a goat's beard, gets the wintry goddess Skadhi to laugh after the gods have killed her father. Perhaps the best commentary on Loki's sexual adventures was made by Alice Karlsdottir in her song on this god:

> They say he's corrupted and wicked indeed,
> 'Cause he mothered the Allfather's whimsical steed;
> It's not he's perverted or easily led—
> Let's just say he's not very choosy in bed.
> He tried to enliven sedate Asgard's halls,
> By tying the beard of a goat to his balls;
> And they say that his tongue's his most effective tool,
> (And that's why all the ladies love Loki the Fool!)

Of all the gods, Loki is most closely associated with Wodan. It has been said before that Loki often seems to act as the agent of Wodan's will, either when expressed overtly—as when Wodan orders him to steal the Frowe's necklace—or when the command is hidden, as in the case of the death of Baldr. Part of the oath of blood-brotherhood which Wodan and Loki swore was that for every horn of drink given to Wodan, Loki should have a horn also. In a very real sense, Loki is Wodan's shadow—though, paradoxically enough, he also seems to embody the sense of humor and lightness of being which is largely absent from most portrayals of Wodan.

Loki also appears in several of the myths as the travel-companion of Thunar; his swift wits often serve to get the stronger god out of tight situations. As Thunar's friend, Loki represents the traditional companion of the hero—the comic, practical "Sancho Panza" figure. As Karlsdottir points out in her article on Loki, both Loki and Thórr are agents of change and even of destruction in their own way—as mentioned above, Thunar does not hesitate to break the standard codes of behavior when he sees the need, even to attacking a guest. Thus, she suggests, the distinction which many moderns seem to draw between Thórr— good/Loki—evil is an artificial line through a very blurred territory.[35] Nevertheless, when Loki goes too far, it is Thunar's might which forces him to make amends; it seems that Thunar is the only one of the god/esses whom Loki really respects, as his speech at the end of "Lokasenna," when Thórr at last comes into the hall, shows. "I've said before Ases and before Ases' sons / whatever whets my thoughts; / before you alone I shall go out, / for I wit that you will strike." Thus, when Loki's presence in your life becomes unwelcome, it is good to call on Thunar to hold him back.

Although the change Loki embodies is often destructive, it is also, quite literally, the source of comic relief in both the myths and the cosmos as a whole. To quote Karlsdottir again:

> To the end of all time he'll run free through the land,
> And all things stir and change at the touch of his hand,
> And when the world's old and no fun's left in store,
> He'll blow it all up and start over once more.
> Now scholars and such say he's captured and bound,
> But just look at the world, you'll see he's still around,
> For to live here without him would be just too cruel,
> Oh Loki, we love you, dear Loki the Fool!

She also mentions that he may be called upon when a complete change in your life is needed, though urges much caution in this—whatever happens may not be enjoyable at all, though at least it won't be boring!

In modern times, Loki has been presented in two different ways: firstly, as the light-hearted jester of many of the myths; secondly, as a sort of "Nordic Satan." Neither of these is true by itself; Loki's fiery light cannot be separated from the shadows it cast. Since he can fairly be neither diabolized nor made holy, this offers a certain problem in dealing with him within the religion. There is no evidence for any worship given to Loki, though he plays a part in many Scandinavian folk-tales which is similar to the comic devil-tales found throughout Europe; he is the bringer of fleas, the sower of weeds, the deceiver who is himself deceived in the end. Nevertheless, because of his mythic prominence and his close ties to Wodan, it is impossible to ignore him, though experience has shown that drinking to him at *symbel* results in minor disasters within the evening (one toaster's glasses fell into the campfire and melted; another, at a later event, broke his carven staff in the very course of making the toast). It is best to call upon him, if you must, together with a call to Thunar and Wodan; or else to call him by the name Lódurr, which speaks of his most helpful and "godly" side—and always remember that you cannot give a horn to Wodan without, at least implicitly, giving it to Loki as well. Remember the wicked fairy of Germanic children's stories, who was enraged by not being invited to the feast—the same thing happens with Loki in "Lokasenna" (Gunnora Hallakarva suggests pouring a few drops of each horn drunk to Wodan into the fire so that Loki will know he hasn't been forgotten).

The only creatures associated with Loki are the spider (in Scandinavian folk-tradition) and the fly, which is a shape he takes at least twice in the myths.

WULDOR (ULLR)

This god, whose name means "glory," is firstly a god of winter; it is suggested that his might is shown by the shifting light-banners of the aurora borealis. He is the son of Sif, stepson of Thunar; his father is unknown, though Wuldor's wintry nature and his many similarities to the etin-goddess Skadhi suggest that this god might be the son of a rime-giant.

Snorri says that "One (of the gods) hight Ullr . . . he is such a good bowman and skier that no one can compete with him; and he is of fair appearance and has the accomplishments of a warrior; he is good to pray to in single combat *(einvígi)*." ("Gylfaginning" 17) He is called "ski-Ase, bow-Ase, hunting-Ase, shield-Ase" in "Skáldskaparmál."

One kenning for "shield" is "Ullr's boat." The tale behind this kenning has been lost, but the term survives in several poems.

Wuldor seems to have held a higher place among the Ases than the Eddic myths suggest. In "Grímnismál," Ódhinn, tortured between two fires, says "Ullr shall bless—and all the gods— whoso quenches first the flames." This combination of "Ullr and the gods" appears in Icelandic place-names as well: Ullarfoss ("Ullr's waterfall") stands next to Godhafoss ("waterfall of the gods"), and Ullarklettur ("Ullr's cliff") next to Godhaklettur. In "Atlakvidha," the oath-ring is called "Ullr's ring." Since single combat often had a particularly holy function, being a means of deciding right in both legal cases and personal quarrels and involving a ritual of invocation of the gods and sacrifice, Wuldor's role as the god of single combat shows that Wuldor, like Tiw and Wodan, may have been called upon as a battle-judge. This is supported by Snorri's specific use of the term *einvígi* in describing Ullr's function; the *einvígi* was the duel carried out to decide a legal question, as opposed to the *holmgang*, which was the duel fought to avenge insult—and sometimes used unfairly by strong men, especially berserks, to gain the property of weaker men either by killing them or forcing them to forfeit. In the *einvígi*, on the other hand, the gods were thought to give victory to the man who stood in the right. Wuldor's association with the oath-ring also implies that he was responsible for enforcing the vows sworn upon it; it is not unlikely that he might have been the "all-mighty Ase" by whom, together with Freyr and Njördhr, oaths were made upon the ring.

The only tale of Wuldor which has survived is in Saxo. Because Wodan had disguised himself as a woman in order to beget Balder's avenger, the gods expelled him for this disgrace. "Ollerus," Wuldor, ruled in Wodan's place for ten years until the gods restored their earlier ruler, after which Wuldor fled to Sweden.

According to Saxo, also, Wuldor was a magician who crossed the sea on a bone inscribed with spells, which some scholars have interpreted as the source of the kenning "Ullr's boat" for "shield." One of the older runic inscriptions includes the name

"W(u)lthuthewaR," which probably is an assumed cultic name meaning "servant of Wuldor"; this may also imply the possibility of an early connection between Wuldor and the runes.

Place-name evidence shows that Ullr was largely worshipped in eastern and central Sweden, as well as southeastern Norway, and suggests that his cult may have reached its height before that of the better-known god/esses. Turville-Petre suggests that Wuldor may have been in the north what Tiw was in Denmark and continental Germany; the early Sky-Father whose place was taken by Wodan in the late Migration/early Viking Age.[36]

Ullr's hall is called "Yew-Dales," and as a bow-god, he is of course strongly associated with the yew from which bows were made. The yew is also appropriate to him as a wintry god, since it is green all through the season of death.

BRAGI

In "Grímnismál," Ódhinn names Bragi as the best of skalds, and he is usually counted among the number of the gods. Of him, Snorri says that "One (of the gods) hight Bragi: he is the most renowned for wisdom and greatest at fluency of speech and skill with words. He knows the most of skaldcraft (poetry), and from him skaldcraft is called *bragr*, and from his name those who have greater fluency with speech than other men or women are called *bragr*-men or -women." "Sigrdrífumál" says that runes are carved "on Bragi's tongue," as they are on other objects of great might, such as Sleipnir's teeth; this probably refers to his immense skill with speech. As an adjective, *bragr* means "first" or "best." The cup of toast-drinking is called the *bragrfull*, "best cup," but also "Bragi's cup," which may be a pun on the fact that oaths and toasts were often expected to be made in poetry.

In "Eiríksmál," Bragi is one of the dwellers in Valhöll; he, together with the two great Ódhinn-heroes Sigmundr and Sinfjötli, gives welcome to the freshly slain Eiríkr Bloodaxe. His position among Wodan's champions implies that Bragi may once have been a living human. Indeed, the first skald of tradition was a man named Bragi Boddason the Old; and Bragi is usually shown as an old man with a long white beard, in spite of the fact that he is wedded to Idunn, keeper of the apples of youth. The historical poet may, then, have been raised into the ranks of the gods after his death, just as other heroes such as Theodoric the Great (see Chapter 7: Heroes) seem to have been. Thus he is no rival for Wodan's place as the god of poetry, but rather a favored fosterling of the god.

In the section of the *Prose Edda* called "Skáldskaparmál" ("The Language of Poetry"), the information about the writing of skaldic verse, together with many of the myths explaining the kennings, is related by Bragi.

IDUNN (IDHUNN)

The goddess Idunn is known as the keeper of the apples of youth. Snorri says that she keeps her apples in a casket and "the gods shall eat of them when they age, and then they all become young, and so shall it be until Ragnarök." The one myth which survives about her is related by Bragi in "Skáldskaparmál." Loki had been captured by the etin Thjazi (the father of the goddess Skadhi), who refused to let him go until he promised to get Idunn outside of the Ases' Garth with her apples. Loki then told Idunn that he had found some apples which she would think worth having, and told her that she should have her own with her so that she could compare the two. Idunn went out and Thjazi kidnapped her. When the god/esses began to grow old and gray, they held a meeting, and found that Idunn had last been seen leaving the Ases' Garth with Loki. They threatened him until he became afraid and promised to bring her back, asking for the loan of Freyja's falcon-hide. Loki flew to Thjazi's cave while the etin was gone and turned Idunn and her apples into a nut, with which he swiftly flew back. Thjazi found his captive missing, turned into an eagle, and followed Loki. As Loki crossed the bounds of the Ases' Garth, the god/esses lit a great fire on the walls, which singed the eagle's feathers and forced Thjazi to earth inside their garth where they slew him.

Both the apples and the nut are, of course, symbols not only of fruitfulness, but of life preserved and renewed; wild apples were used in Scandinavian burial rites from the Bronze Age (ca. 2000 BCE) to the time of the Oseberg ship-burial (ca. 700–800 CE). The fact that Idunn's apples are not freshly plucked, but kept in a casket, implies that she feeds them to the god/esses at a time when apples are not usually ripe—perhaps at Yule, but more likely at Eostre.

The tale of Idunn has several elements which are similar to other spring dramas such as the winning of Gerdhr by Fro Ing ("Skírnismál"), the winning of Menglodh by Svípdag ("Svípdagsmál"), and the awakening of Sigrdrífa by Sigurdhr (Sigrdrífumál"; *Völsunga saga*); the mighty woman held captive in the realm of etins; the crossing of the ring of fire, and the slaying of the guardian etin who embodies winter. It is clear that she is an embodiment of the life-force which must be reawakened each spring—rewon from the world of winter, of sleep and of death; she may be seen as the Norse version of the Spring Bride, the Anglo-Saxon Eostre/German Ostara. As mentioned of Sif and the Frowe, the attempt of the etins to take Idunn for their own is part of the struggle between the giants and the god/esses. Without the might of these holy women, nothing could live or be reborn and the endless winter of Etin-Home would cover the Middle-Garth: it is they, as much as Thunar, who keep the holy garths safe and the dwellers within alive.

Idunn is the wife of the godly skald Bragi.

Fosite (Forseti)

According to the Old Norse sources, Forseti is the son of Balder; Wodan states in "Grímnismál" that he "settles all suits." Fosite appears in none of the Eddic myths, but was worshipped by the Germanic folk around the North Sea, especially the Frisians. His holy place is the island of Helgoland ("holy land," formerly called "Fosete's Land"), which lies between Denmark, Friesland, and Saxony.

According to Frisian tradition, when the Frisians wished to make their law-code, their twelve chosen elders set out to sea in a small boat in order to find a peaceful spot to deliberate. When they had pushed off, a mighty storm drove them far from land. Lost, they called upon Fosite's help; at once they saw a thirteenth man in the boat, who seized the rudder and brought them to an island. He flung his axe onto land; where it struck, a stream gushed forth. The stranger got off and drank of the spring in silence; each of the elders followed him. They all then sat in a circle as this man spoke a code of laws to them. When he was finished, he disappeared, and the elders knew that they had been given their laws by Fosite himself. The island was then declared holy; to this spot the Frisians came for the judicial assemblage of their Thing, always drawing water from Fosite's spring and drinking it in silence before they began. These waters were so holy that they (like the waters of the Well of Wyrd) hallowed whoever drank from them, and even the herds of cattle who drank there could not be slain, but were kept holy to the god.

Fosite hears oaths and keeps the peace between folk. He should especially be called upon in matters of bitter lawsuits, for he, unlike Tiw, is a god of reconciliation, of fairness and mildness in contrast to strict justice.

NOTES

1. "Der nur verdient seine Freiheit / Der täglich neu sie erobert." Goethe, Johann. *Faust*, act II.

2. Turville-Petre, E.O.G. *Myth and Religion of the North*, 42-3.

3. *Völsunga saga*, author's translation.

4. Sweet, Henry (ed.). "Bede's Account of the Coming of the Angles, Saxons, and Jutes" in *Sweet's Anglo-Saxon Reader*, 43.

5. Tacitus, Cornelius; James Chisholm (tr.; ed.). *Germania*, quoted in *Grove and Gallows*, 5.

6. Ibid.

7. "Grímnismál," 20.

8. *The Exeter Book*, Maxims 1:84–92.

9. Nanna Damsholt. "Viking Women."

10. "Lokasenna," 29.

11. Pálsson, Hermann; Paul Edwards (tr.). *Orkneyinga saga*, 36–37.

12. *Snorra Edda*, ch. 33.

13. Chisholm, James (tr.). *Origin of the Lombards*, quoted in *Grove and Gallows*, 27.

14. Ibid., ch. 35.

15. Ibid., ch. 22.

16. Ibid.

17. Grimm, 267.

18. Motz, Lotte. *The Winter Goddess,* 154.

19. Grimm, Jacob. *Deutsche Mythologie,* vol. 1.

20. Sturluson, *Prose Edda,* 82 (Faulkes).

21. Pennick, Nigel. *The Ancient Science of Geomancy,* 46.

22. Pálsson, Hermann; Paul Edwards. *Eyrbyggja saga,* 41.

23. Ibid., 38.

24. Ibid.

25. Turville-Petre, 98.

26. From a votive stone found at Housesteads, by Hadrian's Wall, erected for Germanic soldiers in the Roman army.

27. Turville-Petre, 181.

28. *Snorra Edda,* ch. 13.

29. Such as the idea, put forth in a recent book on "Odinism," that the Ásatrúar set up a manger scene at Yule with Mother Frigga, her Sacred Child in the straw, and three male gift-bringers identified as Odin, Thor, and Loki. The only reason I can see for doing this is to avoid really extreme persecutors and/or keep peace with an intolerant family group. Otherwise, it is simply hanging on to Christian tradition.

30. Saxo wrote in Latin; "Proserpine" would have been the classical equivalent to Hella.

31. Polomé, Edgar. *Essays on Germanic Religion,* 19.

32. Turville-Petre, 151.

33. Fire created solely by the friction of wood against wood; a very important part of early Germanic rituals.

34. Though he is not identified so in the Old Norse sources, this is suggested by his matching against Loge, "wildfire," in the contests at Útgardhloki's hall.

35. Karlsdottir, Alice. "Loki." *Gnosis,* April 1991.

36. Turville-Petre, 183.

Chapter 5

THE WANS

NERTHUS/NJÖRDR

HE FOLLOWING ACCOUNT was written by the Roman Tacitus in the year 98 CE. It is the first direct information we have about the Wanic cult, and contains the chief elements characterizing the Wanic god/esses: the combination of earth and water; the journey by ship; the festive procession in the wain; the association of Wanic holiness with the keeping of *frith* (fruitful peace); the tending of the deity by a holy person of the opposite gender; and the sinking of the gift to the goddess in a holy lake or bog.

The Reudingi, the Aviones, the Angles, the Varini, the Eudoses, the Saurdones, and the Niutones are surrounded by rivers and forests. There is nothing noteworthy about them individually, but they all have in common the veneration of Nerthus who is the Earth Mother. They believe her to be involved in human affairs and that she travels among the folk. There is a sacred grove in an island in the Ocean and it is said that there, there is a carriage dedicated to her and that a sheet is draped over it. One priest has the authority to touch it. When he knows that the Goddess is present in the temple, he follows her in a spirit of profound respect. Then there are festive times in store for those places which she deems worthy of her presence. At this time they conduct no warfare, bear no arms, and all weaponry is put in storage. Peace and quiet are then experienced and loved until the priest finds out from the Goddess that she is satiated with the company of humans and it is time to return her to her temple. After the carriage is returned and covered with the sheet, if you wish to believe it, the carriage and the Goddess herself are washed in a secret lake. Slaves perform this task and are then drowned in the same waters. There is a fear of the arcane attached to this custom for there is a reverence sprung from ignorance about that which is seen only by men who die for having done so.[1]

The name of this North German goddess, Nerthus (coming from a root meaning "under"—possibly the same root that Modern English "north" is derived from), is precisely the same name as that of the Old Norse god Njördhr; only the gender and linguistic form are changed between the Proto-Germanic and the Old Norse. The same deity may have been known as a god or a goddess in different places; Nerthus/Njördhr may have been an hermaphrodite; or else the two, god and goddess, were (like Fro Ing and the Frowe) seen as a pair of twins and lovers. In "Lokasenna," Loki accuses Njördhr of having gotten Freyr and Freyja upon his own sister, and mentions also that the latter pair had committed incest; Njördhr's sister is never named, but it is easy to believe that the two were originally a male/female pair of identical twins. This belief is borne out by the complementary character of the two; while both have islands as holy steads, Njördhr is described as a god of the *sea* in all the Norse sources, while Nerthus is "Terra Mater," "Mother Earth." United, they rule the whole of the world characterized by mysterious depths, fruitfulness, and hidden wisdom and might; the dark Wanic world of earth and water. The mightiest holy steads of the Wans are islands and bogs, where the two come together.

The Wanic cult is as closely associated with the cults of the dead as with the fruitfulness of the land, and for much the same reason: as the rulers of earth and water, Nerthus, Njördhr, and their children receive whatever is put into the darkness, even as what springs forth from it is their gift. The Wanic ship is the means of crossing from one realm to another; it is the funeral ship of the burial as well as the ship of life. This can be seen in the prologue to *Beowulf*, in which it is told how the Wanic king Scyld Scefing

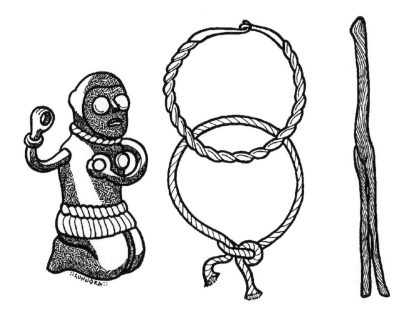

Representations of Nerthus and her sacred torc

("Shield Sheaf-Descended," a name which points to this figure as one of the rulers embodying the might of Fro Ing) was sent over the waters in a ship as an infant—sailing into the land of the living. After a long life as a mighty warrior and great leader, Scyld, on his deathbed, orders that he be put into a boat again and sent out onto the waves, and so his boat is laden with great treasure.

> No less gave they to him   with gifts adorning
> with the folk's treasures   than those did
> who, at time's threshold,   once sent him forth
> alone over waves   a little bairn.

Perhaps for the same reason, the Wanic god/esses are also strongly associated with riches; the dead were buried with their possessions, many of which were very fine, therefore the realm of the Wans was that which held the most treasure. Snorri says of Njördhr that "he is so rich and blessed with wealth, that he may give (to humans) great plenty of lands and things, and he shall be called upon for this," and of Freyr that "he rules also the prosperity of humans."

Although they are not of the kin of giants, the Wans mate freely with these wights. Njördhr and Fro Ing both take wives from the giant race; these wives, Skadhi and Gerdhr are both embodiments of the frozen earth who must be "melted"; and in both cases, the process involves a symbolic emasculation (displaced onto Loki in the tale of Skadhi and Njördhr). The Frowe, in turn, is the chief object of giantish desire, though none of these wights ever succeed in getting her.

The rune of Njördhr is laguz (ᛚ), while that of Nerthus is berkano (ᛒ).

SKADHI

Skadhi, called "the shining bride of gods,"[2] is the daughter of the giant Thjazi, whom the Ases killed after his kidnapping of Idunn and her apples. When her father had been slain, Skadhi came to the Ases' Garth in helm and byrnie with weapons, meaning to avenge him, as was her duty since Thjazi had no sons. The Ases, however, offered her atonement: the first condition was that they should be able to make her laugh; the second was that she might choose a husband from among them, though she was only allowed to choose by the feet. Skadhi wished to wed Baldr, and thus chose the fairest pair of feet; however, it was Njördhr to whom the feet belonged. This motif appears in a number of later "fairy tales," and may go back to the time of the Bronze Age rock carvings, where the imprints of bare feet appear together with other images suggesting fertility. The choosing of a bridegroom by his feet may have been one of the ritual games played at weddings.

The means by which Skadhi was made to laugh also recall fertility rituals. As Snorri describes it, Loki tied one end of a thong to his testicles and the other end to a goat, "and each gave way in turn, and each of the two screeched loudly; then Loki let himself fall onto Skadhi's knee, and she laughed." Loki's mock emasculation may recall the "unmanliness" which was to some degree part of the cult of Fro Ing (see below). Since this story appears in the late *Prose Edda*, it may be that Loki, as a Trickster figure, has been subsituted for Njördhr himself or one of the other gods and the episode deliberately given a more comic slant in the telling. However, Loki also claims that he has slept with Skadhi, so his role in "thawing" her may have been toned down rather than invented! Tales in which a withdrawn or angry god/ess is convinced to laugh by a sexual display also appear in other cultures, both Indo-European and non-Indo-European. The wedding section of the tale of Skadhi and Njördhr is ideally set up to be performed as a folk drama.

The remainder of the story describes the unsuccessfulness of the marriage. Njördhr wished to remain in his home Nóatún by the sea, but Skadhi objected to the sound of the sea-birds; when they went to her ancestral home in the mountains, Thrymheimr ("Home of Noise"), the howling of the wolves was too much for Njördhr to bear. There are various accounts of what happened after this. One is that they compromised by spending nine nights in Thrymheimr and three in Nóatún; this is interpreted as a nature-myth describing the waters from the mountains, which are frozen for nine months out of the year and run to the sea for three months. According to Eyvindr the Plagarist, after the failure of her marriage to Njördhr, Skadhi was married to Wodan (possibly as a second concubine) and mothered many sons, some of whom founded great human dynasties.

Although Skadhi is of giant race, place names show that she was worshipped most of all in eastern Sweden. She is called "Goddess of Snowshoes," and Snorri also speaks of her shooting the bow and hunting wild animals. Her name may mean either "Shadow" or "Scathe." When Loki was bound by the Ases, it was she who hung the bale-dripping wyrm over his face as a last act of revenge for his part in the slaying of her father. Like many of the other goddesses, she has knowledge of what shall become; in "Lokasenna," she prophesies Loki's doom with some glee. The same poem implies that the wise counsel stemming from her goodwill was also prized; she tells Loki that "if first and fiercest in fray you were, / when Thiazi was slain, / from my *wih-steads* and fields shall / cold redes ever come to you." As her name shows, her nature is that of darkness and winter, but still she does not work woe unfairly; indeed, her willingness to accept a husband as atonement for her father's death and the good relations which she maintains with the Ases after the failure of the marriage show her as a surprisingly reasonable goddess, with an interest in maintaining social codes as well as hunting and ruling in her own realm of the wild.

THE FROWE (FREYJA)

The Frowe is unquestionably the most beloved goddess among true folk today, as well as the best-known. Due to the intense sexuality of her cult, a great deal of information concerning her was deliberately lost; even before Iceland was converted to Christianity, writing the love poetry of which she was patroness was considered grounds for lesser outlawry. Unlike that of her twin brother Fro Ing, her true name survives in no sources, though she is sometimes identified with Nerthus, the old Earth-Mother of the North Sea Germans.

The Frowe and Fro Ing are the twin children of Njördhr and his sister, who bears no name in the Old Norse sources. They are the most famed of the Wanic deities.

In contrast to the more domestic and conservative figure of Frija, who embodies the power of the feminine in the social sphere, the Frowe represents the power of the feminine in the realms of nature and magic. She is often a wild goddess; within the terms of society, she was often rebuked for her sexuality, for she holds herself accountable to no one for her loves. In "Lokasenna," Loki says to her that "I know thee fully / ever you are mad after men: / all Ases and Alfs who are in this hall / have had thee to love" (30); while the etin-maid Hyndla says that "you leap about, atheling-friend, outside at nights, / as with the he-goats Heidhrún goes" ("Hyndluljódh" 46, 47). For this reason, also, a Christian skald referred to her as *gray:* "bitch" (he was sentenced to lesser outlawry for this offensive stave).

There is a certain tendency among some moderns to see Freyja as simply a sexual figure, an object of male fantasy. However, the Old Norse sources make it very clear that she was always the one in charge of her relationships—a thoroughly "modern" figure of female sexuality. Although the gods offered Freyja's hand in marriage to giants at least twice, when it came to it, she refused mightily (as a result of which, Thórr had to disguise himself as a woman and take her place to regain his stolen hammer!). "Wroth was then Freyja ... All halls of the Ases shook beneath, / burst then the mighty Brísing necklace. / 'You wit that I a whore should be / if I go with you to Etin-Home!'" ("Thrymskvida" 13–14) Even though she had actually traded four nights of her love to the

Silver amulet depicting Freyja (Sweden, Viking Age)

dwarves in exchange for the necklace Brísingamen, it had been at her own free will; the Frowe shows the might of women to maintain their power over their own bodies and their own alliances, without being coerced into unwanted sex or relationships.

The Frowe is often described as "wife of Ódhr (Wod)," but the constant attempts of the etins and thurses to gain her in marriage shows that the relationship is, at the very least, more casual than that between Wodan and Frija. In many ways, however, she is seen as a feminine counterpart of Wodan. Like him, she has great magical might; both wander often through the worlds, taking lovers among humans and godly wights alike. Though her battle-aspects are not often spoken of in the early writings, the fact that the Frowe and Wodan have an equal share of those slain in strife shows that she is also mighty in matters of war and of challenge. For those whose ritual work is based particularly on balance and polarity, it is within keeping with the Indo-European tradition to couple Wodan and the Frowe as Sky-Father and Earth-Mother, though you should be aware that the "Lord" in the tradition of "Lord and Lady" was never Wodan, but Fro Ing, the twin brother of the Frowe.

The magic practiced by the Frowe is most typically that known as *seidhr* in Old Norse—a magic which is probably the source of the Anglo-Saxon Witch tradition. The modern "Wiccan" and "Witch" both derive from the Old English "wicce." Although popular belief has attempted to connect this word with the root for "wise" (Old English "witig"), there is no possible etymological association between the two. The word "wicce" comes from an Indo-European root meaning "to twist or bend," a root connecting it with the concept of Wyrd. The practice of Witch-Craft according to the Anglo-Saxon/Old Norse tradition is characterized by faring through the worlds and gaining wisdom from the wights outside of the Middle-Garth's walls; by seething things of might in a cauldron and singing magical songs; by working magically upon the minds of others; and by delving into Wyrd to find out what shall come to pass. This skill, as Gunnora Hallakarva suggests, may also be associated with weaving; in this, it is the ability to unravel the twisted skeins of Wyrd and read the pattern of what *should* become. The Frowe is the highest mistress of all these crafts, which she taught to Wodan and teaches to those who follow her.

Unlike Fro Ing, the Frowe is not often a goddess of peace. She first appears as Gullveig, "drunkenness of gold," who stirs strife among the Ases. They burned her thrice and thrice she returned, teaching and working magic under the name Heidhr ("the Glorious"). The first war—the war between the Ases and the Wans—seems to have been fought over her (or possibly at her instigation). Although she is established in the Ases' Garth after that, she does not seem to have been given, like Fro Ing and Njördhr, as a hostage. The "peace-weaver" aspect of Germanic womanhood, associated as it is with the making and strengthening of social bonds and of marriage in particular, is part of the cult of Frija, but not of that of the Frowe. However, many women who were given in marriage as *frith*-pledges often acted as inciters of strife, stirring up the very feuds they had been sent to soothe. According to the tradition of the sagas, romantic love was also one of the chief causes of bloodshed in Iceland; a young man had a higher chance of dying by violence during his courtship (either at the hands of offended family members or in fights with rivals) than he did during a viking raid. As a

goddess of love, the Frowe is no peacemaker; it takes as much bravery to follow her in this aspect as in any other!

In addition to causing strife among the gods, in one version of
the story of the theft of her necklace, the Frowe only gained it back
from Wodan by setting kings to battle so that Walhall might be
filled with their dead. She is also called the chief of the walkyriges,
though this title seems to come more from the similarity of some of
her roles to theirs than from an actual connection between the two.
Like the walkyriges, she rides to battle; she chooses her warriors
and may bring about their deaths in time; Hyndla accuses her of
riding her lover Óttar (whom she has changed into a boar) to his
own slaying (Hyndluljódh 6). Like the walkyriges also, she goes
about pouring the drink for the most worshipful guests in the
Ases' Garth; this is a typical role for atheling-women, particularly
queens, throughout the Germanic culture.

The Frowe was most often worshipped by unmarried women,
divorced women, and widows (though not virgins, who called
upon Gefjön), as Frija was by wives and mothers. However, men
worshipped her as well and made sacrifice to her. The most notable
example is Óttar of "Hyndluljódh," who was at once her lover and
her priest; Frowe-goodmen were probably expected to stand in the
role of lovers or husbands to the goddess, and eventually, as befell
many of the Yngling kings and as the remark in "Hyndluljódh"
implies, to be sacrificed to her.

Freyja is associated with fertility by implication, although her
primary aspect is that of erotic pleasure without a strongly repro-
ductive aspect. She is far more strongly connected with riches than
with the fruitfulness of the fields; the tears she weeps onto land
become gold, while those she weeps into the sea become amber.
Her daughters are named Hnoss and Gersemi, both of which mean
"treasure"; Einar Skulason wrote a poem about a rich gift (quoted
in the Prose Edda) in which he says: "I am able to have the glorious
child of Hörn (Freyja) / we got a dear treasure." The name "Hörn"
means "flax," pointing to an old connection between the Frowe
and the women's mysteries of spinning and weaving (see Frija).

In addition to embodying the might of sexuality, the Frowe
seems to be one of the greatest sources from which the god/esses
of the Ases' Garth draw their life. The giants seek to wed both
Freyja and Idunn, taking them away from the god-kin. As the tale
of the building of the walls of the Ases' Garth show, the need the

gods have for the Frowe is equivalent to the worlds' need of the Sun and the Moon; all three are light and life. (The Frowe is also associated with the Sun, who in some parts of Germany used to be called "the yellow sow.")

The symbol of the Frowe is her necklace or girdle, Brísingamen ("necklace of the Brísings" or "burning-necklace"). This necklace is also called "sea-kidney" or "wave-stone," names which may refer to the battle in which Loki and Heimdallr fought over it in the shape of seals, or may imply that the necklace was made out of amber. The necklace or girdle is the oldest goddess-symbol among the Northern Europeans, particularly in the form of the torc (a collar made out of twisted metal). A great many torcs, too large for human wear, have been found in the bogs in Denmark and southern Sweden, together with huge necklaces of raw amber. In *The Bog People*, P. V. Gløb states that the torc may well have been connected with the strangling-rope with which the Tollund Man was sacrificed before he was buried in the bog; the rope made of twisted strands of hemp and the collar made of twisted strands of thick wire do look very similar (see illustration on page 81). *Ynglinga saga* also describes how the golden necklace which was the inheritance of the Vanic kings of Sweden was used by a Finnish woman to hang her royal husband in one of the many apparently sacrificial deaths which the early Yngling kings suffered.

The Frowe was most usually, though not always, worshipped outdoors; according to Turville-Petre, the Freyja-placenames in Norway are predominantly compounded with the various words for "meadow," though there are three forms derived from "Freyjuhof" (Freyja's temple). There are more of such names in Sweden, with more variation: "Freyjuvé" (Freyja's holy enclosure) and "Freyjulundr" (Freyja's grove) appear as well as many compounds with words for "field/meadow," "rock," "lake," and the like. In Hyndluljódh, Freyja speaks of the harrow which Ottar has built for her from heaped rocks, reddened with blood, and fired so many times that the stones have become glassy.

The Frowe is especially pleased by love-songs; the type attributed to her in Iceland, the *mansöngr*, were so prone to enflame sexuality that even before the conversion it was grounds for legal punishment if a man were to write one of these to a woman. It may also have been feared that such songs could be used for the purpose of sexual magic, enchanting the woman in question to make her fall in love with the poet; there are several references, particularly in "Hávamál," to magic being used for this purpose. Nevertheless, those who follow the Frowe do well to write these love-poems both to the goddess herself and to their earthly loves, for all love is pleasing to the Frowe.

The beasts of her cult are the pig, the falcon, the cat, and small wood-birds in general, especially the swallow and the cuckoo; butterflies are also called "Freyja's hens," and the name "ladybird" ("ladybug" in America) may associate these beetles with her as well. In Westphalia, the weasel was called *froie*, which Grimm connects both with "fräulein" and with the worship of the Frowe.[3] Like cats and mink, these creatures are both extremely prolific and fierce when provoked. The Frowe's wain, according to the *Prose Edda*, is supposed to be drawn by two cats. A picture appears in the Schleswiger Dom (see next page) which shows a naked woman riding on a striped feline and holding a horn in her hand. It is tentatively dated to the twelfth century, which is probably post-heathen for Northern Germany, but it may have been influenced by Scandinavian beliefs (possibly melding with surviving memories of continental German heathenism). The resemblance which the cat bears to a Siberian tiger also implies the possibility of influence from the northeast, which would have reached Germany through the Norse. If this is so, there is little question that it shows the Frowe. A number of scholars have often commented that the cat is particularly appropriate to Freyja because it is the most sensual and overtly sexual of creatures, as well as one of the most beautiful.

The Frowe also rides a boar called Hildisvíni ("Battle-Swine"), who was made for her by the two dwarves Dáinn and Nabbi, and she herself is named Sýr, "Sow." In one of the *Hervarar saga* manuscripts it says specifically that the king Heidhrekr sacrificed a swine at Yule because he particularly worshipped Freyja (the other manuscript makes Heidhrekr's sacrifice of a boar part of the worship of Freyr). As mentioned earlier, she transformed her lover Ottar into a boar and rode upon his back. H.R. Ellis Davidson offers the theory that this may reflect a cultic practice in which the godmen of the Frowe donned masks and/or the skins of boars. Tacitus says that one tribe of Germans on the shore of the Baltic, whom he also knew as the only collectors of amber, "worship the Mother of the gods, and wear, as an emblem of this cult, the device of a wild boar, which stands them in stead of armour or human protection and gives the worshipper a sense of security even among his enemies" (*Germania* 45). Of the next tribe over he says "Bordering on the Suiones are the nations of the Sitones. They resemble them in all respects but one—woman is the ruling sex." This, again, may point to a very strong Wanic influence in the area bordering the Baltic.

The Frowe's act of transforming her lover at night and riding upon him is also closely connected with the Northern European folklore of witches riding men out at night (usually transformed into horses) and returning them exhausted and footsore in the morning. Again, these stories of "Witchcraft" may be survivals of Wanic cult-practice.

The runes associated with the Frowe are fehu (ᚠ), kenaz (ᚲ), and berkano (ᛒ). A runic analysis of her title in the Elder Futhark (ᚠᚱᚬᚹᛗ) is fehu—fire, wealth, sexual energy; raidho—the Goddess' wain and her travels through the worlds; othala—her association with the mysteries of ancestry, death, and the mound; wunjo—again, the mysteries of ancestry as well as her role as the giver of love and joy; ehwaz—the way in which she works in tandem with her twin Fro Ing, as well as the other mysteries of the horse in her cult. Alternatively, the Old Norse form Freyja (ᚠᚱᛗᚲᛁᚠ) adds jera, the rune of the fruitful harvest, and ansuz, referring to her search for *Óðhr* (Wodan in his aspect as Inspiration) and her magical skills.

FRO ING (FREYR)

Fro Ing, like Wodan, is a god of kingship and the ancestor of kings and great tribes such as the Ynglings (the royal dynasties of Sweden) and the Ingvaeones (one of the oldest recorded tribes of Germania). His great importance to the early Germanic people is shown in the names of the runes; the only gods who are named directly in the futhark (runic alphabet) are Ing and Týr (Tiw). The latter's name was deleted from the Old English Rune Poem by a Christian compiler, but Ing was too deeply ingrained in the culture of the Anglo-Saxons to suffer a similar fate.

The Rune Poem says of him that "(Ing) among the East-Danes was first / beheld by men, until that later time when to the east / he made his departure over the waves, followed by his wain / that

The Schleswiger Dom women

was the name those stern warriors gave the hero." The use of the wain is something common to the Wanic cult as a whole, as it has been from the earliest times. "Gunnars tháttr helmings" (in *Flateyjarbók*), the tale of Gunnar Helming, describes how the hero came upon the wagon of Freyr between villages as it was making its yearly rounds. He leapt into the wagon and wrestled with the wooden figure of the god, finally overcoming him and casting him out. Gunnar dressed in Freyr's clothes and continued in his place; there was great joy in the villages when they saw their god eating and drinking, and even more when it became clear that the god-woman had become pregnant with his child. Finally he was discovered and had to flee for his life.

The story of Gunnar Helming is a late and satirical treatment of one of the central mysteries of the cult of Fro Ing: the god's cyclical incarnation in a mortal man who is eventually sacrificed. The first kings of the Ynglings all die in ways which makes it clear that they are Wanic sacrifices: one, as mentioned earlier, is hanged with an ancestral necklace; one, through the working of "witchcraft," is thrown by his horse at the autumnal feast of the idises; one is drowned in a vat of mead; one is smothered in his sleep by a Finnish witch when he refuses to return to his wife; one is slain by a hay-fork; one is given to the gods by his folk because the harvests have been bad. This cyclical slaying of the king who embodies the god keeps the land fruitful. Let no man take the might of Fro Ing into himself who is not willing to pay the price; I know one man who specifically wished to be and remain a Wanic king and the incarnation of the god—taking upon himself the name Ingvar—and who ended by destroying everything around him because he was unwilling even to ritually surrender his leadership for a time.

This sacrifice does not necessarily have to be one of life; the ritual withdrawal, however, is an integral part of the cult of Fro Ing. The poem "Skírnismál" describes how Freyr first withdraws from all company of the gods, then has to give up his horse and his sword in order to win the etin-woman Gerdhr in marriage; this represents the surrender of Ing's manly might either through death or by a ritual relinquishment of power. This was probably seen as a seasonal withdrawal; the god who embodies the life of the earth and the fruitfulness of the fields secluding himself in the dark months from Yule to plowing-time. According to Saxo, Starkadhr was offended by the "unmanly clatter of bells" and the "effeminate gestures" at the Swedish religious ceremonies. It may be that the godmen of Fro Ing actually dressed in feminine garb, or some items thereof on certain occasions, as Tacitus describes the priests of the Alcis doing among the Germanii. However, the prohibition against carrying weapons or riding on a stallion probably served under normal circumstances as token enough of this cyclical Freyic surrender of masculine power.

The rulership of Fro Ing is a rulership of frith (fruitful peace) and joy. The name Frodhi, "The Fruitful," was given by the Danes to several of the kings embodying Fro Ing's might. Of the third of these, Saxo Grammaticus (a Christian Danish historian) reports that he was so beloved by his folk that after his death, his body was preserved and carried about in a wain as if he had simply grown infirm; and that even when he was laid in the mound, he still brought good harvests and peace to his folk. In *Ynglinga saga*, Snorri writes of a king named Freyr that his death was kept secret, and tribute was paid to the cairn where he was laid for three years to maintain peace and plenty, and that "When all the Swedes marked that Frey was dead, but that good seasons and peace still continued, they believed that it would be so, so long as Frey was in Sweden; therefore, they would not burn him, but called him god of the earth, and ever after sacrificed to him, most of all for good seasons and peace."[4] The peace of Freyr, called the peace of Frodhi in Denmark, was remembered by the Norse as a golden age of quiet and plenty, and is often mentioned in Viking Age poetry.

Representations of Freyr

Although Fro Ing is first a god of kingship, peace, and fruitfulness, he is also a warrior, called upon for warding and strength in battle. He is called "protector of the gods" and "ruler of the hosts of the gods"; in "Húsdrápa" he is said to rule the armies.[5] I have been told that the Frey-boar was chosen as the emblem of the Ásatrú Free Assembly's Warrior Guild because of dreams experienced by several major figures at that time. Because of his surrender of his sword, Fro Ing is especially associated with the arts of unarmed combat. He killed the giant Beli (brother of Fro Ing's wife Gerdhr) with a stag's antler, and Snorri says of him that "It was not such a great thing, when Freyr and Beli met; Freyr might have killed him with his hand."[6]

The cult of Freyr was especially strong in Sweden; he is also called "Blót ("sacrifice") god of the Swedes." Given that the royal dynasty was descended from him, this is hardly surprising. Also, Fro Ing and the other Wans are especially connected with the acts and responsibilities of the godmen; Snorri mentions specifically that Njördhr and Freyr were priests and Freyja was a priestess among the Ases,[7] showing that the Wans had a special holy function among the god/esses. Fro Ing was strongly associated with the founding of the great hof at Old Uppsala: both Snorri and Saxo say that Freyr made his dwelling place there.

According to Bede's account of the Anglo-Saxon priesthood, it was not lawful for the high priest to carry weapons or to ride anything but a mare. When Edwin's high priest Coifi chose to convert to Christianity and desecrate his priesthood, he got on a stallion, armed himself, and cast a spear into the hof. These elements of priesthood—the weaponlessness and the taboo against riding a stallion—are associated with Fro Ing's sacrifice of sword and horse; the belief that the hof was profaned if weapons were brought into it recalls the specifically Wanic "frith-garth" (see the chapter on Steads); and the casting of a spear for ritual purpose is a Wodanic act which would indeed be taken as very hostile when directed against a temple of Ing. The worship of Fro Ing, and indeed his priesthood, ran in families; the descendants of the Icelandic Thórdh Freysgodhi, for instance, were all known as the "Freysgydhlingar," "priestlings of Freyr."

The beasts dearest to Fro Ing are horned cattle, horses, stags, and boars. He was usually given an ox or a boar as sacrifice; *Víga-Glúms saga* tells how a man whose son had been slain by Víga-Glúm led an ox into the hof of Freyr and asked the god to take revenge, whereupon the ox gave a loud bellow and dropped dead, showing that Freyr had taken the gift and would answer the call.

The horse also appears as a beast given to Fro Ing; not usually in the sense of a slain sacrifice, but as a living holy creature who was carefully tended and concerning whose care there were several taboos. The most notable of these was the Icelandic Freyfaxi ("Frey-Mane") in *Hrafnkells saga*. Hrafnkell, a Freysgodhi, had sworn to slay any other man who should ride the holy horse; when his enemies came to murder Freyfaxi, they had to draw a bag over the stallion's head so that the might of his gaze would not awe them.[8] *Flateyjarbók* tells how, when Óláfr Tryggvasson went to desecrate the statue of Freyr in Trondheim, he began by mounting the stallion which he had been told was holy to Freyr, while his men got upon the mares. It may also be that this holiness of stallions in general was part of the Anglo-Saxon prohibition against the high priest riding anything but a mare.

The animal which is most central to the cult of Fro Ing, however, is the boar. His own boar is called Gullinbursti ("Golden-Bristled") or Slídhrugtanni ("Cutting-Tusked"); he was forged from an ingot of gold and a pig's hide by Eitri, the dwarf who also made Wodan's ring Draupnir and Thunar's hammer Mjöllnir. This boar is the only beast Fro Ing is ever said to ride, as he had given away his horse Blódhughófi ("Bloody-Hoof"—a name probably implying that Fro Ing rode this stallion into battle). The famous Sutton Hoo helm has gilded boar-heads on the cheek pieces, and the Benty Grange helm (from a burial near Derbyshire) has a bronze boar with garnet eyes standing on its crest; such boar-helms are also described in *Beowulf*. The Swedish King Athils had a helm called Hildigöltr ("Battle-Boar") and a great neck-ring called Sviagrís ("Piglet of the Swedes").[9] These helms of history and literature show that Fro Ing had many worshippers among warriors of the highest rank and kings; the use of the Wanic boar as a protective symbol in battle goes back to the times of Tacitus, as mentioned earlier. The boar is also a sign of troth; at Yule-time, oaths are sworn by his bristles, and only someone of tried and proven bravery can cut the boar's head which is traditionally served at the Yule feast.

Statues of Fro Ing are always equipped with a particularly large and erect phallus, as they have been from the earliest times; such wooden idols from an early period have been found in the bogs in Denmark. Adam of Bremen also mentions that the statue of Freyr at Uppsala was particularly notable for this characteristic, and a small bronze image (clearly meant to be carried on the person) from eleventh century Sweden also displays Freyr's very large phallus. Such a small silver image is also mentioned in one of the sagas. Phallic worship which seems to have a Freyic character also appears in the story called "Völsa tháttr" (from *Óláfs saga inn Whelgi* in *Flateyjarbók*). Óláfr, in disguise, comes to a farmhouse where a strange rite is taking place: the phallus of a horse has been preserved with herbs and charms by the housewife, and each of the members of the household takes it in hand in turn, chanting lewd verses which end with the refrain, "May Mörnir receive this sacrifice!" The name "Mörn" (troll-woman?) is used in kennings both for Gerdhr and for Skadhi, the two etin-maids married to Wanic gods. "Mörnir" is a plural form. Here, the earthly horse-phallus, "Völsi," stands in the stead of Fro Ing's symbolic sword and horse; it is literally a sacrifice of the god to an elemental goddess.

Freyr is said to have gotten his hall Álfheimr as a tooth-gift. This association of Fro Ing with the alfs shows a side of his being which is not often called upon: the mound-god, the lord of the dead who still live within their barrows. As mentioned earlier, his earthly avatars were worshipped within the mound, just as the alfs were. Through his role as god of the barrow and fro of Alf-Home, Fro Ing is also tied to the living might of our fore-gone kin and to the inheritance of udal lands. In the sagas, his friendship preserves the lands of his followers; but when his wrath is roused, he drives men from their lands.

Fro Ing and his father Njördhr are both called upon as the givers of wealth, as described both in *Gylfaginning* and in *Egils saga*. He is also said to have might over "rain, sunshine, and the fruitfulness of the earth."

Fro Ing also has a ship called Skidhbladnir, which was made by the dwarves and can fold up to fit inside a small pouch, or unfold to full size when the god chooses to use it—an obvious symbol!

His rune is the rune Ingwaz, which takes its name from him. A full runic expansion of his name yields fehu (ᚠ) = riches, life-force; raidho (ᚱ) = his aspect as a rider, whether in the wain or ship of his procession or on his horse or boar; othala (ᛉ) = Ing as god of the land and ruler of the alfs; ingwaz (◇) = the mysteries of the god himself. Alternatively, the Old Norse Freyr adds ehwaz (ᛗ) = the horse of his cult; jera (‹›) = the harvest, which is associated with him in the Old Norwegian Rune Poem; and the downward-elhaz as the final r (ᛣ) = the Wanic might rising from beneath the earth and the waters.

NOTES

1. Tacitus; James Chisholm (tr.). *Germania*, quoted in *Grove and Gallows*, 5–6.

2. "Grímnismál," 11.

3. Grimm, *Teutonic Mythology* 1:305–6.

4. *Ynglinga saga*, 10.

5. Turville-Petre, 175.

Boar brooch from Sutton Hoo

6. *Snorra Edda*, ch. 23.

7. *Ynglinga saga*, 4.

8. The blinding of the gaze was often necessary when slaying magicians, or even persons of great inborn *hamingja* (such as Sigurdhr's daughter Swanhild in *Völsunga saga*).

9. Davidson, H.R. Ellis. *Gods and Myths of Northern Europe*, 99.

Chapter 6

GHOSTS AND WIGHTS

S WELL AS THE ASES and the Wans, the Teutonic folk also give worship to many beings of lesser might: walkyriges, idises, alfs, house-ghosts, and land-wights. It is worthwhile to come to know all of these wights and win their friendship, for it is they, rather than the god/esses, with whom we work most closely in the things of daily life. Note that the term "ghost" is used not specifically to mean the soul of a dead person, but rather to refer to any spiritual being which is lesser than the god/esses, as well as to the soul of a living human.

WALKYRIGE (VALKYRJA, VALKYRIE)

The best known of the ghosts of our folk, thanks to Richard Wagner and popular romanticism, is the walkyrige. She is a warrior-woman and far more—she is the teache r of rune-wisdom and bearer of mead; she is the banshee wailing above the storm of battle; she is the shining maiden at the end of the hero's quest and the chooser of the slain, a glimpse of whom means death. Throughout Teutonic tradition, the walkyrige, like the god Wodan whom she serves, appears in shapes ranging from the bloody and terrible wrecker of lives to the sublime guide of the spirit, the *Ewige Weiblichkeit* (eternal feminine) who inspires the hero to rise ever upward.

The name "walkyrige" means "chooser of the slain," and the walkyrige almost always appears in the context of battle—as the protectress of the hero and a warrior herself; as the bearer of the slain to Walhall; and as the maiden who bears ale to the *einherjar* ("single-combatants," Wodan's warriors) within that hall. According to the *Prose Edda*, their duty is "to serve in Walhall, to bear drink and mind the table-service and ale-flagons . . . them Ódhinn sends to every battle; they determine men's feyness and award victory. Gudr and Rota and the youngest Norn, she who is called Skuld, ride ever to take the slain and decide fights." (47–8)

In their earliest incarnation, the walkyriges are, like Wodan himself, spirits of storm and terror, and this is apparently the only form in which they were known among the Anglo-Saxons. The word *wælcyrge* is used as a gloss for *Erinyes* (the Greek Furies) as early as the eighth century, implying wights like the maidens of *Njáls saga*, who weave the fate of battle on a loom on which "Men's heads were used in place of weights, and men's intestines for the weft and warp; a sword served as the beater, and the shuttle was an arrow," chanting a song of slaughter. As Wodan's oldest aspect is that of the god of death and storm, the prevalence of this early form of the walkyrige is hardly surprising; even the loftier walkyriges of the Norse tradition have names like Skögul (the Raging One), Hlökk (the Shrieker), and Hildr (Battle), as described in "Grímnismál." The walkyriges can be seen by the Sighted in times of storm and strife, riding in troops of nine or three times nine. They hover over the heads of their chosen heroes, shielding them from both mortal weapons and woe-working magics; in the Helgi lays, the magical maiden appears in mortal bodies from which she fares forth to ward her destined hero. According to these lays, the hero and his walkyrige can be reborn, meet, and live out their lives several times together.

The walkyrige is sometimes confused with the fetch or one's idises; she bears certain similarities to both, but also certain essential differences. Like the fetch, she is a part of one's being with an apparently independent awareness; the fetch, however, normally has the shape and general character of an animal. It may bear messages to one, but it is not itself a guide to higher wisdom. Like the idises, the walkyrige is a protector and a guide; unlike them, she is

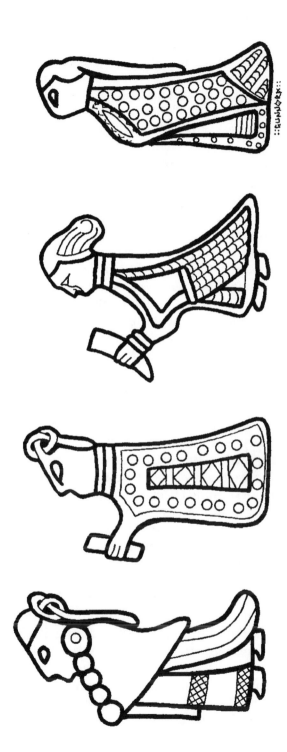

Silver walkrige amulets (Sweden, Viking Age)

not tied to the family line, but to the individual being (although one is usually reborn into one's own line). Also, she is not, as the Old Norse idises seem to be, the spirit of a dead female ancestor, but a part of the individual's own spirit.

On an historical level, it is not unlikely that the belief in the Wodanic walkyrige was a development from the earlier figure of the idis ("goddess" or "noble woman," cognate to Old Norse *dis* but not always necessarily implying a ghost; in Old English the term is applied to the martial heroine Judith and to Grendel's mother). According to the Roman records of battles against our ancestors, Germanic women did not actually fight, but they did come to the battlefield with their men, spurring the warriors to greater courage and readying themselves to die if their men should be slain, rather than becoming enslaved. It is well documented that Germanic women were generally skilled in their own sorts of magic; it is not unlikely that these women who stood beside the battle performed their own magics and/or fared forth from their earthly bodies to ward the men they loved during the fighting, as indeed the Old Norse valkyrjur seem to do. The deeds of these atheling-women, these idises, may have brought our ancestors to their understanding of the feminine warder of the soul.

Old High German did not preserve a cognate word to "walkyrige/valkyrja"; however, the Zweite Merseburger Zauberspruch describes "idisi" acting exactly as the Norse walkyriges do. A band of "idisi" are sitting "above" (presumably over the heads of their chosen warriors). Some fasten fetters and some loosen fetters, which, in the Old Norse sources, is a magical activity exclusively associated with Wodan and the walkyriges; "War-Fetter" is actually a walkyrige-name. The German spell has been taken as a charm to free prisoners of war; but within the context of the deeply rooted tradition of "battle-fetter" as we know it from the Norse, it seems as likely, if not more so, that the chains they are laying and loosening are the magical chains on the soul against which Hár (Wodan) counsels the young initiate Loddfáfnir in "Hávamál." Further, in *Jómsvikinga saga*, the idises Thórgerdhr and Yrpr act in a manner more characteristic of walkyriges than of the Old Norse *dísir* as they appear in other sources; after a man has been sacrificed to them, these women appear in a howling storm with arrows flying from their fingertips and beat off the enemy.

As human awareness of Wodan himself may have evolved from seeing him as a god of death to the god who chooses who shall die to the god who chooses victory in battle, so the awareness of the mighty women who aid their men in battle may have become more and more closely associated with him, till they became known as his handmaidens and the "choosers of the slain." This is likely to have gone together with the growing understanding of Wodan's actions in gathering his heroes together in Walhall against the final battle of Ragnarök. At first this was simply understood as the "endless battle" which appears in its older form even in some of the late Norse works, such as Snorri's account of Högni and Hildr. In this tale, Hildr arranges matters so that her father Högni and her lover/abductor Hedhinn will do battle; every night she goes about waking the dead by magic, and every day the slain warriors fight one another again. As choosers and shapers of heroes, the walkyriges naturally delight in all the strife and battles which forge the soul; as we see later, it is this endless battle which readies the einherjar for Ragnarök.

The association of the Norns with the walkyriges indicates that these wights are closely tied to the power of wyrd, particularly as it affects the individuals to whom they are bound. The act of bearing the cup or horn to the hero is also associated with the determination of wyrd. In this aspect, the walkyrige may be seen as both the receiver and the determiner of those actions performed by the hero which shape his *ørlög*; she is also, as the continual references to the *choosing* of the slain indicate, the being who brings wyrd forth as it *should* be in a particular case; the walkyrige Norn is Skuld, whose very name means "that which should be." In this aspect, she is the embodiment of the *ørlög* of the Wodanic hero; but there is more to her than that.

The walkyrige is known as the *oskmær* of Wodan, a term which is used to mean "adopted daughter" (just as the *einherjar* are Wodan's *osksynir*, "adopted sons") but can also literally mean "wish-maiden." According to Grimm's *Teutonic Mythology*, Wodan was given the name "Wunsch" ("wish") well into Christian times in Germany, as the provider of all good things to humankind; while the Old Norse Oski ("wish") is also a name of Wodan. The walkyrige also appears in Middle German poetry under the name "Wünschelweib" ("Wish-woman"), as in the poem of Staufenberger, in which, "To the knight there shews herself a maiden in *white apparel . . . she has watched over him in danger and war from his youth up,* she *was about him unseen* (332-364); now she becomes his love and is with him *whenever he wishes for her."* (Grimm I, 419) In this form, the walkyrige brings not only battle-victory to the warrior, but dispenses all of Wodan's gifts, including fertility, as in *Völsunga saga* where Wodan sends his *oskmær* Hljódh to Rerir and his queen with an apple which enables them to get a child together. The child who is born from this is Völsi, the father of the heroic Völsung line which culminates in Sigurdhr (Siegfried).

In her shining self, the walkyrige is the maiden who brings the wisdom of Wodan to the Wodanic hero, often through a rune-brewed draught, as described in the *Sigrdrífumál*. She is both the highest and purest aspect of the soul—the very essence of the Self—and the mediator between the human consciousness and the power of Wodan, as shown by her duty of bringing the drink of *wod* (intoxication/inspiration) and knowledge to Wodan's chosen; the soul cannot pass over Bifröst without her aid. To gain her gifts, however, requires a great deal of spiritual dedication. The *Völsunga saga* and the cycle of poems from which it was drawn describe the process by which this may be done. Sigurdhr, having avenged his father—which is to say, won his right to his own inherited powers—goes on to slay the dragon Fáfnir and drink of his blood. By this action, Sigurdhr gains the dragon's unearthly wisdom; he learns to understand the language of the birds, who then tell him of the maiden that lies sleeping on the mountaintop. To the faint of heart, the blood of the dragon or other wild/magical beast traditionally gives a hero's strength and courage; to Sigurdhr, who was already mighty and fearless, this partaking of the world beyond the Middle-Garth gave superhuman understanding and brought him to the point where he might choose to turn his own wyrd—to meet with his own walkyrige and choose for himself whether to receive her gifts, which would, in the course of time, bring him to Walhall.

As a true hero, Sigurdhr chooses to wed Sigrdrífa on the mountaintop where he has awakened her. "One of the greatest goals of the male vitki is to be 'wed' to his walkyrige—to consciously reach her, learn from her, and be lead upward by her; the goal of the female vitki is to become consciously one with her walkyrige—to *be* a walkyrige in the sense that the title is given to mortal women. The subtle will understand that these purposes are not necessarily different, but the human mind is normally so constructed that they call for different forms of symbolic expression."[1] This experience, too, is directly perceived as the cause of the hero's death, as is shown by the plot of the Helgi lays and explicitly stated in *Völsunga saga*'s quote from "Sigurdrífumál," in which Sigrdrífa says to Sigurdhr, "Now you shall choose the choice to you is given / thou tree of true weapons. / Speech or stillness yourself have in heart / meted the meanings all" and the hero replies, "Though you know me fated to fall, I will not flee you. I was never born a coward. Now I will have all your loving rede, as long as I may live."

The duality of the walkyrige appears most clearly in the Lay of Helgi Hjörvardhson. In this lay, Helgi weds the walkyrige Sváva. As his brother Hedhinn is walking through the wood on Yule evening, a troll woman riding on a wolf comes up to him and asks if he is willing to have her. He says he is not, and she replies that he will regret this when swearing on the Yule cup. That night at the oath-making, Hedhinn swears that he will have his brother's wife, an oath which the lay seems to show as having brought about the turning of wyrd which led to Helgi's death in battle with another man. According to the skaldic kennings, the "horse of the walkyrige" is a wolf; although the literature usually makes a distinction between the "troll" or "witch" woman who rides a wolf and the more stately figure of the walkyrige, it is clear that the two are originally the same person. In the poem, Helgi identifies the woman as his fetch (ON *fylgja*), but the wolf-riding troll-woman is an unlikely form for a fetch; it is more probable that Helgi's walkyrige is perceived by way of these two personifications, one of whom wards the hero and one of whom brings about his battle-death through the subtle turnings of Wyrd.

The runes most strongly associated with the walkyrige are elhaz (ᛦ) and the two other runes of its triad, gebo (ᚷ) and dagaz (ᛞ). Elhaz is the rune of the walkyrige herself, as the holy warder and swan-maiden. It is a rune which brings might down from the heavenly worlds; it also represents the fire of the rainbow bridge Bifröst which is crossed with the walkyrige's aid, and the wall of shields or fire which the hero must cross to awaken the sleeping walkyrige. Gebo describes the continual exchange of energy between hero and walkyrige; she wards the hero in battle; his (or her) deeds of honor give the walkyrige more might, so that she in turn can spur him on to greater accomplishments. Dagaz is the moment of the "wedding," the moment when the walkyrige is fully awakened within the consciousness.

One of the main problems which the walkyrige raises is the question of her analogues outside the Wodanic cults. The walkyrige is the only personification of the soul in its absolute form which has been recorded fully in historical sources, and she is invariably associated with Wodan. Nevertheless, it would be ridiculous and even insulting to suggest that non-Wodanists lack such an important and archetypal element of the soul. Both reason and magical experience suggest that walkyrige-equivalents must exist in every person as the bridge between his/her human consciousness and the god/ess to which he/she is most closely tied. The nearest equivalents Eddic writings show to the walkyriges are the handmaidens of Frija, who function in the spheres she rules very much as Wodan's maidens function in his realms, implying the potential for parallel in each branch of the ásatrú. Also, on one runestone, the name of Thórr's daughter Thrudhr is used in a kenning where one would normally expect to find a walkyrige-name, so she may have been seen as taking part in battle in a similar fashion.

In the case of the Wanic cults, I would suggest calling the walkyrige's analogue wight the *fylgjadis* (to distinguish her from the idises proper); in the cult of Thunar she might be named the Thrúdhmaiden; the Tiwic equivalent might be the meotodu (fem. creator/measurer), and so on.

To understand the walkyrige (or her equivalent), it is necessary to know the god/ess from whom she hails and the true Self she expresses; to touch the might of the god/ess and learn your own nature and *ørlög*, it is necessary to wed/become your walkyrige. This is the quest of the true woman or man: to touch the god/ess of your soul through your own holy maid.

Idises (Old Norse Dísir)

The idises are the souls of the women of your family line—the eldest mothers, who still watch over their children through the generations. The first we know about these holy women comes from the Roman frontier in Germania, where a number of votive stone carvings and small (4–6 inches high) terra-cotta sculptures of three women who wear huge round headresses and sit holding

Romano-Germanic "Matrones"

baskets or cornucopias of fruits and grain in their laps have been found. Incense was burned on or before these statues; during feasts, they may have been decorated with garlands and had libations of drink or sacrificial blood poured out before them. The baskets of fruit and ripe grain which they hold suggest that, like the Old Norse dísablót ("blessing to the idises"), their feast was held around harvesttime.[2] These statues bear inscriptions dedicating them to the Matrones—the "Mothers." The round headresses they wear are also very similar to the bridal headress of Norwegian folk tradition, which may emphasize their maternal characteristics.

In the Old Norse sources, these women played a very large role in the religious life of the folk. The festival of Winternights was also called *dísablót*, and there are several references to a special hall being used for this purpose: in Ynglinga saga, Adhils dies when riding his horse around the *dísasalr* ("idises' hall"), and in Heidhreks saga, Heidhrekr's wife hangs herself in the dísasalr. The feast, however, was usually celebrated by family and close friends rather than as a great public ritual—which makes good sense, given that it was meant to show worship to the family's own elder kin. While men often asked special favor of the idises on their own behalf, it was women who led the feasts and reddened the harrow at the *dísablót*.

The idises are firstly concerned with childbirth: Sigrdrífa tells Sigurdhr: "Birth-runes you shall know if birthing you'd aid / and bring from mothers the bairns; / on palm shall you scratch them on span of hand's back / and bid the idises to aid."[3] Snorri speaks of the idises as norns, in the sense that they act to lay *ørlög*: "There are many norns which come to every bairn when it is born to shape its *aldr* ("life-age"—see the chapter on Soul and Afterlife); and some of these are of the kin of gods, and others of the *ætt* (clan) of the alfs, and some are of the *ætt* of the dwarves . . . Good norns from a good *ætt* shape good aldr, but those men for whom it is badly shaped are ruled by ill norns." His reference to the meaningfulness of the *ætt* describes the way in which the idises act, not only as shapers of the family line, but as embodiments and transmitters of its *ørlög* and the whole spiritual complex associated with it. A family, or *ætt*, which is mighty of soul will have mighty idises who look upon its bairns with a kindly mood and give the best of gifts; but if the heritage carries an ill *ørlög*, the idises will bring that down upon the children of the line.

While the idises are usually helpful, they also have a dark and death-bringing side. In "The Greenlandish Lay of Atli," Glaumvör tells her doomed husband Gunnar several dreams she has had; he dismisses them all until she describes the last, in which she saw dead women coming who wanted to "choose" him, and "I say that mighty were the dísir towards you." Then Gunnar can no longer doubt that his *wyrd* is upon him and that his faring to Atli's hall will end in his death. At the end of "Grímnismál," when he reveals himself in wrath Ódhinn tells Geirrodhr that "the dísir are angry"—that is to say, that Geirrodhr's end is upon him.

The idises may appear in two troops, one white and one black. When they are dressed in white, they are weal-bringers and warders; when they wear black, they are the harbingers of death. They often appear mounted on horses. The idises take an active role in warding their living kin, either directly through dream-warnings or through more subtle means. In one saga, for instance, an idis afflicts her descendant with various illnesses in order to keep him from walking into an ambush that has been laid for him.

In a sense, all of the goddesses can be seen as idises of great rank. The Frowe is called "Vanadís," "idis of the Wans," and Hella is named jódís, "horse-idis." Like the goddesses, the idises were given their own temples and statues, before which their children could come to ask for their aid. The idis Thórgerdhr had a great arm-ring on her statue, in which the luck of that clan was held; after her descendant the Jarl Sigurdhr had come and begged her to lend it to a friend of his, she lowered her arm at last so that he could slide it off. A terra-cotta replica of an actual votive statue to the three Matronen can be bought in the Roman-Germanic museums in Bonn and Köln (Cologne), or you can make or find female statuettes which seem to you fitting for your own idises.

The runes of the idises are perthro (ᛈ) and berkano (ᛒ), the runes of birth and of *ørlög*.

ALFS (OLD NORSE ÁLFAR, "ELVES")

The alfs are often seen and called upon as the male counterparts of the idises: the souls of male forebears who see to the weal of their living kin. This is the role which they most often play in the practice of Ásatrú today. There are several different sorts of alfs, however, as the folklore of the Teutonic peoples attests to richly, and it is important to know the difference between them.

Traditionally, the alfs are divided into three sorts: the Light, the Dark, and the Swart or Black. The mound-alfs—the ghosts of dead men—are those classed as Dark Alfs; the Light Alfs, which also come under the rule of Fro Ing, are ghosts of air and brightness, fair to see and dressed in shining colors. The Swart Alfs are also called dwarves; they are ugly to see, but also mighty and skilled craftsmen. The dwarves were made out of the maggots in the flesh of Ymir after Wodan and his brothers slew him. They are spoken of as the children of Dvalin, and it was Dvalin who taught the runes to them.

The Old Norse sources make it clear that many men, once laid in the howe, did indeed become alfs who looked after the udal lands and to whom blessings were often poured and sacrificial meat given when their help was needed. That King Ólafr who was buried at Geirstadhr and called Geirstadhaálfr because of the help he gave his folk after his death is the most notable example of a human actually being identified as an alf within a short time of his burial. Most of the hills at which sacrifice to the alfs were made were indeed barrow-mounds, though this had often been forgotten by the folk who made the blessings there; they remembered only that beings of might dwelt within.

Alfs of this sort are strongly tied to the fruitfulness of the land; it is for this reason that Fro Ing is said to be the ruler of Alf-Home, for he is the greatest of the alfs, just as the Frowe is the greatest of the idises. This particular type of mound-alf is always male; it is these alfs who are the counterparts to the idises, and who are called upon together with the other Wanic powers at the Winternights feasting.

In Sweden, cuplike holes were made in rocks together with carven sun-wheels from the Stone Age through the Iron Age; and folkloric tradition associates these holes with the alfs. Many of these stones, though not all, were placed at burial sites. It has been traditional up to recent times to make blessings by pouring milk or ale into them. Blessings to the alfs are also made by setting a cake under the first furrow plowed or upon rocks where they are known to live—in Europe, usually the ancient standing stones.

The term Dark Alfs seems to cover, not only the mound-dead, but the other sorts of alfs who dwell in wood and stone. These alfs may be homeless ghosts, or a sort of being more akin to the land-wight. They are sometimes well-disposed towards humans, but bring ill just as often. Paralysis and rheumatism are said to be caused by elf-shot, and the Anglo-Saxons had a charm against "water-elf disease," that is, chicken pox. The ill will of alfs is also said to distress and confuse the mind of their victim. At the same time, a human who does a favor for an alf may expect a fair reward and should take it gratefully, though it may not seem so good at first. There are several tales in which such a helper is given what appear to be dead leaves or clods of earth which, when he gets home, turn out to be pure gold. Such tales are often metaphors for the gifts of knowledge and wisdom which, though seldom appreciated at first, turn out of be the fairest gifts possible. The alfs are givers of good counsel and understanding, as shown by the Anglo-Saxon name Alfred—"alf-rede"; the woman's name Ælfgifu, "Alf-gift," also calls on the alfs to befriend the child who bears it.

Unlike the mound-dead, these other Dark Alfs are both male and female, though their breeding is difficult. Sometimes mortal women are asked to come into the mound for a short time as midwives; more often, alfs are disguised as infants and exchanged for human babies. Such changelings are badly behaved and often sickly and stunted. They can be tricked into revealing themselves by the brewing of tea in an eggshell, a pot with a porridge-stirrer long enough to reach the ceiling, or something of similar extraordinary nature. One Icelandic mother, after tricking her changeling into revealing his true origins, beats him until "she sees a woman who was a stranger to her coming into the kitchen with a little boy in her arms ... This stranger gives the child a loving look, and says to the mother: 'We don't act fairly by one another; I cuddle your child, but you beat my husband.'"[4]

Of all the alfs, it is the Dark Alfs who share the Middle-Garth with us who have most to do with humankind. They are human-like in looks, very pale, as one might expect of the dead, and usually richly clad. They are seen most often at night, in the winter half of the year (from Winternights to Eostre, or roughly autumnal equinox to spring equinox).

The Light Alfs dwell in Alf-Home, in the upper airs of the Middle-Garth near to the Ases' Garth; it is these alfs who come to the feasts of the god/esses, as described in the Eddic poems. They are the most beautiful of folk; there was a Norse expression, "beautiful as an alf-woman," which described the height of womanly loveliness, and the Anglo-Saxons had the term "ælfsciene," "elf-shining," as a compliment. In *The Road to Hel*, Davidson points out that Freyr and the alfs are both associated with the Sun, Freyr by virtue of his power over rain, sunshine, and the earth, and the alfs through the name which is given to the Sun in several texts: "Álfrödhull," "Glory of the Alfs";[5] and it is surely the Light Alfs who refer to her as "Fair Wheel," for the Dark Alfs do not care for her light and the Swart Alfs are turned to stone by it. These alfs are helpers to humankind, kindly and well-disposed, though they are seen less often than the Dark Alfs. They appear especially on high places around Eostre-time, as flashes of shining white or as white-clad women.

The Swart Alfs, or dwarves, dwell in rocks and in the depths of the earth. Like the Dark Alfs, they are very close to the dead and perhaps sometimes dead folk themselves, as the dwarf-names Dáin ("the Dead One") and Nár ("Corpse"), imply; Swart Alf-Home overlaps both the lower reaches of the Middle-Garth and the higher reaches of Hella's realm. In German tradition, a race of Swart Alfs was also called *Nibelungen*—literally "kin of the misty darkness," but also a name tying them to the realm of Nibel-Home.[6]

In folklore, the dwarves are always male—they appear as short and sometimes twisted, but thick-thewed and mighty men with gray beards and skins darkened by centuries of working at their forges. However, Snorri also refers to some idises as the "daughters of Dválin," so the dwarf-kind must include females as well. Still, male dwarves lust after both human women and the daughters of the Ases; the Eddic poem "Alvísmál" is spoken by a dwarf who had come to the Ases' Garth in order to claim Thórr's daughter Thrúdhr.

According to the Old Norse tradition, Dválin was the greatest ruler of the Swart Alfs, from whom the dwarves learned the runes; the Swart Alfs are all referred to as his children. In Germany, the ruler of the Swart Alfs was called Alberich (a name familiar to any lover of Wagner); the Old Norse form is Álfaríkr. Since this name simply means "ruler of the alfs," it is probably a title rather than a personal name, so that one might speak of "Dválin álfaríkr," or call upon the might of the Swart Alfs in this name.

Although all the alfs are great craftsmen and magicians, it is the Swart Alfs who are the greatest smiths in the Nine Worlds. The treasures of the god/esses—Wodan's spear, Thunar's hammer, Sif's hair, Fro Ing's ship and boar, the Frowe's necklace, and the ring Draupnir—were all made by them, as was the sword Týrfing, ancestral sword of the kings of Sweden, and many other mighty works of craft. Dwarves also brewed the mead of poetic wod from honey and the heart-blood of Kvasir, the wisest of all wights. The dwarves have been known to teach their crafts to especially gifted human beings at times.

Dwarves are the keepers of all treasures underground; they are sometimes greedy and stingy with their goods, but their ill will is more often due to the intrusions of humans who think they have a right to dig mines and take the riches of the earth without asking the true owners first. If you often work with metal or stone, it is good to make gifts to the Swart Alfs at Yule time, burying a piece of your craft in the earth together with some food and a draught of ale.

Sunna's light turns dwarves to stone, but they are able to fare about by day in the shape of stags. Dwarves can also take the shape of spiders.

A list of dwarf-names can be found in the *Poetic Edda*. In some versions, the "Dvergatál" ("Catalogue of Dwarves") appears as stanzas 9-16 of "Völuspá"; in Lee Hollander's paperback edition, it is treated as a separate poem. Most of these names (such as Bifur, Bofur, Bombur, Thrain, Thorin, Fili, Kili, and Gandálfr) will be familiar to any reader of Tolkien, who drew much of his dwarf-lore from Norse sources.

Dealing with any of the alfs is often rewarding, though it can also carry perils with it. They are swift to take offense at slights and remember grudges for a long time. The alfs, especially the Swart Alfs, are very strongly aware of "a gift for a gift," and they are never satisfied until all scores, both of friendship and of enmity, are evened. If you spend a great deal of time working with any of these wights, you also make yourself likely to take on their characteristics during your lifetime and to join their numbers after death.

The runes of the mound-alfs are wunjo (ᛈ), jera (ᛃ), and othala (ᛜ); wunjo (ᛈ), elhaz (ᛉ) and sowilo (ᛊ) are the runes of the Light Alfs; and kenaz (ᛉ), hagalaz (ᚺ) and the Younger Futhark *ýr* (ᛦ) are runes for the Swart Alfs.

HOUSE-GHOSTS

The folklore of the north speaks of a great many lesser ghosts which inhabit the houses of humans, often attaching themselves to a family and following its members when they leave one place for another. Some of these are helpful, some harmful, though their behavior often has as much to do with the way they are treated as with their basic nature. Most of these house-ghosts are willing to work hard in helping with house and garden work (and maybe even homework for school), though they insist that humans not become lazy; they often pinch and torment sluggards, but they make the work of the diligent faster and easier, and bring luck in all things. An unhelpful house-ghost will hide small things; a helpful one will find them for you and set them beneath your hand when you need them.

Some house-ghosts are not only helpers, but warders, keeping the homes and lands of their families safe from trolls and other such wights.

House-ghosts ask little reward for their work; a bowl or saucer of milk and a bit of food are all they need. Some want to be fed every day; some only on holidays, or once a week. The Norwegian *Napfhans* ("Potjack") likes his saucerful of porridge, a piece of cake, and a glass of beer on feast-evenings. It is especially important to share your feast-food and drink with your house-ghost on Yule, for he thinks of this as his due wages. The house-ghost ought at all times to be spoken of and to with affection and respect, though not with formality; you should think of him as a dear friend.

In Germany, it was often the custom to make little wooden statues called *kobolds* and to keep them in the home; these images served as dwelling-places for house-spirits (the term *kobold* was used for any sort of small home-ghost, as well as for the Swart Alfs in the mines). If you have no house-ghost and want one, find or make such a little figure which seems to express the character you want in your friend and start putting out bread and whole milk (*not* skimmed!) or beer in front of it each evening, saying,

> If weal you wish   with me come dwell,
> and help in my home   to house bring luck.
> I bid you welcome   now be kind to me,
> and milk (or beer) I'll bring   and bread for you.

A cat, especially a tomcat, may also be such a house-ghost in disguise; it is important to treat the house cat well!

The Icelandic house-ghosts called *fylgidraugar* are always woe-workers, sent by malicious sorcerers to attach themselves to a clan and make trouble. These creatures are made from abandoned babies; male ones are usually named Mori because they wear dark jackets, females are called Skotta ("Peaky") because they wear the old-fashioned tall coif with the peak turned backward like a tail. Some Icelandic families are still haunted by these wights. Although they never do good, if they have food left out for them every night they are much less likely to do harm.

There is an Old High German charm against obnoxious house-ghosts, which you can use if you have one that makes trouble and hides things and will not be tamed by regular food and bowls of milk:

> Well know you, wight   that you hight 'wight',
> that you do not know nor can you   say, 'chnospinci'.

This formula, with the magical word "chnospinci" (pronounced *chnaw*-spin-kee; the "chn" is a sneezing sound) which so annoys the house-ghost that it is forced to move away, is very similar to some of the German fairy tales such as "Rumpelstiltskin" in which the discovery and pronunciation of a special word forces a wight to go away and leave its victim in peace. This charm should be saved for a last resort when all your attempts to befriend your house-ghost have failed; don't go around chanting it just to clear the air.

LAND-WIGHTS (OLD NORSE LANDVÆTTIR)

Land-wights are the living embodiment of the might of various features of the natural world. When the Norse came to Iceland, they found it well-filled with these wights, whose friendship they set about gaining at once. The weal of the land and those who dwell within it depends on the might and the happiness of the land-wights; if they are frightened or angered, the land will not thrive and the humans who live upon it will fare ill in all things. When Egill Skalla-Grímsson set up his *nídhing-pole* (a cursing pole, carved with runes and topped with a horse's head) against King Eiríkr Blood-Axe and Queen Gunnhild, he also turned his *nídh* against the land-wights, "so that all of them shall lose their way, none of them find nor reach his home till they drive Eiríkr and Gunnhild from the land." From that time, Eiríkr and Gunnhild had no luck in Norway and were eventually forced to flee to England. The land-wights also ward their own country and lands from human invaders; they dislike the shedding of blood, and they are very loyal to those humans who gain their trust.

Land-wights are most often found dwelling in boulders and bodies of water, especially waterfalls. The friendship of a land-wight is a useful thing to have; it brings prosperity and luck in all your works, even those which would seem to fall outside of these wight's normal realms of nature and fruitfulness of the earth. They can also tell you of what lies ahead in your life and advise you on the best things to do and the best times to do them.

The land-wights appear in various forms. Sometimes they are humanlike; sometimes they appear as trolls, sometimes as beasts. The national land-wights of Iceland, who appeared and drove off the wizard of the Danish king Haraldr Gormsson when he went in the shape of a whale to see if Iceland might be successfully invaded, are the dragon at the northeast, the bird at the west, the bull at the southeast, and the rock-giant at the south. The wizard saw each of these creatures to be of gigantic size and followed by a great host of smaller creatures of the same sort, ready to battle him so that he could not reach the land (had he succeeded in doing so, he would have known that the luck of the Danes was great enough to overcome Iceland's might at that time and King Haraldr would have ordered an invasion).

If you should have to move a large stone from its place, you should make very sure that you have warned any in-dwelling wights well in advance so that they have a chance to move. The same courtesy should be taken whenever you do any sort of major landscaping work, whether it is building a house, clearing trees from an area, draining a marshy spot, or altering the flow of a stream. Many Icelandic farmhouses today have large boulders which they will not plow around nor allow their children to disturb for fear of annoying the land-wights.

To meet with the land-wights, find such a boulder or go to a waterfall or the peak of a hill. Take some food and drink; hallow it to them, eating some yourself and leaving some; then tell them who you are and what you want. Again, remember that politeness is the most important thing in dealing with such wights; they are not like the demons of ceremonial magic, who can (and must!) be dominated and harshly commanded in specific detail, but rather they are free beings who have no reason to wish you ill—or even to deny their help to you—unless you manage to personally offend them.

ETINS, RISES, THURSES, AND TROLLS

These wights are the children of Ymir, dwelling in the wild realm of the Out-Garth. In the religion of the North, they usually embody the forces antagonistic to human kind—the forces of raw nature, which Thunar and Fro Ing ward us against. They are the man-eating fiends that haunt wild places; they are outlaw wights, beings of unholiness. All of them are very closely connected to the realm of death; they are the eaters of the dead, against whom Thunar's hammer hallows the funeral pyre and the memorial stone.

The etins (Old Norse *jötnar*, singular *jötunn*) are primeval beings of great wisdom, able to meet with the god/esses on equal terms—and to breed with them; Wodan's mother was the etin-maid Bestla. They are wise wights, skilled in the crafts of magic. Some are helpful; the wisest of all the etins is Mímir, Bestla's brother, keeper of Mímir's well, to whose head Wodan goes for rede in times of trouble; the goddess Skadhi is herself an etin and the daughter of one of the Ases' Garth's great foes; and the prophetess who speaks to Wodan in the Eddic poem "Völuspá" speaks of having been fostered by etins in the earliest times. Most of the etins are terrifying beings; however, the word "etin" comes from a root meaning "to eat"—like all of Ymir's children, they are devourers of light and life.

Though there is not much evidence for worship given to any of the etin-kind except Skadhi, the two etins Ægir and Ran, who rule/embody the frightful aspects of the sea, are often mentioned in the myths of the North. Ægir is the brewer of ale for the god/esses' feasts; this image may have come first from the ale-froth cast up by the sea. Ran, whose name means "robber," is ever greedy for the souls of the drowned, whom she catches with a silver net and welcomes in her hall beneath the sea. The nine daughters of Ægir and Ran are the nine waves: Himinglaeva, Dufa, Blódhughadda, Hefring, Unn, Hrönn, Bylgja, Bara, and Kolga. If you should be in peril from the sea, these are the wights against whom your workings should be aimed.

The *rises* (ON *rísir*) are the mountain-giants of folklore; the *thurses* (ON *thursar*) are also elemental giants of various sorts: rime-thurses, cliff-thurses, and so forth. The rises may occasionally be helpful to humankind; the thurses are always foes to the Middle-Garth. By and large, rises are not terribly intelligent and thurses are downright stupid.

All ill-meaning or ugly wights of the Out-Garth can be called trolls. Most trolls are man-eaters, though some also kidnap human women or men to be their mates. In one Icelandic folktale, a man who was enchanted by a troll-woman and went to live with her slowly turned into a troll over the course of three years. There are also some indications—such as the nickname "Half-Troll" which appears in several of the sagas, and the insulting accusation that someone has slept with a troll—that briefer affairs between trolls and humans have been known to take place. It is also sometimes possible for the trolls to take over a human mind.

Trolls range in size from giantish to smaller than humans. Daylight always turns them into stone.

In spite of their well-earned reputation for fearsomeness, individual trolls can be friends with individual humans; an Icelandic compliment says that someone is "trusty as a troll." In Swedish folklore, if you can trap a troll into taking a gift from you—tossing a piece of food into its jaws when it opens them to speak or take a bite is a favored method—it must then work weal towards you the rest of its life. In rocky, wild mountain places, trolls and land-wights may overlap to such a degree that it is impossible to make a distinction between them. I myself have one friend who spent a great deal of time in the mountains and got on very good terms with the trolls dwelling there (whom he has also come to resemble a little . . .). The trolls were never worshipped; however, if you should come to befriend one, you might take to leaving food out for it.

NOTES

1. Gundarsson, Kveldulf. *Teutonic Magic.*

2. Helm, Karl. *Altgermanische Religionsgeschichte*, 2:2:223.

3. "Sigrdrífumál," 9.

4. Simpson, Jacqueline. *Icelandic Folktales and Legends*, 30.

5. Davidson, 115.

6. Both the German and the Old Norse tradition later transferred this name (German *Nibelungen*, Old Norse *Niflungar*) to the royal house of the Burgundians—Gunnar, Högni, and Gudhrún—about whom the *Nibelungenlied* and many of the Eddic heroic poems were written. In the earlier German tradition, Hagen (Högni) was the bastard son of an alf, which may have been the source of the connection. See the chapter on Heroes.

Chapter 7

HEROES

 HERE ARE THE HEROES that courage revealed,
The battle-bright warriors who strode to the field
Of the war, their swords a light in the fray?
The heroes are gone, they are all passed away.

Where are the earls who led in the van?
The chieftains and kings who held sway in the
land
Of our fathers, revered in story and song?
They are all passed away, now our heroes are gone.

Where are the unsung who silently strove,
The women and children and all the unknowns
Who were models upon which to pattern our
deeds?
Those heroes are gone, from this life they are freed.

And now in this time of the dark of the sun,
Remember what's ended is only begun.
As Sun sets each evening, she rises at morn,
To the halls of the gods are the heroes reborn.

And we, who with valor must conquer each day,
We too are each heroes as gallant as they,

With truth as our banner and courage our light
We will come to those halls when we tread the long night.

So lift up a toast with the ale-filled horn,
To those who have faced well their wyrd and are gone,
Live well your life and traditions all keep,
Drink to god and to hero this Midwinter's eve."
                ("Midwinter's Toast" by Gunnora Hallakarva)

Knowing the greatest heroes of our folk is almost as important as knowing the god/esses themselves. Their might belongs to the souls of all who choose to follow their ways and take it up; thus we drink their *minne* (memory-draught) at *symbel* and call upon their deeds which we shall match. The list I give here is brief, the account of their works short. As you read and learn more about our tradition, you will find more and more heroes to whom your heart is near, but these are some of the greatest.

HERMANN OF THE CHERUSCI ("ARMINIUS")

The first Germanic hero of whose deeds we have direct historical knowledge, Hermann, whom the Romans called Arminius, served in the Roman army for a long time and then returned to Germany, teaching his tribesmen what he had learned about war. When the Emperor Augustus launched a massive attack to conquer Germany (under the general Varus, Hermann's previous commanding officer), it was Hermann who led the German forces to destroy the Romans at the battle of Teutoberger Wald (9 CE), thereby preserving Germania from the sort of destruction of its native culture which Gaul had already suffered. The Germanic tribes were still singing songs about Hermann more than an hundred years later. A great statue to him currently stands in the middle of the Teutoberger Wald as the sign of German freedom.

WEYLAND THE SMITH (OLD NORSE VÖLUNDR)

The story of Weyland, the greatest of smiths, was well-known to both the Anglo-Saxons and the Norse. Weyland was captured by the king Nithad, robbed of his sword and the ring he had made for his wife, hamstrung, and forced to work for his foe. In revenge, he slew Nithad's two sons, making drinking bowls out of their skulls for the king and brooches out of their eyes for the queen. He also raped Nithad's daughter Bödhvildr. Weyland escaped from his captivity by forging a pair of wings and flying away after he had gained his revenge.

The Anglo-Saxons worshipped Weyland as a lesser god; a shrine to him, "Weyland's Smithy," still stands in England. It is fitting to make gifts to him if you wish help in works of craftsmanship.

The tale of Weyland is told in the Eddic poem "Völundarkvidha," where he is called "wise alf." Images from the poem appear on a couple of Viking Age rock carvings in Gotland and Great Britain; the Anglo-Saxon poem "Deor" speaks of Bodhvild's sufferings after Weyland had left her pregnant. Weyland also appears as a character in *Thidhreks saga*.

THEODERIC THE GREAT
(DIETRICH VON BERN; THIDRIK)

Theoderic the Great was an Ostrogothic ruler who took over the Roman Empire in 493 CE. According to Germanic heroic legend (as opposed to historical actuality), Theoderic had been forced into exile by his rival Odoacer. Accompanied only by his faithful warrior Hildebrand, he had taken refuge in the warband of Attila the Hun, and eventually gathered enough of a host together to retake Rome.

A runestone exists on which Theoderic is invoked as if he were among the hosts of the gods; in medieval German tradition, he is said to lead the Wild Hunt. According to *Thidhreks saga* (the very romantic Old Norse account of his story), he was capable of breathing fire, and said to be the son of the devil. In both *Nibelungenlied* and *Thidhreks saga*, it was Theoderic who single-handedly overcame and captured Högni/Hagen and Gunnar (see below).

BEOWULF

Many hold this mighty warrior, the hero of the Anglo-Saxon epic poem *Beowulf*, to be the most shining of all in both deeds and troth. As a young man, he came to Denmark from his hall in southern Sweden to rid Hrothgar's hall Heorot ("Hart") of the monster Grendel. Beowulf did this not only to win fame, but to pay back Hrothgar for having once sheltered his father. Since Grendel came unarmed and unarmored to wreak havoc in the hall, Beowulf met him on equal terms, wrestling with him and tearing his arm off. After Grendel's death, Grendel's mother came to devastate the hall, and Beowulf had to go down through a fearsome lake to her underwater cave and slay her there to fulfill what he had begun.

When offered the kingship of his own people, the Geats, Beowulf refused, instead supporting the former king's young son. Only when the last heir of the royal line was dead did he take the kingship, reigning well till a great old age.

At the end of his reign, a dragon came forth and Beowulf had to fight it to save his people. His warband, except for the young man Wiglaf, deserted him in this final battle; he slew the dragon, but was mortally wounded in the battle. Of all his deeds, what his death-speech most celebrated was the fact that he had never broken an oath, nor sought out strife, nor raised his sword against a kinsman. Beowulf was buried on a headland where his barrow would still be a guide for seafarers.

I recommend the translations of Ruth Lehmann (University of Texas at Austin) and Burton Raffel (New American Library).

SIGMUNDR, SIGNÝ, SIGURDHR; GUNNARR, HÖGNI, GUDHRÚN

These characters are the main heroes of a massive story cycle which was known to all the branches of the Germanic people. The names I have given are the Old Norse; they may be more familiar from Wagner's Ring Cycle as Siegmund, Sieglinde, Siegfried, Günther, Hagen, and Gutrune. The plot of Wagner's story is a long way from any of the traditional versions.

Beowulf

Two branches of the story exist: the Northern and the German. The German *Nibelungenlied* is probably the less authentic of the two; read the Penguin translation by A.T. Hatto. The Northern version is that of the Sigurdhr-poems in the *Poetic Edda* and the prose work *Völsunga saga*, "Saga of the Völsungs." The best translation is that of R.W. Finch, which has the Old Norse text across from the English; the most readily available is Jesse L. Byock's paperback *Saga of the Volsungs* (University of California Press, 1990).

The story cycle as a whole is too complex to fully relate here. The major events are Sigmundr's drawing out of the sword which Wodan set in the tree called *Barnstokkr* ("child-stock") on the night of his twin sister Signý's wedding; the treacherous slaying of their father Völsi and nine brothers by Signý's husband Siggeirr; Signý changes shapes with a witch-woman and seduces Sigmundr, bearing a son named Sinfjötli. Sigmundr and Sinfjötli run through the wood in wolfskins (as a Wodanic initiation); when this is done, they burn Siggeirr's hall, but Signý insists on dying beside her husband to fulfill her troth. Sinfjötli is poisoned by Sigmundr's wife Borghildr. Sigmundr then weds a woman named Hjördis and falls in battle (against Lyngvi, a rival for Hjördis' hand) when Wodan comes against him and breaks his sword. Sigmundr charges Hjördis to keep the shards for his son.

Sigmundr's son Sigurdhr is fostered by the dwarf Reginn, brother of the dragon Fáfnir, and raised so that he can slay the dragon. Reginn reforges the sword; Sigurdhr first avenges his father's death, then kills Fáfnir. Reginn has him cook the dragon's heart. He burns his finger and tastes the blood, becoming able to understand birds. The birds warn him that Reginn has planned his death and tell him about the walkyrige sleeping on top of a mountain. Sigurdhr kills Reginn, takes the dragon's hoard, and awakens the walkyrige Sigrdrifa (who is apparently identical with Brynhildr, or Brünnhilde). She teaches him runes and other sorts of wisdom and magic.

Sigurdhr goes to the hall of the Gjúkings, where Grimhildr, the mother of Gunnarr, Högni, Gudhrún, and their half-brother Guthormr, gives him a magical draught that causes him to forget the walkyrige and fall in love with Gudhrún. Sigurdhr swears blood-brotherhood with Gunnarr and Högni, then changes shapes with Gunnarr and goes to win Brynhildr for him.

The secret is kept for several years, till Brynhildr and Gudhrún quarrel. At Brynhildr's insistence, Gunnarr ends by plotting Sigurdhr's death and inducing Guthormr to carry it out.[1] Guthormr stabs Sigurdhr in his bed; Sigurdhr kills him and then dies. Brynhildr kills herself and the two are burned together.

Gudhrún is married to Atli (Attila the Hun), who invites Gunnarr and Högni to a feast at his hall. There is a great fight, in which Gudhrún takes up weapons to fight for her brothers; at last Gunnarr and Högni are captured. They refuse to tell Atli where Sigurdhr's treasure is. Atli cuts Högni's heart out and throws Gunnarr into a pit of snakes. Gudhrún and Högni's youngest son Niflung kill Atli in his sleep. Gudhrún then marries again and has several children, all of whom come to horrible ends.

An excellent fictional rendition of this story is Stephan Grundy's well-researched historical novel *Rhinegold* (Bantam, early 1994), which merges several of the major sources but remains in general true to the *Völsunga saga* plot. From a traditional point of view, it is well worth the trouble to become familiar with this tale; our ancestors thought

Sigurdhr reforges the sword and slays Fáfnir (from the church doors at Hylestad, Norway).

the Völsungs and the Gjúkings to have been the highest of heroes, particularly Sigurdhr/Siegfried.

HRÓLFR KRAKI

The national hero of the Viking Age Danes, Hrólfr kraki appears in *Hrólfs saga kraka* and, in a less favorable light, as Hrothulf in *Beowulf*. The nickname "kraki" means a stick; it was given to him by Vogg, a youth of low birth who was surprised to see that the great king was less prepossessing of body than of deeds and reputations, and inadvertently burst out, "Why, he's just a 'kraki'!" Rather than being insulted, Hrólfr accepted the name in good part, giving the youth a gold ring; Vogg, in turn, swore that he would avenge Hrólfr if the king were slain, which he did.

Hrólfr kraki's band included the famous warrior Bodhvar-Bjarki ("Battle-Bear"), the son of a man who had been enchanted into a bear's form by a witch. Bjarki was the most notable of Hrolf's warriors. In the king's last battle, Bjarki went out from his body to fight in the shape of a bear.

Poul Andersson's book *Hrolf Kraki's Saga* is a good rendition of the tale, with only a little fictionalizing to make it read more easily.

HENGEST AND HORSA

These two were, according to English national legend, the leaders of the Saxon conquest of Britain (ca. 449 CE). Their names mean "stallion" and "horse" (or "mare"). There is some question as to whether they were two brothers (as the Venerable Bede recounts) or whether Horsa might have been a woman, either Hengest's sister or his wife—a Germanic man could not be called anything more insulting than "mare." The evidence seems to be weighted fairly evenly, but the tendency in modern times is to see these two war-leaders as a male/female pair. Most histories of the Anglo-Saxons will at least mention them.

RADBOD OF FRISIA

The tale of Radbod, king of Frisia, is found in the Vita Wulframmi (ca. 668 CE):

> Radbod the war-king himself was at last inclined to receive baptism. However, he still hesitated and he bade the bishop that he swear by his oath, where the dead kings and chieftains of the Frisians had their abode: in that heavenly realm, that he was to get if he would believe and be baptized, or in hellish damnation, about which the bishop so often spoke. To this the man of God answered, "Make no mistake, noble prince! By the side of God is the multitude of his chosen ones. But your ancestors, the princes of the Frisians, who died without having received the sacrament of baptism, have verily received the sentence of damnation . . . " As the untrusting war-king, who had already stepped up to the baptismal, heard this, he pulled his foot back away from the source of grace, and said that he could not do without the fellowship of all those who ruled over the Frisians before him, and that he did not want to have to sit around in heaven with a little pack of beggars, and therefore he could not give the new faith any troth and he would rather stay with the one to which he, along with the whole of the Frisians, had held fast. (tr. by James Chisholm)

Radbod then resisted the efforts of the Christian missionaries and worked as strongly as he could to hold the ways of his folk safe.

RAGNAR LÖDDBROK

A great hero of the Viking Age, who led the sack on Paris in 845. According to legend, Ragnar got the name Löddbrok ("Leather-Breeches") by wearing hairy leather breeches as armor when he went to slay a dragon. Ragnar died when he was captured by the English king Aelle and cast into a pit of adders, where he said, "The piglets would grunt if they knew the plight of the old boar," then spoke the poem known as "Ragnar's Death-Song," heroically greeting his death. When Ragnar's sons, led by Ivarr the Boneless, found what had happened to their father, they descended on England, cut the blood-eagle on Aelle, and took a large part of the country. Ragnar's story is told in *Ragnar Löddbroks saga*. An extremely imaginative version (bearing no resemblance to the original except for a few names) was presented in the film "The Vikings," a movie best known for Kirk Douglas' chin and the famous lines "Hail Ragnar! Hail Ragnar's beard!"

EGILL SKALLA-GRÍMSSON

Egill Skalla-Grímsson (d. 990 CE) is the most famous rune-magician of the Viking Age. In addition to his magical skills, he was also one of the best skalds of his time and a warrior of immense might. Egill was an Icelander from a family which had left Norway because of quarrels with Haraldr Harfagri; both the berserkergang and second sight ran in his paternal line. He was a huge man, swarthy of complexion, who went bald early; he was fierce of temper, very ugly, and often greedy. On the whole, he was not greatly attractive, but the beauty of his poetry more than compensated for the faults of his personality and appearance. In return for the gifts of poetry, battle-might, and runic magic, Egill was one of the most dedicated of Ódhinn's followers.

The best-remembered events of Egill's life are his curing of a girl who had been made sick by ignorantly-cut runes; his quarrel with Eiríkr Bloodaxe and his queen Gunnhildr, which led to his raising a nídhing-pole ("pole of insult"; a device for cursing) to drive them out of Norway and, later, to his writing the poem "Head-Ransom" (the first Old Norse poem ever to use end-rhyme!) to save his life; his journeys to England, during one of which he fought in the army of the Anglo-Saxon king Æthelstan; and his wretched old age, in which he went blind and a little crazy, making life very difficult for everyone around him.

The best translation of *Egils saga* is that done by Christine Fell. Both her version and the Penguin Classics edition are available in paperback.

BRYHTNOTH

The hero of the Old English poem "Battle of Maldon," Bryhtnoth was one of the few Anglo-Saxon leaders to stand and fight the Vikings rather than trying to buy them off with Danegeld. He met the Viking troop at a causeway over a tidal channel separating their island from the mainland where his troop stood. The Vikings asked to be allowed over, which Bryhtnoth permitted them because of his great bravery (*ofermod*) and because he knew that it would be easy for them to sail away and attack a less well-defended part of the coast. His surrender of land lost him his life and the battle. After Bryhtnoth was slain and the battle clearly lost, the best of his house-carls (personal retinue) stayed to die beside him; in the poem, the old retainer Bryhtwold speaks the well-known staves:

> Hugr (thought/spirit) shall be the harder   heart the keener
> mood shall be greater   as our main grows less.
> Here lies our leader   all hewed down,
> the good man on ground.   Grieve may he ever
> who now from this war-play   thinks to wend.
> I am wise in life   I will not go from here
> but I by the side   of my loaf-giver
> by such a loved man   think to lay me down.

The full-length poem "Battle of Maldon" can be found in any collection of Old English poetry, both in translation and in the original. The most readily available translation is Kevin Crossley-Holland's *An Anthology of Anglo-Saxon Literature* (Penguin). The battle took place in 991.

GRETTIR THE STRONG

Grettir was an Icelander of immense strength, skill, and intelligence, whose career was destroyed only by his endless ill-luck, which caused him to be outlawed in several lands and kept him from the success his capabilities would otherwise have earned. He is best-known for his victories in wrestling with troublesome undead. The last of these, Glam, cursed him with a great fear of the dark, so that he could not bear to be alone at night; and his need for human society, even after he had been outlawed many times, proved to be his undoing in the end, according to Glam's prophecy. In *Fóstbroedhra saga*, it is mentioned that "Men say that all three stayed together at Reykjahólar, Thórgeirr, Thórmódhr (the fosterbrothers), and Grettir the Strong, son of Asmundr, and the strength of the two of them was about the same as that of Grettir alone. People say too that when Thorgils was asked ... about his winter guests, whether they were not the boldest men in the whole of Iceland and least capable of fearing anything, he answered this by saying that it was not so—'for Grettir fears the dark and Thórmódr fears God'; but he said that Thórgeirr did not know how to be afraid of anything at all." This gripping fear of the dark is not uncommon in Iceland, where the long winter nights have always fed the imagination.

Grettir has long been considered the national hero of Iceland. His story is told in the *Saga of Grettir the Strong*, available in English translations.

HEROIC WOMEN

The ideal of heroism for women in the Germanic tradition is, generally, different from that in the Mediterranean/Christian tradition. According to the ideals of the latter, women could only be heroic by abandoning the female role altogether and taking on the role of men. In the Germanic culture, on the other hand, the role of the woman was recognized as a vital and good part of society— indeed, women were often responsible for keeping the social structure from disintegrating under the continual stresses of feud and war, as the terms "peace-pledge" and "peace-weaver" imply. Feuds were often settled by sending a young woman of one family into another as wife. Such a woman then went unarmed among her foes and lived among them for the rest of her life; each day was a test of her heroism. A woman who wed risked a dreadful death each time she came to childbed as surely as her husband and sons risked death on the battlefield; often, wives would follow their dead men to the funeral pyre. In the ancient times of the Germanic tribesmen, women carried arms to the place where they waited by the battlefield—for if their men were defeated, they preferred death to slavery, both for themselves and for their children.

Because the heroic deeds of women were usually done quietly, and success rewarded not with victory in battle but with the complete absence of battles, such deeds were seldom spoken of in the songs and tales of our ancestors. Most of the women remembered in heroic legend were those who took the role of "Maiden Warrior," taking up arms and stepping into the world of men to

Hervör

fight. However, we can not forget their lesser-known sisters who made peace among men and who suffered and died in silence.

Hervör

The heroine of *Hervör's saga*, Hervör was the daughter of the berserker Angantýr, who was slain and laid in a mound with his eleven brothers on Samsey (a Danish island). Hervör disguised herself as a man and became a highway robber, then the leader of a pirate ship. When she sailed to Samsey to reclaim Angantýr's sword Tyrfingr, her men fled out of fear; but she went to the mound at night and forced her dead father to bring out the ancestral sword, although he told her that it would be the death of her line in time.

Hervör was married to the son of the etin Gudhmundr of Glæsisvellir, and bore the hero-king Heidhrekr, father of the Swedish royal dynasty.

An English translation of her saga was done by Christopher Tolkien.

Wealtheow

Wealtheow was the queen of Hrothgar, spoken of in the epic *Beowulf*. In all ways she was the ideal queen: knowing secret wisdom, giving counsel to her husband, giving gifts to the warriors of their band. In all her deeds, she acts as a peace-weaver; it was largely she who deals with Beowulf and his band of Geats when they came to Hrothgar's hall, and she who urges Hrothulf to remember his troth to his young cousins.

Sigridh the Strong-Minded

This heathen queen of Sweden accepted Óláfr Tryggvason's proposal of marriage, but when he told her that she would have to become a Christian, she said, "I will not go from the faith I have had before, and my kinsmen before me. I will not say anything against thee if thou believe in the god that pleases thee." Óláfr replied to this by saying, "Why should I wed thee, thou heathen bitch?" and struck her in the face with his glove. To this Sigrídhr answered, "This may well be thy death!" And it was; Sigrídhr arranged the collaboration between her husband Sweyn Forkbeard (father of King Canute) of Denmark and her son, the king of Sweden, which brought Óláfr to his final battle and his fall—the fall of one of the greatest and most brutal foes of heathendom in the North. The story of Sigrídhr is told in Snorri Sturluson's *Saga of Óláfr Tryggvason*, which is one of the sagas collected in Sturluson's *Heimskringla* (available in a Dover paperback).

Freydís Eiríksdottir

This woman, the sister of Leifr Eiríksson, was one of the leaders on the expedition to Vinland (North America). When the camp was attacked by Skraelings (American Indians), the men fled, although Freydís rebuked them, "Why are you running from wretches like these? . . . Such gallant lads as you, I thought for sure you would have knocked them on the head like cattle. Why, if I had a weapon, I think I could put up a better fight than any of you." The colonists continued to flee; Freydís, being quite pregnant, was soon left behind. She grabbed a sword from a fallen man, turned around to face the Skraelings, and tore her bodice open, slapping the sword against her breasts. This frightened the Skraelings so much that they ran away. The story of Freydís can be found in Gwyn Jones' *Norse Atlantic Saga* (paperback; Oxford University Press).

NOTES

1. The one point on which the German version seems to preserve a more accurate tradition is Siegfried's death: in *Nibelungenlied*, Hagen spears him in the single vulnerable spot on his back while they are out hunting in the forest. This motif relates Siegfried to Balder as well as to a number of other Indo-European heroes.

Chapter 8

SOUL AND AFTERLIFE

T IS TOLD IN "VÖLUSPA" how, after the creation of the world, Wodan and his brothers Hoenir and Lódurr "found on land little in main, / Ash and Elm, without *ørlög*"—that is to say, still outside the realm of causality. Lacking any power to influence the shape of wyrd, Ash and Elm are still untouched by it; they have no *ørlög* because they have no effective existence. These two trees, the first humans, "possessed not önd had not wod, / nor hair nor shape nor good appearance. / Önd gave Wodan, wod gave Hoenir, / hair gave Lódurr and good appearance." *Önd* is an Old Norse word which can be used for the breath of life or for the soul itself; wod signifies all the higher mental faculties which are awakened through its workings; hair, shape, and good appearance are all expressions of the fiery force of life which appears as both spiritual and physical strength. Hoenir and Lódurr are, in fact, aspects of Wodan himself, which explains how it is that Hoenir gives to humans the gift of wod. As firstly a god of the air, Wodan is responsible for the airy soul, which appears in the earthly world as the breath of life; wod appears as a draught of intoxicating liquid, therefore it is given by the watery Hoenir; the might which Lódurr gives is all characterized by the fire of energy itself.

When Ash and Elm have been given these three gifts, they are no longer "without *ørlög*"; they have *become*, and therefore are both bound by Wyrd and capable of shaping her turnings. To have "soul" is to bear doom and power together; the two are shaped at one time by the weight of what *is*, which determines what *shall be*. From the moment they breathe in the önd of life, they are doomed to die; their *ørlog* is the fourth major component of their "souls." This is the aspect of soul which is given to a child in the naming-ceremony, without which it is not considered human.

In Germanic tradition, these four primal elements of the psychic being were divided into a number of different aspects, which often overlap in some areas but which are nevertheless distinct and important to understand as separate entities. In *Teutonic Magic*, I discussed the aspects of the soul which are most important in magical workings: *hugr* (reason) and *minni* (memory); *hamingja* ("luck", mana); *fylgja* (fetch); *hamr* ("hide" or spiritual form). In addition to these, the soul also bears mood, might and main, *ørlög*, and life-age (*aldr*).

First among these is the *hugr*, which is specifically taken to mean the conscious mind; the verb derived from it, *hyggja*, is generally used for "to think" or "to intend." When contrasted with the *minni*, as in the case of Wodan's ravens Huginn and Muninn, it denotes the intellectual/left-brain process; when used by itself, it seems to encompass both conscious thought and intuition/emotion together. To know something with the *hugr* is to know it, not only intellectually, but with all the awareness of the soul; the *hugr* is often what tells you whether to trust someone or not, or what the results of an action are likely to be. The *hugr* is your courage and the strength of your mind as well as your wisdom. It also denotes the quality of thought and feeling; you can say that your *hugr* is well-disposed or ill-disposed towards someone. The *hugr* of another can be seen in the shape of an animal similar to the fetch; its nature shows the person's character and its actions show his/her intentions towards one.

Closely related to *hugr* is *módhr*. Both are used to describe the quality of feeling or thought; however, *módhr* (the word from which our modern "mood" comes), does not carry the sense of consciousness or thought which is generally shown by *hugr*; *módhr* is generally used to mean "courage," "heart," or "nature." "When Thor is altogether himself, he appears in his godly *módhr* (ásmódhr); the giants put on fiendish *módhr* when they assume their full nature . . . To assume giant's *módhr* or bring it into play is understood to imply all such peculiarities—violence and ferocity as well as features—that show him a being of demon land."[1] To describe his heroism, Beowulf is described as *modig*, which might be translated as "mood-full." If your mood is strong, then you are mighty and brave; if it is weak or low, then activity and strength are lacking.

The three main forms of vital power are called *hamingja*, might, and main. *Hamingja* is often translated as "luck"; it appears as the aura of power around every person. The *hamingja* is what vitalizes the other aspects of the soul such as the fetch and the walkyrige. Unlike the mood, it can be transmitted to other people, sent forth from the body, or even stored in an external item like an electrical charge. It corresponds most closely to the Polynesian concept of "mana," or undifferentiated magical force which can be used for anything, but which certain persons and items have in greater quantity than others. Might and main are unlike *hamingja* in that they represent a combination of earthly strength and soul-force, and they cannot be transferred to another person or thing.

Though our ancestors quite often thought of physical and spiritual strength as being one and the same, this was not always so. One of the greatest heroes of the Danes, the king Hrólfr kraki, was given his nickname "kraki" or "stick" in reference to his small build. Hrólfr was not physically overwhelming, but his great wisdom, mood, and *hamingja* more than made up for his size, although he might have lacked in earthly might and main when compared to some of the warriors such as the bear-hero Bödhvar-Bjarki who fought in his band.

Closely related to *ørlög* is the *aldr*, "life-age," which carries the sense both of vital power and of "fate," as well as of honor. In the *Prose Edda*, it is said of both the three Norns Wyrd, Werthende, and Should, and of the individual norns who come to every child that they "shape *aldr*," and that this shaping determines both the length and the quality of life. The life-age cannot be identical to *ørlög*, because it can be lost or taken; it may, rather, be thought of as a store of might which is kept within from birth, the nature of which determines its keeper's actions and their consequences. Dishonorable deeds lessen it; honorable deeds make it wax and strengthen. It may be seen as the vital essence of the *self*, which determines strength of soul by its quantity and character by its quality.

The fetch (Old Norse *fylgja*) is a semi-independent aspect of the soul, whose shape reflects its owner's true character. Especially strong and noble people often have bear-fetches; the very fierce have wolves; the cunning have foxes, and so forth. The fetch can be seen at any time by folk with soul-sight, but it only appears to those without psychic vision shortly before death. To see your fetch bloody or ill is a sure sign of approaching death; its condition reflects that of its owner. The fetch can be sent out from the body to bring back knowledge, or it is possible to consciously inhabit your fetch's shape when faring away from your body.

Germanic concepts of the afterlife varied between different areas, time periods, and dedication to various gods. Their only really consistent element was the emphasis on the family as a continuous unit spanning the worlds of the dead and the living. One of the most common descriptions of death was that of going to join one's "kinsmen who have gone before";[2] whether spiritually in the halls of the gods or physically within the burial mound.

Most often, the process of death was expressed as a journey. In Anglo-Saxon poetry, it was literally described as "faring forth," or, as in "Bede's Death-Song, "the necessary faring"; in modern German, the word for "ancestors" is still *Vorfahren*—literally, those who have fared before. Throughout Germanic culture, the single image most consistently used in burials was the boat. Sometimes— probably in the cases of very important or royal deaths—a full-sized ship was used, as in the fine burials at Sutton Hoo (England), Gokstad, and Oseberg (Norway). In other circumstances, a smaller boat or boatlike structure might be put in the mound, or a symbolic circle of stones forming the outline of a ship was placed around the body. The image also survives in literature; Egill Skallagrímsson described his father's burial mound by the kenning, "the boat-house of Náin."[3] Náin is a dwarf-name, and the dwarves were very closely tied to the world of death; hence the howe is a "boat-house" for the faring over the waters of death. As mentioned in the discussion of Nerthus/Njördhr, the ship may particularly be associated with the faring to the Wanic realms.

Those who do not sail to the other worlds have to ride or walk. Where it could be afforded, the dead were buried with their horses or even with wagons, as described in the prose to "Hel-Ride of Brynhildr": "After the death of Brynhildr two bale-fires were

Picture stone depicting the journey of death
Top: A rider is welcomed to Walhall
Bottom: Ship faring into the realm of death

Gotland, Viking Age (Lillbjärs III)

prepared: one for Sigurdhr, and he was burned first, and Brynhildr was burned on the other, and she was in a wagon, which was adorned with cloth of gold. So it is said, that Brynhildr rode on the Hel-road with her wagon." The two most frequent images on the Gotlandic picture stones show either ships or warriors riding horses. Sometimes the horse is eight-legged; this figure may represent Wodan himself, or it may, as D. Ellmers suggests, be the dead man for whom "Odin sent his own horse to carry the most honoured guest, as a king or chieftain would do. No greater honour could be shown to those on the path between life and death."[4] For poorer people, Hel-shoes were tied to their feet so that they might be sturdily shod on the long walk.

An odd custom connected with the giving of means of spiritual transport to the dead was the act of ensuring that the ship or shoes could never be used for physical transport. In *Gisla saga*, it is told that the funeral ship was tied to a large rock to prevent it from moving; and this practice is confirmed by the archaeological record. Likewise, the Hel-shoes are tied together as if to prevent the dead man from walking. When a dead person was carried out of the house, either a special "corpse-door" was used which could easily be boarded or bricked up again, or a temporary opening was made in the wall, as mentioned in *Egils saga*. These customs probably stem from the fear that the dead could return from the other worlds through the same means by which they reached them. Thus the ship was tightly moored to prevent the dead from sailing freely into the world of the living, and the Hel-shoes were tied together to keep the corpse from walking out of his/her howe. In Christian times, when Hel-shoes were no longer used, needles might be stuck into the feet of someone who had been suspected of sorcery or was for other reasons likely to be able to walk again.

The aspect of the Germanic afterlife which is best known in modern popular culture is the belief in Walhall (Valhöll), the "Hall of the Slain." As the name and many of the literary references imply, Walhall was usually, though not invariably, seen as the goal of those slain in battle. Wodan sends the walkyriges (valkyrjur) to choose which heroes should fall in a fight and to bring their souls back to Walhall. These warriors—the einherjar or "single champions"—fight every day, coming back to life to feast every night. At the end of all things, they will fight against the giants to make the rebirth of the cosmos possible. It should be noted, however, that

Wodan's halls, Walhall and Válaskjálf ("Hall of Slain Warriors"), were not limited to those who fell in fight. Egil Skallagrímsson says of his son Bödvar who was drowned that "Ódhinn took him to himself . . . My son is come to Ódhinn's house, the son of my wife to visit his kin . . . I remember still that Ódhinn raised up into the home of the gods the ash-tree of my race, that which grew from me, the kin-branch of my wife."[5] The belief in Walhall may have been connected with the practice of cremation. Initiation of this practice is attributed to Wodan in *Ynglinga saga*: "He bade that they burn all the dead and bear their possessions on to the firebale with them. He said that every man should come to Valhöll with such riches as he had with him on the firebale and that each should use what he had himself buried down in the earth. They should bear the ashes out on the sea or bury them down in the earth . . . "[6] The cremation of important persons followed by the burial of the ashes and raising a mound is verified by the great mounds at Old Uppsala; the two that have been excavated both contained cremated bodies together with partially melted weapons and gold ornaments.

The Arab historian ibn Fadlan gives a full description of a cremation carried out by the Rus (the Swedish tribe from whom modern Russia takes its name) along the Volga. The ceremonies are overseen by an old woman whom ibn Fadlan said the Rus called the "Angel of Death," a title which may well have been an Arab's interpretation of "valkyrja." They concluded with the burning of the chieftain and one of his slaves in his ship, at which point ibn Fadlan relates,

> One of the Rus was at my side and I heard him speak to the interpreter who was present. I asked the interpreter what he said. He answered, 'He said, "You Arabs are fools."' 'Why?' I asked him. He said. 'You take the people who are most dear to you and whom you honour most and you put them in the ground where insects and worms devour them. We burn him in a moment, so that he enters Paradise at once.' Then he began to laugh uproariously. When I asked why he laughed, he said, 'His lord, for love of him, has sent the wind to bring him away in an hour.' And actually an hour had not passed before the ship, the wood, the girl, and her master were nothing but cinders and ashes.[7]

It seems to have been generally understood that cremation freed the soul, whereas those who were buried in a howe (burial mound) continued to dwell there, either as well-meaning ghosts or as draugar. This was not always necessarily so; the Second Lay of Helgi Hunding's-Bane describes how the hero and his men rode back and forth from Walhall to their burial mound. Helgi's wife Sigrún goes to the howe and spends the night with him; at dawn he rises and says:

> Time for me to ride on reddening paths,
> on the fallow steed to fly the way.
> I must go westward of Windhelm's bridge
> before Sagolfnir the sig-host wakes.[8]

After this meeting, Helgi and his men do not come back to their barrow again, although Sigrún waits for them.

Njáls saga may show a similar belief in the dead remaining in the barrow for a time before going on to the halls of the gods. When Gunnarr of Hlídharend is slain, he is set upright in a mound, but:

> Rannveig refused to allow his halberd to be buried with him; she said that only the man who was prepared to avenge Gunnar could touch it . . . One night Skarp-Hedin and Högni (Gunnar's son) were standing outside to the south of Gunnar's burial mound. The moonlight was bright but fitful. Suddenly it seemed to them that the mound was open; Gunnar had turned round to face the moon. There seemed to be four lights burning inside the mound, illuminating the whole chamber. They could see that Gunnar was happy; his face was exultant. He chanted a verse so loudly that they could have heard it clearly from much farther away . . . 'There is great significance in such a portent,' said Skarp-Hedin, 'when Gunnar himself appears before our eyes and says that he would rather die than yield to his enemies, and that was his message for us.' . . .
> . . . Högni took down Gunnar's halberd, and it rang loudly. Rannveig sprang up in a towering rage. 'Who is taking the halberd?' she demanded . . . Högni replied, 'I am taking it to my father, so that he can have it in Valhöll and carry it to combat there.' 'But first you are going to carry it yourself,' said Rannveig, 'to avenge your father, for it has just predicted death for someone—or for several.' Högni went out and told Skarp-Hedin of this exchange with his grandmother. Then they set

out for the farm at Oddi. Two ravens flew with them all the way. (pp. 174-75)

Here, the act of revenge is implied to be necessary if Gunnar is to go on to Walhall. The ringing of the halberd, or thrusting-spear, and the presence of the ravens are clear signs of Wodan's presence and blessing upon this mission.

Again, despite the popular conception, not all warriors slain in battle go to Walhall. It is written in "Grímnismál" that "Folkvangr is the ninth (hall) where Freyja rules and chooses who sits in her hall. / Half of the slain she chooses each day the other half Óðhinn has." (58). This stanza may hark back to very ancient beliefs about burial practices and the fate of the soul. Those buried in the earth naturally belonged to the Wanic powers and particularly to the Frowe; given that cremation seems to have been largely associated with the cult of Wodan, the "Grímnismál" passage may be a statement of the spiritual consequences of the fact that the battle-slain dead were burned and buried in roughly even numbers (though this varied widely with place and period).

The popular conception of the Norse afterlife, again, holds that whoever did not die fighting went to the realm of Hel, the grim world below the earth. This conception is largely a product of the *Prose Edda*, in which Snorri puts forth this view, describing Hel's domain in relatively horrific terms.

> Hel he (Óðhinn) cast into Niflheimr, and gave to her power over nine worlds, to apportion all abodes among those that were sent to her: that is, men dead of sickness and old age. She has great possessions there; her walls are exceeding high and her gates great. Her hall is called Sleet-Cold, her dish Hunger; Famine is her knife; Idler, her thrall; Sloven, her maid-servant; Pit of Stumbling, her threshold, by which one enters; Disease, her bed; Gleaming Bale, her bed-hangings. She is half corpse-blue and half flesh-coloured . . . and very louring and fierce. (ch. 34)

However, the poetry of the Elder Edda is not so negative: in "The Dream of Baldr," Óðhinn asks the völva (seeress) "'Tell thou me of Hel . . . for whom are the benches brightened with rings, / fairly adorned with dazzling gold?'" She replies, "'Here stands for Baldr brewed the mead, / a shining drink the shield lies over'" (6–7).

The name of the goddess Hel had already undergone semantic contamination among the Christianized continental Germanic peoples and the Anglo-Saxons, having been superimposed upon the terrible underworld of Indo-Iranian tradition as part of the conversion process. After the identification of Hella's realm with the southern conception of a world of torment, the North was then exposed to the familiar name Hell as part of Christianity, and assimilated the unfamiliar concept of the underworld as a realm of punishment without much difficulty. Thus the Christian concept of Hel's realm almost certainly distorted Snorri's presentation to some degree. In point of fact, the goddess Hella appears in a form which makes her consistent with the nature of the other Wanic powers: she is half-dead and ugly, half-living and beautiful. This description in Snorri seems to preserve a deep understanding of the relationship between the mysteries of death and fertility. On the one hand, Hel is the earth as the terrifying grave; on the other, she is the earth as the mother who protects and nurtures the buried soul-seed, which she may bring to life again. This is precisely the function she carries out on a cosmic scale at Ragnarök; while everything else is destroyed, she preserves the souls of Baldr and his slayer Höder, bringing them forth to live again when the battle is done and the worlds recreated.

To sink down to Hella's realm is to move into a state of potential energy; to rest until you are called forth again. It is the antithesis of Walhall, where the dwellers are in a continuous frenzy of active energy, either feasting or fighting. The passage to Walhall is difficult; those who are not carried over Bifröst by their walkyriges must force their way through a barrier which is described as the great river Thund, "The Noisy": "Thund roars . . . the river stream seems over-mighty / for battle-slain to wade."[9] Hel, on the other hand, is reached by a broad bridge of ice, over which whole troops of warriors may ride with ease, as recounted in the *Prose Edda* description of Hermódhr's ride to Hel in search of Baldr: "Módgudhr is the maiden called who guards the bridge; she asked him his name and race, saying that the day before there had ridden over the bridge five companies of dead men; 'but the bridge thunders no less under thee alone, and thou hast not the colour of dead men'" (p. 74).

Aside from these two major categories, there are references to folk going to the halls of the god/ess to whom their nature best suits them. Snorri says of the goddess Gefjon that she receives virgins in her hall; when Egill Skallagrimsson's daughter Thorgerd announces her intention to die with her father, she says, "I have had no supper, and will have none till I am with Freyja."[10] In the Eddic poem "Hárbardzljodh," Ódhinn (disguised as a ferryman) says to Thórr, "Ódhinn has earls who are slain in battle, / but Thórr the kin of thralls!" To this Thórr replies, "Unevenly you would divide to Ases the hosts / if you had too much power" (24–5). These lines also imply that some sort of division of souls by their nature occurs after death. The claim that Thórr, or Thunar, is a god of thralls is of course a cunning Ódhinnic twisting of fact; it was the carles, or free farmers, who most often counted Thunar as their friend, even as war-drightens gave themselves to Wodan. Nevertheless, this shows again that the literary presentation of Walhall and Hel as the two halls of the dead represents only a limited portion of Germanic belief. The true woman or man ought to expect to fare towards the god/ess whom she or he counts as her or his dearest friend.

Aside from the halls of the gods, many folk also continue to dwell within the howe where they were buried. This existence does not seem to be unpleasant in most cases; *Eyrbyggja saga* describes how Thórsteinn Mostur-Beard and all his descendants dwelt within the mountain Helga Fell after his death, and how, at the death of his son Thórsteinn, "as Thorstein's shepherd was tending sheep north of Helga Fell, he saw the whole north side of the mountain opened up, with great fires burning inside it and the noise of feasting and clamour over the ale-horns. As he strained to catch particular words, he was able to make out that Thorstein Cod-Biter and his crew were being welcomed into the mountain, and that Thorstein was being invited to sit in the place of honour opposite his father" (p. 38).

The howe-dwellers generally remain well-wishing towards their kin and those who treat them with respect, though if they are angered—if someone attempts to dig up their mound against their warning, for instance—they cause death and disaster. A case of this was recorded in the *Old Lore Miscellany* of July 1911, where a farmer's son-in-law told how the farmer had disturbed a howe-dweller's mound and the dead man appeared—complete with Old Norse Hel-shoes "of horse or cowhide tied on with strips of skin on his feet"—to warn the farmer that if he took another shovelful, there would be six cattle dead in his corn-yard and six deaths in the household. "Having said this, the old man vanished and was never seen again; but six cattle actually died in the corn-yard, and there were six deaths in the household. The teller of the story was present when the fourth death occurred, and was told about the mound-dweller and his warning."[11] Most of the time, however, these wights are kindly guardians of their lands and their families.

The Germanic people also believed in several forms of rebirth, although it is difficult to tell how close these are to the modern concept of "reincarnation." After Sigurdhr's death, Högni says that Brynhild must not be hindered from suicide and curses her: "Let no one hold her from the long journey / so that she be never born again!"[12]

The most descriptive references to rebirth in the poetic sources are those of the Helgi lays, a cycle in which three successive heroes named Helgi meet a walkyrige who is protector, lover, and finally the cause of death. Helgi Hjorvardhssonr and his walkyrige Sváva are reborn as Helgi Hundingsbani and Sigrún, who are thereafter reborn as Helgi Haddingjaskadhi and Kára, as the prose of the lays states explicitly. There is no genetic link between the Helgis; the significant element is the continuity of name and, as the prose of the second Lay of Helgi Hunding's-Bane describes, the fact that Helgi's parents deliberately name him *after* Helgi Hjörvardhssonr. The rite of naming, which confers on the child its share in the family soul (kin-fylgja), may therefore have been seen as conferring the individual soul as well. With name and soul come ørlög as well; the Helgis all carry out similar careers which end in the same way, and in *Sturlunga saga* Thórvaldr Gizurarson refuses to name his son after the hero Kolbeinn who had died young because "wise men" had told him that it was unwise to name a child after someone who had been short-lived.

In his *Sigurdhr: Rebirth and Initiation*, Stephen Flowers discusses the fact that various aspects of the soul could be separated from one another and transmitted down family lines. The most important elements of this process are the "hamingja" (luck/spiritual power), "hamr" ("hide" or physical appearance), and "fylgja" ("fetch"; an individual guardian-spirit, which normally appeared in a shape harmonious with the inner nature of the individual). The transmission of all of these is copiously attested to in the sagas. It is not certain whether the individual personality (ON *hugr*) was thought to be reborn; Flowers suggests that "it seems more likely that if the personality were to survive, it would survive in one of these other-worlds rather than in a reborn form" (p. 93). All the references to the rebirth of hamingja, hamr, and fylgja make it clear that these aspects were dependent upon lineage as well as on name; that this form of rebirth is, perhaps, less a form of "reincarnation" than something falling into the provenance of meta-genetics. However, Hogni's curse against Brynhildr seems to be directed at her person; indeed, she had no descendants through whom the inheritable aspects of the soul might have passed in the normal course of things.

The account of St. Ólafr of Norway also seems to point towards an element of individual reincarnation. There was a king named Ólafr who had been laid in a howe at Geirstadhr, but continued to watch over his folk and their lands, and was therefore called Geirstadhaálfr, "The Alf of Geirstadhr." When the queen Ásta is pregnant, a man named Hrani sees the dead Ólafr in a dream and is instructed to break into the howe, cut off the corpse's head, and take a ring, belt, and sword from the mound. The belt he was to put around the waist of Âsta and say that the child should be named Ólafr; the ring and the sword were to be given to the boy as gifts. Later, "when King Ólafr was riding with his bodyguard past the howe of Ólafr the Alf of Geirstadhr, one of his followers, who is not named, questioned him: 'Tell me, lord, were you buried here?' The King answered, 'Never did my soul have two bodies, and it never will have, neither now nor on the day of resurrection. . . . ' Then the courtier said: 'People have said that when you came to this place before you exclaimed, 'Here we were, and here we go.' The King answered: 'I never said that and I never will.' The king was deeply disturbed at heart; he pricked his horse and sped from the place as fast as he could."[13]

As the Helgi lays show, faring to the hall of a god/ess and rebirth are not mutually exclusive. Helgi Hunding's-Bane, in fact, makes the full round of fates; a howe-dweller for a time, taking up permanent residence in Walhall after his last duty to Sigrún is done, he is finally reborn as Helgi Haddingjaskati.

More light is thrown on the transition of the individual soul by the account of the great transition of the cosmos: the final battle, or Ragnarök. Here, all the imagery associated with the death of the individual appears on the cosmic scale; Ragnarök is at once a prophecy of the doom of the worlds and the gods and a description of the process which each individual goes through both in physical death and in the death-process of initiation.

The doom of the gods begins with the bursting asunder of all fetters and the shaking of the physical world; the disintegration of all ordered things into chaos. The ship called Naglfar, "Ship of the Dead," is loosed; the mooring which kept the burial ship within the mound has been broken, so that the dead can, as feared, sail back to the land of the living. The individual has been flung into the realm where life gives way to death.

The beasts who are most associated with individual death— eagle, wolf, and serpent—are prominent figures in the death of the world, particularly the Wolf Fenrir and the Middle-Garth's Wyrm. The serpent or wyrm is connected with the individual burial for obvious natural reasons; "grave-fish" is a kenning for "serpent," and dragons were carved on the lids of the coffins of the Alamannic cemetery at Oberflacht. Serpents who, like Iormungandr, blow poison, entwine the hall of death on Nástróndr ("Corpse-Strand"); as H.R. Ellis Davidson says, "The snake as a symbol of the world of the dead is as recurrent in the art of the North as in its literature."[14] Since it is Thunar's hammer which hallows the dead and protects them from the dangers of the Hel-ways, a projection of this battle between the warder of the dead and their chief attacker onto the cosmic scope follows naturally. This battle is anomalous in the general Indo-European dragon-slaying tradition, a pattern which Thunar's earlier struggle with the Wyrm fits far more closely. Like the serpent, the wolf is very strongly associated with death; in the case of the latter, usually death by battle. Snorri says in the "Skáldskaparmál" section of his Edda that "There is an animal called a *warg*. It is normal to refer to it in terms of blood or corpses in such a way as to call them its food or drink. It is not normal to use such kennings with other animals." The eagle acts as a portent of the destruction to come; he is a deathbird, feeding upon the fallen. "The eagle screams, / his beak slits naked corpses" ("Völuspá" 50).

The three great conflicts of Ragnarök represent the passing of the three major elements of both the human and the universe. When Wodan is swallowed by the Wolf Fenrir, this represents the passing of the highest spiritual and mental faculties. Still, the Wolf's jaws are ripped apart by Wodan's son; this motif, which shows up in a number of fairy tales, implies the survival of the conscious soul, though possibly in a different form. Thunar's single combat with the Middle-Garth's Wyrm is the struggle of fiery vital force and will against the creature which, more than any other, embodies cold and dissolution. His victory is not without a price—he, too, falls from the poison spewed by the Wyrm—but he slays it and outlives it for the space of a significant nine steps, his will overcoming the great enemy of life. Lastly, Fro Ing, the "god of the world," the god who has more than any other to do with the earth and the earthly body, falls against Surt of Muspell-Home, whose flames then consume the cosmos. In this final destruction, we can see the greedy fire of cremation devouring the body—as the Germanic people saw it from their earliest times.

Nevertheless, although the gods have fallen, they are victorious in the end. A new world—a new earthly body—is created, and all the power which Wodan, Thunar, and the others wielded has survived for their children. Modhi and Magni have Thunar's hammer; Vídarr and Váli ward the holy places of the gods; Wodan's runes are remembered. Lastly, Baldr and Hödhr come back from Hella's realm, preserved by her from the destruction of the world, as Wodan had planned it. Here the hopes of transformation and rebirth are shown, as the hall "fairer than the sun, thatched with gold"; ("Völuspá" 64) the gods are reborn in their descendants. This new life is not static; the dragon Nith-Hewer still remains as a reminder that the battle of death will come again; the individual and the world will both continue to evolve till the point of another transformation is reached—and beyond.

NOTES

1. Grönbech, Vilhelm. *The Culture of the Teutons*, 251.

2. Old Norse *framgengena frænda*.

3. Fell, Christine (tr.) *Egils saga*, 196.

4. Nylén, Erik; Jan Peter Lamm (paraphrasing Detlev. Ellmers). *Stones, Ships, and Symbols*, 70.

5. Fell, 197–198.

6. Sturluson, Snorri; Erling Monsen/A.H.Smith (ed.; trs.) *Ynglinga saga*, 6.

7. Smyser, H.M. *Ibn Fadlan's Account of the Rus*, 101.

8. "Helgakvidha Hundingsbana II," 49.

9. "Grímnismál" 21.

10. Fell, 145.

11. Marwick, Ernest W. *The Folklore of Orkney and Shetland*, 41.

12. "Sigurdharkvidha in skamma", 45.

13. *Flateyjarbók* 2:135.

14. *Gods and Myths of Northern Europe*, 162.

Chapter 9

TEUTONIC SOCIETY: CLAN AND TROTH

 HE SOCIAL STRUCTURE of our ancestors was built from the two interlocking concepts of clan, or blood relationships, and troth, or relationships of oath and loyalty. These beliefs have been in large part diminished or lost today; a great part of following the Teutonic way is to bring life back to the honor of our ancestors, requickening it with the warm blood of our clans and the warm breath of our oaths.

The first social unit of the Germanic folk was the *ætt*, the family or clan, which grew into the tribe or *sib*; the very word "king" is derived from the same root as "kin." All clans can ultimately be traced back to the gods, who created us and then came to earth again to father the atheling-lines of kings and heroes. Our ancestral relations are thus our holiness, our might, and our lives; each individual in the clan is quite literally a single branch of a living tree, whose roots are our kinsfolk who have gone before us and the twigs of whose crown are the children who shall spring from us. A taint upon any of its members dishonors the whole; likewise, the strength and deeds of each member of the family shine from the whole. "Every kinsman felt himself as living all that one of his kin had once lived into the world, and he did not merely feel himself as possessing the deeds of old, he renewed them actually in his own doing."[1] Whether you, like the women and men of earlier times, know enough about your ancestry to trace it back to the founder of your line, or whether your written genealogies stop with your great-grandparents, you should nevertheless remember this: you cannot be cut off from your roots, even if they are unknown to you. Everything that you are is shaped by your kin who have gone before you; you may know them by learning to know your own soul.

The unity of the clan is not a spiritual thing alone; every early Germanic lawcode was based on the clan structure. If a member of the family had slain someone and could not pay the were-gild ("man-price"—a settlement set by law and paid to avoid the destructive spiral of feuding) himself, the responsibility fell upon his kindred, according to each person's degree of relationship. Justice within the family was largely dependent on the senior member, who was usually the father but not always; the Icelandic *Landnamabók* also tells of such women as Audhr the Deep-Minded who led her household to Iceland and became a notable chief there in her own right. The head of the household had considerable power over the other members, but this power was not unlimited; it depended on both the head's personal strength and on the respect which the younger members of the family ideally accorded to the elder. As *Beowulf* tells of the growing power of the king Hrothgar, "Such speed of war was sent to Hrothgar / honour of battle, that all his kin / obeyed him gladly, till grown were the youths / the crowd of clansmen" (lines 64–67).

To be cut off from one's clan was to be an outlaw and thus no longer human; a companion to trolls and the other wights of the Out-Garth. The worst fate a Germanic person could imagine was to be separated from kin and society, as the poignant Old English poem "The Wanderer" describes. True to this belief, the Frisian king Radbod, when on the verge of conversion to Christianity, asked whether his ancestors would be with him in heaven. The missionary replied that, being heathens, they would certainly burn, whereupon Radbod declared that he would never consent to any fate which would separate him from his kin in the worlds beyond and, in true horror at this attempt to destroy the souls of his folk, began to hunt the Christians from his lands. Early Christian literature in Germany also reveals the degree to which unity with the clan provided the individual with strength; such Old High German poems as "Muspilli" and the writings of Otfrid constantly repeat and reinforce the helplessness of humans in the face of the Christian god by insisting on the separation between the individual and the kin-group at the time of judgement.

However, the right of birth is not the only factor in kinship. A child has to be ritually accepted into the clan by the ceremony of name-giving; likewise, the rite of blood-brotherhood grants the same spiritual and social rights and duties as those of birth. In *Völsunga saga*, Grimhild says to Sigurdhr when she is encouraging him to swear this oath to her sons Gunnarr and Högni, "King Gjúki shall be your father, and I your mother, and Gunnarr and Högni and all who swear the oath shall be your brothers." Ritual adoption is spiritually just as valid as birth into a family. This ritual joining of a new member to the clan is also a great underlying aspect of the rites of marriage, which bind two clans in soul as well as in society. For this reason women given in marriage are frequently called "frith-weavers," weavers of peace; the most effective method of ending a feud in our ancestors' time was through the marriage which united the quarreling clans. If strife should occur between them afterwards, however, the wife was expected to maintain her loyalty, not to her husband's clan, but to her father's above all. It should be noted that the custom of a wife taking her husband's last name is not Germanic, but Roman in origin; only the Romans and Greeks regarded their women as chattel, a practice which was encouraged by the doctrines of mainstream Christianity. In Iceland even today a married woman does not change her name, but remains the daughter of her father all her life. Though the line of the father is more often thought to be the primary line, this was not always so; the son of a notable mother might well take her name rather than his father's, especially in Sweden and those areas of Iceland settled by Swedes.

Although the tendency in Germanic society was towards male rule, Teutonic women enjoyed a great degree of freedom and power, particularly within the spheres of home, craftwork, and spiritual influence. Within the clan, although women were nominally subordinate to the head of household, this was not solely due to their gender, but to the fact that the father had a certain degree of legal authority over his whole family, male and female alike. Further, it seldom seems to have been the way of things that the "patriarch" was able to force any of his family members to obey his will against their own. A father had the legal right to choose his daughter's husband, but in the vast majority of sagas which recount marriage alliances, the woman is always given the final choice. Nor might a man expect to discipline his wife with impunity; the Germanic woman did not take to insults any better than her brothers, and might be expected to avenge any mistreatment. In *Njáls saga*, Gunnarr of Hlídharend's wife Hallgerdhr provokes him into slapping her and "Hallgerdhr said that she would remember that slap and pay him back if she could" (p. 125). Later, when Gunnarr is trapped inside his house by his foes, he says to his wife Hallgerdhr, "'Let me have two locks of your hair, and help my mother plait them into a bowstring for me.' 'Does anything depend on it?' asked Hallgerdhr. 'My life depends on it,' replied Gunnarr, 'for they will never overcome me as long as I can use my bow.' 'In that case,' said Hallgerdhr, 'I shall now remind you of the slap you once gave me. I do not care in the least whether you hold out a long time or not'" (p. 171).

The woman of the house held all the housekeys; indeed, one sign of the married woman was the ring of keys dangling from her belt. The ideal Germanic woman brewed ale and mead, baked bread, spun wool, wove and sold cloth, and, if her person or home were threatened, could take up weapons and fight for herself at need. She was responsible for all the economic and internal affairs of the household, and had the right to inherit property—even to speak for herself at the Thing-assemblies if she had no immediate male kin. A single woman was both mistress, and, if she were a woman of property and household, a chieftain such as Aud the Deep-Minded or Geirrid of Iceland, who "was not grudging of her food to men: she had her hall built straddling the highway, and would sit on a stool outside and invite guests in, and there was always a table standing indoors with food on it."[2] She could divorce her husband without a great deal of trouble, and the laws saw to a reasonable division of property between the two—a considerably better position than women held under the law in America and England less than an hundred years ago. If this sounds unimpressive in contrast to the place of women today, you should consider the normal state of affairs in the Christian West from the time of the Roman Empire through the age of Victoria. Indeed, the Germanic folk were less patriarchal than the people of any other Western culture (and infinitely less so than the Eastern folks), with the possible exception of the Celts.

The Germanic woman was also responsible for making sure that her male kinsmen and her husband always acted in an honorable fashion. The Icelandic sagas are filled with women who made sure that vengeance was taken for their kinsmen and those of their husbands at need; the courage of Germanic women was often an inspiration to their men and sometimes proved to be the greater, as is recounted of Freydís in the saga of Eiríkr the Red (see Chapter 7: Heroes).

This aspect of our ancestors' culture offers us a guideline for the relationships between men and women in our own. The protection of women which, because they were only to fight in self-defense, ended by excluding them from most matters of politics, is no longer necessary; the population situation today is now such that the particular value of women as the bearers of a few children is hardly a factor to be considered. Rather, it is important to be aware of the importance which women's counsel played in the social and which their labor played in the economic lives of our ancestors. If, in a time when conflicts were often decided by the fighting from which women were largely exempt, women could still become chieftains and figures of power—even deciders of policy at the highest levels—how much more so now? Women were never considered inferior among the early Germanic folks; their courage, strength, and wisdom were always praised as highly as those of men, and respect and responsibility given to them accordingly.

The Germanic kin-grouping counts as close kin up through the third or fourth cousins; however, within this grouping, certain relationships are more important than others. The first degree of relationship is considered to be that of grandparents and grandchildren; parents and their children, and brothers and sisters, are thought to be effectively the same person. A single word, "sunufatarungo," which has no English equivalent but might be roughly translated as "son-father-kinship line," is used in the Old High German poem "Hildebrandslied" to describe this relationship. The belief, in spite of Christian teachings, survived at least into the thirteenth century even in Germany; Wolfram von Eschenbach has Parzival's half-brother say to him, "both my father and you and I, we are surely all one ... so the wise man sees the kinship between father and child, if he wishes to find the truth."[3] Of all duties, that of avenging one's father was thought the most holy; for only by that vengeance could one's own honor be restored and the soul of one's clan saved from shame.

The role of the mother is no less important; she is the bearer of power from one generation to another, the keeper of the sword which embodied the ancestral soul, as in *Völsunga saga* where Sigmundr bids his wife to take the shards of the sword which he drew out of the pillar-tree called the Barnstock and to keep them till the son she carried had grown old enough to reforge them. Significantly, Sigmundr's wife is named Hjördís—"the *idis* of the sword"—a name exactly signifying her function. Sigurdhr's reclamation of the sword from his mother is an action corresponding precisely to his father's drawing of it from the Barnstock; Hjördís is the human embodiment of the "Bairn-Stock," the fruit-bearing *ætt*-tree around which the hall of the Völsungs was originally built. *Ørlög* and soul descend equally through the mother's line and the father's; *Völsunga saga*, in which the hero Sigurdhr is the reincarnation of his father Sigmundr, shows the masculine side, but in *Hervarar saga ok Heidhreks*, Heidhrekr, the hero of the second part, is shaped almost wholly by the inheritance of name, soul, and the ancestral sword Tyrfingr, all of which he gets from his mother, who had reclaimed the sword and the might of her line from her slain father in her own right, by going to his barrow and forcing the dead man to bring out the ancient weapon.

After the parents, the next most important relative is the mother's brother. This may be a remnant of a matrilinear system in which inheritance and relationships were mostly counted through the mother's line, making the mother's brother the child's nearest male kin. Matrilineality, which survived to some degree in the north and to a much larger degree in Scotland through the twelfth or thirteenth century, should not be confused with matriarchy, for which there is no evidence from any period of Northern Europe outside of the romantic imagination (although the "Venus" statues may imply worship of a goddess, this does not mean that the prehistoric culture that made them might have been matriarchal, any more than the common worship of Mary in medieval Catholicism was a sign of the matriarchy of medieval Christian countries).

The mother's brother is particularly responsible for the education and spiritual initiation of his sister's children. In "Hávamál," Ódhinn describes how he learned nine mighty songs from "the son of Bolthorn Bestla's father"—which is to say, his own mother's brother, since Ódhinn was the son of Bestla the daughter of Bolthorn. *Völsunga saga* shows the education of the young warrior Sinfjotli by his mother's brother Sigmundr—an education which takes place while the two of them are separate from society and climaxes with Sigmundr's initiation of Sinfjötli into the mysteries of berserkergang and Ódhinnic death/revival.

The relationships of troth were precisely as important as the relationships of blood—neither more nor less. This dichotomy is the source of many of the greatest Germanic tragedies, in which sworn oaths inadvertently bring blood-kin into mortal combat.

The first relationship of troth was that of the oaths sworn within the *comitatus*, or warband. Such groups were led by a drighten, who was personally responsible for all of its members and who dealt out not only gold, but also weapons and armor, to his warriors. In return, they owed him their loyalty up to death; even well after the Christianization of the Anglo-Saxons, it was considered exceedingly shameful for such sworn warriors to survive after their drighten's death in battle. The relationship between drighten and thane should serve as a model for the intensity of loyalty which the ways of the North demand, not only between god/esses and humans, but between whoever swears oaths to another, whether leader and follower or comrade and comrade.

The essence of troth is this true behavior in every relationship: the word unbreakable until—and sometimes after—death; the fulfillment of every vow, however great or small; this full and endless loyalty to one's friends, comrades, and kin, and to the god/esses who are the elders of our clan. A person without troth, or a breaker of troth who turns against his/her comrades or fails to keep her/his sworn word, is a *nithling*: a cowardly object of shame and disgust, not fit to live among free folk.

Because the exchange of oaths between drighten and thane was marked by the giving of gifts, a king or leader was commonly referred to as ring-giver; the act of giving and receiving constituted the oath in itself. A gift is also a pledge, which, if it is given in good troth, bears some of the giver's hamingja within it. The concept of giving without expectation of return does not exist among the Germanic people; as the very shape of the rune gebo—"gift" (X), which demonstrates the equal flow of might between two folk, shows each gift was expected to be met with another gift, whether earthly or of the soul. The early Germanic folk were open-handed with their possessions, but always expected return; to get and not to give was thought of as frightful. This is why, for instance, even traditional Christian houses leave out cookies and milk for Santa Claus (a thoroughly heathen figure); and also why the "Hávamál" advises against too much sacrificing: "Better unbidden than over-blóted / for gift ever looks for a gift. / Better unsent than over-spilled" (138).

Related to the idea of open-handedness is that of guest-friend-liness (hospitality). One of the worst insults that could be given to someone was to say that he or she was stingy with food. From the tales we know, we can see that this side of troth is especially dear to the god/esses. Those who show it shall wax well in their sight; those who do not shall wither. Often the god/esses come in the shapes of strangers—or even of folk you know.

The first rite of guest-friendliness is always the bearing of drink to the one who has entered your home. In the old days, the frowe of the household would bring the guest a horn or cup of ale, mead, or wine. The giving and taking of this drink shows that the guest is fully welcome within the house and has gained the guest-right of safety and good treatment. Until the guest has partaken of his/her host's drink, his/her soul has not truly passed within the garth, as is shown in "Skírnismál" where Gerdhr does not offer Skírnir drink until he has forced her to agree to wed Freyr. As token of her acceptance, she makes Freyr's messenger welcome at the end of the poem with the words, "Hail rather, warrior! with this rime-cup[4] / full of the old mead" (37).

For ordinary occasions, this drink does not have to be brought out in a horn, nor does it have to be alcoholic. Most of the time, it is enough simply to ask your guests what they would like to drink as they pass over your threshold. This seemingly simple politeness, deeply rooted as it is, is still current and natural within the modern context; before I ever knew much about our tradition, my mother (who is of Scandinavian descent) impressed on me in the strongest of terms that the first thing I should always do when guests came over was to offer them something to drink. It is best for the frowe of the home to be the one who brings drink, if possible; however, men may do this if it is needful. You should note that this is not a servile role; rather, it is a sign of the high nobility of the woman that she bears the drink to heroes and athelings. The frowe's act of bearing drink rises from the fact that she is the very source of life and wis-dom for her men and the guests within her hall. At an Ásatrú feast, however, the purpose of everything you do is to bring you closer to the god/esses and your elder kin, and thus a brief traditional Rite of Welcoming should be carried out (see Chapter 16: Rites).

When a guest has been welcomed, that person must be safe within your walls for the term of his/her stay, no matter what he/she says, does, or has done in the past. The host/ess has the absolute duty of making sure that all guests are treated well and honorably. If a conflict is necessary, it must take place outside.

The great strengths of the soul are so closely bound to troth that there is hardly any distinguishing between them. In addition to openhandedness and guest-friendliness, the Germanic folk hold as the highest things bravery, truthfulness, and freedom.

By bravery is meant not only physical bravery—most of us do not have to engage in bodily combat very often—but the bravery which it takes to risk everything for what you know to be right; to face ugly truths, even about yourself, and to deal with them boldly; and to overcome the fears which everyone holds within. Every such act strengthens your soul; though no one but yourself knows of them, they are yet *tir-fast*—"glorious"—deeds. To wrestle with social pressure sometimes asks the strength of Beowulf wrestling Grendel; to battle with financial difficulties may call for the brave mood of Sigurdhr slaying Fáfnir. Be sure that these are deeds worthy of boasting at *symbel*, and never back down before another just because she/he may seem to be stronger or better placed.

Truthfulness is not necessarily the obsessively literal telling of "the truth, the whole truth, and nothing but the truth"; rather, it is the steadfast willingness to stand by your word and not to falsify it. This is especially needful when you have sworn an oath—the oath-breaker is the worst sort of nithling. While a Wodanist might swear an ambiguous oath, this was never considered really honorable; it was not an act of troth. The *true* word is a word that is more binding on the speaker than any legal contract; the worth of your truth is the worth of your soul.

To the Northern peoples, only a free person really existed as a full human being; to have worth and troth, to be able to make a boast or swear a valid oath, to carry weapons were things that only the free could do. While the Germanic folk believed that their leaders were more closely descended from the gods than most folk, a leader who made unreasonable demands on his followers or tried to lift himself too high above them swiftly found himself displaced and/or dead. It is not in the Germanic soul to follow blindly where troth is not returned; those warriors who die with their drighten fall as free men who have chosen their own end, not as soldiers "following orders." Although literal slavery is no longer a legal institution, there are many ways in which you may still be unfree: addiction, ignorance, cowardice, or whatever keeps you from showing all the might and troth of a free wo/man are slavemasters as much as any human owner; likewise, any sort of dependence upon another (whether financial or emotional) is a kind of unfreedom. The dividing lines between freedom and thralldom are not so clear now as they were in the old days, but if you look closely, you may still see them.

NOTES

1. Grönbech, 122.

2. Jones, Gwyn. *Norse Atlantic Saga*, 169.

3. *Parzival* 15:752.

4. *Hrímkalkr*, "ice-cup," was a phrase used by both the Old Norse and the Anglo-Saxons to describe crystal chalices—thus Gerdhr is bringing Skírnir the best vessel in the house, full of the best mead (mead seldom survives to get very old!). Since etins are described as possessing crystal cups in more than one tale, it might also be taken in its literal sense; that is, these wintry wights drink out of cups of ice.

Chapter 10

PRACTICING THE
NORTHERN WAY

HE PRIMARY DIFFERENCE between religion and magic is that in magic, you must have absolute control at all times and are responsible for your slightest failure, whereas in religion, the ultimate decisions belong to the god/esses; it is they who decide whether they will give their power to blessings or curses, or answer the folk who call upon them. For this reason, experience and intensive training are not nearly so vital in performing religious rites as they are in performing magical rites. The only great dangers lie in the possibilities of either offending one of the god/esses directly or of making a commitment that one is not then prepared to live up to; minor mistakes in the wording or handling of a rite are usually unlikely to have this effect. Whereas magic is like working with the raw and impersonal forces of electricity or fire, where an error can cause great damage, religious activity must be understood as working with other personalities, who understand your situation and to whom things can be explained.

In my experience, many people who have turned from Christianity back to some other religion, whether it be a traditional and historical faith such as Ásatrú or a modern creation along archetypal lines such as Wicca, often begin as solitary practitioners who found or join groups after they themselves have become more comfortable with their non-Christian faith. Although the Northern tradition has a very strong social orientation, and generally group observance of the major festivals and so forth is thought to be the ideal, there is nothing at all wrong with practicing the Teutonic faith as a solitary. Many of my own most intense spiritual experiences took place during the rites I performed by myself during a year of travel and study in Scandinavia, Britain, and Germany, equipped with only the most basic of ritual tools and companioned only by the gods and goddesses.

There are certain advantages in working alone, especially for someone who feels unsure about his/her metaphysical community or is concerned about the consequences of his/her heathenism becoming known. Aside from such potential difficulties, which will be discussed in detail at the end of this chapter, starting out as a solitary will allow you to gain your own sense of the presence of the god/esses without any distractions, especially if you are not a performer by nature. Nothing detracts from spiritual experience so quickly or unpleasantly as wondering whether you might be making a fool out of yourself in front of a bunch of other people. Also, a group which is largely directed by one or two people with strong personalities and a good deal of spiritual experience may tend to focus more on the aspects of the god/esses to which the leaders themselves feel comfortable and allow slightly less scope for individual development. Unlike those religions in which the leaders are intermediaries between their god and the rest of humanity, each walker of the Teutonic way is expected to be a friend of the god/esses, responsible first to his/her own soul. Therefore, if you should feel uncomfortable about working with others at first or be unable to find folk of like minds and souls with whom to study and keep the holy feasts, don't be too greatly concerned. With the exception of the dramatic rites for Winternights, Yule, and Ostara, to which I have provided alternate rituals for the solitary or small kindred, and the social rites such as the Wedding and Name-giving, there is virtually nothing in this book which you cannot do alone just as well as you could in a group.

Although solitary practice is very good and especially helpful in some cases—as well as often being forced by circumstance—the larger group is the ideal. Within Ásatrú, these groups are normally called "kindreds," a term which implies a social bond of loyalty and troth between the members. Most of the kindreds currently existing run between four and fifteen people, with the average probably being about six to eight active members and another two or three warm bodies and friends who show up at a couple of major feasts throughout the year.

If there are no groups currently practicing Teutonic tradition in your area, or those which are there are for some reason unsuitable to your needs, and you still wish to work with others, you may want to start your own kindred. Probably the best way to do this is to advertise through your local metaphysical bookstores. For reasons which will be discussed at the end of this chapter, I do not recommend beginning with advertisements for a kindred and especially not anything which gives out your home address or phone number. The technique which I have found to be best is to begin by holding a study group in some neutral territory until you get to know the people with whom you are dealing and decide that you want to work with them on a close and personal level. Once you have gotten a core of trustworthy and solid heathen friends, you can probably be more comfortable about inviting the occasional friend of a friend or interested stranger into your study meetings or rituals; remember, there is safety in numbers. However, personally screening your guests before inviting them is always a good idea.

The principle of safety in numbers also applies if you wish to hold rites in outdoor places which are extremely out of the way. Trusting in the god/esses is a very good thing, but the god/esses of the Northern tradition place little value on fools who neglect basic safety precautions. Our ancestors were particularly fond of worshipping on top of mountains, beside waterfalls, and in other such areas. Such dramatic natural features are the most powerful of natural holy places, but often difficult and dangerous of access. The "difficult and dangerous of access" also, quite often, goes for such places as city parks at night. Whether you are hiking into the wilderness to get to your holy place or braving the dangers of local inhabitants, it is generally much safer to go in a group than by yourself.

On both the spiritual and the social level, the rewards of working with a kindred can be considerable. One of the beauties of the Northern way is the fact that it has always been meant to unify the god/esses, the individual, and his/her society. The Germanic culture is defined and upheld by the bonds of friendship and troth which bring humans and god/esses together, to share each others' joys and help in times of trouble. Modern society, especially urban modern society, has tended to move away from community and towards isolation. On a daily basis, forming and working with a kindred gives you the chance to exist in a community of like-minded people, upheld by friendships based on a great common interest, culture, and belief.

The structure of our modern kindreds is partially based on the structure of the ancient clan and partially on the clan-like legal groupings created by the loyalty-bindings of the warbands and the institution of fostering. As has been discussed (in Chapter 8), the family was the foundation of early Germanic law and culture—not the nuclear family, but the extended family, in which all of the members stood in a much closer relationship to one another than is usual today. Modern Western culture, by contrast, has moved farther and farther towards the isolation of the individual from the clan, both from those kinsfolk who are still living and from those who have gone before—especially in America, where only the fortunate can name their forebears past three or four generations. To come back into a truer and healthier relationship with the living clan—especially in this culture, where the dysfunctional family seems to be rapidly becoming the norm rather than the exception—is often difficult and sometimes downright impossible, especially within the context of a religion which other family members may not fully understand or appreciate. Additionally, most Westerners are no longer tied to their udal (ancestral) lands, but are comparatively highly mobile, and thus the adult members even of a nuclear family are more likely than not to live at a considerable physical distance from each other, gathering together perhaps once or twice a year.

It is this isolation to which the kindred structure seeks to provide a solution. Rather than a group bound by the earthly ties of blood, the kindred members are committed to one another through such oaths of loyalty as they may choose to take towards one another, and through the fellowship created and strengthened by joining together in the rituals which we share with each other, with the gods from whom we are descended, and with our kinsfolk who have gone before us. As members of a kindred, we owe each other troth, help in times of trouble, aid in the battles which we all have

have to fight in one way or another, guidance, and affection. The kindred should be set up like the battle-fellowships of our ancestors in that it is woven from members of different backgrounds who are there by choice more importantly than by birth and is maintained by the troth and friendship which the members bear to one another. It is more like the clan, however, in that there should be no absolute and undisputed authority-figure or drighten/ine to whom everyone else is bound by the oaths of follower to leader, but rather all should be considered basically equals, with differing degrees of individual influence being dependent on differing degrees of knowledge, capability, and willingness to put time and effort into making the kindred a working entity.

It is a good thing to keep new would-be members on a sort of probation (three, six, or nine months) while the kindred gets to know them and make sure that they won't cause difficulties within the group. Probational members should be allowed and encouraged to participate fully, especially concerning matters of taking responsibility for feast preparation, clean-up, and other chores which sometimes cause dissension. If possible, each probationer should be "fostered" by some established member of the group with whom he/she forms a close bond and who is responsible for teaching the new person lore, proper behavior, and so forth. At the end of this period, if everyone in the group agrees, a full rite should be carried out in which the new member is given a name by the kindred's leader (either reaffirming his/her own name and ancestry or taking a Nordic name of choice). One rite for this is given in Thorsson's *Book of Troth*. His version is a reversal of the oath which the continental Saxons were forced to swear at the time of their conversion; the first part of Thorsson's vow contains a renunciation of the Christian god and angels, the second is an affirmation of trust in Wodan, Thunar, Frey and Freya. Another is given here in the chapter on Rites.

In the due course of time, members who are called to be godsmen or -women will come forth and take up their tasks of providing spiritual and intellectual guidance; however, they should probably not be given the privilege of having the unquestioned "final word" in all things; that way lie rampant egotism, personal power struggles, and the other trolls which continuously beset heathen groups.

MONEY AND THE KINDRED

(Wealth) is good to him who has it . . .
    —Anglo-Saxon Rune Poem

Once a group has been assembled, the question of finances will eventually come up. Ritual tools will be necessary; the responsibility of hosting feasts for a whole kindred on a roughly monthly basis cannot be avoided; and if the kindred wishes to take on extra projects, such as building or renting a space to use as a hof (temple), putting out a newsletter, etc., the money for these will have to come from somewhere.

How much of a problem this question will be is directly related to how large and ambitious the kindred is, as well as the financial status of its members. The simplest method, and probably the most useful in the vast majority of cases is to keep everything on a purely volunteer basis, with individuals providing whatever they feel to be needed. For instance, someone with a strong affinity for Thunar (whether he/she feels called to become a godwo/man or not) might purchase or make the kindred Hammer, while another person might bring the blessing bowl, and the kindred Wodanist, if there is one, could reasonably be expected to make mead for the major feasts and supply the horn or cup out of which it is to be drunk—though the whole kindred ought to pitch in on buying the materials for the mead or ale.

Experience has proven that for one person to host a full feast by him/herself can be grossly expensive, especially if beer and wine are included. By far the most reliable method for handling the feasts is to hold them as potlucks, BYOB (Bring Your Own Beverage). It is highly recommended for the kindred members to establish at least a week beforehand what each person intends to bring; the feast (held by a certain unnamed group) in which there were four very rich desserts, two giant bags of chips, a salad, and no main dish at all will live in infamy forever! Since the large main dish is usually the most expensive part of the feast, especially if it is meat, it is good either to have a rotation of responsibility or for two people to go in on it together.

Probably the least efficient method of financing anything for the kindred is for one person or household to purchase something and ask for donations after. In theory this sounds good; in practice, it only works if the buyer doesn't really expect to get a substantial portion of the price back. Asking for cash donations in any circumstances is potentially embarassing for the lower-income members of the kindred and can often lead to resentment, especially if it happens on a regular basis.

If you decide to ask for membership fees, be aware that this will involve you in a lot of paperwork. It will, at that point, become necessary to designate one member as an official Reeve (treasurer) and to have very clear guidelines on how and when the money can be spent, as well as a definite policy on nonpayment. Clear and accurate books must be kept, because the group will be a potentially taxable entity at that point, and good records will also stave off any possible accusations of non-payment, misuse of funds, etc.

For a relatively small and informal group such as most kindreds tend to be, regular membership fees will probably be more trouble than they're worth. In general, they will only be worthwhile for kindreds which have taken on some sort of chronic and predictable financial responsibility such as the renting of a hofspace or the production of a newsletter. In such cases, membership fees are a virtual necessity if one person is not to risk being left holding the responsibility for the whole kindred.

Exceptionally successful kindreds may eventually decide that members are contributing enough material donations, either as money, as artifacts, or as skilled labor, to make applying for tax-exempt status worthwhile. This decision should not be come to lightly, as the process of getting this status is lengthy, complex, and requires a solid lump sum for the filing fee (in Texas for 1990, the fee was roughly $150). However, if members are donating enough to make a difference in their personal taxes, the possibility should, perhaps, be considered. For those who wish to become a tax-exempt group without going through the difficulties of making personal applications, a viable alternative is to consider becoming a subsidary of a larger group which already has this status, such as the Ring of Troth.

KINDRED ACTIVITIES

The first and greatest duty of the kindred is to hold the seasonal blessings together. The most important of these are Yule, Eostre, and Winternights, followed by Midsummer's, Loaf-Fest, Charming of the Plough, Feast of Thunar, and Walpurgisnacht. If you keep all the seasonal feasts, you will be gathering roughly once every month/month and a half. In our kindred, we usually hold a gathering on the weekend before the feast to talk about the meaning and traditions of the celebration and to plan how we will arrange it: what everyone needs to bring for the rite and/or the potluck, earthly details such as location and carpools, and so forth.

One of the problems which kindreds often run into at feasts is the question of clean-up. Be aware: the host/ess has already gone to some trouble to arrange the feast; it is not good guest-manners to leave him/her with a big mess to clean up. In early times, the folk paid a *hoftollr*, "temple-toll," to a semi-professional godwo/man; today, the way for you as a kindred member to do your fair share is to help prepare the meals, to mow your host/ess' lawn and do a little basic yardwork for outdoor rites, and to wash dishes and generally pick up after a feast.

The more often you meet, the more cohesive you will be as a group; the more time you put into keeping the tradition, the more you will get out of it. The ideal is to hold weekly group-meetings for the purpose of studying together and building your friendships. To this, you may wish to add smaller "special-interest" gatherings during the week. These might include study of the magic of the runes; practice of traditional arts and crafts (weaving/spinning/sewing, leatherwork, brewing, metalwork, carving, or whatever else you can do); practice of martial arts, swimming or rowing, fencing/swordfighting, archery—or even just working out at the gym together.

Neither the seasonal feasts nor the weekly meetings should be limited to solemn study—the feasts in elder times certainly weren't. Rather, they should be opportunities for each member to show off his/her skills and, most of all, to have fun together. A good Germanic feast should include boasting—preferably in alliterative verse; displays of physical prowess such as wrestling, shooting, or racing; and a showing of crafts and poetic skills or storytelling. These are best done when couched in the form of challenges, as at one feast in the Orkney isles where Earl Rognvaldr Kali challenged a man named Oddi to make a verse about the warrior embroidered on a wall-hanging—adding that Oddi would have to make his poem after the Earl had spoken his own on the same subject, and to make it in the same span of time, and not to use any word that the Earl had used (it might be added that Oddi met the challenge successfully!).

One of the best ways to teach lore and stretch your wits at the same time is to engage in games of knowledge—either riddle-games or the sort of lore-competitions which appear in the Eddic poems "Vafthrúdhnismál" and "Álvismál." A good example of the traditional Germanic riddle-game appears in *The Hobbit*—the chapter "Riddles in the Dark," where Bilbo and Gollum compete in riddle-knowledge is drawn directly from the Northern tradition! The Anglo-Saxon *Exeter Book* contains a number of riddles which can serve as a good starting-place for your own, as does the chapter "Heidhrekr's Riddles" in *Hervör's Saga*. A few other examples (from Gunnora Hallakarva's article "Riddles," *Mountain Thunder* I, i) are:

> I am the herald of battles to come.
> I am the last to leave the field.
> The hanged one knows my every thought,
> And memory my name shall yield.[1]

> The oak shall serve my supper,
> The forest-hall's my bed.
> The swords are shining ivory,
> My eyes are crimson red.
> Upon the helm my image rides,
> All shining like the sun,
> But black the surcoat that I wear,
> When I am on the run.[2]

> What has four feet and one hand?[3]

The riddle-contest can go on until everyone runs out of riddles or until someone asks a question that no one can answer. But if one of your kindred seems suddenly wiser than you had thought him/her to be, beware: Wodan has been known to take the shape of a living human and come to play riddle-games in that disguise . . .

Lore-competitions are also great fun, as well as being educational. The easiest way to do these is in circular form, in which each person asks the person to his/her left a question. Anyone who cannot answer is eliminated, leaving the next person to answer the same question. In the first rounds, simple questions should be asked: "Name the Nine Worlds"; "Where did Wodan lose his eye?"; "Who was the father of the Middle-Garth's Wyrm?" As the less learned contestants are eliminated, the questions should gradually get more and more challenging, until two or three people are left displaying a really impressive level of knowledge: "Name all nine of Aegir's daughters"; "According to Saxo's version of the tale, who avenged Balder?"; "How did Sigurdhr name himself to Fáfnir when first asked, and what was the lineage he gave?"[4]

To make kindred competitions, both physical and mental, more interesting, small but desirable prizes should be offered. A good bottle of mead is always welcome; arm and finger rings can also be made easily and cheaply out of copper or silver wire. Giving such gifts, especially rings, is also the traditional way to show your appreciation for a poem, tale, or deed which has particularly impressed you.

WHERE MONSTERS LURK

Nothing worth doing is done without struggle of some sort, and everything has its own intrinsic dangers. Some of the problems you are likely to find along the Teutonic pathway are problems that any religious group—especially smaller religions—will suffer from; some belong to us alone.

The most obnoxious and recurrent blight on the recovery of our Germanic heritage is the spectre of Nazism. For obvious reasons, it is still considered very uncouth to use one of our holiest symbols—the swastika—in situations where it might be misinterpreted, which means any and all public contexts. To anyone who knows the true meaning of this sign and is aware of its long and honorable history in Germanic spirituality before it was misused within the context of the Third Reich, this constraint is infuriating. Nevertheless, the degree of psychic and personal distress which public use of the swastika will cause to innocent persons ought to make responsible Ásatrú folk unwilling to display it outside of closed rituals.

No matter how circumspect you are in your use of symbolism, however, when you make your awareness of your Teutonic heritage known to others, you are probably going to have to deal with the occasional accusation of Nazism. Expect it and don't be upset;

instead, use the opportunity to educate. It is a fact that many aspects of our heritage were grossly misused and attached to a vile racial ideology which has no part in the Northern tradition; it is our duty to cleanse ourselves of that association and to be able to present ourselves with as much pride in our ancestral culture—and respect for those of other peoples—as any other ethnic group is regularly able to boast. It is our great fortune to have a mighty current of ancestral myth and symbol bearing us up; it is our greatest misfortune in this century that the power of this current was used to bring authority and success to the most generally vilified figure of modern history. This is something with which we must deal, always maintaining the awareness that what the Nazis did with early Germanic culture, while it may have rotted a branch of our ancestral World-Tree, has in no way poisoned its roots.

It is unfortunate that much of Ásatrú today is perceived as ultra-right wing or racist even by other heathens. It is even more unfortunate that, in a few cases, there are some grounds for this perception. Like every faith, Ásatrú has its own fringe groups and crazies; for us, these are usually racists or neo-Nazis concealing themselves beneath a dogma of quasi-Nordic spirituality. If you make yourself known as a practitioner of Ásatrú, the chances are good that at some point you may receive attempts at communication from this sort of person. This is one of the main reasons why getting a post office box, not inviting strangers to your home, and not giving out your legal name or personal phone number on a general basis is a good idea. The best thing to do with people like this is to ignore them; indignant responses only encourage them.

As a non-establishment religion, openly avowed followers of the Teutonic troth naturally face certain difficulties. Unless you live off in the backwoods surrounded by rabid and violent fundamentalists, physical attacks on your home or person by Christian terrorists are not particularly likely. However, it is well to be circumspect when holding gatherings and performing rituals in isolated places, especially if the public at large knows about it; there have been some instances of pagan and New Age gatherings which were disrupted and/or terrorized by drunken locals looking to harass the "weirdos"—sometimes with guns or threats of physical violence.

The first concern which most heathens have when it comes to a question of going public or not is, "How will it affect my job?"

Quite a lot of the time, this is a valid concern, particularly if one works in a conservative or high-pressure field. On the other hand, there is also the fact that the more "respectable" heathens will admit and stand up for their religious beliefs, the more generally acceptable heathenism will become. Martyring yourself to make a gesture which has no particular benefit for the larger community is not a good thing; although the courage is admirable, the stupidity is not. However, conforming to Christian expectations in order to avoid any degree of social friction isn't particularly admirable either. In general, the best thing to do is not to openly flaunt your belief in the gods of your ancestors, nor to shove it down the throats of your coworkers. However, if the question of religion should come up (if you are in a position where you can afford to do so), you should state your beliefs quietly and firmly, and be able to defend and discuss them as well as you can. Remember, however, that arguing with someone who not only believes totally in their faith but thinks that everyone else must as well is probably going to be like arguing with a drunk: utterly without benefit.

Ultimately the question of how far you can go in presenting your troth to those who do not share in it is going to be a question of your individual judgement. No matter how free speech and the practice of religion are supposed to be, the fact is, if you come out publicly and announce your heathenism to the world at large, you are likely to be labled a "crackpot," or, at worst, a "devil-worshipper." This attitude has shifted considerably over the last two decades and is still shifting, thanks largely to the courage of those who have defied the general pressures of society and spoken up for non-Establishment beliefs. The problem is still there, however, and has to be reckoned with.

In addition to threats from outside, every gathering of humans is going to have some degree of internal friction. Personal ego-clashes and the struggle for power or position are probably the worst enemies with which heathenism as a whole has to deal. Discrepancies over ideology can usually be resolved with a minimum of conflict if there is no underlying personal problem; however, bitter ideological struggles within a group are often no more than smoke screens for a personal battle. When it comes to this, the most important thing to remember is that, if we are ever to be accepted as a "legitimate" religion, a general heathen unity and solidarity is more important than one's personal position. However, it may be that there are two or more people in the kindred who, for whatever reason, are wholly incompatible. In this case, separation is often the best thing, even if it splits the group down the middle. Having two different kindreds in the area who have no contact or minimal contact with one another is infinitely preferable to having a single group which is eating itself out from within through the ills of secret un-*frith* and troth-breaking. If you are forced to break a kindred, however, that should be the end of it; do not yield to the wish to muddy the names of other heathens, because that ultimately reflects ill upon Ásatrú. The worst ill our ancestors could think of was kin-strife; if it comes to that, total silence is better.

Even if you should suffer from a conflict of belief which cannot be overcome—such as that which now exists between the more reputable Ásatrú groups and the racist contingents—the answer does not lie in personal attacks upon those perpetrating an untenable belief, but rather in positive response and action, such as the verbal and written expression of one's own views with the historical documentation to prove what our ancestors' thoughts on the idea in question were. You should also remember that there is room for many ways within the Teutonic troth; our ancestors were no more bound to a single set of ideological beliefs than they were to a single god. Incompetence and stupidity are ultimately self-defeating, after all. The solution is not the destruction of those who practice them, but rather to preserve yourself from malice and misinformation without being drawn into destructive and pointless political struggles.

NOTES

1. Wodan's raven Muninn, "Memory."

2. A wild boar.

3. The Wolf Fenrir—who took Tiw's hand . . .

4. Detailed rules for one such competition were set out by Jeff Burke in his article "Head Games at Mimir's Well," *Idunna*, 2:4. His version featured a "High One" who asked all the questions in the first round, then exchanged questions with each of the folk remaining until he/she missed one, at which time the questioner became the High One and the round continued.

Chapter 11

HOLY FOLK

 ITHIN THE TEUTONIC TRADITION, there are a number of titles which bespeak special traits or describe roles which the bearer plays in religion and in society as a whole. Some of these holy folk are not necessary to a kindred to gathering; their titles denote special skills or gifts of the gods which were rare even in the time of our ancestors. Other titles describe social positions which may have religious aspects, but which require no uncanny craft.

GODWO/MAN (OLD NORSE GODHI/GYDHJA)

Godman or godwoman is the term which we use to describe the person who would usually be called a "priest/ess" in other traditions. The title means just what it looks like: a person who is closer than others to one or more of the god/esses.[1] In Iceland, this office also had a strong earthly role; the *godhi* was the local chieftain as well as being the religious leader of the community, and the *godhordh* could be bought and sold. The *godhi* was responsible for maintaining the hof, making sure the holy feasts were held as they ought to be, and so forth. Often the hof would be the home of the *godhi* himself, and this is the way it is usually done in modern Ásatrú. The *gydhja* or *hofghdhja* seems to have played a solely religious role, such as Steinvör in *Vápnfirdhinga saga*, who was given the title *hof-gydhja* and was responsible for maintaining the temple and receiving its dues. Turville-Petre comments that "It is clear that such women did not wield political power, but it is possible that they could inherit the godhordh and exercise religious function which went with it" (p. 261). However, women were occasionally chieftains, even in those days when leadership often depended on skill with a sword, and there is no reason why any distinction should be made between the roles of godman and godwoman today.

If your kindred is not lucky (or rich) enough to have a separate building serving as a hof, it is the normal course of things for the godwo/man to host most of the holy feasts. S/he should also be responsible for organizing the rituals, and should generally bring focus and a certain degree of structure to the kindred—though not too much, as it is the way of the Northern folk to be free spirited and not take well to arbitrary orders and sundry guff from their leaders.

Among Ásatrú organizations, only the Ring of Troth has a settled process and set of standards for establishing godwo/men, as discussed below. Otherwise, the most usual means is self-selection: i.e., "This back yard belongs to my friend Frija and me, so I am the Kindred godwoman and you will come to my feasts." At least in the Old Norse/Icelandic context, this seems to be a perfectly valid and traditional means of establishing yourself. The first qualification is to feel especially close to one or more of the god/esses, as described in Thórolfr Mostur-Beard in *Eyrbyggia saga*, who "was a close friend of Thórr." Thórolfr asked his god's rede about going to Iceland and was advised to go, so he settled in Iceland, claimed land, and set up a great hof there, of which he and his family were the hereditary keepers.

The process of initiation is one which will depend very much on your individual circumstances. The best traditional guide to initiatory ceremonies is the *Elder Edda:* many of the poems in this work offer outlines for various sorts of initiation. Grimm's fairy tales and other such Teutonic folk sources also present a vast number of initiatory tales. The most famous initiation of Norse literature is Ódhinn's ordeal on Yggdrasill, described in "Hávamál": in one modern initiation based on this, the Wodanist was tied outside for three hours on Yule-night between two posts, arms out-stretched; though his feet were safely on the ground, this position was considered to fill the needs of a symbolic hanging. An initiation centered on Fro Ing might be expected to involve a symbolic death, burial, and springtime rebirth; while a Frowesgodwoman could be asked to dance erotically with four men representing dwarves, who then present her with a necklace betokening Brísingamen, the symbol of the Frowe's might.

Such initiations are not necessary for you to function as a godwo/man; performing the holy blessings is something which can be done by anyone. The purpose of these is firstly the soul-growth of the individual and only secondly the good which such growth will bring to her/his Kindred. If you do this, you do not need a "superior" spiritual figure to initiate you: should the god/esses want you, they themselves will watch over the rite.

However, since one of its primary purposes is to teach and spread lore on a basis of solid historical knowledge, the Ring of Troth has a two-level training and certification program for its leaders. The basic level is that of godwo/man. To gain this title, you must have a good, solid grounding in the Eddas and sagas (and other source material such as *Beowulf*), a basic knowledge of the history of the Germanic peoples, a reasonable knowledge of the secondary literature (works such as those listed for further studies in the back of this book) and be both capable and experienced at working rituals and leading a kindred. The Troth is set up to give teaching and advice to the folk who wish to reach this standard.

The highest level of lore within the Ring of Troth is that of the Elder. The Elder is someone who not only has significant experience and ability in leading a group, but also has a deep and broad knowledge of the religion, culture, history and archaeology of the Teutonic people, along with a general background in philosophy and theology. The current Elder training is somewhat based on that given in Edred Thorsson's *A Book of Troth* (Llewellyn, 1989), but has been considerably reworked since. The list of subjects which an Elder-trainee is required to study includes, among other things, Norse and Common Germanic Mythology; Prehistoric, Migration Age, Viking Age, and Teutonic Revival History; Teutonic Culture (with brief overviews of Indo-European and general World Cultural History); Heroic Legends; Major Sagas; Folklore; Modern Conceptions and Misconceptions of the Teutonic Path; Methodologies and Critical Theory; Theological and Philosophical Principles; and Basic Principles of Ritual, Mythology, and Religion. Learning Old Norse and at least one modern Germanic language other than English is highly encouraged, as is the practice of traditional skills and crafts. No previous degrees are required, although university work will count for full credit in whatever subjects it is applicable to. The training of the candidate is overseen by either the Warder of the Lore or whichever Elder is either physically closest or specializes in a candidate's particular fields of interest. Certification is given by a panel consisting of the Warder of the Lore and the Masters of the Lore (officers appointed to help examine candidates for Eldership). A certified Troth Elder is legally considered to be an ordained minister, capable of performing marriages and funerals.

Those who are interested in the Troth or its training programs should write to the address given at the back of the book for more information.

The other sorts of holy folk for whom titles are known are not necessary to a kindred; it is the gift of the gods which will bring them to you, should they be needed. Nevertheless, it is well to recognize them, for their works are deeply meaningful and helpful in following the ways of our folk.

VÖLVA

The ancient Germanic people were well known for their "priestesses" such as the Veleda, holy women whose words were heeded by all the leaders of the folk. The völva is closer to the worlds of the gods and ghosts than other people; her inspiration is what might be described as shamanic in character, rising from visionary trance states which reveal what shall become if a given course of action is taken. Strabo describes the holy women of the Cimbri, a Germanic tribe living at the beginning of the Common Era: "The Cimbri reportedly adhere to a custom in which their women embark on campaigns with the men and among them there are priestesses with prophetic powers. These priestesses are hoary and dressed in white and wear flaxen mantles attached with brooches. Their belts are wrought of bronze and they go barefoot."[2] This gift, a detailed and thorough foresight, is inborn and quite rare; there are no references to it being something that could be taught or trained, except that, according to the saga of Eiríkr the Red, there were certain songs which could be learned and had to be sung while the völva was in her trance. She also had a special stool on which she sat, possibly similar in function to the thule's seat (see below).

There were spae-men as well as women, but they did not usually have such clear visions, nor were they honored in the same way. The high degree of foresight shown by the völva seems to have been almost exclusively a female thing. Even Wodan himself had to ride down to the gates of Hella's realm and raise such women up from the dead in order to ask them about what should become! Frija and several of the goddesses are described as knowing *ørlög*: it is their might and that of the Frowe, drightine of witchcraft, that the völva reflects in the world of the Middle-Garth.

The völva clearly played an important advisory and ceremonial role in the society of the Germanic peoples, of which modern Ásatrúar should be aware. If your kindred should be lucky enough to include a strong psychic, the greatest honor should be shown to her and heed given to her prophecies. Among the continental Germans, these women had a very clear position as officially established "priestesses," with a great deal of direct influence on the course of political doings, so that the Romans were sometimes forced to deal with them as well as with the tribal drightens. In the more settled society of the Old Norse, however, spae-women lived outside of the usual social structure; some, like the völva in *Eiríks saga rauda*, traveled from stead to stead; some dwelt a little apart from their community. Should you reach a point where you (as an individual or a group) feel the need of more direct information than you can gain by yourself about the worlds beyond the Middle-Garth's ring, or about what should become of a particular affair, it is very traditional to seek out a professional psychic, or invite her to a special kindred ceremony for the sake of asking her advice.

THULE

The thule stands in the same relationship to Wodan that the völva does to Frija and the Frowe: just as the völva embodies the might of those goddesses during her trances, when the thule sits upon the thule's seat and speaks, he is the earthly embodiment of Wodan's wisdom and wod-filled speech. In "Hávamál," where Wodan is specifically fulfilling this side of his being, this god calls himself "Fimbulthul," the Great Thule.

The work of the thule is characterized by "inspired" speech; that is, speech flowing from the worlds beyond the Middle-Garth. To "thylja," "speak as a thule," may imply some prophetic capabilities, though not of the same high degree as the völva's; it is certainly a term describing great wisdom expressed in a framework which has considerable ritual significance. This appears in "Hávamál" where Ódhinn, shifting his focus from the general audience and earthly wisdom to the young initiate Loddfáfnir and wisdom of a more magical/spiritual character, states suddenly: "It is time to speak as a thule on the thule's seat, / at the Well of Wyrd." When the speaker moves into the special seat, his words become imbued with the lore of the god/esses flowing through him: he speaks with the full authority of the Ases' doom-stead at the Well.

Unlike the spae-woman, the thule seems to have held an official social and possibly legal position among both the Anglo-Saxons and the Old Norse. In *Beowulf*, the hero's antagonist Unferth is described as a thule, which the Christian scribe glosses as "orator"—that is, he speaks for the king, testing Beowulf's right to make the heroic challenge against Grendel. Probably because of the influence of Christianity, Unferth appears as a very diminished figure in the version of *Beowulf* which has survived; his ritual/religious function does not appear at all, but a hint of the great worship in which a thule was held appears in the lines which state that Unferth had a special place at the king's feet even though he had killed his own kinsman. The thule in whose memory the Snøldelev stone was set up was "thule on the Sal-howes"; this is to say, he spoke officially from the top of certain barrow-mounds, probably those in which his ancestors or the ancestors of the rulers of the area were buried, and gained much of his inspiration from the wights within. This aspect of the thule's role is also similar to that of the Icelandic Lawspeaker, who pronounced law from the promontory known as the Law-Rock at Thingvellir, and who, at least in the case of the Lawspeaker Thórgeirr, also could call on inspiration from the worlds beyond in speaking his decrees.

Other figures described as "thules" are the etin Vafthrúdhnir and Sigurdhr's foster-father Reginn, both wights of great age and wisdom whose primary purpose seems to be the preservation and transmission of ancient lore to younger beings. As well as being an inspired speaker, then, a Kindred thule should be well and deeply versed in the history and lore of the Northern folks, and able to bring that lore forth to those around him. In many ways, his role is similar or identical to that of the Elder of the Ring of Troth[3]: he is a trained figure whose knowledge of the tradition is authoritative (though not absolutely so).

VITKI

"Vitki," meaning "wizard" or "magician," is a title given to those skilled in magical lore, particularly the lore of the runes. The title does not denote any social placement or authority, aside from the respect which ought to be given to a mighty mage; it is not, properly speaking, a religious title or one which ought to be made an office within a purely religious kindred.

DRIGHTEN/DRIGHTINE (ON DROTTIN/DROTTNING)

This social title was originally used to describe the leader of a small, usually elite, warband. In Old Norse, where the complementary term "freyr" (see below) had developed into a taboo-name for a single god, this term filled the gap and came into use as a generic word for king *(dróttinn)* and queen *(dróttning)*. The drighten is characteristically a Wodanic figure, a leader in battle rather than a full-time ruler. In modern times, "drighten" is used for the leader of any elite group united more by loyalty and a single common purpose than by blood; the Rune-Gild, for instance, originally had "drighten" as its highest rank, with the "Irmin-drighten" ("Great Drighten") as its leader (though this structure has recently been changed).

Fro/Frowe (ON Freyr/Freyja; German Frau)

"Fro" or "Frowe" may originally have been the title given to the ruler of a settled area; it implies the judicial qualities of rulership in peacetime, as contrasted with the goal-directed leadership of the drighten/ine. It is also a generic title of respect, which can be applied to any atheling ("noble").

NOTES

1. . . . although there are, it must be admitted, a few who think that they themselves rank among the gods.

2. Strabo in Chisholm, 1.

3. See Edred Thorsson's *A Book of Troth*, p. 207, for more details.

Chapter 12

RITUAL TOOLS

THE HORN: DRINKING AND SYMBEL

HE GREATEST RITUAL TOOL of the Teutonic peoples is, and has always been, the drinking horn. From the depths of our earliest prehistory through late into the Christian Era, the act of drinking from the horn has remained the central act of religious devotion, particularly in the custom known as *minne*-drinking, or drinking to the memory of a god, ancestor, or hero. The earliest records describing our ancestors spoke of the aurochs-horns which they adorned with silver and precious stones at the rims and at the tips.[1] Two of the greatest treasures of Denmark, which unfortunately were stolen and melted for the gold in the last century, were the Gallehus horns. These drinking horns, which had probably been made between 400–450 CE, were made of several pounds of solid gold, embossed with religious symbols and scenes. One of them was also graven with a line of runic verse: "Ek Hlewa-gastiR HoltijaR horna tawido"—"I Hlewagast, son of Holte the horn made."[2] Some horns had proper names, such as the two pairs held by Óláfr Tryggvason, the Grims and the Hyrnings (the first of which had been brought to him as a gift from the etin Gudhmundr of Glæsisvellir).

The words ALU ("Ale") and, less frequently, MEDU ("Mead") appear in runic inscriptions, where they seem to signify not only the actual drinks, but the whole freight of spiritual/magical power and "luck" which our ancestors saw the fermented beverages as holding. In *Beowulf*, the king Scyld Scefing is described as taking away the mead-benches of his foes, which is to say, depriving their souls as well as their bodies of all their power, while the giant Hrungnir's threat (described below) to "drink all the ale of the Ases" is meant in the same sense: he means literally to drain them of this drink of might.

The drinking horn appears frequently in the stone-carvings of both the continental Germans and the Norse, always in a religious or magical context. Its most frequent occurence is on the Gotlandic picture-stones, memorial stones set up for the dead. On the Lill-bjärs stone (p. 141), as upon a number of the other stones, a walkyrja is shown bringing a horn to greet the dead man upon his entrance to Walhall; beside the walknot, symbol of Wodan, a device of three interlocked drinking horns appear. These three interlocked horns are also carved on the Danish Snøldelev stone, together with a swastika and the inscription "Gunvald's stone, son of Roald, *thul* on the Sal-mounds." The precise role of the Thul is discussed in the previous chapter; the specifically religious context shows the degree of holiness attributed to the sign of the horn itself. The three interlocked horns seem to be specifically associated with Wodan; however, the horn itself is hallowed to all the gods and goddesses. One of the two "Luftreiterinnen" ("wind-riding women") in the Schleswiger Dom rides a giant cat, which shows her clearly to be a Frowe-figure, but in her hand she holds up a drinking horn (p. 91). In the Baltic countries, particularly among the Wends, the horn appears on stone carvings together with the cross, seemingly in an attempt to unify the symbol of the native heathenism with that of Christianity.

Although the cup often fulfilled the same role as the horn, especially in the later literature, the importance of the specific horn-shape is shown by the use, not only of actual cattle-horns, but of horn-shaped metal vessels such as the Gallehus horns and the Romano-Frankish manufacture of glass "horns." Several of the German glass horns were imported to Scandinavia from the Rhineland, where they were preserved carefully and eventually buried with dead chieftains as great treasures. *Orkneyinga saga* also describes how, even after the Christianization of the North, the men drank cups at the beginning of the evening, but "after they had carried on drinking for some time, they went out for Nones (the evening Mass), then came back and drank *minne* from horns." Here, the distinction between the simple drinking of the feast and the ritual drinking of the religious toasts (which had been to gods and ancestors, but were usually made to saints such as Martin and Gertrude whose names had replaced those of Wodan and the Frowe in the North after the conversion) is made clear by the change in vessels, from the more modern cup to the ancestral horn.

The drinking horn functions as the pivot of social/earthly ritual, of the communication between humans and the gods, and of the human involvement in the turnings of Wyrd. As an earthly action, the sharing of the horn was the gesture defining membership in the human community. A drinking horn would be brought to the guest as a sign of welcome, after which it was necessary to treat him with hospitality, as is described in the *Prose Edda* when Ódinn invites the giant Hrungnir into the Ases' Garth.

> And when (Hrungnir) came to the doors of the hall, the Ases bade him to drink; he went into the hall and asked for drink; then were taken the goblets, from which Thórr was accustomed to drinking, and Hrungnir drained each of them. And when he became drunk, then there was no lack of great words; he said he should take Walhall up and carry it to Etin-Home, but bury the Ases' Garth and slay all the gods, and he wanted to take Freyja and Sif and have them at home with him. And Freyja alone dared to bring him drink then, and he declared that he would drink all the ale of the Ases. And when the Ases became tired of his boastings, they spoke the name of Thórr. At once came Thórr into the hall and had his hammer raised up and was greatly wroth, and asked whose rede it was, that cunning etins should drink there, and who had given Hrungnir safety in Valhöll, and why Freyja should be serving him drink as if he were at the feast of the Ases. Then answered Hrungnir and looked at Thórr with unfriendly eyes and said that Ódinn invited him to drink and he was under his protection.[3]

Because Hrungnir has been given drink, Thórr cannot strike him while he is within the hall, despite his provocations.

It was considered the right thing for the hostess or highest-ranking woman in the hall to bring the drink to the guests, as is shown in every hall from Walhall to the Middle-Garth to Hella's realm. In Walhall, the walkyriges carry drink around to the heroes, as Wodan says in "Grímnismál":

> Hrist and Mist to me will bear horn,
>   Skeggjöld and Skögul,
> Hildr and Thrúdhr, Hlökk and Herfjötur,
>   Göll and Geirölul,
> Randgridh and Rádgrídh and Reginlief:
>   they bear the einherjar ale. (36)

In Etin-Home as in the Middle-Garth, this is done by the frowe of the hall: Hymir's wife greets Thórr and Týr with a drink, and Gerdhr gives a cup of mead to Skírnir after he has finally forced her to give him welcome. In *Beowulf*, the queen Wealtheow pours out the drink for the warriors; the image of the woman bearing the horn to the guest or honored hero appears throughout Germanic literature and sculpture.

As well as representing social integration, the holy act of drinking was the act which, more than any other, integrated humans with the gods. In the *Vita Sancti Columbani*, it is described how the Alamannic tribe (Germans in the Black Forest/Bodensee area) carried out their sacrifice: a cauldron was filled with beer and set in the middle of the folk; by drinking from this, "they wished thereby to bring a sacrifice to their god Wodan, whom others name Mercurius."[4] The drinking of the gods' *minni* was one of the most definitive acts of Germanic heathendom. In *Ynglinga saga*, it is described how Sigurdhr the Jarl prevails upon the Christian King Hákon to drink at Yule-time: "And when the first bowl was poured out, Sigurdhr the Jarl spoke and blessed it in the name of Ódhinn and drank to the king from the horn. The king took it and made the sign of the Cross over it. Then said Kar of Gryting, 'Wherefore does the king so? Will he even now not sacrifice?'" The next year, when Hákon's great men were rebelling against Christianity, "The first day of the guest feast the bonders thronged about the king and bade him make the offering and otherwise threatened him with force. Sigurdhr the Jarl went between them and it came about that King Hákon ate some bits of horse liver and then drank all the *minni*-bowls which the bonders poured out for him, without making the sign of the cross."[5] It is also described how, at Yule-time, the first horn was drunk to Wodan or Thunar, the second to Njördhr, and the third to Fro Ing, while in the life of St. Hamrham it is written of Bavaria that the folk had not yet given up heathenism "in that they often enjoyed the blood of Christ and the heathenish sacrificial drink out of one chalice."[6] In his Gothic translation of the New Testament, the bishop Ulfila also interprets a section of I Corinthians as "one cannot drink alike from the chalice of the Lord and the chalice of the Devil," which Grimm takes as an unmistakable reference to the heathen practice of drinking as a sacrifice to the gods.

At most feasts, the folk would drink in pairs, two friends of the same gender or, sometimes, a man and a woman sharing a horn. At the holy feasts, however, a single horn was carried around the hall, most often by the frowe of the hall.[7] The round of the horn was the focus of the feast itself: it was the opportunity for each person in turn to speak a toast to the god/esses or make a boast before the gathered folk. By sharing the horn, those within the hall also showed that they shared *frith* and fellowship with one another, strengthening the bonds of troth that bound them.

The third level of the power of the horn is that of its use in the rite of symbel (of which I write more in Chapter 16: Rites) and its association with Wyrd. Many of the mightiest oaths of our ancestors were spoken as they drank from the hallowed horn, as it tells in the Lay of Helgi Hjörvardhsson: "That evening was the swearing of oaths. The best boar was led in and men laid their hands on him and swore oaths at the hallowed drinking." An oath sworn while drinking from the horn is an oath that has to be fulfilled, no matter what came of it. The reason for this is that the filled horn is itself an earthly representation of the Well of Wyrd: its depths contain all of that-which-is, while the mighty liquid that froths forth from it is the force which shapes all that is becoming and all that shall be. Words spoken over the holy horn are laid into Wyrd as surely as if the Norns had graven their runes into the bark of Yggdrasill; they are known through all the worlds, heard by gods and humans alike. The same holds true for the cup, but to a much lesser degree: it is the horn, our eldest and holiest vessel, which has always unified our folk from root to flower.

THE OATH-RING

The arm-ring was the holiest symbol of troth to our ancestors; the *baugeidhr*, "ring-oath," the holiest of oaths. It was through the giving and getting of the golden ring that a thane was bound to his drighten with a bond as strong as (and sometimes stronger than) the bonds of blood. According to *Eyrbyggja saga*, the oath-ring always lay on the harrow, and had to be made of at least an ounce of precious metal. The godhi was expected to wear it on his arm at the Thing (law-meeting) and at other times when he called upon the might of the gods or touched them most closely; the rest of the time it was kept in the hof. Sometimes it was on the arm of one of the statues, as it was at the Jarl Hákon's harrow where the ring that embodied his own luck was kept by the image of his ancestral idis Thórgerdhr Hörgabrúdhr (or "Hölgabrúdhr) till he made sacrifice to her so that she allowed him to lend it to his friend Sigmundr. Oaths spoken on the ring were spoken "to Freyr and Njördhr and the mighty Ase." The last of these gods may have been Wuldor, Thunar or Wodan; the ambiguity was probably deliberate, so that the same oath could be sworn by all, no matter to which god/ess they owed their greatest troth.

The oath-ring is also called the "ring of Ullr" (Wuldor), implying that that god was particularly responsible for the vows sworn upon it. It may have been worn as a part of *einvígi* (the judicial duel) or other combats in which the might of the gods was expected to play a decisive role. The Hunninge picture stone shows a spear-wielding man on a horse with a male figure flying above him and holding a ring towards him, probably as a sign of the "luck" which was to bring him victory.

The might of the oath-ring is not necessarily bound by place, but rather makes the place where it is holy. The Anglo-Saxon Chronicle recounts how the Vikings in England swore oaths to Alfred the Great on the ring which they had brought with them, on which they had never before been willing to take an oath to non-Norsemen. Although the men of this mobile army of raiders probably had no set holy places in England at this time (876 CE), they had brought their oath-rings with them from Denmark, probably both because of the great luck in them and to fulfill the need for a focus of worship.

The oath-ring should be worn at all blessings and sprinkled with the ale or mead of the rite each time. Yule oaths can be sworn on this ring in place of the Yule boar; wedding oaths and legal contracts alike can be concluded upon it.

For directions on making your own oath-ring, see the section on Rings in Chapter 17: Crafts.

THE HAMMER

The Hammer is the sign of Thunar's might, which both wards the realm within the garth from the wights without and hallows the realm inside. To swing the Hammer over something is to fill it with holy power; thus it is swung over the dead on the bier and laid in the lap of the bride at the wedding. Although it is used little in magic, the Hammer is one of the main tools of the Teutonic religion.

A plain sledgehammer, as heavy as you can comfortably swing about, makes a good Thunar's Hammer for ritual use. The handle may be painted red and/or have a runic inscription such as Thunar Hallows (ᚦᚢᚾᚨᚱ:ᚺᚨᛚᛚᛟᚹᛋ) or Thórr, Warder of the Wih-Stead (ᚦᛟᚱᛏ:ᚹᛖᛗᛏᚱᛏ) graven on it. A better woodcarver may carve a Thunar-mask with staring, fiery eyes on the Hammer's handle, or the Middle-Garth's Wyrm ringed about it. For private use, if you are comfortable with the symbol, it is also appropriate to adorn the Hammer with a swastika, either on the handle or on the head. A good woodcarver can also make a full-sized Hammer out of oak.

If you should be lucky enough to have a stone axehead, you can fit it into an oaken handle and use that whenever ritual usage calls for a Hammer.

For more portable ritual kits, the silver or bronze Hammer you wear about your neck can also be used in place of a full-sized hammer. This is also useful if you are caught by a thunderstorm on the road, or in any other circumstances where you need to do an impromptu hallowing. One Texan of my acquaintance drives with a small Hammer of enameled bronze hanging from her rearview mirror to ward her car against hailstones and tornadoes! Such a Hammer can easily be sawed out of a small piece of oak; oak from a lightning-struck tree is the mightiest of all.

For hallowing your Hammer, it is good to sprinkle it with water from a thunderstorm and best to take it out and hallow it during the storm. The hammer can also be buried for nine nights and then dug up, making it into a true "thunder-stone" (see the chapter on Thunar).

The Blessing-Bowl

Like the Hammer, this tool is seldom used in magic, but very often in religious rites. The blessing bowl holds the god/esses' portion of the drink which is shared about at the ritual; it is the focal point of the hallowing, and should stand in the middle of the harrow.

The best wood for a blessing bowl is that of a fruit- or nut-bearing tree, followed by oak and then by ash. Because you will probably use it to share drink with all the holy wights, any symbols and/or inscriptions you carve on it should be extremely general in character. Something like, "To the holy ones" (ᛏᛟ⁝ᚦᛖ:ᚺᛟᛚᛃ⁝ᛟᚾᛖᛋ) or "Gods and goddesses all" (ᚷᛟᛞᛋ⁝ᚨᚾᛞ⁝ ᚷᛟᛞᛖᛋᛖᛋ⁝ᚨᛚ), is an appropriate runic inscription. For the same reason, animal images are not really appropriate, unless you use several of the godly beasts together (i.e., boar, horse, goat, and raven or eagle, or whatever combination you find fitting). You might also carve the walknot, the Hammer, and the sun-wheel on the rim at an equal distance from one another; the swastika, in either its straight-armed or its swirling form, is also a good general-purpose holy sign which may be scratched either within the bowl or on its base, as is the trefot or triskelion (see Appendix II: Runes and Holy Signs).

If you do not want to put any special inscriptions or symbols on the blessing bowl, but would like to adorn it with carving nevertheless, you can use any sort of knotwork design. Several of these are given in the chapter on Crafts; or you can consult any book on Celtic or Germanic art. The best of these is Iain Bains' *Celtic Knotwork*.

Blessing-Twig (Hlaut-Teinn)

A fresh twig is often used to sprinkle the drink from the blessing bowl over the harrow and the folk. This twig ought to either be from an evergreen or from an oak. When gathering this twig, it is best to do the "Rite of Tree-Gift" (described in *Teutonic Magic*, pp.

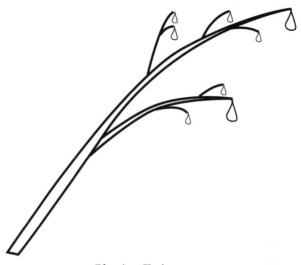

Blessing-Twig

284–285). The essential elements of this rite are asking the tree for permission to take its twig; pouring out a draught of mead or ale to it and setting a piece of bread at its roots; pouring healing might into the wound after you have taken the twig; and saying a blessing of thanks to it.

If you do not want to use a fresh twig every time, you can strip a slightly larger branch of its bark and leaves and dry it. If you do this, you should be careful to save all the little offshoots so that you will have something for the droplets to hang on (see illustration).

SAX (KNIFE)

In religious rites, the hallowed sax is used for the symbolic "sacrificing" of the bread figures which represent the animals slain by our ancestors at their blessings. A sax which is used solely for this work might be inscribed, like the blessing bowl, with more general signs or runic sayings, or it might be graven with a name such as "Giver" (ᚷᛁᚠᛘᚱ) or "Blessing-Blade" (ᛒᛚᛗᛋᛁ ᛒᛚᚨᛗᛞᛥ These runes can be carved into the hilt or engraved on the blade.

The other use of the sax is for carving runes or signs on holy items; in this, it is firstly a magical tool.

A sacrificial sax may be either single- or double-edged; one which is used for carving will, for obvious practical reasons, need to be single-edged. Larger blades are preferred for sacrifices, especially if your rites are more dramatically oriented; smaller ones are easier to carve with.

The sax may be as ornate or as plain as suits your aesthetic sense and your pocketbook. Most cutlery shops carry quite a range; there are also several knife/sword catalogues which sell replicas of museum pieces, and Renaissance Faires usually have one or two booths with medieval weapons of all sorts.

WEAPONS

There is some debate about whether or not it is fitting to carry and/or use weapons in ritual. The argument against it is that weapons were traditionally not allowed into the holy space, though it is not certain whether this was because the weapons themselves were thought to be offensive or whether it was forbidden as a means of preventing fighting inside the holy stead, which was certainly offensive, as it broke the peace of the *frithgarth*. Also, since the shedding of blood was definitely considered to defile a *wih-stead*, it may have been that weapons which had been used to shed blood were also unfitting to the holy place. On the other hand, the spear certainly had a strong sacral function; the Hammer, which is one of the great tools of Germanic holy workings, can be classed as a weapon; and so much emphasis was placed on the sword as the embodiment of the family hamingja/ørlög that it is impossible not to think of these things as holy. In Norway, ancestral knives and axes were used for magical healing up into the modern era. Grönbeck suggests that "both sword and spear and shield must possess the entire luck of the clan, also its healing power, fertility, food-luck, and wisdom" (vol. 2, p. 31). Further, the right to carry weapons was the mark of a free man among the Germanic folk, and arms were properly brought to the assembly of the Thing. The Ásatrú Alliance, indeed, has held at least one Týrsblót in which both medieval and modern weapons were brought forth for the blessing of the god!

In practice, the choice of bringing weapons to a ritual or not may depend heavily on the rite in question. If you are giving worship specifically to the Wanic god/esses, especially if you are calling on them for *frith* and riches rather than asking their help in a fight or if you are treading within a *wih-stead* which is hallowed to them, you will probably do better not to go armed. In a rite to Wodan, however, it is far better to have weapons than not to have them: the statue of the god himself in the hof at Uppsala was armed and ready for war. As he counsels in "Hávamál," "From his weapons should no one on field / step a stride away; / 'tis uncertain of knowledge soon becomes on the ways outside / a spear what the warrior needs" (38); in the "Second Lay of Helgi Hundings-Bane," Ódhinn gives Dag a spear to kill Helgi within a hallowed grove. The use of weapons in our rites also shows the god/esses (and reminds us) that we have not forgotten the warrior-soul of our foregone kin.

In choosing your weapons, you should think first of their battle-worthiness. Although you never mean to lift them against another human, a blade that is badly wrought or blunt will never have any luck in it; it will be the weapon of a *nithling* from the beginning. A good keen knife of fine steel is far more honorable and mighty in rite and magic than is a sword or spear of pot-metal.

The spear is the weapon of Wodan or Tiw; the axe or hammer that of Thunar; the sword that of Fro Ing; the bow is used by Wuldor and Skadhi. Swords are also strongly associated with the cult of Wodan. These attributions are not exclusive; a follower of any god/ess can bear a sword to ritual as a personal weapon, for instance. However, the weapons actually used in making a *sig*-blessing to Wodan (for instance) would be firstly a spear and then, possibly, a sword.

A true weapon should have its own name, and with the name you give it *ørlög*, and a character of its own; its use and the bravery of the person who carries it will build its *hamingja*. Many of these names were graven upon the blade in runes, and when the name is given, the hilt should be sprinkled with water as if it were a nine-day-old child. The *ørlög* given to many of the swords in legend were as much frightful as promising: several, for instance, could not be sheathed without having first been covered in a human's warm blood; others, after their making (particularly after they had been taken from the rightful owner), were cursed to bring death to the clan of their wielder. Great power often calls for a great price ...

NOTES

1. Caesar's *De Bello Gallicae* and others.

2. That this was meant to be a line of verse is proven not only by the alliteration, which might have been coincidental, but by the word-order and stress-patterns.

3. "Skáldskaparmál" 25.

4. Jung, Erich. *Germanische Göttern und Helden in christlicher Zeit*, 252.

5. Sturluson, Snorri; Monsen and Smith, trs. *Ynglinga saga*, 89-90.

6. Jung, Erich, 253.

7. Grönbeck, 160.

Chapter 13

HOLY STEADS

HE TEUTONIC PEOPLE worshipped the gods and goddesses in a number of different kinds of steads, both natural and made by human hands. Which of these you choose for your own will probably depend entirely upon where you live and what you have available to you. I myself have called upon the high ones in every setting from the inside of a small and cluttered apartment in Dallas to the top of one of the great pillars of living stone known as the Externsteine in Germany and the mounds of Old Uppsala where the greatest heathen temple of Scandinavia once stood. Wherever you are, there is always a way!

WIH-STEAD (VÉ)

This term, meaning "holy/taboo enclosure," can be used for any holy stead which is set apart from daily life, particularly a *frith-garth*, grove, enclosed field, or hallowed hof. The word "wih" shows that the stead is so filled with the might of the gods that it may be perilous to tread there; that the god/esses dwell there and humans are but guests in the holy garth. It is no more (and perhaps less) than half in the Middle-Garth; it stands half (and perhaps more than half) in the hidden worlds. Wooden images of the god/esses are often kept in the *wih-steads*. These images need not be finely carved—many of those made by our elder kin look rather crude by modern standards, and the earlier ones were natural pieces of wood given only a little carving to emphasize a shape which they bore already. For making simple images, see the chapter on Crafts.

Most often, if your *wih-stead* is not marked out by features of the landscape, you will want to mark its bounds with either a fence or a ring of stones (perhaps carven with runes or other holy signs) so as to set it more clearly apart from its surroundings in the Middle-Garth and so that all will know when they have crossed the border into the realms of holy might.

In general, silence should be kept within the *wih-steads* except when speaking the words of the blessing. These are steads of awe; a careless word spoken or a clumsy move made here can echo through the worlds and bring ill back down upon you. In the hof, as will be spoken of, a separate room is used for the feasting; otherwise, it should take place outside the bounds of the *wih-stead*.

Unhallowed weapons should *not* be brought into the *wih-stead*. However, ritual weapons are acceptable. Tacitus describes how "certain totems and emblems are fetched from groves and carried into battle"; some of these may have been battle-standards, other weapons such as Wodan's spear, which might have stood in the hand of the god's image.

FRITHGARTH

Groves, fields, and hofs were alike surrounded by an enclosure, or garth, within which holiness was maintained. An English law against heathenism condemns the *"fridh-geard* (fence of frith) on any man's land about a stone or a tree or a spring or suchlike ungodly foolishness." Within this garth, weapons were not to be drawn and blood might not be spilled on the ground, nor was it permitted to relieve oneself. The *frithgarth* is particularly associated with the Wanic god/esses.

The traditional boundaries of a ritual *garth* ("enclosure"— *frithgarth* or otherwise) are hazel stakes.

GROVES

The earliest holy places of our ancestors were outside; Tacitus says of the Germanic folk that "They consecrate groves and woods and with the names of Gods refer to remote places which they only behold when in a state of religious awe."[1] Nearly every Roman and Greek source which describes the religion of the Germanic tribes refers to the holy groves where they made sacrifice and hung the captured standards of their foemen. According to Claudianus' account of the Gothic war, the Visigothic king Alaric who conquered Rome in 413 claimed that "The Gods also drove me to these actions. Birds and dreams are not for me; but a plain voice was emitted from the sacred grove. 'Cast away all delays, Alaric. Cross the Alps of Italy bravely and you shall penetrate to the city!'"[2] There was one grove which was thought so holy that no one could enter it without being bound in fetters, and if he were to fall, might not stand, but had to roll himself out. Wooden images of the gods might be kept in these groves, and these images were brought forth sometimes to go into battle with the folk. There might or might not be a harrow of heaped stone in the middle of the grove. Sometimes the groves were enclosed to mark them off as holy and ensure that no one entered them unwittingly.

Some groves, especially in Scandinavia, were particularly holy to one or another of the gods. In Sweden stands a grove called the Ódhinslundr and (particularly in Eastern Sweden) several others whose names go back to an original Njardharlundr (Njördhr's grove), Freyslundr (Fro Ing's grove), Freyjulundr (the Frowe's grove), or Skadhalundr (Skadhi's grove); several groves called Thórslundr are found throughout Scandinavia, and Wensley (Derbyshire, in England) is derived from the older form Wodnesleie.[3] These are groves in which the presence of a particular god/ess was felt so strongly that it was marked out as holy to that one.

In finding your own holy grove, your chief guide should be the sense of awe which comes over you when you step into it. You should be able to sense that you are standing in a stead beyond the realm of humanity, where the god/esses dwell upon the earth and where the least word spoken will echo through all the worlds. The holy grove is most likely to be of oak and/or ash, but other kinds of trees may also form such a grove. If you have chanced upon a place where one of the god/esses has taken up dwelling more strongly than any other, you may expect to know about it through a mighty sign or vision; a grove where you see two ravens perching on a tree, for instance, is likely to be holy to Wodan, while forest cats (or even large domestic cats) are a sign of the Frowe's presence, and so forth.

The rites which are most effectively performed in groves are works of divination, inspiration, and communion with the god/esses. Gifts should also be left there. Groves are not the best places to hold feasting or more "community"-oriented rites, because their holiness and might are such that the unprepared should not enter into them. Remember that these are not places which humans make holy, but places which the gods themselves have hallowed as their own dwellings; for them to be kept so, it is only needful that we treat them with all the awe and love we feel towards our elder kin.

MOUNTAIN, FIELD, AND WILD PLACES

Our ancestors often worshipped the god/esses on the tops of mountains; Germany, Britain, and Scandinavia are full of mountains and hills whose names still remember the high ones to whom they are holy. These most often show the presence of either Wodan or Thunar, who seem to have been more worshipped on mountains than the other deities. Germany has the Godesberg (Wodan's Mountain) near Bonn and several Donners- or Thuneresbergs; Thorsborg stands in Gothland; in Shetland, off the island of Papa Stour, there is an isolated pillar of rock called "Frue Stack" or the Frowe's Stack. The Old Norse name of Wodan's seat, "Hlidhskjálf," implies that the god looks out over the worlds from a seat high on the side of a mountain, and the "-skjálf" element, meaning "crag" or "rocky pinnacle," also appears in the name of one of Wodan's halls, "Válaskjálf" or "Crag of the Slain." The place-name Ódinsberg is fairly widespread in Sweden and Denmark; in "Reginsmál" the god names himself "Karl af bergi," "(old) man of the mountain." Words spoken from a height were known to have a particular might to them; at Thingvellir in Iceland there stands a crag from which judgements spoken became law, and the laws of Sweden were spoken from the great mounds at Uppsala. Any high place, mountain, mound, or ridge, is almost by its very nature well fit for dealing with the gods and goddesses on, as climbing up it brings you to a point where the mights of the earth and the heavens spiral together, filling the place with power and bringing you closer to the high dwellings of the Ases' Garth in both body and soul.

Fields were often enclosed in a *frithgarth* and set apart as holy places. In "Lokasenna," Skadhi says to Loki that "from my holy places and fields shall / cold redes ever come to you" (51). These fields were especially holy to Fro Ing and to Njördhr, who took vengeance if the *frith* was broken within their bounds or the field defiled in any way. The law against spilling blood on the ground there was particularly strong. One Odinsakr (Wodan's Field) also exists, as well as several fields named Thórsakr. These fields may have been places where the gods were particularly invoked in their aspects of fruitfulness; one *frithgarth* which Fro Ing was particularly staunch in defending was called "Vitazgjafi," "the certain giver." This field was defiled when the outlaw Víga-Glúmr slew a man within its bounds, an act which made Fro Ing his foe. In general, fields are best suited for working with the might of the Wans.

Many wild places are marked out by natural formations which show their power. Rocks with natural holes in them and crags standing alone are very strong places for worship and magic. The feeling of awe that comes over you whenever you stand in a wild place and are overwhelmed by its beauty and its might is a good marker of the presence of the god/esses there.

RIVERS, WELLS, AND HOLY WATERS

Our ancestors were well aware of the might of the waters, and often worshipped at waterfalls, rivers, streams, and wells. Running bodies of water, particularly waterfalls, were known to have their own indwelling wights. The Alamanns (a South German tribe, living in the Black Forest area) and Franks were particularly known for worshipping rivers and fountains; at the brink of the fountains they lit candles and laid down gifts.[4] The modern practice of throwing a coin into a fountain "for luck" comes from the old heathen gifts which were given to the wights who dwelt within.

Living gifts were especially given to rivers; it was still said frequently in the last century in Germany that various rivers demanded one life every year (most often on Midsummer's), and if their usual sacrifice was not given to them, they would take it for themselves. In the wiser parts of the Germanic countries (or those less overwhelmed by Christianity), the folk did, and in some parts still do, throw flowers and bread into the river, sometimes made in the shape of a human being.

Running water is filled with holy power; all running water takes part in the might of the water which springs forth from the Well of Wyrd, by which the World-Tree and all within is strengthened, healed, and made holy. Grimm recounts that "Water drawn at a holy season, at midnight, before sunrise, and in solemn silence, bore till a recent time the name of *heilawâc, heilwâc, heilwæge*" (vol. 2, p. 585). This water was used in magic and holy ceremonies by both the continental Germans and the Anglo-Saxons, as we still use it today in many of our rites. Just before sunrise is the best time to draw the water from the stream or river; when drawing it, you must go to the stead in silence, draw it in silence, and not speak till you have laid it on the harrow or wherever you mean to keep it.

Waterfalls and whirlpools are even more mighty than rivers, as anyone who has ever stood beside one will know. The holiness of the waterfall appears as a mighty image for the storm in the first Lay of Helgi, "holy waters fell from heaven's cliffs," where the clouds have become the high mountains and the rain is the torrents streaming down from them. This sign shows, as surely as the screaming of the eagles and the great wyrd-weaving of the Norns, that a hero—someone filled with more than the usual portion of the might of the gods, is being born; the hero's very name, "Helgi," means "the Hallowed One," and may have been a title before it was a personal name. More than one waterfall in Iceland bears the name "Godhafoss," "god-falls" or "god-force." In a magical, as well as an earthly sense, waterfalls are great generators of might; as the Old Norwegian Rune Poem says, "(Water) is what falls from the fells, a force." They are the very embodiment of the *ur*-might of the rune laguz (ᛚ), the yeasty waters of life which flowed from Nibel-Home at the beginning of time. Gifts to the god/esses can be cast over the falls. A whirlpool on the waters is a sign of a mighty wight beneath, a place of power which must be treated with respect and caution.

Nerthus and Njördhr were especially worshipped on islands, which, being neither fully land nor fully water, are steads of great power. Some true folk still hold their outdoor rituals on piers or jetties, which also stand between the realms.

HOF

The word "Hof" seems to have originally meant a large farmhouse, without a specially holy nature. In continental German, it continued to mean "farmstead," "garden," or "court," describing earthly enclosures, normally on high ground; in Anglo-Saxon, the term was sometimes used for a temple, but that use was probably derived from or at least influenced by the Viking invasions. In Old Norse, on the other hand, the term was almost always used to describe a place where a number of folk gathered to keep the holy feasts.[5] This place was usually a farmstead in a central location, often the dwelling of the godman himself. A great many place-names in Iceland are compounded with the "hof-" element. One of them is described in *Eyrbyggja saga*:

> Thórolf established a great farm at Hofsvag which he called Hofstad, and had a large temple built there with its door in one of the side walls near the gable. Just inside the door stood the high-seat pillars with the so-called gods' nails (ON reginnaglar) fixed in them, and beyond that point the whole building was considered a sanctuary. Inside the main temple was a structure built much like the choir in churches nowadays, and in the middle a raised platform like an altar. On this platform lay a solid ring weighing twenty ounces, upon which people had to swear all their oaths. It was the business of the hofgodhi (temple priest) to wear this ring on his arm at every public meeting. There was a sacrificial bowl on the platform too, with a sacrificial twig shaped like the priest's aspergillium for the blood of animals killed as offerings to the gods to be sprinkled from the bowl. Inside the choir-like part of the building the figures of gods were arranged in a circle right round the platform. (ch. 4)

The descriptions in *Landnámabók* and *Heimskringla* also tell of a similar arrangement: there was a bowl for catching the blood of the sacrificed animals and a twig or rod for sprinkling it about. The raised altar, called a *stallr*, was kept in one room with the images of the gods, and the actual feasting took place in the other.

The pillars supporting the roof of the hof had a great deal of religious significance. It is suggested that the "gods' nails" might have been used with flint for striking the holy fires. These pillars were also tied to Thunar and to Tiw (see the chapter on "Knowing the God/esses"), as well as being earthly embodiments of the World-Tree, similar to the Irminsul of the Saxons.

The greatest hof of the Northern peoples was that at Uppsala, which was apparently inhabited by a number of full-time godwo/men. The Icelanders also seem to have had hofs which did not serve primarily as dwelling places, but rather were built solely as places of worship. This may be a late development from the more ordinary Scandinavian practice; however, the Anglo-Saxons also had buildings in which the gods were worshipped. Many of these steads stood near or in woods which had been recognized as holy long beforehand and did not lose any of their sacral nature to the temple, but were rather considered to be part of the hallowed garth.

HOME

Whether your home is a hof where many heathens gather to hold the high feasts, or whether you and your family alone keep your troth there, it is one of the holiest places you will ever know. The stead where you dwell is the first seat of your might and that of all your clan.

When moving into a new home, the first thing which must be done is to carry fire widdershins (counterclockwise) all around its boundaries. This marks them out on a spiritual as well as an earthly level, claiming them as yours and keeping out unwanted wights.

The roofs of our ancestors were held up by the house-pillars with the images of the gods carved into them. Among their many functions, these pillars often served as the embodiment of the *barn-stokkr*—the "Bairn-Stock," or family tree, which held the luck of the family line and at the branches of which women in labor would clutch as they bore their children forth. In *Völsunga saga*, the house pillars and tree were combined into the single great "Barnstokkr," a fruit-bearing tree which stood in the middle of the hall and whose branches held up the roof.

If it is possible for you, you should get a pair of poles or a single great one which reaches from floor to roof and set your pillar(s) up in the most central place of your house—not necessarily the most physically central, but the place which you feel to be the heart of your house. If you should be lucky enough to have a house with a nice fireplace and hearth, that is where they should stand; the hearth naturally holds all the *hamingja* (luck) of the household, embodied by the coals brought from the hearth of the old house into the new one and the fire carried around the land.

If you have no hearth, you should trust in the god/esses and your elder kin to guide your house-pillars to the place where they should go. When you move, the pillars go with you; when Thórolfr Mostur-Beard came from Norway to Iceland, he "threw overboard the high-seat pillars from the temple with the figure of Thórr carved on one of them, and declared that he would settle at any place in Iceland where Thórr chose to send the pillars ashore."[6] For instructions on making house-pillars, see the chapter on Crafts.

Beside the house-pillars is the high seat, the seat where the master or mistress of the home sits to assert his/her rule in the house. After the death of the previous head of the household, the heir would not seat him/herself in the high seat until the memorial *arvel* (funeral drinking-feast) had begun, whereupon s/he would ritually take that place to show that he/she had taken possession of the full lands and inheritance.

Should you have a free room, this can be made into a *wih-stead* where you keep the images of the god/esses and all your holy things, and in which you carry out your blessings. Otherwise, the place where you put your house-pillars—the heart of your home— is the place where you should hold your rites.

To ward the doors and windows of your house, you can either rist (carve) and redden a hex-sign (see Appendix II) above each or, if you live in an apartment, draw the hex-signs in red ink upon small pieces of paper and tape them above each opening. Such signs can also be carved on small disks of wood and hung up over doors and windows. Some plants, such as Sunnaswort (St. Johnswort), rowan, oak, and many others, can be either hung up inside or planted around the house to ward off ill wights and draw in weal-working might.

It used to be customary to bury an animal skull in the foundations or under the threshold of the house as a warder. A similar custom is that of setting up antlers above doors, as described in *Beowulf* where the hall Heorot ("Hart") is adorned with gilded antlers. To this day, Norwegians customarily decorate the doors and roofs their cabins in the Jotunheim ("Etin-Home") mountains with the horns of deer and elk. Other traditional means of warding through adornment are the old German farmers' gables which were carved into the shapes of animal heads; the Fachwerk houses (see illustration) with wooden beams forming the shape of the rune elhaz (ᛉ) on a white background, and the hex signs of the Pennsylvania Dutch.

HOWES OR BARROW-MOUNDS

The Northern European landscape is studded with howes (burial mounds), each of which has its own dweller; most small hillocks in the Germanic and Celtic countries are actually grave-mounds. In the oldest days, the kin were buried on their land; some of the early Germanic laws required, as proof of land-owner-ship, that one be able to find the barrows of one's ancestors and name them. Howes were often placed at the bounds of the land, perhaps in hopes that the dwellers within would sit as guards of the safety and rights of their descendants.

It has always been traditional to pour out ale at the howes of kinfolk on feast-days and to bring them food; in the cases of kings or other folk of special might, gifts of money were also brought to lay within the mound. This practice is different in modern times; the combination of public, rather than private, burial places and extensive mobility often makes it difficult to bring gifts to the barrows of the kin. Therefore, you may wish to take some earth from the graves of your favorite relatives to betoken the mound itself. If you have your own land, you can heap up an actual mound of earth over this sod near the border and call upon the howe-dweller there; otherwise, you will wish to keep it carefully tucked away in a box lined with black linen and to bring it out on feast-days—perhaps even to incorporate it into your house-pillars or harrow.

In times of confusion or need, it was also traditional to sit out on a barrow-mound overnight, in hopes that the ancestor within the mound would give rede and help. Most of the references to this in the sagas make it a practice specificially of kings—the king gets his authority from his ancestor within. However, the folklore tradition also shows that other folk do this for the sake of gaining

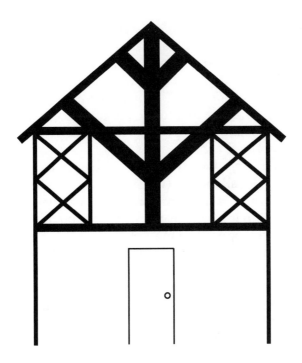

*Fachwerk house—typical traditional
germa dark wood beams against white background*

knowledge from the dead. If you need to do this, and cannot (for whatever reason) sit on the actual grave of your kinswo/man, you can set some grave-earth beneath your pillow after making a gift of ale or mead to the howe-dweller by hallowing a horn or cup to him/her, then moistening the dirt well with some of it and drinking the rest of the draught in two gulps. The safer method is then to sit awake upon the pillow; it is more chancy to fall asleep over the mound-earth, for then you yourself wend into the realm of ghosts where you may more easily be harmed if you have misjudged the good will of your kinswo/man.

HARROW (HÖRGR)

The harrow is the Teutonic equivalent of an altar. Traditionally it is set outside, in the middle of a grove or field; such a harrow ought to be made of heaped stones. A natural single boulder can also be good, as long as you have assured yourself first that either no wights dwell within it already or that the ones which are there are friendly towards you and towards the god/esses. The ale of the blessing is poured out on and about the harrow, as the blood of the sacrifice was in the older days. Holy fires are traditionally lit there, though some of the true folk in the modern world, mindful of the risk of starting fires outdoors, will set a small grill on top of their harrow to light the fire in.

For indoor use, a wooden harrow is easier to deal with than a stone harrow. A small cabinet (waist-height or a little lower) makes a good harrow and is quite practical because the hallowed tools can be kept within it when it is not in use, if you have reason not to leave them in the open. The mantel above a fireplace can also be used, although it is less workable in ritual practice because you have to keep turning about to pick things up and put them down, which can interrupt the flow of your rite. Whatever you make your harrow out of, try to use one with a top wide enough to hold all your ritual tools at once; otherwise you may want a small table beside it so that you won't have to fumble about.

If you are cramped for space or travel a great deal, a useful alternative to a permanent harrow is to hallow a small stone or carven plate of wood which you can set upon a desk, bed, or table as your circumstances allow. The best stone for this purpose is probably natural (unpolished) Baltic amber, the holiest and mightiest gem of the North. Other stones which make excellent portable harrows are "snake-stones," that is to say, stones containing fossils of any of the various spiral-shells such as ammonites, which embody the whirling wyrm-might of the earth; crystals of "sunstone" (Iceland spar, a transparent calcite); and "thunderstones," that is, stone axe-heads or arrow-points. Nearly all fossil-stones hold a great deal of *hamingja*. Malachite, especially a piece in which a hollow has been made (such as are sold for ashtrays in many rock shops), shows, in its layers of light green and dark green, the being of the Well of Wyrd, and this is also fitting for a mighty harrow-stone.

GREAT STEADS

The ancestral holy places of continental Scandinavia were deeply important even to those Northerners who had gone west to Iceland; *Landnámabók* mentions how "Lopt made a voyage to Norway every third summer, on his own account and that of his mother's brother Flosi, to sacrifice at the temple which Thórbjörn, Flosi's mother's father, had tended at Gaular."[7] Likewise, we who dwell in lands far from the earlier homes of our kin should remember the great steads and go to them when we can, or at least speak of them at *symbel* when it comes time to remember the might of the elder days. Though most of the heathen hofs of old no longer stand in the Middle-Garth as they did, they are mighty still in the hidden depths of the Well of Wyrd; they are the spring from which the ancient holiness still flows forth to shape the hofs and halls of today.

Denmark

Lejre, on Zealand, is perhaps the holiest stead of Denmark: Thietmar of Merseburg (a German chronicler writing ca. 1012 CE) describes sacrifices there which were very like those carried out at Uppsala. Lejre had been the traditional seat of Danish kings at least since the Migration Age; the Skjolding dynasty (Hrothgar of *Beowulf* and Hrolf Kraki, among others) ruled there for many years. A short distance outside the modern town is Gammel Lejre, where you will find a large Viking Age burial site and a great and hallowed mound from the Iron Age, possibly the seat from which the Skjoldings called on the god/esses and ruled their folk.

Two of the holy steads of Denmark are found on the island Fyn, a small isle between Zealand and Jutland. The name of the chief city on Fyne is Odense, which is derived from "Ódhinn's Vé," Ódhinn's holy stead. Another small town on this island is called "Gudme," derived from Godheimr, "World of the God." This particular stead is best known for the great numbers of small, thin gold plaques stamped with figures who appear to be gods and goddesses or holy folk; often seen is the image of an embracing couple, an image interpreted as the wedding of Freyr and Gerdr. Very lately, the foundations of a great hall were also discovered on Gudme, suggesting that this stead was both a cultic center and ruler's hall (a usual combination, as Scandinavian rulers were usually religious leaders as well). There is little left to see in either Odense or Gudme, though slightly north of Odense is a reconstructed Iron Age village.

Mosegård Prehistoric Museum (a short bus ride out of Århus, the main city on the eastern coast of Jutland) is not precisely a holy stead, but it does have a room which can be counted as a shrine of sorts, where both the body of Grauballe Man (who was probably killed as a sacrifice before being interred in the bog which preserved his body for some 1500–2000 years) and a long fork of wood, lightly carved to make it into the general image of a tall, long-legged goddess, which had also been preserved by the peat waters of the bog in which she originally stood, have been set up.

Finally, Copenhagen has not only the National Museum, which contains a vast number of Danish holy artifacts, but the Gefjon fountain, which is one of the most awesome pieces of Nordic art. This fountain shows the goddess Gefjon with her four wild oxen—her sons by an etin—plowing the island of Zealand free from the Swedish coast to drag it out to sea. Before her plow are great serpents, which the Danish children often pet for luck. This fountain is a good place to take a beer or two and pour a blessing to the goddess, who cares particularly for young maidens and who founded and watches over Denmark's largest island.

Norway

The brutality of the conversion in Norway has left us with very few steads that are known to have been major religious centers in heathen times. In *Heimskringla*, Snorri describes a great temple in Trondheim, with an image of Thórr adorned with gold and silver, one of the sagas also mentions an image of Freyr there. There is little left in Trondheim today; the city is considered to have been officially founded by Óláfr the Traitor (Óláfr Tryggvason—best known for the appalling tortures he visited upon those Norwegians who refused to convert to Christianity) in 997 CE, and a statue of this wretch stands on a high pillar in the middle of the city.

In Skogn, there is a great burial mound called Alvshaugen just north of the town's church; this grave has been dated to 300–600 CE, and is thought to have been the religious/political center of the canton.

Place names give us some hints about holy steads. In the old days, as Magnus Olsen describes in *Farms and Fanes of Ancient Norway*, names compounded with "hörgr," "haugr," or "vangr" are likely to have originally been holy steads, and frequently appear for the sites where Christian churches now stand. Some of the god/esses' names have also been preserved, such as Torshov (the hof of Thórr), a name which appears in Jevnaker (Hadeland area) and Gjerdrum (Romerike area), and Norderhof (the hof of Njörðr) in the middle of Ringerike.

Although Norway has no sites to compare with Lejre or Uppsala, a great deal of it is still wild mountains and forest land, and the land wights, trolls, and etins are stronger there than any of the continental Scandinavian countries. Perhaps the most powerful area of the country is the Jotunheimen Mountains, a vast and awesome range within a few hours' drive from Oslo. As the name "Etin-Home" suggests, many of the greatest (and most dangerous) of the wild wights dwell there. Being very high and full of might, these mountains are also a great place from which to call on the god/esses and make blessings.

Sweden

The greatest holy stead of the Northern folk is Gamla Uppsala, or Old Uppsala. Adam of Bremen describes the temple there: its roof was adorned with gold; outside stood a huge evergreen tree and beneath it a well in which sacrifices were drowned; sacrifices, nine of every kind, were hanged from the trees about it. No one is quite sure where, precisely, the temple stood, but from the description of the hills which formed a sort of natural ampitheatre about it, it was probably close to the three great mounds. It has been suggested that the old temple was in or very near to the place where a Christian church stands now.

All that is really visible of Old Uppsala now is the mounds. You can get there by bus from the modern city of Uppsala, and the mounds are within sight of the road. The first and the last have been dug into; they held partially-cremated bodies with rich gravegoods. These bodies were clearly noble; they may, as legend and tradition have it, have been among the first kings of southern Sweden. The middle howe has not been broken yet, and it is in this one that the most might still lives. Beneath it on the westerly side is a wide depression with a huge tree growing from it. If this tree is not the same holy tree described in Adam of Bremen's account of the earlier temple, it is, nevertheless, a mighty embodiment of the World-Tree.

Iceland

Iceland has many mountains called "Helgafell," "Holy Mountain." Of one of these, out on the peninsula, it is said that if you can climb up it to the top without looking back or speaking, you will be granted a wish. This fell is, unfortunately, difficult of access, as it does not lie on the Ring-road and so a special bus must be taken to reach it.

Thingvellir, the place where the Thing was held in the ancient times, is a highly honored place. Near the Law-Rock is a waterfall.

One fall which is deeply meaningful to heathens today is Godhafoss (the Waterfall of the Gods) in the north of Iceland. After the lawspeaker Thórgeirr declared Christianity as the official religion of Iceland, he went back to his home, took his household statues of the gods, and threw them into this waterfall. This act may be taken as a last heathen gift; the images of the gods were cast into the Well of Wyrd, as at the well at Uppsala—not destroyed, but hidden, sunken like the Rhine's gold in the waters, lest they should be desecrated by the new faith. They have lain long in those depths, their might waiting beneath the waters for the time when Wyrd should turn again and bring them forth to a time when they would be known again as of old. Now it is fitting for whoever goes to Iceland to wend his/her way up to Godhafoss; to cast some gift and pour out hallowed drink into the waters, and to call upon the holy ones who are wakening again in that stead.

The easiest way to reach Godhafoss is to take the tour from Akureyri, if you don't mind the other tourists giving you funny looks as you make your gift. The noise of the falls is likely to drown out anything you have to say if you speak softly, at least. To get close enough to throw anything over the actual falls, you need to be brave, agile, careful, and wearing shoes with a good grip. The access is through a rather dangerous glacial river, and the rocks, as your tour guide will warn you, are slippery. Alternatively, if you are not feeling particularly heroic (suicidal?) that day, you can throw your gifts into the river, which will carry them over the falls anyway.

In the national park in the south, you have a chance to visit both the waterfall Svartifoss ("Black Falls") and the glacier Vatnajökull. The latter is the place to go if you have any desire to communicate with etins and rime-thurses, or wish to see for yourself the earthly shape of the well Hvergelmir and the baleful rivers flowing from it. A limb of the glacier reaches down about 45 minutes' walk from the main campground. If you walk along the path, you will pass some little birch trees and then get to the foot of the glacier where a wild and murky river flows. This river is actually bubbling and seething like a great boiling cauldron at the point where it froths up from the glacier. It is possible for the brave and agile to cross the river and walk on the glacier, but this is a massively stupid thing to do, especially if you are alone, inexperienced, and/or not equipped for keeping your footing on the ice. You can expect to slip and fall; if you are very lucky, you, like the not-so-bright Teutonic magician who tried doing this a couple of years ago, will only bruise your butt and your dignity. However, as a number of signs along the way will warn you, you can pretty well expect that falling into the river will be fatal. If, however, you have come equipped and accompanied, you, like Thunar, can cross the river into this earthly extension of Etin-Home and deal with the wights within. Otherwise, you can shout across it. Just a good sense of Etin-Home is enough for most people anyway. There are also tours which will take you out driving and walking on the glacier with an experienced guide, if you feel the need to get closer to it. The presence of the rime-thurses can also be felt strongly on the great barren rock-field which lies before this tongue of the glacier, where the stones are all shattered by the might of their passing.

Germany

Germany is filled with holy places whose names still bear witness to the gods and goddesses worshipped there. In my own experience, the mightiest stead in Germany is the group of natural stone pillars which are called the Externsteine. These huge towers of living rock stand above a lake in the Teutoberger Wald, near to the place where Arminius drove back the Roman invasion of Germany. The Saxon Irminsul also stood very near to the Externsteine until Charlemagne's army destroyed it near the end of the eighth century.

The best way to reach the Externsteine is to take the train to a small town called Horn, which is near Detmold. (I stayed in Detmold, because I had been told that the Externsteine were "nearby." They are, for someone with a motor vehicle. They are not so near for someone riding a bicycle uphill, especially an hour and a half before dawn on a very frosty Ostara morning.) Then it is not so far to bicycle or walk to the stones. There is a nominal visiting charge if you go during normal hours; otherwise, you can duck under the chain. The middle pillar has steps hewn into the rock leading up to a platform from which walls of stone soar up all around. There is a hole in the wall on the eastern side, just above a small anvillike structure. I do not know how recently any of these were carved out, but it makes a perfect place to perform a rite.

Near Bonn are two holy mountains, the Godesberg (Wodan's Mountain), where the Franks used to worship Wodan, and Drachenfels (The Dragon's Crag). According to legend, Drachenfels is the place where Siegfried (Sigurdhr) slew the dragon Fáfnir. Unfortunately, modern tourism has had a detrimental impact on both of these. Godesberg is crowned by a resturant and Drachenfels is riddled with all sorts of little tourist shops and places to eat, not to mention hordes of tourists, locals having picnics, and the Drachenfels train which takes the lazy up to the top of the mountain. Nevertheless, you can still feel the might of the mounts beneath the modern tinsel.

The Godesberg serves as a nexus point for lines of energy radiating from the Siebengebirge ("Seven Mountains," of which Drachenfels is one); this power can be felt most strongly at sunrise or sunset. It is easy to reach; all you need to do is to take the U-Bahn from Bonn and walk through the town center to the mountain.

The best place to know the might of Drachenfels is, surprisingly, a rather strange little structure called the Nibelungensaal ("Nibelung-Hall") about halfway up the footpath. This item is a combination of Wagner temple and snake zoo: you pay your money, you get to see a shrine full of huge paintings from the Ring Cycle and listen to a tape of scratchy music from same, then, to escape, you walk through a long tunnel, observe a cement dragon, and go through the snake zoo. Once you have gotten into the snake zoo, you can (or at least I did) sit and meditate for hours on the might and mysteries of the great wyrms who still coil beneath the earth—remember Fáfnir and think of the Middle-Garth's Wyrm who rings the world, of the dragon beneath the mound who holds the wisdom of our elder kin in his hoard.

Great Britain

Great Britain is richer in folk traditions and local holy steads than any other country. Many of these sites were first barrows or menhirs set up by the folk who dwelt in Britain before the coming of the Celts. The Celts continued to hold these steads holy, as did the Anglo-Saxons after them. With the coming of Christianity, many of the names were changed and Christian churches built on the sites where the heathens had held their blessings, as Pope Gregory ("the Great") directed his first missionary to England in 586: "Since (the heathen English) have a custom of sacrificing many oxen to devils, let some other solemnity be subsituted in its place ... On such occasions they might well construct shelters of boughs for themselves around the churches that once were temples, and celebrate the solemnity with devout feasting. They are no longer to sacrifice beasts to the Devil, but they may kill them for food to the praise of God, and give thanks to the giver of all gifts for His bounty." As this absorption of heathen ways into nominally Christian practice had elsewhere, the conversion of holy sites smoothed the process of conversion, but also made sure that the ways of the folk still lived on in "local tradition."

The mightiest stead of the Saxons, and the most beloved, is the White Horse Stone. The White Horse was the banner of Hengest and Horsa; it is the traditional sign of the Saxons. This stone stands near Uffington, in Oxfordshire, and is the site of many of the Odinic Rite's rituals.

Beneath the eye of the White Horse is a conical hill known as "Dragon Hill." This is associated with the English legend of "St. George"—a tale which may in its first Anglo-Saxon form have dealt with Thunar's battle with the Middle-Garth's Wyrm.

Near Uffington also stands a chambered barrow known to the Anglo-Saxons as "Weyland's Smithy." If a horse were left here with a piece of money beside him, the owner would return to find the money gone and the horse new-shod. This place is a mighty stead for craftswo/men to make blessings; it is also fitting for anyone to come and drink *minne* to Weyland's heroism as well as his skill (see Chapter 7: Heroes).

Lovedon Hill in East Anglia was the site of one of the greatest heathen Anglo-Saxon burial places. The hill held over 2000 heathen burials, some with goods (such as a carven whetstone scepter similar to the one in the Sutton Hoo burial) showing that one or more of the early Anglo-Saxon kings may have been buried there. After the conversion, the town moot (council) still met upon the hilltop. This hill is a good place to go for making blessings to the alfs and idises, or to sit out at night in search of redes and wod. The nearest towns are Grantham, Gelston, and Hough: from the A607 Grantham—Lincoln road, turn north to Hough, then left to Gelston. A footpath leads downhill from Gelston to the northwest; Loveden Hill is to the left of the track. The burial ground was under the flattish area on the near side of the plantation on top.

Wansdyke, "Woden's Dyke," is an early Anglo-Saxon cultic center. This extensive earthwork, though partially destroyed, stretches from Bristol to Marlborough. The most complete section is the part south of Marlborough, which runs (roughly) from A-361 to A-345.

At Yeavering in Northumbria is the site of a great Anglo-Saxon hof. Modern archaeological excavations have found the places where an "Irminsul," a great holy pillar, was set up to the northwest of the building; where the inner pillars had stood; and where the skulls of the sacrificed oxen were heaped up in a long pit. Here the English gathered to give worship to the god/esses of their ancestors, probably led by the kings who dwelt at Yeavering in the last quarter-century of English heathenism.

The hill known as "Arthur's Seat," in Edinburgh's Holyrood Park, has been a holy site since ancient days. One folk tradition associates it with the Romano-British King Arthur of Celtic myth; another extremely dubious etymology suggests that the name is derived from a mix of Gaelic and Norse elements: the seat of "Ard Thórr," "The High Thórr." One of its slopes (perhaps the most difficult to climb) is known as "Raven Rock." "Arthur's Seat" is the focus of the lines of earth-might in the whole surrounding area; it is also a place at which the alfs are mighty. In the last century, a class of schoolboys stumbled upon a cave in which a great number of small mannequins were interred in miniature coffins; the oldest were quite decayed, while the newest were in good enough condition to have been put in that year. No explanation for these has ever been given. Climbing "Arthur's Seat" without rest stops is the standard test of good fitness in Edinburgh; it is also a stimulating test of will, especially if (as you ought) you climb it without looking back until you have reached the peak.

The Orkney Islands, which were settled by the Norse in the late ninth century, are rather inaccessible to the casual traveler but hold several sights worth visiting. They can be reached by sea from Aberdeen or by air from Edinburgh. If you are there on Midsummer's night, the sky never becomes darker than twilight; the islands are relatively unspoilt, so that if you go only a little distance from the towns, you can see them as the Norsemen who settled there did.

The first holy site on Orkney (coming by sea) is the island of Hoy, "The High Island." The name may be derived from the Ódhinn-title Hár, "The High One." Off the shore of this island, about an hour's walk from the nearest town, is a "stack"—an isolated rock standing out of the sea—known as the Old Man of Hoy. This stack is a mighty Wodanic stead. It cannot be climbed except with special equipment; however, the mainland juts out into a point behind it where workings may be done (I held my own Midsummer's rite there in 1990). Hoy is also the island where the walkyrige Hild awakens the slain hosts of her father Högni and her lover Hedhinn to fight every day, as she will till Ragnarök—an earthly reflection of Walhall.

The Ring of Brodgar, on mainland Orkney, is approximately the same age and size as Stonehenge, though neither so sophisticated nor so well-preserved. As the Norse name suggests, the Vikings used this ring as a holy site. At least in the 18th century, the Ring of Brodgar was called "the Temple of the Sun" and the nearby circle known as the Standing Stones of Stenness was called "the Temple of the Moon." According to the eighteenth-century antiquarian Dr. Robert Henry, a pair of lovers would plight their troth in these two: the woman would get on her knees before the man and pray to "Wodden" in the "Temple of the Moon," after which he would do the same in the Ring of Brodgar.

A stone with a natural hole in it, known as the "Stone of Odin," used to stand in Stenness (on mainland Orkney). It was used for both magical and religious purposes. The most common use was for lovers to take "the oath of Odin" (the words to which were unfortunately never recorded) while clasping hands through the hole in the stone. Sadly, the stone was broken in 1814.

Fewer traditions are preserved in the Shetland Islands; the only place which might have been an old holy stead is the crag known as "Fruwe Stack" ("the Frowe's Stack") off the island of Papa Stour. An agile person can easily climb this stack without any special training or equipment, though it can only be reached by boat (the keepers of North-House, the only bed-and-breakfast on the island, will take their guests out to it on request).

America

The lands of the New World have as much claim to Germanic holiness as did Iceland when the Scandinavians first began to settle it in 870 CE, or Britain when the Saxons came in 448 CE. The only difference is that during the settlement of America, there were no (or few) folk who still followed the elder ways, so there was no one to set aside mountains to Thunar or Wodan, or fields to Fro Ing and Njördhr. This does not mean that our god/esses do not dwell in this land; only that there are no great steads which, as in Iceland and Britain, have been hallowed by generations of worship and history. It is our generation who must find these places, set aside the *wih-steads*, and build the great *hofs*.

In seeking holy places in America, care must be taken not to rouse the wrath of the Native American gods and ghosts, but rather to respect their being. Still, many of the great Germanic holy places in Britain were steads of worship before the Saxons or the Norse ever came to their shores; if local lore does not make a place taboo to non-Native Americans, then there is no reason why, after fitting respect has been paid to the indwelling wights and their permission gained, you should not call upon the god/esses of the North and hallow the lands to them as well.

NOTES

1. Tacitus; Chisholm (tr.). In *Grove and Gallows*, 3.

2. Claudianus in Chisholm, 10.

3. Turville-Petre.

4. Grimm, 2:584.

5. Markey, Thomas L. "Germanic Terms for Temple and Cult," in *Studies for Einar Haugen*, 366.

6. *Eyrbyggja saga*, ch. 4.

7. Grönbeck, 2:131.

Chapter 14

ELEMENTS OF TEUTONIC RITUAL

NE OF THE MOST IMPORTANT things to remember about the Teutonic tradition is that it is not a tradition of absolute practices any more than it is one of absolute beliefs. The rituals in this book, or in *A Book of Troth* or any other book on the Northern ways, are not rites which must be worked word for word and gesture for gesture, but may be changed to fit your needs.

In Teutonic religious practice, there are some elements which are fairly consistent throughout most rituals. These are elements of which you should be aware in constructing your own rites; they should serve as loose guidelines, though not as necessities. The outline which I offer here is the simplest form of a "basic" Nordic ritual, which you can incorporate into whatever personal workings or dramatic enactments of myth you wish.

GATHERING THE FOLK

When it is time for the rite to start, you may wish to have a more ceremonious gathering than just shouting, "Hey, get over here!" Favored methods have included the sounding or striking of an instrument, banging of a sword or spear against a shield, and a singer or herald with a loud voice calling out a few ritual lines of invitation. Such a gesture is not needful, but it is useful for setting the ritual mood and getting everyone into their places in the shortest possible time.

THE HALLOWING

This part of the rite is performed when you are working in your home or other such place where everyday life usually takes place. It serves to create a ritual space in which you may work more directly with the god/esses and ghosts—a place that stands half in the Middle-Garth, half in the worlds beyond, and into which no unholy or unfriendly wight may tread; on a psychological level, it heightens your awareness of things of the soul and blocks out distractions which might interfere with your communion with the god/esses. For this reason, the hallowing is not necessary in any of the places which are considered wih-steads (see the chapter on Holy Steads). The hallowing, indeed, can be seen as creating a temporary garth of the soul around the space where the ritual is taking place.

In many ways the hallowing is similar to the circle-casting of the magician, but the level of energy is not usually so intense, nor does a great danger exist if the bounds of the garth are crossed during a religious rite. Indeed, as you will notice, several of the dramatic rites for the greater seasonal blessings in this book specifically integrate a figure bringing a holy gift from the realms without into the community of folk inside. In the rituals here, the figures embodied are Wodan (bearing the mead of poetry and leading the ghosts of the kin) and the Spring Bride (Eostre/Idunn, bringing the golden apples of new life). In the Eddic myths, Thunar also fares to Etin-Home to gain or reclaim treasures for the god/esses (such as Ægir's brewing-cauldron and his own hammer); any of these tales can be used as models on which to build a like dramatic rite.

The Hallowing which I describe in this book—the tracing of the Hammer-sign at the *ættir*—is the simplest form possible. The four-quartered circle was not unknown to the Germanic folk—it appears, for instance, in Anglo-Saxon charm spells where the names of the evangelists set at the quarters have probably been subsituted by Christian writers for the names of the heathen god/esses. Since the *frithgarth* is firstly an affair of the Wans, you might choose to call upon them at the quarters thus: Fro Ing in the east, the Frowe in the south, Njördhr in the west, Nerthus in the east. Otherwise, if you wish to make a rite which is specifically given to the Ases, you can call upon Thunar in the east, Tiw in the south, Heimdallr in the west, and Wodan in the north.

THE SETTING

Sometimes, especially if you are dealing with a group of folk who are not deeply versed in Teutonic tradition, you may find it well to speak a few words about the history and lore of the feast you are holding. Such a statement should remind the folk gathered there that their ancestors stand beside them in the garth; that the stream of tradition flows unblocked, though sometimes hidden, from the first celebration of the festival to you and all who have come together to keep it with you; and should generally serve both to inform about the feast and set the mood you want for its beginning—a mood which will vary from holy day to holy day. At Eostre, for instance, the feeling should be one of an anticipation, which the rite will fulfill; at the feast of Thunar, the beginning of the rite should be darkened by a mood of uncertainty and an awareness of the lowering threat of the rime-giants—a mood which the rite will banish.

THE CALLING

The Calling is simply an invocation of whichever god/esses and/or ghosts you wish to work with in the ritual. In your Calling, it is good to look up the various names and titles by which your god/esses are called (see the appendix on Kennings) and incorporate whichever of those are appropriate to the aspect which you wish to have turned towards you. This is especially good if you are calling Wodan, many of whose faces can be dire!

If you are doing a rite given to all the god/esses, it is probably simplest to speak a line or two for each of the chief ones—Wodan,

Frija, Thunar, Fro Ing, and the Frowe, and then simply add, "and gods and goddesses all" or some such inclusive formula.

SHARING OF DRINK

The passing of the horn is also central to most Teutonic rituals. This is usually done as a part of the blessing, in which whatever is left in the horn after the folk have all drunk from it is poured into the blessing bowl and used as the "blood" of the sacrificial bread animal, if you have one. Usually the godwo/man hallows the horn first; each of the folk then makes the sign of the walknot (Wodanic), Hammer (for Thunar, or just as a general sign of hallowing), or sun-wheel (Wanic) over it and speaks a toast. The frowe of the hall, or a woman who chooses to fill the role of walkyrige, may carry the horn from person to person; otherwise, it can simply be passed. In most rites, it is passed about deosil, though when the Wanic powers are specifically being called upon, it can also go widdershins. This sharing of drink should not be neglected in solo rites, either; here you are drinking with the god/esses as a close friend, giving them half of your own horn or cup.

A *symbel* may be included as part of the ritual. This should be distinguished from the act of drinking with the god/esses; when you drink at *symbel*, you are taking part in the work of the Norns by shaping wyrd. If you do *symbel* as part of the rite, it takes place after the sharing of drink with the holy ones and the blessing. Most of the time, however, it is done as a separate rite, usually after the feast.

THE BLESSING (BLÓT)

In all the sources dealing with all the Teutonic folk, the heart of all religious workings is the making of a gift to the god/esses, either as thanks for something they have done or as a request for something you would like for them to do, or (as in the seasonal blessings) both. In earlier days, this gift was a living sacrifice which bore the message to the gods; now, it is more commonly an animal made out of bread or biscuit dough (recipe and directions in the chapter on Crafts). The type of animal varies according to the rite: a boar is traditionally used at Yule, cattle or horses at Winternights and Midsummer, a goat at the Feast of Thunar, and so forth; while a human figure made of bread might be used either at a Wodans-blót or as the symbolic "Frodhi-King" at Winternights.

This part of the rite offers the opportunity for each of the folk to put their hands on the creature and speak their own wishes or thanks to the god/esses. Thus charged, the symbolic "killing" of the bread beast by the godwo/man releases the might and the words which have been set into it by this part of the ritual, sending them straight to the god/esses.

Because the sprinkling of the sacrifice's blood upon the harrow, the stead, and the gathered folk was a primary aspect of the blessing among the Old Norse, it has become customary to subsitute wine, mead, or ale poured into the blessing bowl and sprinkled about with a twig of oak or pine. This may be done whether or not a bread-creature is actually used; if you do not have a symbolic animal, then the wishes/thanks should be spoken or whispered while the horn is being passed around. The remainder is then poured out over the harrow (if the rite takes place outside) or else taken outside at the end of the blót and poured onto the earth, preferably at the roots of a tree (although the first Steersman of the Ring of Troth, when doing rites in his home, often flung the contents of the blessing bowl out the window into the garden with a great dramatic gesture).

The meaningfulness of the blessing to Teutonic ritual cannot be over-stressed, because this gift of might which flows back and forth between humans and the god/esses is the primary form of interaction between the realms. It is vital that we show them our thanks for the gifts we have gotten from them—the gifts of life, might, mind, and luck—and all they do so that the things of our life may go well for us. In this way we keep our troth with them and keep their friendship as well. As Wodan says in "Hávamál" 41-2, "Giver and returner remain longest friends / if that (the exchange of gifts) is able to turn out well. / To his friend should a man friend ever be / and pay back gift for gift." The giving and getting of these gifts is a vow in its way; to make the blessing is to swear your troth to the gods and to strengthen the bonds between you, just as gifts in the earthly realm are the tokens of alliance and loyalty.

Other ways to make gifts to the god/esses are to hang things on hallowed trees, (especially in the case of Wodan, though this can be done for any of the god/esses) perhaps attached to a wish or note of thanks written in runes; for Wanic sacrifices, the gift should be tossed into a body of water or sunken in deep mud; an Ase-sacrifice, particularly to Wodan, can be burned. Such gifts can be bread- or cookie-dough animals, or else small figures betokening the issue in question (to give thanks for surviving a car wreck, for instance, or to ask the god/esses' help concerning problems of your vehicle, you might hang up a small model car). Decorating a special tree with colored ribbons and flowers (real or artificial) on feast days is also a very traditional way of giving worship to the god/esses and wights of the land. This is done, not only at Yule, but also at the beginning of summer, usually on the various feast days between the equinox and Midsummer's.

The Closing

It is often good to have some sort of short speech or gesture which marks the shift from the specifically ritual part of the event to the feasting and celebration. This can be as complex as a specific formula of thanks addressed to each of the god/esses who were called upon at the beginning of the rite, or as simple as a chorus of "So mote it be," a blast on a blowing horn, or the striking of a staff against the ground, etc. If the folk still remain quiet, leave them be for a few moments; a mighty rite should give rise to a feeling of awe. If this silence lasts too long (again, especially if you have guests or new members), they may not realize that the rite is over; the godwo/man should then make some remark to betoken the return to spontaneous activity (the favored one in the North Texas Kindred was "Rite's over, folk—let's party!"). Alternatively, if you wish to emphasize the sense of continuity, a brief formula inviting all the wights present to the feast of celebration can be added at the end of the rite proper.

It is not needful to ceremoniously take down the circle after a simple Hammer-hallowing. However, if you have called upon the god/esses to ward the garth, you should give them spoken thanks either at the end of the ritual proper or when the feast is over.

Other Comments

Memorized rites are better than rites read out loud. Write your rituals well ahead of time and, if more than one person is involved in the performance, PRACTICE. Don't try to get too complicated, especially the first few times.

From experience, I have found that lengthy readings from the Eddas tend to bore most people who are not already closely familiar with, and emotionally tied to, the legends of our folk. If you wish to do the poetry of the *Elder Edda*, it is much better to adapt it for a dramatic rendition; many of these poems may originally have been meant as scripts for folk-drama, and thus translate very easily into that medium. This does not mean that readings from the Eddas are not a good thing; they hold much might in and of themselves, and are very powerful if performed for folk who understand their meaning or read in solo rites. It is also perfectly all right to read a fitting exerpt from an Eddic poem rather than struggling through the whole thing.

A brief homily on one or more of the strengths and goods of our folk—troth, bravery, or such—or on the nature of the god/esses being worshipped at the rite is not inappropriate, if you feel the need of one; this may serve to remind those who are gathered there of the most important reasons why they follow the Northern way, and of what they must do to be worthy. If you do this, remember to keep it very short. Use only words which come from Germanic roots. Try to avoid reminding the folk of a sermon in a Christian church.

Music with the rite is, at least in theory, a very good thing. Until someone collects a heathen songbook, however, the choices are pretty much limited to (a) what you can write yourself, (b) folksongs with a strong heathen flavor such as "John Barleycorn," and (c) Richard Wagner's *Ring Cycle*. If you can find or write folksongs, be sure everyone has the music and words well in advance so that they can all sing along.

The use of Wagner's music at Teutonic feasts is something that can best be described as part of the living tradition, Wagner being a Late Romantic and his music bearing no resemblance to anything our ancestors might have recognized (not to mention the fact that his plot mutilates the basic myths pretty grossly). Nevertheless, the *Ring Cycle* is the only generally available music dealing with the Germanic culture, and historical or not, it is awesomely powerful.

If you want to incorporate Wagner into your rites, be sure you know the Ring Cycle pretty well—Wagner had a rather negative attitude towards the god/esses he wrote the operas about, and some bits are just not really appropriate, or are only appropriate under very particular circumstances. My personal suggestions: "Ride of the Valkyries" should be reserved for Wodan-centered rituals, rites commemorating the dead, and calling the Wild Hunt on Yule (a foolhardy pastime at best). For the feast of Thunar, Donner's solo at the end of *Das Rheingold* (beginning with "Schwüles Gedünst schwebt in der Luft") is good, and even better if you have a godman with a strong baritone or bass voice to perform it live. For Eostre, the wakening of Brünnhild at the end of Siegfried is the most appropriate (begins with the music of *Siegfried* passing through the ring of fire). If you want to do a Spring Drama and don't have the people to act it yourself, you can use the whole of *Siegfried* on videotape or audio instead, starting it 4½-5 hours before sunrise; the plot corresponds pretty generally to the basic structure of the Germanic spring drama. For waking up the sluggards who did *not* keep watch the whole night long on Eostre, I recommend the "Reforging of Nothung" from *Siegfried*, Act I (begins "Nothung! Nothung! Neidliches Schwert!"); played as LOUDLY as you can stand it, or louder, this will awaken everyone with a great charge of true *wod* (and may even cause you to be treated to a live performance of berserkergang). The best music for Walpurgisnacht is the Spring Song from Act I of *Die Walküre* (from "Winterstürme wichen dem Wonnemond" to the end of the act). For Loaf-Fest, play either "Siegfried's Rhine Journey" (*Götterdämmerung*, orchestral interlude at the end of Act I) or the first scene of *Das Rheingold*, but in the latter case be sure to cut it off *before* Alberich begins his cursing of love (which starts with "Der Welt Erbe gewänn' ich zu eigen durch dich?"). The beginning of Act III of *Siegfried*, Wotan's dialogue with Erda, is fitting for Winternights, as is "Siegfried's Funeral March" (*Götterdämmerung*, orchestral interlude in the middle of Act III).

The ultimate recording of the Ring Cycle is Sir Georg Solti's London (Decca Record Co. Ltd.) recording with the Vienna Philharmonic, starring such notables as Kirsten Flagstad (Fricka in *Das Rheingold*), Wolfgang Windgassen (Siegfried), Gottlob Frick (Hunding and Hagen), Hans Hotter (Wotan in *Die Walküre* and *Siegfried*), and Birgit Nilsson (Brünnhilde). This version is available in both records and CD.

The finest piece of heathen music yet written is Grieg's operatic fragment *Olav Trygvason,* opus 50, (released on CD by Unicorn-Kanchana Records, London, 1992), of which only the invocations of the Norse gods, the speech of the Völva, and a choral scene of heathen worship and rejoicing were actually completed. Many of Grieg's instrumental pieces are also appropriate ritual music, as are most of the works of Sibelius.

Some kindreds also use recordings of natural sounds such as thunderstorms, howling wolves, and so forth as very effective enhancement for ritual performance.

Chapter 15

RITUAL POETRY

riginally performed as a lecture at the Ring of Troth's
Ostara feast in March of 1991.

Galdor means "croaking"   the cracked raven's voice
calling on winds   'twixt the worlds that blow
deep in the mound-burg   mutter the voices
of dead men within   who dwell in the stone.

Wodan 'twas first   went to Etin-Home
brought forth the mead   from mountain's dark roots.
Eagle, he sprang forth   awesome, flew from there
the song-shining mead   gold seed fell from his beak.

Blood of wise Kvasir   blended by Dáinn's kin
wod whirling forth   from worlds of night!
Well may you work it   well may you craft it
well may you wield it   Wodan's high gift.

Among our ancestors, poetry served two primary functions.
The poetry which has survived best are the songs of heroic deeds,
which preserved the memories of the greatest among our folk from
generation to generation. As well as their social function, these
songs may be seen as having a certain sacral function: they are

memorial stones graven in words instead of rock, which preserved the might of the hero's honor and memory to live wakeful in his descendants. Less well preserved, but probably the eldest, was the purely sacral word-craft: the galdor, or spoken incantation, poetry used for the purposes of magic and/or religion. This was the poetry of the thule (see Chapter 11: Holy Folk) as described in "Hávamál": "Time to speak as a thule on thule's seat / at the Well of Wyrd." The words spoken by the thule are not "at the Well of Wyrd" physically, but in the spiritual sense: because he, when seated on the holy stool, has passed into a realm beyond that of mundane existence and is speaking in a state of inspiration, transmitting wisdom across the marches between the worlds, his words are therefore set into Wyrd as are the words of the gods when they sit at judgement before the Well.

Our tradition makes it clear that poetry is the gift of Wodan to humankind. A number of Old Norse sources describe the story of the making and winning of the mead of poetry, called *Wod*-Roarer (ON Óðhroerir). After the war of the Aesir and the Vanir, the gods chewed berries and mingled their spittle in a vessel. From this rose Kvasir, the wisest wight in the Nine Worlds. Kvasir was slain by a pair of dwarves, who brewed mead from his blood. The etin Suttung in turn forced the dwarves to give him the mead, which he set beneath the mountain Hnitborg in the three cauldrons Wod-Roarer, Son, and Bodn, guarded by his daughter Gunnlödh. Wodan transformed himself into a serpent and bored his way beneath the mountain. He stayed with Gunnlödh three nights, then drained the cauldrons and flew away in the shape of an eagle. Suttung followed him, but Wodan made it back to Ásgardhr and disgorged the mead again. This mead of skaldcraft he deals out to those humans whom he especially favors; but a few drops fell outside the gates of the Ases' Garth, and those are the share of bad poets, which can be picked up by anybody. From this account, poetry is called the sea of Wodan's breast, the seed of the eagle's beak, and a number of other names which all refer to this tale.

In the Celto-Germanic tradition, it is also possible to become a poet by sitting out on a dead person's mound all night. In the course of this ordeal, the sitter receives the force of inspiration from the dead. Those who are able to control and shape it become poets; those who are not go mad. As the god who travels between the worlds more than any—particularly from the realms of the dead to the realms of the living—Wodan was naturally understood as the master of this force from an early time, so that the Germanic word for fury or madness—*wod*—from which his name is derived came in its later Scandinavian form, *ódhr*, to mean poetic inspiration. The wod-word was also used by Ulfilas in his translation of the New Testament to denote demonic possession; whether or not the Goths were aware of the personified Wodan, which is a matter of some debate, they clearly understood *wod* as a spiritual might which could rush into and overwhelm the individual mind. The name Wodan/Ódhinn itself means "master of *wod*": the shaper and controller of this violent fury—hence the poet who shapes inspiration by means of poetic forms and will. In a sense, everyone who undertakes this task seeks to become a little "Wodan."

For sacral uses, the power of poetry lies in the fact that it is not something native to the realm of ordinary life, but rather brought from the worlds beyond the Middle-Garth—the world of the dead. Truly inspired words are, therefore, words which roar through all the realms of being at once, as if they had been carved in runestaves and stained. This simultaneity is also important as a psychological element of ritual, because the combination of the sense of the words, which affects the mind, the sound and rhythm of the words, which affect the physical being, and the magical or spiritual power of the words, which affect the various levels of the soul, creates a synergistic effect which works deeply and profoundly upon the participants, bringing them into a state of awareness in which they may touch and see the might of the gods and goddesses.

As the various uses of the word *wod* show, its might alone is not enough to create poetry, but rather it must be carefully crafted and controlled to have its full spiritual effect. In the "Skáldskaparmál" section of the *Prose Edda*, Snorri Sturluson has Bragi, the god of poetry, dividing all poetry into two categories, language and verse-forms. Both of these must be considered carefully.

The primary distinguishing characteristic of Germanic poetry is alliteration: stressed syllables beginning with the same letter. You can get away with writing rituals that do not use strict Teutonic rhythmic forms if you have good alliteration. End-rhyme is not native to the Germanic tradition, but is, rather, a southern innovation. This is not to say that using it is wrong or even grossly detrimental to Germanic practice; it was the greatest poet of the Viking Age, Egill Skallagrímsson, who was first to use end-rhyme in Old

Norse verse. However, it should not be forgotten that he did this in a moment of desperation, to save his head by writing the praise-poem "Head-Ransom" for Eiríkr Blood-Axe, about whom he was not overly enthusiastic.

> Fremr munk segja   ef firar thegja;
> frágum fleira   til frama theira.
> Oextu undir   jöfra fundir,
> brustu brandar   vidh bláar randar.

> (More I must tell   if men are still
> more we've learned   how bravery burned.
> Wounds were waxing   at battle-boars' clashing,
> burst the brands   on shield's blue rounds.)

Even in this poem, Egill maintained strict skaldic alliterative and metric form as well as adding the end-rhyme; while in his most powerful poem, "Sonatorrek" (his lament for his drowned son), he kept entirely to skaldic metre.

The alliteration of Germanic verse is fairly simple. One needs only to remember that all vowels alliterate with each other. Also, if one is working with Old Norse names in English poetry, I have found it perfectly effective to alliterate those such as Ódhinn and Urdhr with the English w, since those are forms which originally had an initial w. However, since English equivalents (Wodan, Wyrd, and so forth.) generally exist, this really should not present a problem.

Alliteration is particularly helpful if you are trying to incorporate runic forces into your ritual, since the extra stress on the alliterated syllables can easily be used to evoke the might which the initial sound embodies, as "Geiri undadhr   ok gefinn Odhni," calls up the force of gebo, the rune by which, as the line itself describes, Ódhinn is sacrificing himself to himSelf.

There are two major divisions to the poetic aspect of word-choice. The first is vocabulary; the second is that known as the kenning.

Even such orthodox Christian churches as the Episcopalians teach their priests to use words based on Anglo-Saxon when writing sermons and prayers. To them, this is important because the Anglo-Saxon words are the first learned by most children; they are the words which speak directly to the deepest levels of the consciousness. To us, this is three times more important because the word-hoard of our elder kin speaks to our blood and our souls; the truest and deepest runes of our folk can only be spoken forth in our own speech if their ringing is not to be warped. Our words are the words through which our earlier kin knew the Nine Worlds and the mights and wights dwelling in them; and thus they must be the words through which we work to rebuild the wisdom of our kin who have gone before us.

Writing ritual poetry in English is often frustrating because English is essentially a bastard language filled with a number of non-Germanic words—and often the most important words, at that. Thus we have no native word for inspiration/fury, no native word for honor, none for victory, vengeance, and so forth; while many of the Anglo-Saxon words remaining to the language are so archaic as to be difficult of comprehension—such as the "Hollanderese" of the best-known translation of the Poetic Edda. Further, some of the words which survive have taken on a meaning which is no longer that of the original; to be "modig" ("courageous") in Anglo-Saxon is not the same as to be "moody" in modern English. The problem, then, has two possible solutions: either to use foreign words when needful, or else to resurrect—sometimes to invent—a Germanic English vocabulary for ritual use. I myself have almost always found the second to be a better way, calling as it does on all the rich heritage of our people. Although the sword of our speech has become rusty in places, it is not for us to hide it away, but rather to clean it carefully so that it may shine in its full might. In Appendix V: Word-Hoard, I have prepared a brief list of some of the words which are best to use in Germanic ritual in place of their more usual modern counterparts. Some of these are rather archaic Modern English; some are actual reconstructions.

The kenning is the last, and most specialized, element of Germanic poetry. Briefly described, it is a way of referring to something without naming it directly, yet bringing in a wealth of descriptive imagery and understanding of its being by the elliptical way in which the subject is spoken of. In the runic materials, kennings begin to appear quite early, as on one fifth-century item which speaks of gold as "the Welsh (foreign) grains." The gold is "foreign" because it has presumably been gotten by raiding; it is described as "grains" both because of the color which gold and ripe grain share and because both are the very embodiments of fertility and riches. Thus, in a ritual meant for bringing riches, the speaker might bury a golden item in the earth for a time, saying something like, "I sow the Welsh grains   grant me harvest bright!" The combination of spiritual understanding with beautiful imagery and the magical intensification which is caused by this verbal concealment makes the kenning one of the most effective tools of ritual poetry.

Kennings are also particularly useful in invocations, where a kenning can be chosen to invoke the specific aspect of a god or wight upon whom you wish to call. To invoke Thórr in his fertility aspect, as the bringer of the storms which help the grains grow and the lightning that is said to ripen it, you would call him by the kenning "husband of Sif," because his golden-haired wife Sif is thought (on one level of being) to be a personification of the golden fields of grain. However, to invoke him for protection, you would call him Warder of the Middle-Garth or Slayer of Trolls; for hallowing or warding, Mjöllnir's Wielder and Wih-Warder; while to call upon him for strength, you would name him as Father of Magni ("Main-strength), Father of Módhi ("Courage"), or Father of Thrúdhr, "Strength"). The second part of Snorri Sturluson's Prose Edda, "Skáldskaparmál," gives a number of kennings for all of the gods and most things in the world. If this should fail you, you can make up your own kennings (a car, for instance, might be called "steed of the stone-path," since cars are usually driven on paved roads).

Similar also to kennings are *heiti*, the use-names by which many of the gods—most especially Ódhinn—are called. These names are especially useful for invocation: Ódhinn, for instance, can be invoked as Sigfadhir ("Father of Victory"); Yggr ("the Terrible"); Farmatýr ("God of Cargoes"); Grímr ("Masked"), All-Father; and by many other names.

The basic format of Germanic poetry is that of the "Old-Lore Metre" or "Epic Measure," which appears in the early Primitive Norse runic verse as well as in Old Norse, Old High German, and Anglo-Saxon. This form, according to Winifred Lehmann, was probably standardized at least five centuries before the first surviving Germanic verse was written down. This measure is characterized by the two half-lines bound by alliteration, with two stressed syllables and a variable number of unstressed syllables in

each half-line. An example is the inscription on the famous Gallehus horn: Ek HlewagastiR HoltijaR horna tawido—I Laegast, son
of Holte, made the horn—or the beginning lines of *Beowulf*:

> Hwaet! We Gar-Dena   in gear-dagum
> theod-cyninga   thrym gefrunon
> hy dha aethlingas   ellen fremedon.

One of the stressed syllables in the first half-line, generally the
second, though it may be either or even both, must alliterate with
the first stressed syllable in the second half-line. The last stressed
syllable of the full line should not share the alliteration; this only
appears in the later Eddic verse.

The old-lore metre is pretty well the simplest metre to write
in. When strophes are used, which they generally were in the Old
Norse, though not in Anglo-Saxon or Old High German, the strophe is made up of four full lines, each divided into two half-lines,
as in "Völuspá":

> Hljódhs bidh'k allar   helgar kindir
> meiri ok minni   mögu heimdallar
> vilt'at ek, Valfödhr   vel framtelja
> forn spjöll fira   pau fremst um man.

> (To hearing I bid all   holy children
> higher and lower   of Heimdallr's kin.
> Thou wilt that I, Walfather   well tell forth
> of fore-gone wisdom   which first I mind.)

In the Old Norse, also, the number of unstressed syllables was
generally restricted to two per half-line.

The most specifically magical metres from the Old Norse are
the ljódhaháttr—song or spell-metre—and its subset of galdralag
or incantation metre. The basic ljódhaháttr is made up of a four-line
strophe, of which the first and third lines are divided into two half-
lines connected by alliteration as in the Old-Lore Metre, and the
second and fourth are single lines with three stresses, of which two
must be alliterated. Many verses of "Hávamál" show this pattern:

> Deyr fé   deyja frændr,
> deyr sjálfr   it sama;

ek veit einn   at aldri deyr
dómr um   daudhan hvern.

(Cattle die   kinsmen die
you shall also die;
I know one thing   that never dies
how each dead man is deemed.)

The beginning of the runic section of this poem, in which Ódhinn describes his ordeal on Yggdrasill, also shows the ljódhahattr pattern of rhythm and alliteration:

Veit ek, at ek hekk   vindga meidhi á
nætr allar níu
geiri undadhr   ok gefinn Ódhni,
sjálfr sjálfum mér,
á theim meidhi   er manngi veit
hvers hann af rótum renn.

(I wit that I hung   on the windy tree
all of nine nights
gored with a spear   and given to Ódhinn
self by self to me
on that tree   of which none knows
from what roots it rises.)

This passage, however, adds an extra half-strophe to the normal ljódhahattr pattern for the purpose of creating the magical pattern of three triads.

The galdralag, as its name implies, is particularly effective for magical songs. It is similar to ljódhahattr but marked by the repetition of one of the single lines, usually the last in the stanza. The repeated line normally changes just slightly, reinforcing and strengthening the magical effect of the galdr. The form of "För Skírnis" shifts from ljodhahattr to galdralag for the stanzas in which Skírnir is actually cursing Gerdhr:

Heyri iötnar   heyri hrímthursar,
synir Suttunga,   siálfir áslidhar:
hvé ek fyrb'ydh   hvé ek fyrbanna
manna glaum mani,
manna nyt mani.

(Hear the etins   hear, rime-thurses
the sons of Suttung   Ases' sibs all:
how I forbid   how I foreban
    men's love to the maid
    men's joy to the maid.)

The repetition is not limited to the last single line, but rather is characteristic of the entire passage; the effect is that of an upward-spiraling intensity. This repetition also appears in the Anglo-Saxon and Old High German charm spells, as in this one against a magical "shot" causing sickness in which the charm lists all the possibilities for the shot's lodging place—flesh, blood, bone, limb—and origin: shot of Aesir, shot of elves, shot of hags, then states its effectiveness against all of them.

Gif dhu waere on fell scoten   odhdhe waere on flaesc scoten
odhdhe waere on blod scoten   odhdhe waere on ban scoten
odhdhe waere on lidh scoten   naefre ne sy dhin lif ataesed.
Gif hit waere esa gescot,   odhdhe hit waere ylfa gescot,
odhdhe hit waere haegtessan gescot,   nu ic wille dhin hilpan.
This dhe to bote esa gescotes,   dhis dhe to bote ylfa gescotes,
dhis dhe to bote haegtessan gescotes,   ic dhin wille helpan.

Or, as in the Second Meresburger Charm:

thu biguol en sinthgunt,   sunna era suister;
thu biguol en friia   uolla era suister;
thu biguol en uuodan,   so he uuola conda:
sosa benrenki   sose bluotrenki,
   sose lidirenki
ben zu bena   bluot zi bluoda
lid zi geliden   sose gelimida sin.

(Then chanted Sinthgunt   Sunna her sister;
Then chanted Frija   Volla her sister;
then chanted Wodan   as he well knew how to:
so as the sprain of bone,   so as the sprain of blood
   so as the sprain of limb,
bone to bone   blood to blood,
limb to limb,   so be the binding.)

Skaldic poetry was far more highly controlled than the older forms, both in language and metre. A number of metres with precise syllabic counts were used, all of which are detailed thoroughly in the "Skáldskaparmál" section of the *Prose Edda*. The looser chant-metres are, however, preferable for most ritual use, as well as being considerably easier to write. The essence of skaldic verse was the way in which it showed off the cleverness of the poet; the poems are riddles in and of themselves. The skaldic techniques can be very useful in the hands of a skilled vitki; for general religious use, they are better left alone.

The better you are able to use these elements to craft your wod, the mightier your songs and rites will be. Use them well!

Chapter 16

RITES

HE GREATEST RITES of the Teutonic way are those of the seasonal holy feasts: Yule, Eostre, Midsummer's, Winternights, and the other feasts which mark the changing of the year-tides. In addition to these, there are several rites which can be performed at any time during the year, as there may be need. The greater of these are the rites of passage—birth/naming, initiation, wedding, and death. The rite of blood-siblinghood is also holy and rare. There are also smaller and more simple rites which should be carried out whenever they seem to be fitting. Some of these are workings for individuals or between two people; some, such as the *symbel* and Hammer-Hallowing, are rites to be done as part of rituals or at feasting.

BIRTH AND NAMING

In ancient times, when a woman began to give birth, she would clutch either to the trunk of a fruit tree or to the house-pillars. The tree or wooden pedestal was called the *Barnstokkr*; as has been discussed before, it embodied the entire family line. By holding onto this stock, the woman called upon the whole might of her kin to aid her in the birthing. When her waters broke, she would begin to weave a red three-stranded cord with which the child's umbilical cord would be tied off; this cord, and the remnants of the umbilical, she would keep carefully. After the birth, the placenta was buried beneath an alder tree.

Some, or all, of these elements of birthing-ritual are often difficult to carry out in the modern world, especially for those who do not have lands of their own. Where it is needful (particularly if you are giving birth in a hospital rather than in your own home) other ways can be used. If you have no fruit-tree and have not been able to find or make even a symbolic house-pillar, you should, instead, hold an apple or a pear in each hand when labor begins. These fruits should be carefully dried and kept until you can plant the seeds in your own land. Most hospitals will refuse to tie the umbilical with a hand-braided cord; in modern Norway, the cord is tied around the child's wrist instead until after the name-fastening when its *ørlög* is set. If you have the bravery to ask your doctor for the placenta, he/she will probably give it to you! A couple I knew did this, explaining that what they were going to do was a traditional custom from the husband's Swedish ancestry; it raised a couple of eyebrows, but no more.[1] If you have no living tree under which to bury the placenta, take it to where your dearest dead are laid and bury it over their graves. Should there be a conflict between woman and man over this, it is the maternal kin which has the right to claim it.

As you hold to the Bairn-Stock (or its fruit), say thrice,

> *Idises all   shall aid me now!*
> *Might of my kin   in me shall flow,*
> *As I bring forth   the fruit of loved lines,*
> *hale and whole   hold me and my bairn.*

When you braid the triple strand, say thrice,

> *Idises all   shall aid me now!*
> *Thrice I wind   weal for my bairn*
> *Thrice I braid   bright wyrd for my bairn*
> *Thrice I weave   to ward my bairn aye.*

When you bury the placenta, say thrice,

> *Idises all   awesome, I hail!*
> *Mothers watch   and ward my bairn,*
> *Warn her/him if   aught woe shall threaten,*
> *Wisdom bring   bright through his/her life.*

The newly-born child is not thought to have a true soul until it has undergone the rite of naming, which cannot be done until nine days have passed. In olden times, a child who was unhealthy or deformed was often set out to die during this period. This was not because our ancestors were cruel or heartless (and, despite some popular belief, female infants were never exposed on account of their sex), but because the scarcity of resources, particularly in Iceland and Greenland, made it impossible to waste food on a child who might not be able to survive, or who would be a drain on the community all its life. After the coming of Christianity, perfectly healthy children who happened to be born out of wedlock were also exposed fairly often. These children, called *útburdhir*, became particularly horrifying and malicious ghosts. Nevertheless, it is also said in Iceland that if one meets with one of these creatures and calls out a name three times, then the child will take it for its own and be satisfied—that is to say, it will have become part of the namer's clan. Of course, the danger in this is that the child may have been exposed for a reason, and thus likely to bring weakness or deformity into the namer's line if it is taken in.

As these legends show, it is the act of naming which makes a child part of its clan; as discussed in the chapter on the Soul, it is also this which gives it its *ørlög* and character. The importance of choosing a name which is an ancestral name and/or bears a history which you wish for your child has been spoken of already; you must think carefully upon it! Since many names drawn directly from traditional sources sound odd to modern English-speakers (especially Germanic women's names, which mostly do not sound so nice to the contemporary ear) you may wish to use a modern form, to give the child its "true name" as a legal middle name, or else to give it a middle name by which it can be called in ordinary circumstances (I myself went to school with a boy named Thorwald William Anderson; no one had any clue that his first name was *not* Bill till the day he graduated from high school, when his full name was listed on the graduation roll).

The naming-rite and feast are the events in which the *ørlög* is laid for the child's entire life; it is at this time that the "norns," or rather the family's idises, come to speak its wyrd. This belief has survived in the legend of Sleeping Beauty, in which the naming-feast has become a "christening" and the idises who give the infant all her gifts of beauty, intelligence, etc.—and determine the length of her life—are called "fairies."

As many members of the family and close friends as possible ought to be invited to the naming feast. They should be told in advance to choose a gift for the child which will embody a characteristic which they wish to bestow upon it—preferably one which is strong in the giver him/herself. The favored gift in my Kindred has been a hardbound and finely illustrated copy of the Grimm Brothers' fairy stories, which represents the remembering and passing on of the ancient wisdom and tales of our folk. This particular gift will also provide the child with a great deal of enjoyment in later years, as well as laying the basic conceptual groundwork for it to understand the ways of our folk. For courage and strength, a weapon of some sort (even if only symbolic) is equally appropriate for both boys and girls. Symbolic jewelry or jewelry graven with a fitting runic inscription can also be given—a pendant in the shape of a raven for intelligence; a Thunar's Hammer for troth and strength of body and will; something in the shape of a boar will bring warding and safety throughout the child's life, and so forth. If it is thought appropriate for someone to bring traditional presents such as a cup or spoon graven with the baby's name, and if you prefer to use Roman letters rather than runes for this, the giver should be told of the meaning of the name and what qualities you wish it to give to your child. Filled with mead, a cup may also betoken *wod*; filled with ale, luck and strength; filled with food, it becomes a sign of fruitfulness (you should wet the child's lips with the drink or give it a crumb of the food, and then drink or eat the rest of it yourself to the worship of whatever god/esses are most fitting). A spoon may likewise have a bit of food or a coin in it to bring frith and wealth, or drink for *wod*. If you wish your child to have a warrior's soul, however, the first food it tastes after its name has been given it should be meal and salt given to it on the blade of a sword or knife.

This rite may also be carried out with an adopted child; Sig-urdhr Fáfnir's-Bane himself was sprinkled with water and given his name by the king Hjálprekr who had taken his mother in after the death of his father Sigmundr.

Naming Rite

Time: Nine days after the birth of the bairn.
Tools: A horn or cup filled with water drawn from a running stream; a leek; whatever gifts the guests have chosen to give the child.

When all the guests are gathered before your hearth, house-pillar, or whatever other feature you have chosen as the heart of your home, the Mother should carry the child forth, stopping before the Father.

> MOTHER: *I have borne you this bairn, hale and whole. Will you know him/her as your own, born of your clan? Or shall he/she be cast clanless out of the garth, to live or die with troll and warg?*

(The Father looks the child over carefully, searching for ills and deeming its strength. If he deems that it is worthy to be taken into his clan, he raises his arms and takes it from the Mother, hold-ing it high. Should he see anything of note—great strength, the adder-keen eyes of the hero, mighty soul, or aught of the bairn's fetch, he should speak a few words about it here).

> FATHER: *All worthy in might   ween I the bairn,*
> *Come he/she now   to clan of my blood.*
> *High ones and holy   hear now my words,*
> *This name I give   good wax my child!*

(The Father dips the leek's leaves into the horn or cup and sprinkles the child with the water, speaking its name and the *ørlög* which he wishes that name to lay upon the bairn. If he wishes to give it its first food from a blade, he does so now. He then gives it whatever gift he has chosen, telling the god/esses and the gathered folk what it shall mean. The Mother gives the child her gift, fol-lowed by each of the guests according to rank.)

INITIATION INTO THE KINDRED

The Kindred should be gathered about the harrow. The new member, here spoken of (regardless of age) as the CHILD, stands outside the circle, behind his/her FOSTERER. The welcoming can be done by either a woman or a man, but it is more traditional to have it done by a man. If this is done on a holy day, it should take place after the Call, but before the sharing of drink and the blessing.

The special tools which are needed are a gift for the GOD-WO/MAN to give the CHILD, a leek, and water drawn from a running stream. The CHILD ought to be dressed in a plain white garment. The most traditional gifts would be a weapon (symbolizing adulthood); a spindle and distaff (for a woman); or a twisted armring (the emblem of troth).

(If this rite is not being done as part of another, the rite begins with the usual Hammer-Hallowing and the GODWO/MAN's Call to all the god/esses.)

GODWO/MAN: *Wodan mighty   and wise Frija,*
Thunar, Warder,   we call all you!
Sif and Tiw   shining Idunn,
Balder and Bragi   be here with us!
Fro Ing we call   and Frowe bright,
Njördhr and Nerthus   now come to our garth!
Skadhi and Wuldor   we call upon you,
Heimdallr holy   and all high ones, we hail!
Gods and goddesses   we greet you here,
Look well upon   the works we do,
At Wyrd's Well high   where ørlög is laid.

FOSTERER (stepping forward): I *have a foster-son/daughter, young in the ways of our folk but worthy, whom I wish to bring into our kindred.*

GODWO/MAN: *Is he/she known to all here?*

FOSTERER: *He/she is.*

GODWO/MAN: *Do any here find this youth/maiden unworthy to be made one of us—a free wo/man to work with us in frith, a sibling to stand by our backs in strife, a kinswo/man to share all our clan's troth?*

(Any objections must be made here, and the challenge dealt with. The kindred may choose to have its thule or other designated speaker make a challenge of lore—perhaps of ancient knowledge; perhaps concerning the duties of a kindred member—which the CHILD must answer to the satisfaction of all present. When this is satisfied, the GODWO/MAN speaks again:)

(Mundane name), *step forth.*

(The CHILD moves to stand at the edge of the circle, facing the GODWO/MAN. S/he still does not step inside.)

GODWO/MAN: *Why do you wish to come into the garth of our kindred?*

(The CHILD answers with his/her personal reasons for wishing to join.)

GODWO/MAN: *What name shall be the sign of your troth, and what shall it mean?*

(The CHILD shall here speak the name he/she has chosen. If it is his/her given name, he/she should also recount his/her ancestry as far back as he/she knows it; otherwise, he/she should explain the reasons for his/her choice. The GODWO/MAN swings the Hammer three times over the CHILD's head, then embraces the CHILD—lifting him/her up, if possible, and either carries or pulls him/her into the circle of Folk.)

GODWO/MAN: *Now, before the holy gods and goddesses, I give you the name (chosen name). Bear your name well, (chosen name), for so shall true folk ever know you. Holy waters, drawn from Wyrd's Well, shape you shining lifeage, (chosen name).*

(As s/he speaks the name the third time, s/he should use the leek to sprinkle the CHILD's head with the hallowed stream-water). So I give you this naming-gift: be welcome to our kin, thou true wo/man of the Folk. (S/he gives the CHILD the gift. The CHILD takes it in the left hand and lays his/her right hand upon the oath-ring or the Hammer).

> CHILD: *I*, (chosen name) *take this gift as a sign of my troth: troth to the gods and goddesses; troth to my fore-gone kin; troth to my kin who are here. So shall it be.*

> ALL: *So shall it be.*

(Each person shall then embrace the new member of their kindred in turn.)

WEDDING

For the Teutonic peoples, a wedding was more than an affirmation of individual love and commitment; it was an economic and social transaction through which political alliances were made and the futures of the two people involved and their children was provided for. While divorces were relatively easy to obtain—equally easy for husband and wife—the financial terms were set beforehand to be sure that both would be well provided for and the children always well supported. Social stability and the healthy continuance of the family line were more important to the Germanic folk than romantic love; marriages were generally made for practical reasons (though often broken by personal problems).

Traditionally, the woman came with a dowry (usually equivalent to her share of her family inheritance) which remained her own possession; though her husband might manage and invest it, it reverted to her upon divorce or upon the death of her husband. The dowry was also expected to include the bed, dishes, linen, and all the other household goods. The husband paid a bride-price to the family of the bride, which was designed to compensate them for the loss of her work—a daughter, especially in Iceland where spinning and weaving were so important to the economy, was a valuable asset to the family. The morning after the wedding was consummated, the husband also gave his wife a "morning-gift" of considerable substance which, again, represented an investment towards her future. The bride-price and the morning-gift amounted to a goodly sum; the fact that a young man was able to amass this quantity of cash or goods showed that he would be able to support his wife and family. In case of a divorce, the husband was always responsible for the full support of all his legitimate children.

In modern times, the dowry can be replaced by life and health insurance policies, which protect husband and wife financially in case of the death, sickness, or injury of one or the other. Since few daughters contribute to the support of their family today to the degree that they did in early Germanic households, the bride-price is no longer necessary; however, a symbolic gift from the groom to the bride's family, of a quality indicating his financial capabilities and prospects, is still appropriate. For the morning-gift, in addition to a nice piece of jewelery as a symbolic present (Gunnora Hallakarva insists that a big chunky amber necklace is the very most appropriate morning-gift, and certain to bring the newlyweds' household the blessings of *frith* and riches), a high-yield bond or other investment made in the wife's name should fulfill the same function that the morning-gift did among our ancestors. In the same vein, it is also appropriate to set up the beginnings of college funding for your children; and a marriage-contract clarifying financial terms and division of the property in case of divorce is a good thing. If you cannot meet these requirements together, you may need to consider postponing the marriage until you are able, not only to survive together, but to provide for your own future and your children's—this is how our ancestors did it.

Different states have different laws concerning what is classified as a legal marriage. If your area is particularly strict, or if your relatives are not understanding, you may wish to have a civil ceremony in addition to your Ásatrú marriage to be sure that everything is fully in order. However, many states require only two or three folk (including the wedding couple) who accept the person performing the rite as a valid religious leader.

If you have a non-establishment standard living arrangement which is not expected to produce children, but which you wish to hallow in a traditional fashion, the rite of blood-siblinghood involves an equal (or greater, since it, unlike marriage, is virtually indissoluble) level of commitment and is more appropriate under such circumstances than the marriage rite, which is *specifically* aimed at the continuance of the family line.

A proper Germanic wedding requires an ancestral sword (for the groom to give the bride), a wedding crown, two rings, and several companions of both sexes, including at least one on either side who is either related or willing and qualified in some manner to stand in for that person's family.

If you have no inherited sword, an ancestral sword can be made by carving your family name in runes into the blade and hilt of a new-made sword and dyeing it with your blood and/or other genetic material. This sword is the earthly embodiment of the might of your ancestral line—it should be the great treasure of your house. The sword symbolizes not only the life of the groom's line, which he is entrusting to his bride, but also that she is expected to be his partner, standing beside him through all the battles and hardships of life.

The wedding crown, worn by the bride, should likewise be something that can be passed down through the generations. It represents her maidenhood; the groom will remove it before the witnesses when they are brought to bed as a symbolic defloration.

The rings are the traditional unbroken circle of gold, embodying the holiness of the oath.

For wedding clothing, you should wear traditional early Germanic garb (see Crafts, pp. 331–353), preferably embroidered by the bride herself (and perhaps the groom as well). The bride should wear a white shift with an overdress in a bright color: red, bright blue, yellow, or green. The Eddic poem "Thrymskvidha," in which Thórr is dressed as a bride so that he can regain his hammer, also mentions a linen hood as part of the regalia—a hood which was deep enough to veil his face and bright red beard effectively!

The first ceremony of the wedding is the groom's reclaiming of his ancestral sword, which takes place the night before. If it is possible, a barrow-site should be set up with an older man costumed as a dead man, who will impersonate an early ancestor of the groom. The groom will then be taken to the site in darkness and told that he must take the sword out of the howe. When he touches the sword, the *draugr* should rise up and challenge him to give his name and lineage. If the groom accomplishes this successfully, his "ancestor" should then give him wise counsel on marriage and life in general before letting him take the sword.

Should this prove too complex to arrange, the sword should instead be secured in a large tree (preferably fruit- or nut-bearing). Each of the men present should try to draw it out and fail before the groom succeeds.

The wedding ceremony itself is performed the next day. It is overseen by an ELDER, who may not necessarily be a godwo/man but should be someone who knows the couple well and is considered worthy in wisdom and might. The wedding rite ought to be done outdoors in a place of natural beauty.

(The BRIDE's family stand on the left side with her; the GROOM's to the right with him. Unrelated women stand with the BRIDE, men with the GROOM. The GROOM has brought his ancestral sword, his ring for her, and all his paperwork; the BRIDE has brought her ring for him, her paperwork, and a weapon of some sort for him. There is also a horn and bridal ale.

The ELDER begins with the Hammer-Hallowing:)

ELDER: *Gods I hail   and goddesses all,*
Ases and Wans   alfs and idises here.
Look well upon us   this wedding bless.
Hail to Frija   frowe of the home,
Holy mother, hear us!
Keeper of keys   keeper of distaff,
keeper of Wodan's cares,
highest of wives   and holder of vows
bless the work wrought this day.
Who stands for the groom?

GROOM'S NEXT OF KIN: *I do.*

ELDER: *Who stands for the bride?*

BRIDE'S NEXT OF KIN: *I do.*

ELDER: *What is the worth of this man, and what bride-gift is paid?*

(GROOM's NEXT OF KIN describes the groom's good qualities and worthy deeds at as much length as possible, then details
his financial contribution to the wedding. Another witness, not
related, should then be called upon to attest to the truth of the
NEXT OF KIN's words of praise and to add praises of her/his
own.)

> ELDER: *What is the worth of this woman, and what dowry
> does she bring?*

(BRIDE'S NEXT OF KIN describes the bride's worth of character and deeds and her financial contribution; another witness is
likewise called, as above.)

> ELDER: *Are both clans satisfied with the terms of this wed-
> ding?*

(Both NEXT OF KINs speak their assent—or disagreement, if
there is any.)

> ELDER (to the BRIDAL COUPLE): *Then nothing may
> stand in your way! Now speak your wedding-vows.*

> GROOM (holding his ancestral sword out to the BRIDE
> together with the ring—if possible, the ring should be
> slipped onto one of the quillions. The BRIDE brings
> her ring for him up to touch the other ring and the
> sword):
> *I bring you this sword   the soul of my line,*
> *bear it well, my bride!*
> *In battle and frith   to be by your side,*
> *as shall I stand by you aye.*
> *On these rings   my oath I swear:*
> *love and worship to my wife.*

> BRIDE (bringing up her other hand, in which she has the
> weapon for him):
> *I bring you this weapon   wield it mightily,*
> *and hold it well, my husband!*
> *In battle and frith   to be your strength,*

> *as shall I stand by you aye.*
> *On these rings   my oath I swear:*
> *to my husband, hallowed love.*

(The GROOM takes his weapon as the BRIDE takes his ancestral sword; he puts the ring on her finger, she puts the ring on his.)

ELDER: *Now Frowe Var   to witness I call,*
> *who keeps all contracts made*
> *and Sjófn   sweetest maid*
> *that law be held by love.*
> *Frija's handmaids   hold your oath all,*
> *and aye give joy of it.*
> *Now let bride-gift and dowry be given.*

(The BRIDE and GROOM exchange their paperwork, which each then hands to the corresponding NEXT OF KIN to hold for the rest of the ceremony. If there is a wedding contract and this can be officially done now, they should sign the contract at this time. The ELDER pours the first horn of bridal ale and makes the Hammer-sign over it.)

ELDER: *Hallowed for bride-pair   this horn shall be,*
> *I deem your days shall be good.*
> *Frith be in this ale   and fruitfulness great,*
> *when you have drained the draught.*

(The GROOM drinks half of the horn, then gives it to the BRIDE, who finishes it. They give the horn back to the ELDER, who refills it, making the sign of the Hammer.)

ELDER: *Hallowed to bride-pair this horn shall be,*
> *speak all your wishes for weal!*

(The ELDER makes a toast, then passes the horn deosil. All drink except the BRIDAL COUPLE. Each person should make a toast to the good of the bridal couple and their future children before drinking. The ELDER pours what is left into the blessing-bowl when the horn has made its round, refills it, and hallows it again.)

ELDER: *Hallowed to bride-pair   this horn shall be,*
    and to gods and goddesses all!
  Holy ones, hear!   here blessing we ask,
    for a wedding filled with weal.

(The ELDER drinks; the BRIDAL COUPLE drink; the ELDER pours what is left into the blessing-bowl, then lifts it up.)

ELDER: *Frija, Frowe, Fulla, Sjófn! Var and Vor, Syn and Hlín, Snotra, Gna, Lofn! Hlíf and Hlífthrasa, Thjódhvarta, Björt and Bleik, Blithe and Frith, Eir and Aurbodha! Thunar, Sif, and all ye others, gods, goddesses, and wights, who look well on the Middle-Garth's weddings; alfs and idises of the clans of* (ELDER names the BRIDAL COUPLE). *I hallow this bowl to you all* (making the Hammer-sign over it). *Cast friendly eyes on the marriage of* (GROOM) *and* (BRIDE): *grant that it be fruitful, filled with joy and frith, and that their children be worthy of the best of their line, mighty in luck, wisdom, and main. Hail!*

ALL: *Hail!*

(The ELDER sprinkles the harrow, the *ættir*, and the BRIDAL COUPLE with the ale, then pours it out over the harrow or onto the earth before it.)

ELDER: *Hail* (GROOM) *and* (BRIDE)!

ALL: *Hail* (GROOM) *and* (BRIDE)!

ELDER: *Hail the gods and goddesses!*

ALL: *Hail the gods and goddesses! HAIL!*

(The men and women should then divide. When the ELDER gives a signal, they should race either back to the hall where the feast is being held or, if this is not possible, to their cars. If the men reach the goal first, the women must serve the drink at the feast; if the women reach it first, the men must serve—in earlier times, the men were sometimes mounted while the women ran on foot,

Gold amulet depicting the marriage of Freyr and Gerd
(Denmark, 6th century CE*)*

which made sure the race would have the correct outcome. The GROOM must stand at the door of the hall to block the BRIDE's entry; he must then take her arm and guide her over the threshold to make sure she doesn't stumble, which would be an exceptionally bad sign.

The BRIDE's first duty at the feast is to bring her husband a horn of bridal ale or mead.)

> BRIDE: *Ale I bring thee,   apple of battle* (or: "*Mead do I bring thee,   mightiest boar*").
> *Hallowed be horn we share.*

(The GROOM should then drink from the horn and give it to the BRIDE; the two of them alternate draughts till it is empty.

The ELDER hallows the GROOM with the hammer, then gives the Hammer to the GROOM, who makes the sign of the Hammer over the BRIDE with it, then touches it to her womb.)

> GROOM: *Hammer hallow you holy bride,*
> *bear men and maids of might!*

(At the feast a holy cake ought to be shared about—perhaps baked in the shape of a boar, a horse, or other fitting beast. After the feast, the BRIDE and GROOM are then given a large cup of mead[2] apiece and their attendants lead them away to ready them for bed. The BRIDE is stripped down to her shift, with the bridal crown still on her head, and put into the wedding bed; the GROOM is then brought to her. If it is dark, this procession must be accompanied with torches; there must be at least six witnesses as he takes the bridal crown off. The witnesses then go away and leave the BRIDAL COUPLE together all night to consummate the wedding. In earlier times, the witnesses would settle themselves outside the door to the bridal chamber, drinking and shouting ribald suggestions to the newlyweds . . .

When the BRIDAL COUPLE wake up the next morning, the GROOM should give the BRIDE her morning-gift. At this time also, the GROOM gives the BRIDE a bunch of keys which she ties at her belt. Ideally, a morning-feast should be held with the guests at which the gifts are given.)

GROOM: *I give you these keys: my house is yours to rule. Hold them well, my wife.*

BRIDE: *I take these keys: well and wisely shall I use them ever.*

FUNERALS

The funeral customs of the Germanic folk are exceedingly diverse (see the chapter on Soul). As a general guideline: Wodanists and persons whom you suspect may walk after death should be cremated, while most others should be buried and a mound thrown up over them. The ashes of the cremated may also be laid in a mound. If a real boat cannot be gotten, it is appropriate to put a model Viking ship in the coffin for cremation, or in the howe. There is only one literary reference to the "Viking ship funeral" where the dead person is sent off to sea in a burning boat; however, boats were burned on land and buried with the dead. A ring of stones in the outline of a ship may also be set around the body.

It is important to make sure that the dead person is provided with some means of transport, good walking shoes, and a warm cloak or coat; it is a long and cold way to the halls of the dead. Beyond this, some of the dead person's treasures and weapons should be burned or buried with him/her; these should be sufficient in quantity and quality to reflect the status of that person in life. In early days, the hawk, hound, and horse of the deceased would be slain and put into the mound or onto the pyre. Models of these may be subsituted for modern usage.

If music is desired at any time during the ceremony, appropriate selections are: the crossing of the gods into Walhall at the end of *Das Rhinegold*; "Ride of the Valkyries" (especially for Wodanists); Siegfried's Death and Funeral March from *Götterdämmerung*, and Brünnhilde's lament for Siegfried and Immolation scene at the end of *Götterdämmerung*. For a ship-burial, "Siegfried's Rhine Journey" from *Götterdämmerung* is also fitting.

The Funeral Rite should be held with the burning or burial as its climax. It is fitting for the godwo/man and all who attend to dress in black as a sign of mourning.

Funeral Rite

Tools: ritual Hammer, a Hammer amulet to lay in the coffin with the dead wo/man, ale or mead and a horn, blessing-bowl and blessing-twig. Whoever wishes may also bring a gift to lay in the coffin. Among the gifts should be three apples and nuts, preferably hazel-nuts ("filberts" in America).

(The GODWO/MAN begins with a Hammer-Hallowing.)

GODWO/MAN: *Wodan, drighten of the dead, ferryman, I call thee—show the way to the worlds beyond.*
Frija, in thy sunken hall, hear my voice.
Thunar, Warder, Friend of Men, be with us—lend your Hammer's holy might.
Heimdallr, open the Ases' Garth's gate; worthy steps shall sound soon on thy bridge.
(or: "Hella, ready the bench; set a shield of gold over your ale; set a fine feast, for a worthy guest comes to your hall.")
Fro Ing, bring frith to the mound: a fair life within, and friendship to the living aye.
Frowe, bear the mead forth: well should you greet this guest, and roomy-seated is your hall.
Idunn, here is one worthy to eat of your apples: I ask you to grant that food freely.
Idises and alfs, greet your kinswo/man kindly.
All ye holy ones, gods, goddesses, and wights, hail (name of dead) who comes among you; help him/her to the hall of his/her soul.

We have come here to speak farewells to our beloved friend and kinswo/man (name of dead), who goes forth from us now on the farthest of farings—that need-faring which all must make in time. Far is the faring to the halls of the holy ones; long is the way, and there are many who wait for the traveler. (Name of dead), this Hammer hallows you and your pathway. Thunar ward you from the etins, thurses, trolls, and all other wights of ill on the way; Thunar ward you from wyrm and wolf. (GODWO/MAN makes the

Hammer-sign over the DEAD with the amulet, then
lays it upon the chest.) *"Cattle die; kinsmen die; you
yourself shall die. But fair fame shall never die, for the one
who gets it well. Cattle die; kinsmen die; you yourself shall
die. One thing I know that never dies—how each man dead
is deemed."*[3] *Now let those speak who knew* (name of
dead); *say, what shall be remembered of her/him by kin and
friends in the days to come.*

(Each person who is willing and able should then speak hon-
estly of the dead person: his/her deeds, his/her character, the
legacy of children and/or works which he/she has left behind. If
someone has written an elegy, this is the time to read it. When
everyone who wishes to has spoken, the GODWO/MAN should
then fill the horn with ale.)

GODWO/MAN: *Now I hallow this horn to our friend and
kinswo/man,* (name of dead). *Drink to this in friendship
and frith: that he/she come well to the hall of* (whichever
god/ess the DEAD was closest to), *and be reborn into
the Middle-Garth in time.*

(The GODWO/MAN passes the horn deosil: all drink, repeating the toast or some variation of it. The GODWO/MAN pours
what is left into the blessing bowl and hallows it with the Hammer.)

GODWO/MAN: *Now whoever has gifts for* (name of dead)
*to take with him/her to the holy halls, it is time that they be
given. The tide is rising; the ship is waiting; the steed stands
on the shore.*

(Those who have gifts come forward and lay them in the coffin. If the DEAD is being buried, it is especially important to supply him/her with plenty of food and drink.)

GODWO/MAN: (laying the right hand over the Hammer amulet on the DEAD's chest.)
*Fare thou well   forth on thy path,
where no sorrows scathe.*

Thunar ward thee   weal be with thee,
  on the wet ways thou far'st,
  in the hallowed god-halls.
To (the hall of whichever god/ess the DEAD was closest to) *send we thee forth.*
Hail (NAME OF DEAD)!

ALL: *Hail* (NAME OF DEAD)!

(The GODWO/MAN pours the contents of the blessing bowl
out over the closed coffin either before the first dirt is dropped on
it or before it is put in for cremation.)

After the funeral, it is necessary to have a memorial feast. This
is known as "drinking the funeral *arvel*." At this time, the dead person's heir should sit down in the high seat in full view of everyone.
Rounds of toasts to the dead person should be made as long as the
gathered folk are able. Remember that the funeral is the time for
grieving: the feast the time for fond remembrances.

SYMBEL

The *symbel* is and always has been the most beloved rite of the
Germanic people. At the feasts of old, when all the food had been
eaten, the tables would be carried away and the serious drinking
and speaking would begin. A *symbel* is characterized by the passing
of the drinking horn and the speaking of words of great meaning;
the making of oaths, the singing of songs, the reciting of poetry, and
the voicing of boasts. Of all the rites of our ancestors, this is the one
which has lived the most strongly—the speaking of toasts with a
draught comes straight from this custom. This is also the rite which
calls most strongly to those who have not studied the Northern
ways or chosen to follow the god/esses of the Teutonic folks; many
of the finer *symbels* which I have led have included considerable
participation by Christians or people with no particular religious
orientation. The appeal of the *symbel* is that it allows each person
present to speak words which he/she knows that everyone there
will hold to be meaningful; that he/she is able to express, if only for
a moment, those things which are most meaningful to him/her.

In doing a *symbel*, it is best to use a single horn, preferably one which is hallowed to the use of the kindred as a whole. By its very being, the horn symbolizes our oneness with our kin who have gone before: it is the vessel of the Northern tradition. Having a single hallowed vessel which makes the round of a circle focuses the attention of everyone present upon the person holding the vessel; it is, as much as a royal scepter or a judge's gavel, a symbol that the holder is the most important person in the room for a moment.

Words spoken at *symbel* are more full of meaning than words spoken at any other time, except for the oath made on the boar's bristles at Yule-time, which is just as meaningful. The reason for this is that the horn of ale or mead embodies the Well of Wyrd; it binds the frothing, holy liquid which holds hidden all that *is* and gives might to all that becomes and shall become. Thus words spoken over it are laid into the Well of Wyrd, becoming *ørlög*—they shape what shall be, and there is no getting out of it, no matter whether the speaker meant his/her words fully or not. For this reason, oaths are often spoken at *symbel*: the Norns, the god/esses, and the folk all stand to witness the vow that has been made, so that every realm of being shall act not only to compel, but to aid the speaker in fulfilling his/her oath.

The highest art of the Germanic wo/man is, like the hero Starkadhr to whom Óðhinn gave his many gifts, to be able to make poetry as fast as he/she can speak. This skill is best displayed at *symbel*, where the full attention of everyone there is on the skald. If Wodan has not gifted you with this swift craft, it is nearly as good if you can memorize either your own poetry or staves of the ancient skalds and be ready to speak them when the horn passes to you. Likewise, if you have any skill at singing, the *symbel* is the time to show it. Among the Anglo-Saxons, it was a shameful thing to be unable to play the harp and chant or sing any verse; the great poet Caedmon, before he met with the ghost who gave him his art, began by fleeing from the hall whenever *symbel* started so that he would not have to admit before the gathered folk that he could neither sing nor make poetry.

Both the oath and the poetic art are combined in the fine art of the ritual boast. Most people, oppressed by the Christian injunctions against pride and the modern culture which makes modesty a virtue, are uncomfortable with early Germanic writings such as

Beowulf in which the hero proudly states his own worth and skills without exaggeration or affected self-deprecation. The essence of the boast is to present your own worthiness to its fullness, without ever stating abilities beyond the bounds of what you can fulfill. One who over-boasts (especially under the influence of too much drink) is an object of contempt; but it is no better to present yourself to the god/esses and your friends (and/or foes) as anything less than the best you can be. It is the part of the hero to make great boasts and then to fulfill them, driven by the need to prove the worth of his/her words. The best boasts are made in poetic form and deal both with deeds done and deeds which you mean to do soon, so that all the folk may know how you carry out the things of which you speak. The best example of ritual boasting in the poetry of our elder kin is in *Beowulf*, where Beowulf enters Hrothgar's hall, tells of his past deeds, and states his intentions of meeting Grendel in single combat on equal terms—words which he makes good that very night.

The *symbel* can take place at any time, with any number of people; the best and most inspired *symbels* at which I have been present were actually spontaneously held by small groups of three to four folk who were well-versed in the old lore of the North. It is, however, most customary to have a *symbel* after a feast, with the whole kindred (and any guests who have come) taking part in it.

The format followed in modern times is: the first round is drunk to the god/esses, the second to ancestors and heroes, the third (and following) round/s to whom or whatever you wish. It is best if, to open the *symbel*, the godwo/man or whoever is held the highest in the kindred holds up the horn and speaks thus:

> *Now gather 'round   in ring of eld,*
> *at the holy well   at Wyrd's mighty seat.*
> *Words of might   shall we now speak,*
> *wary be all   who ørlög lay!*
>
> *First to the high ones   the horn we shall raise,*
> *then to elder kin   the old heroes gone.*
> *The third round to wish   our wills all speak,*
> *we may say what   whets then our hearts.*

The horn then goes its rounds until you run out of time, inspiration, or ale. At the end of the last round, the person who began the *symbel* should say,

> *Now words are writ   in Wyrd's mighty burne,*
> *Hail to all who have heard!*
> *Wend now our ways   we shall to all homes,*
> *Free shall we fare in frith,*
> *wise shall we fare on our ways,*
> *holy fare we to our holds.*

(Note: it was, and is, considered rather uncouth to get very drunk at *symbel*. If the horn has passed a few times too many, DO NOT LET THOSE WHO ARE DRUNK DRIVE. At some of our events at which drinking was expected, the hosts simply claimed all keys at the door and only surrendered them to the sober at the end of the night. The same preparations for dealing with transport and such should be taken at a holy feast as at any other party—perhaps more so, since some of our god/esses and ghosts have been known to choose their own sacrifices on occasion.)

BLOOD-SIBLINGHOOD

As described in Chapter 9: Clan and Troth, the rite of blood-siblinghood is a very solemn one. You must take care not to enter into this relationship with a person of lesser worth, for in working this rite, each person takes on something of the other's *ørlög* and might, so that the greater gives strength to the lesser, but the lesser can also drag down the greater (if there is a question of a serious disease being shared with the blood, this rite should not be done in any case). Thus a nithling's deed on the part of one blood-sibling shames the other and taints his/her soul and worth. Each blood-sibling has the same claim on the other as do siblings born. If one blood-sibling turns against the other, it is sure to bring an ill doom—it is the same as the crime of kinslaying.

In many ways, the rite of blood-siblinghood is more of a committment than the rite of marriage; divorces were even easier to obtain in the time of our Germanic ancestors than they are now (all it took was repeating "I divorce you" three times, at bedside, front door, and outside; and then proclaiming the reason for the divorce at the Thing), whereas the bond of blood-siblinghood is virtually unbreakable. It can be dissolved only by the outlawry of one of the members, which separates the outlaw from his/her clan of birth and from all human oaths; the mere death of one blood-sibling does not end the other's responsibility to him/her. The only occasion I have ever known of someone attempting to break the bond of such an oath occured in modern times: a man who felt shamed by his blood-brother's actions went before the god/esses, ritually renounced the other, and then virtually exsanguinated himself upon the harrow (he had to be hospitalized and given a transfusion to save his life afterwards).

The most traditional form of this rite is that in which a long strip of turf is cut intact, with the two ends still attached to the earth so that the turf-strip can be propped up as an unbroken arch. If this is not possible, the two blood-siblings should, at the appropriate point in the rite, each take up a clod of earth from behind him/herself and cast it in an arc over the head of the other.

Blood-siblinghood is usually performed between persons of the same gender—between persons of the opposite gender, such a lifetime committment is usually solemnized by the rite of marriage.

Tools: One horn of drink; an oath-ring (if possible); a sharp weapon. If a turf arch is being used, it should have been cut and propped up before the rite begins.

(Hammer-Hallowing. The SIBLINGS speak together. Different calls are given here; however, if the SIBLINGS are of mixed sex, the lines should be alternated, with the man hailing the gods and the woman the goddesses. After the Call, the rite will be the same for both genders. Mixed sexes should subsitute "sibling" for "sister" or "brother.")

(MALE SIBLINGS' CALL)
Hail to Wodan   highest god,
hail to Thunar   holy ward.
Hail we Wuldor   oath-warder mighty,
Hail the gods,   high goddesses, all.

(FEMALE SIBLINGS' CALL)
> *Hail to Frija   first of queens,*
> *Hail the Frowe   holder of life.*
> *Hail we Var   oath-warder mighty,*
> *Hail the goddesses   and high gods all.*

(The SIBLINGS speak the oath in turn. If there is an oath-ring, they should both hold it for the entire course of the swearing.)

> *Before all Ases   and all Wans wise,*
> *   I, (name), swear this oath*
> *Troth to (sibling's name)   true I'll be ever,*
> *   My clan shall be your kin,*
> *   My father and mother thine.*
>
> *Should this bond   e'er broken be,*
> *   then spill the sister's/brother's blood*
> *in rivers run   red to the earth.*
> *   Warg be the word-breaker*
> *   trolls take the troth-breaker*
> *   Hella have oath-breaker.*
>
> *So shall it be!*

(The SIBLINGS then cut their arms, holding the wounds together and mixing the blood, then letting some of the blood flow into the horn of drink, which is held by a WITNESS. The SIBLINGS speak together.)

> *From Mother Earth's womb   wend we forth again,*
> *Sisters/brothers as sisters/brothers born!*

(They crawl through the turf arch or fling clods of dirt over each other's head. Linking arms, they take the full horn from the WITNESS and speak together.)

> *Now sworn is troth   true we shall be,*
> *   born new as kin in blood.*
> *This holy draught   drink we brothers/sisters to gods,*
> *   and mighty goddesses aye!*

(The SIBLINGS each drain a third of the horn, then together pour the remainder beneath the turf arch and lower the arch back in place, or else simply pour the drink onto the earth.)

So it is wrought. Hail!

RITE OF WELCOME

A brief description of the right thing to do when a guest enters has already been given in Chapter 9: Clan and Troth. This Rite of Welcome is meant to be used at times when you wish to do more than simply offering drink to your guests. The most appropriate occasions are when greeting heathen guests who have come from a long way off; when someone who also treads the traditional pathway will be staying at your house overnight (or longer); and, most especially, at Ásatrú feasts.

The especial importance of carrying this rite out at a feast is based on the awareness that the god/esses and your elder kin are your guests as much as (if not more so than!) the living humans you have bidden to greet them with you. Thus everything you say and do should be meant to bring you and they together and to make sure that everyone gets joy of the occasion. When the frowe (or, if there is no woman in the kindred who will take this part, the fro) of the hall brings drink to the guests, she is welcoming them, not only into the earthly garth of the household, but into the greater garth of the timeless realm which we share with the god/esses and our kin in the hidden worlds.

Tools: The working of this rite will depend very much on what the members of the kindred have and want to do. In some groups, everyone brings his/her own horn or cup to rites; in others, the host is expected to provide drinking vessels. Ideally, you should have a small horn (such as most people can empty in one or three draughts without being overcome) or a hallowed cup to use for greeting your guests, after which they can drink from their own vessels or whatever is offered. If, for whatever reason, there is a problem with everyone drinking the draught of greeting from the same horn, then you should have a pitcher full of drink by the door and let each of the folk use their own horn/cup.

As the Guest steps over the threshold, the Frowe gives him/her the greeting horn or fills his/her vessel with ale, mead, or wine,[4] speaking as she pours. The drink will determine which greeting she speaks, thus:

> (Ale) *Ale I bring you ash   (or "elm") of true weapons*
> *Hail, thou guest in our hall!*

> (Mead) *Mead I do give thee   thou mighty boar (or "frowe")*
> *Hail, thou guest in the hall!*

> (Wine) *Wine I do give thee   thou wise and well-famed*
> *Hail, thou guest in our hall!*

In all cases, the Guest ought to reply by lifting the horn/cup towards the frowe and/or fro of the hall and saying,

> *Hail to the giver   who greets me here,*
> *Hail, host/ess in the hall!*

The Guest should then drink the horn/cup dry in one or three draughts.

HAMMER-HALLOWING

It is fitting to start off every great rite with a Hammer-Hallowing, which calls upon the might of Thunar to ward the garth within which you work and sets the holy stead apart as a soul-hall in which the god/esses join with humankind.

Those who have read my book *Teutonic Magic* will recognize this as a shortened form of the Circle Rite. For religious purposes, the full runic circle is not necessary and, I have found through experience, often bores participants who aren't themselves runesters.

The Godwo/man takes the Hammer in both hands and makes the sign of the Hammer towards each of the *ættir* with it, beginning at the north and turning deosil. With each Hammer-signing, he/she repeats: "Hammer ward our works without."

The Godwo/man traces the Hammer or swastika above his/her head, saying: "Hammer hallow our works within." He/she then traces the same sign below, repeating "Hammer hallow our works within."

The Godwo/man stands with feet together, raising head and hands upward and crying out, "Above us Ase-Garth's awesome might!" He/she then spreads his/her feet to shoulder width, crying out, "Below us roots in Hel's black hall!" Bringing feet together again and spreading arms directly out to the sides, he/she calls, "The middle is Middle-Garth's might!"

OVER FOOD OR DRINK

You should trace the sign of the Hammer or a swastika over food or drink to hallow it, saying or whispering, "Hammer hallow this food/drink to my might." This may be shortened, especially in company, to simply making the sign of the Hammer.

For a full blessing of food, as at a feast, the host/ess should stand at the head of the table. Trace the walknot; say, "Wodan bring wisdom to our drink." Trace the Hammer or swastika; say, "Thunar hallow this food to our might." Trace the sun-wheel; say "Hail to the Wans, from whose wealth this food sprang. Be it strength to us as we eat; be blessed by the Ases all." The guests should then answer, "Hail!"

YULE

Yule is the holiest feast of the Teutonic year. It begins on December 20 and lasts for 12 nights, the 12th being New Year's. These 12 nights are the Wih-Nights—a space of time set apart between the old year and the new, in which the greatest workings are wrought and the greatest wyrds turned. The god/esses are called "Yule-wights," for their might is greatest at this time.

During the nights of Yule, the doors between the worlds are open. Wodan's Wild Hunt and the Perchtenlauf both ride at this time, and the dead walk freely in the land of the living. For this reason, we give worship especially to our kin who have gone before us, for they stand unseen about our hearth.

Putting greenery of all sorts up inside the house is an *ur*-old heathen tradition—the holly and fir or pine embody the might of the soul which lives through the winter. Although yew is very fitting as Yule greenery, you must be careful if you have small children in the house, because both the berries and the leaves are extremely poisonous. The same precautions should be taken with mistletoe and holly to keep children or pets from eating their berries.

The stocking full of gifts is part of heathen tradition; accounts of the guest who comes in the night to fill it are different in different areas. The two most favored bringers of gifts are Frau Holda (or Berchta) and Father Thunar. The stockings should be put up on Mother-Night. They can be filled on whichever night of the Yule season you think is most fitting—Mother-Night, Yule proper, Twelfth Night, or even the Christian Christmas—for Frau Holda and Father Thunar are abroad for the whole of the season.

Mother-Night

The first night of Yule, Mother-Night, is hallowed to Frija, Frowe Holda (or Berchta), and the idises.

On the day before the day of the solstice, the family/kindred should make a wreath from holly, ivy, evergreen branches, fruit, and nuts (see Crafts for full instructions). Each person should write his/her wish for the coming year in red runes on a strip of paper, which is then to be woven into the wreath. The ring-shape shows the rings of the Middle-Garth and the Ases' Garth; it is also the holy oath-ring and the wheel of the Sun, which will be burned at dawn at the end of Yule's last night. The wreath should be hung above the hearth or wherever you hang your stockings, or else laid upon the harrow. It will stay where you have put it until the sunrise ending Twelfth Night.

The Mother-Night rite should be worked by the frowe of the household or by one of the women of the kindred, even if there is no chosen godwoman. The part of the Father should be played by the fro of the house or by the kindred godwo/man (if there is one); the Child should be either the youngest or eldest child in the family or else the youngest member of the kindred. The Mother-Night ritual takes place at sunset. It can be worked as a solitary rite at need, with the worker simply speaking all of the parts and leaving out the distribution of presents.

Tools: Blessing-bowl; a bowl from your kitchen; a horn of ale; enough whole milk[6] to fill the kitchen bowl; and a small gift, perhaps a cookie or an ornament, for each person to hang on the Yule tree (given out before the rite). It is best if you can actually get a spindle which is wound full of spun yarn; otherwise, you should have some symbol that the work of the year has been fully wrought, and a skein or ball of yarn which you have wound yourself. The Mother should be dressed in either dark blue or white, with a symbolic whip (perhaps as simple as a piece of string tied to a broom handle) stuck through her belt. She should have a bag with a present for each person who will be there.

The MOTHER calls the folk into a ring about the harrow or hearth by rapping on it three times with the handle of her whip.

MOTHER: *Come swiftly in, as the day is darkening!*
Come to the harrow (hearth), heart of our hold!
Kinfolk all, I call you round.

(She takes the skein of yarn from the harrow and strings it deosil around the gathered folk, saying as she does,)

Frija weave   the web of frith,
frowe of   our highest home.
Mother's work   weave children safe,
of our kin   key-keeper bright.

(She twists the end of the yarn back into the skein and lays the yarn on the harrow again, careful not to disturb the ring.)

Idises, I call,   ur-mothers dear,
Come to our kindred's hold.
Frija, I call,   frith-weaver wise,
Come to our kindred's hold.
Frau Holda, I call,   holy and bright,
Come to our kindred's hold!
Now the year's work is done—

Wound is the spindle, stilled the loom.
The bread is baked for the feast.

FATHER: *Now the year's work is done—*
The beasts are in byre, the harvest brought home.
The farmers come in from the field.

CHILD: *Now the year's work is done—*
The apples are picked, the goose is plucked.
Tonight is the time to feast!

(The MOTHER fills the horn with ale and lifts it high.)

MOTHER: *Hallowed women of the home,*
I raise the horn to you.
Frau Holda, riding forth this night,
Look kindly on our home,
Berchta, beldame of the wheel,
Spin us good wyrds to come.
Frija, who winds the distaff full,
Fill our house with joy.

(She drinks and passes the horn around. Each drinks in turn, hailing Frija, Holda, Berchta, or the idises. The MOTHER pours what is left into the blessing bowl, tracing an outward spiral like the winding of thread upon its surface. She then calls each of the FOLK by name. When each steps forward, the MOTHER gives him/her a light tap with the whip in her left hand, saying "That for the year's woe—may it wane in the year to come." She then draws that person's present out of the bag with her right hand and gives it to him/her, saying, "That for the year's weal—may it wax in the year to come." When all have returned to their places, she pours the milk into the kitchen bowl.)

MOTHER: *Now you shall bring forth your gifts.*

(Each of the FOLK lays his/her Yule ornament on the harrow for a moment and dips a finger into the bowl of milk, saying, "To the Mothers." When all have done this, go together to the Yule tree and hang the gifts upon it. The MOTHER winds up her skein, then takes the two bowls and leads everyone outside, where she pours the ale out on the earth and sets the bowl of milk beside the main housedoor. If you live in a place where this can be done easily, everyone can then put on a mask and run around making noise in a wild "Perchtenlauf" before coming back to the house.

The milk should be left outside all night. In the morning, a few drops may be sprinkled on whatever or whoever needs to be blessed; the remainder is given to children and/or animals to drink, or else poured out on the earth where you poured the ale the night before).

Dramatic Yule Rite

The chief feast of Yule takes place on the night of the solstice— the darkest night of the year. If the Yule tree was not fully adorned the day of Mother-Night, any remaining decorations should be put on in the course of Yule day.

This rite is divided into three parts: sunset, midnight, and sunrise. It is not needful for any single person to stay awake the night through, but someone should be awake at all times, both to watch and ward the kindred and to make sure that the Yule candle or fire does not set the house aflame.

Ideally you should be using a Yule log. However, since not many houses have a fireplace large enough to hold a log that will burn continuously all night, a 24-hour Yule candle will do as a symbolic replacement.

The Harrow should be set up with the Yule candle (black or dark green) in the middle, ringed with evergreen branches. If you have no log, this candle must be large enough to burn the whole night through. On the Harrow should lie a boar made out of bread, the kindred horn or cup, the blessing bowl, blessing twig, and hallowed sax.

This rite can be carried out by workers of either gender in either part. The Sunset and Sunrise parts can be performed by a single person speaking both parts at need; I include an alternate Midnight for solo workers. If your kindred has no one who is personally close to Wodan, you may wish to use the solo Midnight ritual rather than the dramatic, simply subsituting "we" and "us" for "I" and "me."

Sunset

(Hammer-Hallowing)

WODANSGODWO/MAN: *Sunna sinks down   into the
dark sea
wolf and wind howl   outside the walls
now Holda shakes   out her snowy bed
now are life-fires   hid in yew-night.
From Thrymheim Skadhi,   shadow-black, skis
Wodan's gray steed   leads ghosts on the wind
trolls fare from cliff-halls   harry from rock-caves
the etins arising   from ice and stone.
Ye who would watch   this night, ward ye well!*

WANAGODWO/MAN: *Sunna sinks down   into the dark
sea* (She lays hands on the holy boar)
*But Gullinbursti   gleams bright in the hall.
Well are we warded   who watch this night
by boar tusk's thrusting   by Thunar's strength.
In this high hall   stand all holy kin,
from sib-roots to branches   runs hidden fire.
Thunar's stark hammer   this hall has hallowed
Alfs and idises   the dark and light kin
Fro Ing and Frowe   share now frith and might!*

TOGETHER: (lighting the Yule candle) *We kindle the yew-
flame to year's Yule-night!* (If you have an actual fire
laid, it should be lit at this time.)

(WANAGODWO/MAN comes forth. She refills the horn.)

WANAGODWO/MAN: *Now feast in highest   and hallowed frith
Our joy to gods   we give this night
that while worlds sleep   they wax in main
from midnight growing   greater ever towards dawn.*

(WANAGODWO/MAN makes the sign of the sun-wheel
over the horn and passes it thrice deosil around the flame of the

Yule candle. She drinks and passes it deosil to the FOLK, each of whom should think silently on some side of their being which they wish to wax in might. A little ale should be left in the horn by the time it reaches her again.)

> WANAGODWO/MAN: *So shall it be!* (She pours the ale into the blessing bowl, hallowing it with the runes ing-waz (◇)—berkano (ᛒ)—jera (ᚼ) and the signs of the walknot, Hammer, and sun-wheel, then bears it in silence to pour it out at the roots of the Yule tree, not speaking till she stands before the harrow again.

> WANAGODWO/MAN: *Give your gifts   in good and joy,*
> *Then shall the feast begin!*

> FOLK: *Hail!*

(The FOLK then exchange Yule presents. If you have a large kindred or unexpected guests, you may want to have a basket of apples and cakes out so that whoever came unprepared will have something to give everyone else).

Midnight

WANAGODWO/MAN stands in the center with the FOLK ringed (or half-circle) around her. The WODANSGODWO/MAN shall be hidden in the darkness somewhere outside the circle.

> WANAGODWO/MAN: *Now Sunna stands   in her lowest stead*
> *Lost is all light   sleeping all life*
> *the hoar-cold wights   have icy rule.*
> *We hail the might   that howls now from north.*
> *Wuldor, from Yew-Dales   at Yule-tide haring,*
> *Shield-god, ward us   with thy strong bow*
> *Wuldor-might shining   in winter sky*
> *banners bright cast   to burn through the dark.*
> *Now Sunna stands   in her lowest stead*
> *lost is all light   sleeping all life.*
> *Etin-Skadhi   skis from the north*

Huntress, give us   thy holy rede
Where wrong is wrought   wreak thou revenge
as with thy weapons   weregild thou won.
Frowe's might hold us   here in our garth.
Fro Ing's might   hold us in frith.
All of ye gods   and goddesses high,
from darkness we hail ye   from dragon-deep roots
where Sunna fares   forth through the waters
her shining shield   shall ward us still
lead us through darkness   through all dire dooms.

(A moment of silence. The WODANSGODWO/MAN begins to drum in a triple rhythm, slowly and softly. When he feels the moment, he gives a wolf's howl.)

WANAGODWO/MAN: *Who waits without   the walls of*
    the garth
who, wolfish, runs   and wanders dark roads
when hidden is Sunna's   shining might?
when dead men fare   on dire wind-ways?

WODANSGODWO/MAN:(coming to the northern edge
    of the circle)
I, who have walked   in the dragon's dark ways,
Who wisdom have won,   in the howes-of-the-home,
the ghosts fare behind me   grim the gray spirits
ride on the wind   in my wild train
we hunt over hilltops   and howl through the pines
where the mad storm   whirls the hanged men.
Do you know me,   ye kin in this garth?

WANAGODWO/MAN: *Our oldest hold   in howe-mounds*
    high
from Bairn-stock's roots   rise kin this night.
Well do we know you   Wanderer dark
ancestor old   of Ase and man.
First of our kin   come within the garth's walls!

(The WANAGODWO/MAN opens her arms, as if opening a door. The WODANSGODWO/MAN steps within, carrying a horn of mead or hard cider.)

WODANSGODWO/MAN: *I bring the wisdom from Well's deep roots,*
I bring the runes   that roar in the mead,
up from the Bairnstock's   eldest roots.
Your kin who have fared   forth, come in with me,
Drink with them, hallowing   draught to the gods!

(He makes the sign of the Walknot over the horn.)
Hail to Wodan   wisdom's drighten
Sig in our strife send this year!

(The horn is passed deosil and all drink, either repeating his toast or saying, *Hail to Thunar thurses' bane / In my might and main I trust!* The Wanagodwo/man pours what is left into the blessing bowl and refills the horn.)

WANAGODWO/MAN: *Hail Fro Ing   frith's mighty god,*
High be the harvest this year!
Hail to Njordhr with holy drink,
Winds blow well to us this year!

(The horn is passed deosil; all repeat the toast. WANA-GODWO/MAN pours what is left into the bowl and refills the horn; both put their hands on it and speak.)

WODANSGODWO/MAN: *Hail to the alfs   all ringed around us,*
the fathers of our folk.

WANAGODWO/MAN: *Hail the idises   all ringed around us,*
the mothers of our might.

WODANSGODWO/MAN: *Hail our kin   in hidden lands*
Hail the Yule-wights high!

(First the WODANSGODWO/MAN, then each of the FOLK makes a toast to a dead kinswo/man; the WANAGODWO/MAN makes the last toast and empties the horn into the blessing bowl. She lifts the holy bread-boar.)

WANAGODWO/MAN: *At Wyrd's great well   we all are met,*
>   *where the gods gather to deem.*
>   *Now by the boar's holy   bristles swear oaths—*
>   *Deeds you shall do this year.*

(Each of the FOLK, beginning with the WODANS-GODWO/MAN, puts a hand upon the boar's back and swears an oath beginning *By the bristles of the boar, I swear...* When the WANAGODWO/MAN has made her own oath, she takes the sax into her right hand and says:)

>   *Now bear our words   to god-world high,*
>   *thou golden boar   glitter oaths on your back.*
>   *All we have sworn   swiftly you'll bear*
>   *our oaths must shape   what shall soon be.*

(The WANAGODWO/MAN slits the boar's throat and holds it over the blessing bowl, then chops the boar's head off and crumbles it in. She takes the blessing-twig and sprinkles the harrow, the eight ættir, and each of the FOLK in turn. The full bowl is left upon the harrow, where it will stay until sunrise. The WANA-GODWO/MAN carries the boar about deosil, each of the FOLK eating a piece. Any leftovers should be placed on the harrow beside the blessing bowl.)

WANAGODWO/MAN: *So it is wrought.*

ALL: *So it is wrought.*

Midnight (Alternate; for Solo Worker)

The room is dark except for the Yule candle.

WORKER: *Now Sunna stands   in her lowest stead,*
>   *lost is all light   all life is asleep,*
>   *the hoar-cold wights   have icy rule.*
>   *I hail the might   that howls now from North,*
>   *Wuldor, from Yew-Dales   at Yule-tide haring,*
>   *Shield-Ase, ward me   with thy strong bow.*

Wuldor-might shining   in winter sky,
banners cast bright   to burn through the dark.
Etin-maid Skadhi   skis from the north,
Huntress, give to me   thy holy rede.
Where wrong is wrought   wreak thou revenge,
as with thy weapons   weregild thou won.
Frowe's might hold me   here in my garth,
Fro Ing's boar-strength   in frith hold me yet.
All of ye blessed   Yule-wights high,
From darkness I hail ye   from dragon-deep roots,
where Sunna fares   forth through dark waters,
her shining shield   shall ward me aye.
lead me through darkness   and dire dooms all.

(Pause, listening to the sound of the wind till you can hear voices and the howling of wolves down it.)

Now Wodan rides   in the Wild Hunt
leading the ghosts,   gray, down the wind.
My oldest hold   in howe-mounds high,
from Bairn-Stock's roots   rise kin this night.
Well do I know   the Wanderer old,
eldest the father   of Ase and man,
wisest of kin   Wodan, I hail thee!

(The WORKER pours the horn full of mead or hard cider.)

Wisdom rising   from Well's deep roots,
Runes of might   roar in the mead,
up from the Bairn-Stock's   eldest roots.
My kin who have fared   forth, come to me,
I drink with you, hallowing   draught to the gods!

(Make the sign of the Walknot over the horn, saying, "Hail to Wodan   wisdom's drighten / Sig in my strifes send this year" or else make the sign of the Hammer, saying, "Hail to Thunar thurses' bane / In my might and main I trust." Drink; pour some into the blessing bowl; refill the horn.)

Hail to Fro Ing   frith's mighty god,
*   High be the harvest this year.*

> *Hail to Njördhr   with holy drink,*
>   *Winds blow well for me this year.*

(Drink; pour a draught into the bowl; refill the horn.)

> *Hail to the alfs   all ringed around me,*
>   *the fathers of my folk.*
> *Hail the idises   all ringed around me,*
>   *the mothers of my might.*
> *Hail my kin   in hidden lands*
>   *Hail the Yule-wights high!*

(Here, if you choose, you may make one or several toasts to a specific dead kinswo/man. When you are done with this, empty the horn into the blessing-bowl. Lift the holy boar high.)

> *To Wyrd's wide-flowing   well, I've come,*
>   *where the gods gather to deem.*
> *Now by the boar's holy   bristles I swear*
>   *The oath I'll fulfill this year.*

(Put one hand on the boar's back and swear your oath.)

> *Now bear my words   to god-world high,*
> *thou golden boar   my oath gleams on your back.*
> *All I have sworn   swiftly you'll bear*
> *my oath must shape   what shall soon be.*

(Slit the boar's throat and hold it over the blessing bowl. Take the blessing-twig and sprinkle the harrow, the *ættir*, and yourself.)

> *So it is wrought.*

Sunrise

(The WODANSGODWO/MAN carries the Yule candle; the WANAGODWO/MAN carries the blessing bowl and the remains of the boar. If you used a Yule log, you should light a candle to carry out from its flame. Together they lead the folk outside and stand facing eastward.)

WODANSGODWO/MAN: *Our Yule-glow   that gleamed all night,*
   now kindles the keen fire.
   Sunna's flame   flares bright again,
   upon the heavens' hearth.

(He blows out the candle in the direction of the sunrise)

WANAGODWO/MAN: *Sunna's fire   flares bright again,*
   the darkest night is done,
   the holy gifts are given.

(She digs a small hole in the earth and buries the boar, then pours the contents of the blessing bowl over it.)

BOTH: *Hail the gods and the goddesses! Hail the Yule morn!*

ALL: *Hail the gods and the goddesses! Hail the Yule morn!*

Twelfth Night (New Year's Eve)

Twelfth Night should be, as is traditional everywhere, marked by feasting, partying, and the making of lots and lots of noise at midnight. The Yule-Wreath should still be hung where everyone can see it—by this time, it ought to be very dry and able to burn nicely. It is not needful for anyone to keep a full night's vigil, but someone ought to be awake at all times. The rite itself is held at sunrise.

In the Christian calendar, Twelfth Night is actually held on January sixth. This is because the Yule festivities were displaced to December 25 for Christmas; thus the Christian "holy nights" are several days behind the heathen season.

Tools: Yule wreath (and a safe place to burn it where flying sparks cannot catch anything else on fire), matches or other fire-lighter, one bottle of high-alcohol drink (100 proof or better—I recommend Rumpleminze Peppermint Schnapps), horn.
Time: Sunrise.

GODWO/MAN: *Now go all ghosts   to grave-holds dark,*
  etins fare back to East.
Sunna has won   her way through the night
  and we yet live in this world.
Drink we and hail   the high ones once more,
  with wish-words for this year.

(The GODWO/MAN fills the horn with the drink, makes a toast hailing his/her chosen god/ess for a gift in the year to come, drinks, and passes the horn deosil. When it has made the round, he/she pours the rest of the alcohol over the Yule wreath.)

GODWO/MAN: *New is the year   new is the day,*
  Sun-wheel, burn in the sky!

(He/she sets it on fire. The FOLK clap, cheer, blow on noise-makers, and are generally rowdy until the wreath has burned away.)

GODWO/MAN: *Go forth in might   gods' blessing on all,*
  The new year has begun.

FEAST OF THUNAR

The Feast of Thunar takes place in January. The Sun is waxing in strength at this time, but the cold is also getting stronger—mid-January to mid-February is the true peak of winter. Thus, at the Feast of Thunar, we hail the Thunderer for driving back the darkness, but we also need to call on his aid to protect us against the rime-thurses (frost giants) whose might grows with the cold and who are no friends to humans. In this icy and miserable time of the year, we also need to be strengthened by the fire of Thunar's courage and the thunder of his laughter as he reminds us that our bravery, might, and strength—his children Módhi, Magni, and Thrúdhr—are enough to see us through all the trials of the winter.

Tools: Hammer; horn; three hornfulls of ale; blessing bowl; oak twig; candle; goat cheese molded about a wire skeleton or framework in the shape of a goat, or else a goat-costume for the designated Goat, who hides a quantity of goat cheese beneath his hide.

Workers: GODWO/MAN, GOAT, and FOLK or single GODWO/MAN. This rite may be performed solo simply by replacing "we" with "I" at appropriate points and having the performer speak all parts.

Hammer-Hallowing

(GODWO/MAN, still with the Hammer in both hands, swings it upward and around the circle, finally facing east.)

GODWO/MAN: *Fierce are the rime-thurses   frost's wildest sons*
all beating against   bare Middle-Garth's holds.
Where is the warder   'gainst winter's rough kin?

ALL: *Thunar, Thunar!   Thunderer, we call!*

(GODWO/MAN swings the Hammer around deosil.)

GODWO/MAN: *Etins and trolls   are waiting without*
where draugs ride the roof-tops   in darkness of day.
Where is the warder   'gainst wights dark and dead?

ALL: *Thunar, Thunar!   Thunderer, we call!*

(GODWO/MAN swings the Hammer deosil.)

GODWO/MAN: *And Loki within   leaps up to betray*
fiery etin   to eat the house-walls
Who shall hold house-pillars   hallowed and whole?

ALL: *Thunar, Thunar!   Thunderer, we call!*

(A moment of silence. The GODWO/MAN turns towards the east as if listening, then speaks again, beginning softly and rising louder and louder.)

GODWO/MAN: *Hark! We can hear now   wain's rolling wheels,*
far in the east   in etin-home deep.

Thunar the Warder   wends his way here,
Thunar the Hallower   has heard our call.
Goats' teeth are grinding   goats' teeth are gnashing
Thunar's fierce steeds   wain thunders behind,
Look to the lightning   lashing above them,
Mjollnir is raised by   Earth's mightiest son!
Hail to the hammer!   howl now the thurses,
Thunar is striking   sons of the ice.
Flee shadows from bright   flash of the lightning.

(GODWO/MAN kindles the candle swiftly, holding it over his/her head in one hand and the Hammer over his/her head in the other.)

Hail to Wain-Thunar   Warder of earth!

(The GOAT enters, frisking around and acting goatish for a few minutes; or else GODWO/MAN holds up the cheese-goat.)

GODWO/MAN: *Thunar, we give thee   goat for thy faring*
We mind all your help   for Middle-Garth's wights.
This gift for that good   and good yet to come.

(ALL place hands to the GOAT together, thinking silently of something for which they thank Thunar and something in which they wish his help.)

GODWO/MAN: *So we give thee to Thunar!*

(GODWO/MAN mimes cutting the GOAT's throat and takes the cheese from beneath his hide or divides the model goat into pieces. ALL eat.)

GODWO/MAN: *Tooth-Gnasher,   Tooth-Gritter   though eaten your flesh,*
the Hammer of Thunar   hallows hide and bones
Arise now, thou goat!   Thunar rides in the wain!

(GODWO/MAN swings the hammer thrice deosil over the GOAT, who arises and acts goatlike for a little while longer; otherwise, the cheese "goat" is raised to its feet again.)

GODWO/MAN: *Hail to Thunar!*

ALL: *Hail to Thunar!*

(GODWO/MAN pours the horn full of ale and holds it up. He/she will make the sign of the Hammer each time he/she speaks Thunar's name over the horn.)

GODWO/MAN: *Hail to Thunar   house-pillars' god!*
   Hallower of   all highest things.

(The horn is passed; it should not be quite emptied, but some should be left to pour into the blessing bowl.)

   Hail to Thunar   thurse's stark foe!
   Mjollnir's wielder   thy might and main!

(The horn is refilled, passed, etc.)

   Hail to Thunar   who hallows the fields,
   brightens Sif's hair   brings grain-harvest good!

(The horn is refilled, passed, etc. GODWO/MAN lifts the blessing bowl.)

GODWO/MAN: *Three draughts deep   for Thunar drained,*
   We hail thee, strongest god   hold us through winter long.
   Thy blessings be upon us.

(GODWO/MAN Hammer-signs each of the FOLK and sprinkles them with ale.)

GODWO/MAN: *Now let us feast to Thunar's might!*

(Throughout the night, when each person eats or drinks, they must drop a little food and some of their drink into the blessing bowl. At the end of the feast, the GODWO/MAN should pour it out.)

GODWO/MAN: *Thunar, our thanks   have, Thunderer, ever.*
Hail to Thunar high!

CHARMING OF THE PLOUGH

This feast, also known as Disting (the Thing or Meeting of the Idises), takes place at the beginning of planting season when the days are getting longer and longer. It marks the beginning of the end of the winter's stillness and rest. At this time, the frozen earth is just beginning to thaw and to be broken by the might of Fro Ing so that she can bring forth new life. This is the earthly meaning of the Eddic poem "Skírnismál." Fro Ing sends his messenger Skírnir, "the Shining," to woo the etin-maid Gerdhr for him; she refuses his bribes and threats alike until he menaces her with the rune thurisaz ("thurse" or "giant") and its magical threat of rape by one of these elemental beings. Then Gerdhr agrees to meet Fro Ing in nine nights at a certain grove, where they will be wed.

Gerdhr herself, whose name means "enclosure" (cognate to the English "garth"), is the embodiment of the wintry earth; she is an etin, filled with the *ur*-power of her ancient kindred, but unwilling to use that power for weal. Although Fro Ing desires her, she will not let herself be made fruitful. Skírnir is described as "not alf nor Ase nor a wise Wan"; his nature is left unclear. However, he is acting as the plow who breaks the first furrow so that the earth can be planted; we know that the ancient Germanic people believed that humans learned to plow from watching the boar, and the boar is the beast of Fro Ing himself. His own boar is named "Gullinbursti," or "Golden-Bristle," and described as shining: "He might run over air and water, night and day better than any horse, and it would never be so mirky at night or in the mirk-worlds that it would not be light wherever he fared; so his bristles shone."[1] It may be, then, that Skírnir is the human personification of Fro Ing's boar; it is to him that Fro Ing gives up sword (the boar's tusk) and horse for the sake of winning Gerdhr. The use of the rune thurisaz (ᚦ) is both the thrust of the boar's tusk which breaks through the frosty earth and the threat of what will happen if she does not allow Fro Ing to warm her: Gerdhr, the "garth" of the world, will be abused by the rime-thurses who embody the most woe-working aspects of winter. At the end, she gives him a "hrimkalkr," which means "crystal cup" but is literally an "ice-chalice" full of mead; Fro Ing's messenger is welcome in the etin's hall as her ice begins to melt. The "nine nights" is a magical measure of time, signifying the delay between the breaking of the first farrow and the celebration of the feast of Ostara, where the god is finally united with the spring maiden.

Like many of the poems in the *Elder Edda*, the poem "Skírnismál" may have been originally created as the script for a ritual drama, its interspersed prose being a rendition of the directions for the actors and the poetry itself being the part spoken. If your group is large enough to make it feasible, this piece may either be performed before or after the "Charming of the Plough" ritual, or else subsituted for the part of the ritual between "As Wodan the drighten deemed" and the entrance of the BEGGAR.

The basic text for "Charming of the Plough" comes from an Anglo-Saxon charm spell. As it was originally written down, the spell mixes Christian and heathen elements with blithe thoroughness; I have attempted to restore it to something bearing more closeness to a theoretical heathen original.

Tools: One plow (real or model)/shovel/roto-tiller or whatever you use to turn the earth in your garden, four sun-crosses (equal-armed) made of aspen wood if possible, oil, honey, yeast, milk, part of every kind of tree growing on your lands or in your general area except for oak and alder, part of every herb, etc. except for burdock, four sods of turf cut from your yard, water drawn from a running spring or river, a loaf roughly the size of the palm of your hand, baked with flour of three different grains, milk, and the hallowed water, recels ("incense"), fennel, soap, and salt. Each person participating should also bring a packet of seeds. In addition, you will need "unknown seeds"; this can be achieved by having two or three people bring seeds and mixing them without telling the others what has been brought, so that no one will know everything in the mixture. If you have no yard to charm, a similar effect may be achieved by setting four potted plants at North, South, East, and West, and making the furrow in the earth of the easterly one. Likewise, if you have no running spring or river nearby, the water of a running tap is not nearly as good, but it will do at need if you strongly visualize a running stream while you draw it.

Workers: GODWO/MAN, BEGGAR, FOLK. This rite may be performed solo simply by having the GODWO/MAN read all parts and leaving out the section with the BEGGAR altogether.

At dawn on the day of the rite, the GODWO/MAN should take the four sods from four sides of the land. Then at dawn take the oil, honey, yeast, milk, and the parts of the trees and herbs, and pour the water on them, and let it drip three times on the bottom of the sods while saying, "Wax and become manyfold, and fill the earth." Then set the sods on the harrow with the green sides down.

Take the four sun-crosses and carve the runes on them thus: on the one which will lie in the east, the name FRO ING; on the one which will lie in the south, FROWE; on the westerly one, NJÖRDHR; on the northerly one, NERTHUZ. While the runes of each are being carved and colored, the FOLK shall stand about in a circle chanting the name for each. This may be done either inside or outside.

If the carving was done inside, ALL shall go out and stand in a ring about the yard. The GODWO/MAN shall take the sun-crosses and put them where the sods were taken, and then lay the sods back over them, saying:

> *Wax, with the blessings of Fro Ing. Wax, with the blessings of the Frowe. Wax, with the blessings of Njördhr. Wax, with the blessings of Nerthus.*

The GODWO/MAN shall then turn to the east and say,

> *Eastward I stand, for favors I ask,*
> *I bid the mighty Fro Ing, I bid the mickle drighten,*
> *I bid the holy Heavens'-Warder,*
> *and the Frowe, most fair and true,*
> *and the heavens' might and high hall,*
> *that I may this galdor, with Wodan's gift,*
> *well through my firm will speak,*
> *wax up these crops, to our worldly good,*
> *fill this earth with fast troth,*
> *make fair these farmlands, as the wise one said,*

and that one shall have weal on earth,
who deals it out well, as Wodan our drighten deemed.

(The GODWO/MAN shall then turn three times deosil and stretch himself out along the ground. At this point, the one chosen to play the BEGGAR shall slip away, putting on rags and getting the handful of "unknown seeds.")

GODWO/MAN: *What ails Fro Ing   where does he wait,*
   the world's well-known god?
Long is the winter   but lighter the days
   though fetters of frost be harsh.
His eyes light on   the etin-maid
   in longing and in love
But Gymir's daughter   Gerdhr is icy,
   and hard as stone her heart.

FOLK: *Who will come   to woo the maid,*
   to free the frozen earth?

GODWO/MAN: *The shining hero   shall ride bright,*
   Boar-tusk break the sod.
Then the rime-cup   shall be raised,
   ice melt to brimming mead.

FOLK: *Weal and blessing   be to the land,*
   Weal to the wights within.

GODWO/MAN: *Hail the shining one   hero of day!*
   Nine nights the wedding hence.

FOLK: *Weal and blessing   be to the land,*
   Weal to the wights within.

GODWO/MAN: *Hail Fro Ing   and etin-maid,*
   betrothed for bright dayspring.

FOLK: *Weal and blessing   be to the land,*
   Weal to the wights within.

(The GODWO/MAN raises hands and head towards the east, spreading his/her feet widely at the same time. This is the cue for the BEGGAR to come out, his/her face shadowed by a cloak. He/she speaks in a cracked voice.)

> BEGGAR: *Atheling-fros, good frowes, what have you got to give me? It's cold on the roads, yes, the winds are cold at winter's end and the earth is frosty. What can you give an old beggar-man (or "beggar-woman")?*

> GODWO/MAN: *What have you brought with you on the wet wilderness ways? You are far from house and hall; the fetters of ice have locked earth to you. Yet a gift aye asks for a gift; what do you hold?*

> BEGGAR: *Atheling-fros, good frowes, I carry seeds, very good seeds, gathered on the many ways.*

> GODWO/MAN: *What manner of seeds does a beggar bring? From what stem are they sprung; what shall spring forth from them?*

> BEGGAR: *The roots from which they rose are unknown, but weal shall spring forth, as Wyrd has turned it.*

> GODWO/MAN: *Then give us the seeds, and take our own in turn.*

(The BEGGAR distributes unknown seeds to the GODWO/MAN and each of the FOLK, who in turn give him/her at least twice as much as they got.)

> BEGGAR: *Now the gods and goddesses bless you all! May the dwellers in Wan-Home and the Ase's Garth look upon you with friendly eyes, and your planting bring harvests of weal.*

> GODWO/MAN: *May the gods and goddesses bless your faring, and bless the seeds you bear with you.*

(The BEGGAR turns and goes away with the seeds, which he/she hides before taking off the costume and returning to the FOLK. Meanwhile, the GODWO/MAN bores a hole in the tail of the plow and puts the recels, fennel, hallowed soap, and hallowed salt in it.)

GODWO/MAN: *Now set your seed upon the plow.*

(As the FOLK do this, he/she continues to speak.)

> *Erce, Erce, Erce, earthen mother,*
> *may the god of the world give you*
> *fields waxing in weal*
> *shining shafts of millet-crops*
> *and of the broad barley-crops,*
> *and of the white wheat-crops*
> *and of all the crops of the earth.*
> *Give these the eternal drighten*
> *and the holy ones of the heavens,*
> *Keep the harvest in frith, against all foes*
> *and hold it against every harm*
> *which witchcraft may sow through the land.*
> *Now I bid the ruler who shaped the world*
> *That no woman be so speech-strong, no man so crafty,*
> *That they may wend away the words thus spoken.*

(The GODWO/MAN drives forth the plow, cutting the furrow from east to west.)

> ALL: *Hail to thee, earth, mother of men,*
> *May you be fruitful, warded by Fro Ing,*
> *Filled with food for the need of all.*

(The GODWO/MAN passes around the cake. All lay their hands on it, filling it with their thanks and prayers. The GODWO/MAN lays the cake under the furrow.)

> *Field full of food for human-kin,*
> *brightly blooming, blessed be thou,*
> *In the holy names of the heavenly gods,*

and gods of the earth where we dwell.
Fro and Frowe, Nerthus, Njördhr,
Grant us the gift of this growing,
that each grain may fill our need.
Hail the gods and the goddesses!

FOLK: *Hail the gods and the goddesses!*

GODWO/MAN: *Hail the all-giving earth!*

FOLK: *Hail the all-giving earth!*

GODWO/MAN: *So it is wrought.*

EOSTRE

The Ostara season is the brightest and most joyful of the Teutonic year. It is at this time that we celebrate the victory of Thunar over the rime-thurses, of the Sun over the wolves that follow her, and of Summer over Winter. At the feast of Ostara, we hail the gods and goddesses for bringing us alive through the winter and for a good season to come.

This feast takes its name from the goddess Eostre (Old High German Ostara), of whom little is known, except that she must have been a goddess of spring, fertility, rebirth, and the rising sun; her name is etymologically connected with both the east and with a word for "shining; glorious." Her might was so strong in the souls of the Anglo-Saxons that even the Christian conversion was not able to extirpate her name from the holy year; Bede recounts that the Christian Paschal feast was called Eostre after the heathen goddess Eostre, and so this celebration is still named Easter among the Christians.

The name Ostara/Eostre does not seem to have been known in the Scandinavian countries, but the feast at the beginning of summer was still celebrated as the sigrblót, or blessing for victory. With the planting all done and the harvest most of a season away, this feast marked the beginning of the time when battles could be fought and glory won, while the seeds planted in the fields at home were growing.

The symbol which modern culture associates most thoroughly with Easter, the egg, goes back to heathen times. Painted clay eggs (white with black and red stripes) were found in a Germanic cemetery in Worms (ca. 320 CE) as part of a child's burial goods. The egg is, of course, one of the mightiest symbols of new life, fertility, and "good luck." It should be noted that among modern Germans today, "Eier" or "eggs" is still a slang term for a man's testicles. In the Norse-settled islands north of Scotland (the Orkneys and Shetlands), it was the custom to rub a bull's testes before going out to gather eggs from the cliffs, saying, "I rub the bull's eggs, and I get the gull's eggs . . . " The bird's eggs and the other generative organs (ovaries may be assumed as well as testicles) hold the same store of *aldri* and *hamingja*; they are the very source of life. In Sweden, eggs were thrown over the field during plowing, and in Germany, they were hurled in the air before the sowing began "to ensure that the grain would grow as high."[8]

In the Orkneys and Shetlands there were certain traditions concerning the Easter eggs. On several days during the Easter season, "Boys went around . . . with a mitten begging eggs and would get one or two from each family . . . On Sunday a lot of them lit a fire in the hills and boiled their eggs near some plain green, threw up their eggs to see which ones would be longest unbroken, and then ate them." On the Orkney island of Rousay, "children were always given eggs to eat. Well-off families encouraged each child to eat as many as it could; in poorer families children often had to share an egg."[9]

This belief in the might of eggs eaten at Ostara time also appears in Germany. In Oldenburg it is said that a weak man should "eat a few more Easter eggs" and a 17th-century Rhineland source quotes the local proverb, "Auf Ostern iss hart gesotene Eyer, dann bist du das gantze Jahr gesundt"—At Easter eat hard-boiled eggs, then you'll be healthy the whole year.[10] This is particularly so if the egg is eaten just before sunrise on Ostara, which will ward off illness.

The custom of "Pace-egging" or Paschal-egging, in which the performers of the Easter mummers'-plays went around in costume, begging for eggs before the play, was part of Lancastershire tradition. In the north of England, colored eggs were rolled down slopes on Easter Monday, "and at Chester cathedral the bishop and the dean are said to have engaged in an egg-throwing match with the choir boys when the antiphon *Quem quaeritis* was sung on Easter day."[11] In Heidelberg, schoolchildren would go about singing "Winter heraus / Sommer herein!" (Winter out / Summer in!) and be given pretzels and eggs. In German Moravia, after the children had carried an effigy representing Death out of the town, they would beg for eggs "as payment for carrying away Death."[12]

The Ostara hunt for the egg is also an originally German tradition. In South Germany, the eggs were deliberately put in a place where the children looking for them would be stung by nettles or scratched by thorns before they were able to reach them. This, like the mock switchings or beatings with green branches which are also common at Ostara time, symbolizes the awakening of the soul through the prick of the thorn—the bright counterpart to the dark "sleep-thorn" of Norse legend. Likewise, the Easter hare or bunny is a German tradition; German children still build nests for this creature to lay its eggs in. A rich buttery bread, decorated with almonds or currants, is often baked in the shape of a hare. It is not certain how this tradition originated, except that hares and rabbits are fairly obvious symbols of fertility.

One of the chief Ostara traditions which has survived in modern Germanic culture is the coloring and painting of eggs at this season. This, as far as I can tell, is only done in Germanic countries, Slavic countries, and America. In Scotland and Ireland the custom is virtually unknown and the feast passes with little remark. During my stay in Scotland, I had to make my own dyes out of beets (red), onions (yellow, sort of), and food coloring. No one there, except for the other students from America and England, had ever heard of painting eggs for Easter! In Germany, on the other hand, the bakery windows were filled with the most beautifully and elaborately painted eggs, which were hung on flowering branches to make "egg trees." Easter is celebrated there more enthusiastically than it is anywhere else in the world; the Germans seem to love this festival as dearly as they love their Weihnachten ("Holy Nights" or Yule/Christmas) celebrations. The German Easter decorations went up a good month before the festival was due, and friends with whom I was staying there told me that they would often have parties, egg hunts, and so forth weeks in advance of Easter itself. It was even possible to buy pre-colored hard-boiled eggs in all the stores at that time.

The artistic and careful decoration of the eggshells and their preservation ofter the Ostara feast becomes even more significant when one considers that all over Germany, the Easter eggs or shells were kept all year to ward the family and cattle against harm. These eggs were also used very specifically as a charm against hail and lightning.

The eggs for Ostara can either be hard-boiled or the innards blown out and the eggs hung up, as in the German egg trees. In Denmark, such eggs are strung together to make garlands which are put on the roofs of houses, schools, and churches. This can be done as much as a month before the actual Ostara rite is held, whenever it seems that winter is starting to end and summer to begin. Directions for making and coloring such eggs, together with a few traditional patterns, can be found in Chapter 17: Crafts.

A custom which recalls earlier fertility rites was also carried out in the north of England. On Easter Monday and Tuesday, groups of women would surround any man they came across and "heave" him three times over their heads, then sprinkle him with water and kiss him. The next day, the men would do the same thing to the women. This may go back to the name-giving rite in which the newborn was lifted up and sprinkled with water, and at which time he/she could also be given "luck" and surrounded with magical protection, as described in the runic section of "Hávamál": "I ken that thirteenth if a young thane I shall / throw (hallowed) water upon, / he will not fall though to war he goes / nor shall the hero sink before blades" (158). Since Ostara is the time of rebirth, that springing might can be used so that the community can bless its folk as if they, too, were reborn.

In several rural villages in Germany, a spring drama is still carried out in which a straw figure representing Winter is beaten and burned or drowned, after which Summer is enthroned. This forms the basic structure of the Ostara dramatic ritual which I present here. Some of the Eddic poems, most notably "Svipdagsmál" and perhaps also "Sigrdrífumál," are also likely to have been spring dramas. The basic plot of this is thus: a hero, disguised as an outlaw, troll, or such *útlanding*, goes into Etin-Home to seek a bride, who dwells (or sleeps) on top of a mountain ringed about with fire. He meets with a giant who wards the way to the maiden's mound. This giant, who may be the maiden's brother or other close kinsman, but in any case represents the might of Winter, challenges the hero. They fight and the hero slays or subdues the giant, then continues through the ring of flames where the maiden greets him as her beloved. This drama, to which I present a script adapted from "Svipdagsmál" and "Sigrdrífumál," can be carried out on the evening before the sunrise rite or else worked into it, if you choose to write your own ritual.

There is no specific date on which the Ostara feast must be held. The three mightiest times at this turning of the year are the equinox itself and the new and full moons following the equinox. It is probably better in general to celebrate Ostara during the waxing moon.

Spring Drama

Players:

SVIPDAG (the hero, whose name means "swift day"). He is clad in tunic and breeches of white, gold, and/or light blue, which are hidden beneath a dark cloak with a hood that also cloaks his face. In his hand he holds a stag's antler.

FJOLSVITH (an etin). A large and frightening figure, shaggy, dressed in dark and wintry clothing. Possibly snowflakes may be attached to his garb to symbolize his role as Winter. He is armed with a spear, with which he continuously menaces SVIPDAG.

MENGLOTH (the Spring Maiden). She is dressed in a white shift with a belt of gold, which again is covered with a dark cloak. She must wear a splendid necklace; amber and/or gold are ideal, but otherwise it can be made of anything except silver, which is the metal of ice. She has either a clear glass cup or a horn filled with mead.

Set: Ideally, you will have an area with a raised place for MENGLOTH's mound; otherwise, one area should be marked off in some way, perhaps with flames of paper or cloth. MENGLOTH should be lying down in the middle of this, covered completely beneath her cloak. FJOLSVITH stands before the only entrance as a guard, holding his spear to bar the way. SVIPDAG comes to stand before him. As SVIPDAG and FJOLSVITH speak, they raise their weapons and spar slowly, each casting down the other's weapon and menacing him in turn.

> SVIPDAG: *What is that foul wight   who stands before fore-gates*
> *hovers before flickering fire?*

FJOLSVITH: *What led you here   what look you for?*
and what will you, friendless one, know?

SVIPDAG: *Who is that foul wight   who stands before fore-*
gates
and bids not the wanderer welcome?

FJOLSVITH: *I hight Fjolsvith   for wisdom famed,*
but free I am not with my food:
Within the garth   will you never come,
Warg, go now on your way!

SVIPDAG: *I see the garth   with gold gleam bright*
here would I make my home.

FJOLSVITH: *Say to me: of whom   were you, warrior, born,*
and who are your kinsmen all?

SVIPDAG: *Windcold I'm called   Spring-Cold was my sire,*
Very-Cold was his father.
Say to me, Fjolsvith   for I would ask,
and I wish to wit,
Who has rule   and who rules here,
great lands and goodly hall?

FJOLSVITH: *Mengloth she hight   whom her mother got,*
with Svafrthorin's son.
She has rule   and rules here
great lands and goodly hall.

SVIPDAG: *Say to me, Fjolsvith   for I would ask*
and I wish to wit,
what hight the hall   all hedged about
by the flickering flame?

FJOLSVITH: *Lýr it is hight   and long it will*
stand high on sword's point;
of this wealthy hall   have men only
through hearsay ever heard.

SVIPDAG: *Say to me, Fjolsvith   for I would ask,*
and I wish to wit,
what the berg hight   where the bride I see,
the dearest maiden dwells?

FJOLSVITH: *Healing-Mount hight   it has long been*
help for the sick and sore.
whole will be ever   —though hopeless she seems—
the woman who wins its might.

SVIPDAG: *Say to me, Fjolsvith   for I would ask,*
and I wish to wit,
what the maids hight   who before Mengloth's knees
sit as sisters together.

FJOLSVITH: *Hlíf hight the one   Hlífthrasa the second,*
the third is Thiodhvarta,
Bjort and Bleik   Blidh and Fridh,
Eir and Aurbodha.

SVIPDAG: *Say to me, Fjolsvith   for I would ask,*
and I wish to wit,
to those who pour blots   blessings give they,
when they have need of help?

FJOLSVITH: *They give blessings ever   when blots are poured*
standing in holy stead,
there is never a need   that nears a man
but they heed and help.

SVIPDAG: *Say to me, Fjolsvith   for I would ask,*
and I wish to wit,
if to any man   Mengloth will grant
to sleep in her soft arms?

FJOLSVITH: *There is no man   to whom Mengloth grants*
to sleep in her soft arms
except Svipdag alone   to him sunbright bride,
was given for his wife.

(SVIPDAG and FJOLSVITH fight fiercely for a few moments; at last SVIPDAG overcomes FJOLSVITH and presses him to the ground with one hand, casting his own cloak aside with the other.)

> SVIPDAG: *Let gape the gates   and give wide space,*
> > *here may you Svipdag see.*
> > *now fare with in   to find it out,*
> > *if Mengloth gives me love.*

> FJOLSVITH (gestures as throwing gates open; calls within): *Hear thou, Mengloth   a man is come*
> > *go thou to greet the guest.*
> > *the hounds give welcome   the hall-gates unlock*
> > *it seems that Svipdag has come!*

(FJOLSVITH turns away, sinking into his cloak and down to the ground. SVIPDAG treads slowly up towards MENGLOTH where she lies sleeping.)

> SVIPDAG: *Now fare I over   the fire bright*
> > *that shimmers in rainbow-sheen*
> > *upon the mound   the maid to wed*
> > *Mengloth, sun-bright bride!*
> > (He stops before the covered body.)
> > *Still as ice   and stone as death*
> > *no greeting gives me here*
> > *but cold she lies   as corpse in mound,*
> > *the dark time is not done.*

(SVIPDAG raises his weapon, lowering it slowly till the point of a tine touches between her breasts.)

> > *Awake! Awake!   Arise to swift day,*
> > *freed from fetters of ice!*
> > *Awake to my love   too long you have slept,*
> > *in brightness dawns the day!*

(He flings the cloak from her in a single movement. MENGLOTH rises to a sitting position, reaching rapturously out to him.)

MENGLOTH: *Whence fared you forth   from whence came you,*
   how hight my wakener bright?
   Your ætt and name   all must I know,
   before I become your bride.

SVIPDAG: *Svipdag hight I   Solbright hight my father*
   I fared windcold ways to you.
   the words of Wyrd   withstands no man,
   though loathly his lot be.
(Mengloth stands and embraces him. They sing together.)

SVIPDAG and MENGLOTH: *Hail, Day!   Hail, ye day's sons,*
   Hail, Night and the daughter of Night.
   Look down upon us here   with loving eyes,
   Sig grant to those sitting here.
   Hail the Æsir!   hail the Asynjur,
   hail earth who gives at need.
   Goodly speech and human wit   may you grant to we, the mighty,
   and hands of healing, while we live.
   Hail!

MENGLOTH (giving Svipdag the horn or cup of mead):"
   Ale I bring thee   apple of battle,
   well-come within my walls.
   Long I slept   on Lyfja Mount
   and waited through dark days.

   Heartsick I was   to have your love,
   while your mind turned towards me.
   now that is sooth   that Svipdag, we shall
   live together in love.

Dramatic Folk-Rite

Workers: GODWO/MAN; DEATH-BEARER/SPRING BRIDE (must be female).

(The FOLK are gathered around the harrow, on which a fire of nine different kinds of woods is laid, but not lit. Each holds a green switch.)

(Hammer-Hallowing)

GODWO/MAN: *Dark was the winter   and woeful the days*
    Thunar strove hard against thurse.
  Our seeds now are sown   saved through winter's night
    bare now are barn and bin.
  Winter has taken   his woeful toll
    the eater of light and life.
  Let etins and thurses   to east now fare,
    flee, before Sunna's fair light!

(The DEATH-BEARER, cloaked in black and carrying the figure of Winter on a stretcher of dry twigs before her, treads slowly from the north. She stops before the harrow and speaks.)

DEATH-BEARER: *Words will not do   if Winter you'd slay,*
  he still lays fast   his fetters of cold.
  Sig over etins   is harder to grasp,
  Now you should kneel   to know him your fro.

GODWO/MAN: *We shall not kneel   know Winter our fro,*
  this uncouth carl   keeps rule too long!
  Let Summer beat him   lash him from our doors,
  let him not linger   no longer he stays!

(The FOLK all whip Death three times deosil about the harrow, singing and calling out or whispering the names of things they want to be rid of or have ended. The song is:)

  Summer wax   and winter fall
  light the day   to life awake
  sorrows gone   for Summer's king
  Sunna wake   Sig-drightine high!

(The DEATH-BEARER lays Winter on top of the fire and withdraws outside the circle.)

GODWO/MAN: *Winter is dead!   We hail thee, Summer!*

FOLK: *Winter is dead!   We hail thee, Summer!*

GODWO/MAN: *Now let the day-flame   from darkness burn,*
Let Sunna rise   her siege to take
Swan-white, the day-maid   at Delling's door,
Glimmering, rises   to glow in the dawn.

(While this is taking place, the DEATH-BEARER casts off her cloak to reveal herself as the SPRING BRIDE. On no account must the cloak be touched again until it has been cleansed by sprinkling with some of the water borne by the SPRING BRIDE. She takes up a horn of mead or ale, a second of water drawn from a running spring with a leek springing out of it, a fire-lighter, and a basket with enough golden apples, colored eggs, and Eostre cakes[13] for everyone. [She may find it easier to draw some of these things behind her in a small wagon.] Slowly, she treads towards the east and in to stand before the edge of the circle.)

GODWO/MAN: *Who waits there outside   white-clad and fair*
Who is the mighty   maid at our doors?

SPRING BRIDE: *I am the Day-Queen   the drightine of light,*
Awaked by the call   of Eostre's bright dawn.
I am the Bride   and I bring the flame
Apples of gold   and ale's might.

GODWO/MAN: (going to the edge of the circle and stretching his arms out to touch her)
Come here within   and welcome be,
of holiest kin   thou queen beloved.
Thou Bride, we greet thee   bright maid of day!

(As the Spring Bride steps within the circle, the GODWO/MAN sings the "Hail to Day" from "Sigrdrífumál":)

Hail, Day! Hail, ye Day's sons!
Hail, Night and the daughter of Night.

Look down upon us here   with loving eyes,
   and sig grant to those standing here.

Hail to the gods! Hail to the goddesses!
Hail to all-giving earth!
Goodly speech and human wit   grant to us, the well-
   known,
   and hands of healing, while we live.

Hail!

SPRING BRIDE: *Ale I bring you   apples of battle,*
   and ale to the awesome gods.

(She drinks, gives the horn to the GODWO/MAN, who drinks and passes it about the circle, then pours what is left into the blessing bowl.)

Water I sprinkle   sprung from the depths,
   a leek I have laid in the cup
   no bale shall be your bane.

(She rounds the circle, using the leek to sprinkle the GODWO/MAN and each of the FOLK in turn.)

Bread to you all   bring I for life
   and eke an egg for luck.
And golden apples   to awe your souls,
   Shine they in Sunna's sig-light
   Shine for you the shapes of this year.

(She rounds the circle, giving a bread, an egg, and an apple to each. All take at least one bite from the bread and the apple, holding the egg carefully.)

GODWO/MAN: *Now let the flames' might   flare in the*
   day,
   Hail to Sunna on high!
Winter is gone   and withered to naught.
   Let wane all seeds of woe

let wax all seeds of weal
as shining year-dawn shows!

(The SPRING BRIDE lights the fire to burn Winter. Each of the FOLK in turn steps forward to pass his/her egg over the flames, whispering what he/she wants to wreak during the year. When this has been done, the GODWO/MAN blows thrice on the horn or rings a bell thrice, and all leap in the air as high as they can, then toss their eggs up and catch them again. Other horseplay, such as everyone switching members of the opposite gender with their switches, is also fitting.)

Eostre (Single Worker)

This rite can be done as a solo rite or for a kindred if you are not able to do the dramatic folk-rite.

Tools: Hammer; horn of ale/mead; blessing bowl; blessing-twig one golden apple, one piece of bread, and one colored egg for each person there; three candles—white, red, and black or dark blue.
Time: Sunrise.

(The WORKER begins with the Hammer-Hallowing as usual.)

Long was the winter   wolf's dark realm,
*   while etins held the earth.*
Long was the night   long slept the maid,
*   life is long to the sad.*

Awakened now   are all bright souls,
*   from night and need and mist.*
Now day-fire on hearth   and high harrow flames,
*   Bright rises springtime bride.*

(The WORKER lights each of the candles in turn, saying,)

White flame burn   for birth of day,
*   fair is the fire of dawn.*
Red flame burn   for rule of day,
*   fair is the noontide flame.*

Black flame burn   for fall of day,
  fair is the sunset fire.
Three times set   and three times lit,
  woven this braid for weal.

(The WORKER fills the horn; holding it in the right hand, he/she raises hands and head, facing East.)

Hail, Day!   Hail, ye Day's sons
Hail, Night, and the daughter of Night!
Look down upon me/those here   with loving eyes,
  and sig give to me,/those standing here.
Hail to the gods!   Hail the goddesses!
  Hail to all-giving earth!
Goodly speech and human wit   grant to me/us, the well-
  known,
  and hands of healing, while I/we live.

Hail!

(The WORKER drinks from the horn; if others are present, he/she passes it deosil. When the drinking is done, the WORKER pours the contents into the blessing bowl.)

Hail, Eostre mighty   maid most fair,
to Sunna taking   her springtide seat,
to Wodan for sig,   for strength, to Thunar,
Hail the Wans   wise earth-kin all!

(The WORKER then hallows the bowl with the Hammer and sprinkles the aettir and each of the true FOLK there in turn.)

Now Idunn bring   her apples gold,
and bread that's made   with main of earth.
Eat all for might   in months to come,
that strength and life   stand ever high.

(Each person eats of his/her apple and bread.)

Blessed now   be Eostre's dawn,
Dark fled before the fair light.
Holy hence,   home fare all wights.
Shall wax all my/our seeds of weal,
shall wither all my/our seeds of woe,
shall my/our works of might be all wrought!

(Each person throws her/his egg up in the air as high as possible and tries to catch it.)

WALPURGISNACHT
(with apologies to Goethe's *Faust*)

Tools: Boy Scout bow and drill firelighting kit, red candle, ale, horn or cup.
Workers: WANAGODWO/MAN, ASAGODWO/MAN, FOLK.
(This can also be performed as a solo rite by having a single Worker speak all the parts.)

(The WANAGODWO/MAN shall perform the Hammer Rite, using the snowflake form of hagalaz and chanting, "Hexe-Heidh hallow the heroes here!")

WANAGODWO/MAN: *Hail to Heidh, mistress of magic!*

ASAGODWO/MAN: *Hail to Wodan, magic's master!*

BOTH: *Hail ways hidden, awake on this night!*

WANAGODWO/MAN: *The fire burns in the flood-tide, flaming over gold's glow.*

ASAGODWO/MAN: *The wind is wandering wild, through this night's open ways.*

WANAGODWO/MAN: *Fair is the field's green fire.*

ASAGODWO/MAN: *Fair are the glimmering stars.*

BOTH: *Hail to Wodan and Heidh!*

ASAGODWO/MAN: *Here, this night, we pass the gateway,*
Into magic dreams and mazes
Lead us well and win our praises
Speed us on our courses straightway
Through the vast enchanted spaces.
Earth-strong tree with tree enlaces,
Past each other swiftly scudding,
And the cliffsides sharply nodding,
And the rocky crags sharp goring
Howling wind and dark clouds lowering.
Down through sward and pebbles pouring
Rill and rivulet are springing
Hear them bubbling, hear them singing,
Sweetest water-maidens' chanting
To the faithful memory granting
Magic songs of godly might,
Echoing through this haunted night,
Rising wyrd called forth again.

WANAGODWO/MAN: *Hear the wood-birds' howling call,*
Screech-owl, cuckoo, falcon all,
Witch-wings flying through the dark.
Newts among the rootwork crouching
Where the river earth is touching
Serpent roots, their reptile creepers,
Up through rock and bracken wending,
Weirdly writhing loops extending,
Bent to scare us, snare us, keep us,
From their sturdy tendrils sloping,
Sending wyrm-lithe fringes groping
For the wanderer. Fire glimmers
In the air, a shifting sheen,
Weird seidh-women's lightning-shimmers
Following Heidh's flames, I ween.
Flame points on the earth are sparkling,
Golden sand-grains scattered low.
See, Heidh's seething, hidden fire,
Quickening life with her bright glow.

As the goddess rides forth now,
Seated on her mother sow.

ASAGODWO/MAN: *Now is the night of need.*

WANAGODWO/MAN: *I call the need-fire forth.*

ASAGODWO/MAN: *Where in darkness weird is written*
Where the word of weird is turned
Should is often shadow-sorrow,
Shadowed is the face of Wyrd.
Turn the need-flame, turn again,
Bring Frowe's hidden fire forth.
Need's narrow grip upon the folk
Needs the might to set us free.

(Silence, till the fire is kindled and the candle lit.)

WANAGODWO/MAN: *Now the fire keen is kindled*
Who would work Wyrd's ways again?
Who shall use its might?

(Each in turn, by rank, passes their hands through or over the flame, thinking of a particular situation in which they need the might to turn wyrd.)

WANAGODWO/MAN: (filling the horn with ale)
Alu fill the symbel-horn,
Frothing, seething, water's wyrd.
Mighty are the streaming wave's ways,
Froth from the well and flow back down.
At symbel stand around the fire
Hero-folk to make their boasts
Need-fire strengthens streams of ale,
Wyrd's waters turned by need-fire's glow.

(The *symbel* shall proceed in the usual manner. If the participants who touched the need-fire are willing to speak their purpose in public, they should make their boasts concerning that matter; if not, they should whisper them silently into the ale before drinking. When the *symbel* is done, the WANAGODWO/MAN fills the horn again.)

ASAGODWO/MAN: *Alu mighy   with elder kin,*
   share we this shining night.
Gods and ghosts   of our great folk,
   drink with us holy draught.
Hail to all   the holy ones dear,
   who stand in steads of our hearts.

(The Horn is passed once more. The WANAGODWO/MAN pours what is left into the blessing bowl; the ASAGODWO/MAN hallows it with the Hammer.)

ASAGODWO/MAN: *Mjöllnir hallow   the holy gift,*
   with Thunar's springtide might.
Hallow and bless the true!

(He/she sprinkles the harrow, the aettir, and each of the FOLK with the ale.)

GODWO/MEN: *So shall it be!*

FOLK: *So shall it be!*

MIDSUMMER

Tools: Blowing horn, drinking horn, twig, blessing bowl, ale, mead, two bread horses, mead, harrow-fire laid with nine different kinds of wood, mugwort, juniper.

(The GODWO/MAN calls the FOLK together at the harrow with three blasts of the horn.)

(Hammer-Hallowing)

GODWO/MAN: *Hail to Sunna in her height of the year,*
   To the Sun in her high siege, hail!
Árvakr and Alsvith draw her bright wain
Round in the shining ring.
Now shall the holy fire flame forth
Hallow the harrow's heaped stones
Where here we hail the Sun!

(The GODWO/MAN lights the harrow's flame.)

Let the blessing-blaze before us
Burn weal to our works, woe to strengthen our wills.

(Sprinkle mugwort and juniper on the coals; each of the FOLK shall step forward in turn to pass his/her hand through the smoke.)

Hail to Wodan, wisest of gods
Runes dyed red and ravens' cries
Be sig-staves writ on sun's bright day.
Hail to Heimdall, highest-minded,
Let us rightly rewin the worlds of Rig.
Hail to Tiw at the height of the Thing-tide
One-Hand's spear shall set our measure
Battle's boldness lay our laws.
Hail to Frija, seeress secret
Woman's wisdom wedding well
Truest hearts with holy ties.
Hail to Thunar, thane of the thunder,
Whose hammer hallows, wards the walls.
Hail, Idunn, whose apples' might
Give life and light to the forth-springing folk.
Hail to Fro Ing, hallowed ruler,
Life of the land, the fruitful Wan.
Hail the Frowe, fiery love-queen,
Witch-wife, warrior, woman of seidh.
Hail the gods and goddesses all,
Ases and Wans most wise.

(The GODWO/MAN takes up the horses.)

We give these gifts to the gods of our folk,
For blessings bright, a gift for a gift,
In thanks for things that are and shall be.

(The horses are passed around, the stallion deosil and the mare widdershins. Each person touches them in turn, whispering or thinking silently a message which he/she wants to send to one or all of the gods.)

Now horn we raise to the holy gods,
At height of the day where they deem at Wyrd's Well,
Hail gods and goddesses all!

(GODWO/MAN fills the horn with ale, hallows it with the Hammer-sign, and passes it around. All drink. GODWO/MAN fills the blessing bowl with what is left.)

Thus we give these gifts.

(The GODWO/MAN cuts the throats of the horses and sprinkles the harrow, the FOLK, and the aettir with the ale. He then passes them around and everyone takes a little piece and eats of it. This is followed by the filling of the horn with mead.)

Hallowed mead, Wod-Stirrer hight
Gift of Wodan, Gunnlödh's loss
Drops from Heidhdraupnir's head
Drops from Hoddrofnir's horn
Wod roaring in rune-red might
Flows to fill the folk.

(Trace and sing the runes of ODHROERIR (ᛟᛞᚱᚨᚱᛁᛉ) over the draught and hallow with two ansuz-trefots (). Pass the horn around deosil; all drink. The GODWO/MAN drains the horn dry if any is left.)

Let the harrow-fire hallow
Our food and all who feast here.
Let the feast begin!

(The GODWO/MAN blows three blasts on the Horn, strikes three times on the harrow, or other similar gesture to close the rite.)

Loaf-Fest

This Anglo-Saxon festival takes place on the first of August—roughly midway between Midsummer's and Winternights. It is called Loaf-Fest because this was the time when the first grain could be harvested and made into bread—possibly the first bread that had been eaten for several months, after the previous year's grain had run out. Loaf-Fest marks the beginning of the harvest season: a time of hard work, but also of rejoicing; a time when the wishes written at Yule and the seeds planted at Charming of the Plough should be starting to bring forth fruit. At Loaf-Fest, we look back to the beginning of the year and forward to the efforts and fulfillment of harvest which lie ahead of us. Loaf-Fest also marks the ending of the rest and relative freedom of the summer and the beginning of a period of hard and intensive labor in preparation for the winter.

Because this is the time of the cropping of the grain, and also the month most prone to summer thunderstorms, Thunar and Sif are especially called upon. At this time, Thunar acts in the third Dumözilian function, swinging his hammer to bring fruitfulness to the land and to cause the grain to ripen properly. The tale of the cropping of Sif's hair also reminds us that harvest comes in many realms besides that of agriculture; from the stolen "harvest" of Sif's hair come, eventually, the greatest treasures of the gods—a mighty harvest indeed.

In *Practical Magic in the Northern Tradition*, Nigel Pennick suggests that the English folk song "John Barleycorn" should either be sung, recited, or acted out as a folk drama in the course of this festival. It was also traditional on Loaf-Fest to give worship to the holy wells and springs and to the wights dwelling within them.

In Iceland, gatherings were held at this time during which one of the major activities was horse-fighting. A similar practice took place in Sweden, as shown on the Haggeby Stone from Uppland, which has two fighting horses behind whom men with goads stand. As well as being entertainment, these horse-duels may have had a holy meaning: Summer is beginning to age and Winter is mounting his first challenge. These fairs were lively events, at which goods were sold and marriages were arranged.

Loaf-Fest Rite

Time: Sunset
Worker: GODWO/MAN, two HORSE-GOADERS (if done as a kindred event—if this rite is done alone, the godwo/man should simply hold one horse in each hand and raise each in turn while speaking the corresponding horse-goader's lines).

Tools: Hammer, one home-baked loaf or biscuit for each person, a horn of ale, two horse-images—one dark and one light (small plastic horses, such as are sold in any toy store, will do perfectly, the more so as you can usually find a couple in the rearing position), red ribbon, one copper coin for each person. If you have no nearby spring or well, draw water from the nearest outdoor source you can find in advance and have a bowl of it sitting on the harrow.

(The gathering begins with the singing or recitation of "John Barleycorn" by the GODWO/MAN or a chosen skald—music can be found in most collections of English/British folk songs.)

> SINGER: *Three men came out of the West,*
> *Their fortune for to try,*
> *And they swore a vow and a solemn oath,*
> *John Barleycorn must die.*
>
> *They took a plough and ploughed him down,*
> *Threw clods upon his head,*
> *And they have sworn a solemn oath,*
> *John Barleycorn was dead.*
>
> *But the cheerful spring came brightly on,*
> *And showers began to fall.*
> *John Barleycorn got up again,*
> *And sore surprised them all.*
>
> *The sultry suns of summer came,*
> *And he grew thick and strong,*
> *His head well armed with pointed spears,*
> *That no one do him wrong.*
>
> *The sober autumn entered mild,*
> *When he grew wan and pale,*
> *His bending joints and drooping head,*
> *Showed he began to fail.*

Then they hired men with sickles sharp
To cut him off at the knee,
And the worst of all they served Barleycorn,
They served him barbarously.

Then they hired men with pitchforks,
To pitch him onto the load,
And the worst of all they served Barleycorn,
They bound him down with cord.

Then they hired men with thrashels
To beat him high and low,
They came smick-smack on poor Jack's back,
Till the flesh began to flow.

O they put him in the maltin' kiln,
Thinking to dry his bones,
And the worst of all they served Barleycorn,
They crushed him between two stones.

Then they put him into the mashing-tub,
Thinking to scald his tail,
And the next thing they called Barleycorn,
They called him home-brewed ale.

John Barleycorn was a hero bold,
Of noble enterprise,
For if you do but taste his blood,
'Twill make your courage rise.

He'll make a maid dance round the room,
As naked as she was born,
He'll make a parson pawn his books,
And a farmer burn his corn.

The whole world over men worship him,
No matter friend or foe,
And where they be that make so free,
He's sure to lay them low.

So put your wine in the glasses fine,
Your cider in the can.
Put John Barleycorn in the old brown jug,
For he's proved the strongest man!

(By this time, the FOLK should be gathered around in a circle. The GODWO/MAN does the Hammer-Hallowing or setting of the Frithgarth as usual.)

GODWO/MAN: *Hail to Thunar!   Thunder of summer,*
    Hallow the shimmering sheaves,
Hallow fair Sif.   Hail, Thunar's bride!
    Golden-haired, glistening grain.
Now the first fruits are plucked,
The first of the fields are shorn.
Sif's shining hair has been cropped—
The Thunderer rages on high.
But deep in the earth   delve the Swart-Alfs
    Shaping beneath the stone.
Forging a harvest   higher than grain,
    and good for all the gods.
For Sif golden hair   the Hammer to Thunar,
Ruler's spear, Wodan,   and richest of rings.
To Fro Ing, boar shining   and ship of the finest,
Good is that harvest   gained by the gods.
The first bread is baked   first beer is brewed,
We hail Fro Ing   for harvest-year good!
Let all bring forth   the fruits you hold,
And say, what seeds   have sprung so well.

(Each of the FOLK brings the loaf in his/her hand forward and lays it on the harrow, telling of some deed or work which has begun to bear fruit.)

GODWO/MAN: *Then let us drink   to the loaf-givers great*
    In ale born of the bright grain.

(He/she fills the horn with ale till it froths over and raises it high, tracing the Sun-Wheel and saying as he/she does so "Fro Ing—Frowe—Njördhr—Nerthus". He/she then makes the sign of the hammer, saying, "Hail to Thunar and Sif." The GOD-WO/MAN drinks and passes the horn around clockwise, pouring what is left into the blessing bowl at the end of the round.)

> GODWO/MAN (sprinkling the aettir, the harrow, and each of the FOLK with the ale from the blessing bowl):
> *ALU-might bless   all who are here,*
> *good harvest give to all.*

(The HORSE-GOADERS step forth into the middle of the circle with their steeds.)

> DARK: *Your golden* (or *"white"*) *nag's getting old—his mane's turning gray. You can't beat me now.*

> LIGHT: *My stallion's at the full of his strength. Your mangy black colt can't stand up to him. Come and try it!*

(The HORSE-GOADERS circle each other for a moment, then clash, miming a fight between the two horses they hold. At last the LIGHT overcomes the DARK, who slinks back to his place in the circle.)

> LIGHT (holding his horse high): *The golden stallion is still king—fair days for the harvest to come.*

(The FOLK clap and cheer; he/she sets the horse on the harrow and returns to his/her place)

> GODWO/MAN: *Now unto the wells   be worship given*
> *from which holy waters flow,*
> *and unto the springs   whence sprout all that grows*
> *and to the wights within.*

(If there is a nearby spring, well, or lake which you have chosen, the FOLK should go there at this point; otherwise, the rest of the rite will take place around the bowl of water on the harrow.)
(The GODWO/MAN ties the red ribbon around the bowl or around the branch of a tree growing by the spring.)

314 / *Teutonic Religion*

GODWO/MAN: *Deep in the water   are wisdom's roots,*
    and the wise ones sleep within.
   Cast for blessing   the coin in your hand,
    and whisper, what you will see.

(Each person drops his/her coin into the water, murmuring a question or wish.)

GODWO/MAN: *Hail to the gods   hail to the goddesses,*
    Hail to the harvest's first fruits!

(He/she pours the contents of the blessing bowl into the water, then either casts the loaves in or drops a symbolic crumb from each into the bowl.)

GODWO/MAN: *So it shall be.*

ALL: *So it shall be.*

(If a bowl of water was used, after the rite the GODWO/MAN should take the water back to its source and cast everything in, including the remainder of the loaves.)

WINTERNIGHTS

The feast of Winternights marks the end of the summer half of the year and the beginning of the winter half. At this time, those cattle who could not live through the winter were sacrificed and their meat either eaten at the feast or preserved as food for the winter ahead. This killing of cattle was not a gratuitous blood-sacrifice: rather, it was our ancestors' way of hallowing the fall slaughtering which all agricultural societies (especially in lands with harsh winters) have to do and of giving worship to the beasts whose lives would give them life in the cold months to come.

Winternights also marks the end of the harvest season which began with Loaf-Fest. It is the greatest harvest festival of the Northern folk. Thus the feast should be exceptionally rich, with autumnal fruits and nuts of all sorts served as well as meat and bread. Thanks are especially given to Fro Ing and the Frowe at this time, as well as hopes for a good harvest next year.

In many ways, Winternights is the Germanic equivalent of the Celtic Samhain.[14] Both are the turning point between summer and winter; both are nights on which worship should be given to dead kinswo/men and on which the dead may return to claim their portion. For this reason, Winternights was also called Álfablót ("Alfs' Blessing") and Dísablót ("Idises' Blessing"). The Wild Hunt begins to ride on Winternights and continues throughout the winter until Eostre; from Winternights onward, ghosts, trolls, and other such dwellers in the Out-Garth gain greater and greater might in the darkness.

The timing of Winternights, like that of Eostre, is open to considerable variation. The Anglo-Saxons called this feast "Winterfyllith"—"Winter Full-Moon," and thus the favored date for holding it is on the first full moon after the autumnal equinox (or the nearest weekend). You may choose to go by other seasonal changes (turning leaves, first snowfall if you live far in the North or first frost if you don't), but Winternights ought to come sometime in late September or in October.

Dramatic Winternights Rite
(by Kveldulf, Ertha, and Eiríkr Malmstrom)

Tools: Harrow, one horn of mead, two cups of elderberry wine or ale, one bread stallion, one bread human (crowned and phallic), one sword, one loose stag's antler or good symbolic imitation, one blessing-twig, one knife.

Workers: FROWESGODWOMAN, INGSGODWO/MAN, WARG/WODANSGODWO/MAN (or GODWOMAN), FOLK.

Garb: The FROWESGODWOMAN should be clothed in a long garment of dark green and/or black and crowned with elder or birch branches, the INGSGODWO/MAN should be clothed in a sky-blue tunic with yellow belt and crowned with stag-horns or oak branches. The WARG/WODANSGODWO/MAN should have a dark hooded cloak, a wolf's mask or something similar (we used a werewolf head-mask, which should be easy to find at this time of year), and an eyepatch.

(The FOLK gather around the harrow, men forming the southern half of the circle and women the northern half. The FROWESGODWOMAN and INGSGODWO/MAN stand at the West; the

WARG waits concealed outside of the circle to the north, his mask hidden by the hood of his cloak. Ideally none of the FOLK will have seen it before he reveals himself!)

(Men walk deosil behind the INGSGODWO/MAN; women walk widdershins behind the FROWESGODWOMAN. Each hugs as he/she passes the others. All chant:)

> Circle of light, fire of night,
> Around us glow the shield-ring bright.

(The circle is walked three times; GODWO/MAN and GOD-WOMAN meet in the West again.)

FROWESGODWOMAN: *Through time and tide we are met once more, to hold these Winter-Nights holy. So our ancestors did; so we come to honor them at this holy feast.*

INGSGODWO/MAN: *We gather the harvest; pass, summer to winter. We honor the dead.*

FROWESGODWOMAN: *Hail the Frowe! Hail, idises of our house!*

INGSGODWO/MAN: *Hail to Fro Ing! To the alfs, all dark and light!*
Hail to Day and his sons!

FROWESGODWOMAN: *Hail to Night and her daughters!*

TOGETHER: *Hail, Earth that givest to all!*

FROWESGODWOMAN: *Draw close in the circle of shining light*
Inside the garth, be glad together,
For outside the winter's wolves are waiting,
Woe to the heedless who hearken not to me!

(The WARG flings back the hood of his cloak to reveal the wolf's head. Waving the sword, he runs from north to east, snarling and menacing the FOLK, who begin to chant again.)

FOLK: *Circle of light, fire of night,*
Around us glows the shield-ring bright.

WARG (from the East): *I am the eater of weal and wealth,*
I am hunger that withers, wilts, and wastes.

INGSGODWO/MAN: *Hunger that withers, wilts, and*
wastes,
Fruits of Frodhi fend thee far.

(WARG runs from East to South, menacing the FOLK, who chant as before. He stops in the South.)

WARG: *I am the bane of wholeness and health,*
I am the sickness that sears and slays.

FROWESGODWOMAN: *Sickness that sears and slays, I say,*
The Frowe's hands shall heal thy hurt.

(WARG runs from South to West, etc.)

ALL: *Circle of light,* etc.

WARG: *I dog the door of the last faring far,*
I am the dealer of darkness and death.

INGSGODWO/MAN: *Doom-laden dealer of darkness and*
death,
Ing's völsi defeat you with his life-might.

(INGSGODWO/MAN raises the stag's antler and fences with the WARG for a short time, finally overcoming him. WARG runs from West to North, all chanting as before.)

WARG: *I am the Warg, forest-goer, fen-walker*
Banefullest blood of the Out-Garth's dark dwellers.

FROWESGODWOMAN: *Idises ward us from thee and thy*
kindred,
Idises ward us from Out-Garth's dark dwellers!

ALL: *Circle of light*, etc.

(The WARG roars once more in defiance, but flees to the North. Raising his hood, his back turned to the circle, he removes the wolf's head and puts on the eyepatch as the FROWESGOD-WOMAN continues to speak.)

FROWESGODWOMAN: *Wod is gone with the wind's wild wandering,*
Weeping, I seek in sadness my love.

INGSGODWO/MAN: *Where is the wisdom to guide world's god?*
Where is the hidden hand that helped mine?

FROWESGODWOMAN: *Where is song's might to withstand winter's cold?*

INGSGODWO/MAN: *Where the mighty king-stallion's shadowy twin?*

(A moment of silence. WARG, now WODANSGOD-WO/MAN, turns, the horn of mead in his hand, and walks slowly towards the circle, face still hidden by his hood.)

INGSGODWO/MAN: Who are you?

WODANSGODWO/MAN: *I am Hroptr, the hidden king and creator,*
I am Yggr, the eagle, serpent, and wolf
I am Wodan, bearing Wod-Stirrer mead.
Drink to the Fro and the Frowe!
Wisdom roar into the world!

(WODANSGODWO/MAN spills a few drops from the horn onto the ground, drinks, and passes it deosil around the circle. As INGSGODWO/MAN and FROWESGODWOMAN receive it, each speaks in turn before drinking.)

INGSGODWO/MAN: *The Hidden One's wisdom guides Freyr's hand,*
Twin stallions ride and rule together.

FROWESGODWOMAN: *Wodan's wisdom rewards my wandering,*
Earth is wedded to wind again.

(The horn is passed back to WODANSGODWO/MAN, who shall not speak again except as one of the FOLK.)

INGSGODWO/MAN (raising the stallion):
Hail Fro Ing for the fruitful fields,
Hail the Alfs for their help and gifts!
Where the year is winter-turning,
We give thanks for harvest good.
Favor ask we of alfs again,
Dream-wisdom guide dark winter days.
We ask again the favor of Ing
Fields ripe with riches in years to come.
Hail to Fro Ing, fro of Alf-Home!

(The INGSGODWO/MAN passes the stallion around the circle deosil. Each of the FOLK touches it in turn, speaking or whispering their thanks and wishes and ending with the spoken "Hail Fro Ing!")

INGSGODWO/MAN: *In thanks for gifts and hope of growth,*
We send this stallion for Ing's might.

(He slits the horse's throat and sprinkles the wine from the bowl upon the harrow with the blessing-twig, then to the eight winds and over each of the FOLK in a deosil circle. He passes the stallion around deosil and each of the FOLK takes a bite from it.)

FROWESGODWOMAN (raising the king-figure):
Hail the Frowe, giver of good,
Hail, idises of our kin!
Where the year is winter-turning,

We give thanks for harvest good.
Idises, dream-queens, warn us of woe,
Work for our weal in winter's dark womb.
Frowe, favor us with thy fiery joys,
Hold us and heal us through the dark days.
Hail the Frowe, Wanadis high!

(She carries the figure of the King around widdershins. Each of the FOLK touches him and whispers or speaks the name of something they wish to be rid of, ending with "Hail to the King!")

FROWESGODWOMAN: *Unto the women of the earth,*
  We give as gift our King.

(She castrates the figure and slits its throat over the blessing bowl, then crumbles the phallus into nine pieces, flinging one to each of the winds and eating the last. She sprinkles wine from the bowl over the harrow and around the circle widdershins, then passes the King around. Each of the FOLK takes a bite.)

FROWESGODWOMAN: *Hail to the Frowe! Hail our idises!*

(She spills a few drops of elderberry wine or ale on the earth and passes the cup counterclockwise. When the circle is rounded, the INGSGODWO/MAN pours what is left into the blessing bowl and refills the cup.)

INGSGODWO/MAN: *Hail Fro Ing! Hail to the alfs!*

(He spills a few drops and passes the cup deosil; when it has rounded, the FROWESGODWOMAN pours what is left into the bowl.)

BOTH: *Hail to the passing year!*

GODWOMAN: *Idises of help, hold us in holiness. Bless our*
  houses and all within.

GODWO/MAN: *Alfs all aid us in wisdom and deed. Bring*
  us brightness and weal in our works.

GODWOMAN: *Frowe fill us with fires of life.*

GODWO/MAN: *Fro Ing hallow our hopes till next harvest.*

BOTH: *Blessed be all who are here,*
  Warded from winter's woe.
  Hail to the gods!

ALL: *Hail to the gods!*

GODWO/MEN: *Hail to the goddesses!*

ALL: *Hail to the goddesses!*

GODWO/MEN: *Again we hail the earth!*

ALL: *Again we hail the earth!*

GODWO/MEN: *So mote it be.*

(Together they pour the blessing bowl out over the harrow as the FOLK chant, "So mote it be.")

Winternights (Godwo/man and Godwoman or Solo)

This rite can be performed either by a man and a woman or by a single worker of either sex. If it is done solo, the only changes which need to be made are to replace "we" with "I," and to change the commands "Bring forth," "Now let all eat," etc. into the declarations "I bring forth," "Now I eat," etc. If you are doing it as a solo working and do not yourself wish to call upon Wodan, leave out the entire section beginning with "This night we step through winter's door" and go straight to "Now the gifts are gathered all."

Tools: Hammer, gandr, hlaut-teinn, bread mare, ale, horn, blessing bowl, blessing twig, three hornfulls of ale, sheaf of grain, basket of apples.

GODWO/MAN: *The summer is ending; the time of harvest*
  is done. We stand at winter's door, at the sunset of the year.

Now it is time for us to turn our eyes within our souls: to look back upon the works we have wrought and seek out again the wisdom of our kinsmen who have gone before, who shape still what we are. So gather around the holy stone, the bone of the earth in which we are rooted, and come to honor the gods and the ghosts of our ancestors.

(GODWO/MAN traces a circle three times around the FOLK, chanting:)

See the shining   shield-ring round us
Bifrost's rainbow   bright the fire
*   holds out all wights of woe.*
Hammer ward our works without

(Continue Hammer-Hallowing as usual.)

(GODWO/MAN stands with feet together and hands upraised; GODWOMAN stands with hands at her side and feet spread. A single worker should both raise hands and spread feet to draw might both from below and from above.)

GODWOMAN: *We call you, idises   clan's ancient mothers.*
    Bright-clad and holy   bring us your weal
    Dark-clad and woeful   withhold from us ill.
    Your wisdom and warnings   warding our ways
    Keepers of kin-folk   we call you now.

ALL: *Idises, we hail you! The idises are among us!*

GODWO/MAN: *Alfs, we call you   old howe-dwelling kind.*
    Light Alfs frithful   Fro Ing's shining kin,
    Mound Alfs mighty   memory's warders
    Swart Alfs, rock-dwellers   dwarves, matchless smiths,
    From your wide worlds   we call on you now.

ALL: *Alfs, we hail you! The alfs are among us!*

GODWOMAN: *We call thee, Frowe   Freyja, Wan-idis.*
    In thy cat-drawn wain   wend thee to our hold.

Bright on thy breast   Brisingamen shining,
Spae-wife and warrior   womb and dark howe,
Thou keen-eyed goddess   now call we on thee.

ALL: *Frowe, we hail you! The Frowe is among us!*

GODWO/MAN: *We call thee, Fro Ing   fruitful year's Fro.*
Thy golden boar bright   bring thee to our hold.
Stark in thy hand   thy stag's horn shining
Hero of gods   with hart and boar's might,
Keeper of frith   we call on thee now.

ALL: *Fro Ing, we hail thee! Fro Ing is among us!*

GODWO/MAN: *Ases and Wans,   and holy wights all,*
We call you at Winter's Eve,
We hail you for harvest's gifts.

ALL: *Ases, Wans, we hail you, gods and goddesses among us!*

GODWO/MAN: *Bring forth to the harrow the signs of the*
harvest which you have reaped this year; aloud or silently,
speak your thanks to the gods and wights who have helped
you in it and your hopes for the year to come.

(One by one, all bring forth works and lay them upon the harrow. When they are done, the GODWO/MAN takes the Horse and holds it aloft.)

GODWO/MAN: *As this mare rides into the hidden worlds,*
let her bear on her back our thanks for the gifts we have got-
ten and our needs for the year to come, that the high ones
bless those seeds and help to bring them to fruit by next har-
vest. As you touch the mare, speak or whisper your thanks
and your wishes, that they may be loaded upon her for her
faring. (Pass the mare around widdershins, letting
everyone touch her.) Fro Ing, Frowe; alfs, idises; you holy
gods and goddesses, you wights of help, we give you this gift
in thanks for all you have given us.

(The GODWO/MAN holds the mare and the GODWOMAN slits her throat.)

GODWOMAN: *Now let all eat of the hallowed horseflesh, as our elder kinsmen did to show their troth.*

(She bears the mare around widdershins, letting everyone tear off a hunk of bread and eat of it. The GODWOMAN pours the ale into the horn; the GODWO/MAN raises it, tracing the sun-wheel.)

GODWO/MAN: *Hallowed this horn to the alfs   holy our hidden kin!*
Light Alfs, awe us   with Ase-Garth's brightness
Dark Alfs, bring memory   and might from the howes
Swart Alfs, smite steel,   smith our wills to shape!

GODWOMAN: *Hallowed this horn to idises   holy our hidden kin!*
You ward-wives who follow us   our foes you shall awe,
that no will overcome us   no weapons shall scathe
your clan who here hail   high Mothers, our kin.

(The horn is passed around and each person traces the sun-wheel and says, in turn, "Hail the alfs and idises," then drinks. When this is finished, there should be some ale left, which is poured into the blessing bowl. The GODWOMAN fills the horn with ale again.)

GODWO/MAN: *We hallow this horn to gods' harvest-might!*
(She/he traces the Hammer.)

Harvest holds the good year; I say that Fro Ing was generous.

GODWOMAN: *Bright shines the sun-gold sow; secret is Ertha's womb.*
North are the roots of might; Njördhr and Nerthus give gold.

GODWO/MAN: *The Hammer hallows the grain; hail to Thunar and Sif! Hail harvest-gods all!*

(The horn is passed around; each traces the Hammer and says "Hail harvest-gods all!" The ale is poured into the blessing bowl.)

GODWO/MAN: *This night we step through winter's door. From this night, Wodan shall lead the Wild Hunt on his eight-legged, wind-gray steed. The ghosts shall ride on the winter's wind behind Yggr, the drighten of draugs; wolf and raven shall rule the wintry wood. We leave this last sheaf of grain to the leader of the hosts of the restless dead, the Hunt riding out from the Hall of the Slain.*

(GODWOMAN fills the horn with ale; GODWO/MAN holds it up in his left hand and the sheaf in his right.)

Hail to Wodan, lord of the wind! Galdor-Father, Sig-Father, Wal-Father; runes' first rister, ravens' ruler; One-Eyed, Awesome, keeper of skaldcraft's mead; Wodan, I hail thee!

(The GODWO/MAN traces the walknot over and drinks from the horn.)

Let those who dare now come forth. Drink of this horn, lay your hand on Sleipnir's sheaf, and ask for Wodan's boons— word-craft, wod, will, and sig. But ask not lightly, for he is a fearsome god and a gift ever asks for a gift.

(Those who will come forward and do this. The GODWO/MAN pours the ale into the blessing bowl.)

GODWO/MAN: *Now the gifts are gathered all. Be blessing to the eight winds, blessing on harrow and folk.*

(GODWO/MAN sprinkles the ættir, harrow and FOLK with the ale from the bowl.)

GODWOMAN: *Now the gifts are gathered all. Be given to gods and wights!*

(GODWOMAN sprinkles the ættir and harrow, then pours the ale out before the north side of the harrow.)

> GODWO/MAN: *As we step through winter's door, let us eat these apples and remember how death and life are woven together. Idunn brings her apples to the godly kind to bring them life and youth everlasting; from the eating of hallowed apples comes the birth of heroes. Our ancestors also placed wild apples in the barrow with the ships that bore their dead from this world to the worlds unseen. The flower must fall so that the fruit can swell; the fruit must rot so that the seed which bears the soul may grow. Now we share these apples with our kin, living and dead; though we fall and rise again, our clans are unbroken and the river of our blood runs mighty from our roots.*

(GODWOMAN bears apples to all; all eat of the apples in silence.)

> GODWO/MAN: *Now wend your ways, all gathered here, back to the worlds of your homes. Let us feast now; let our joy give worship to all those who have given us life, harvest and frith.*

NOTES

1. Some people do much less socially acceptable things with placentae. Basically, if you've just given birth, the placenta is part of your body and it belongs to you and your child, so you have the right to do as you please with it.

2. Here, the drink ought to be mead if possible. The term "honeymoon" derives from the custom of drinking mead for the first month after the wedding to encourage fruitfulness.

3. "Hávamál" 76-77.

4. If you have someone in your kindred who is allergic to alcohol or a confirmed teetotaller, whatever non-alcoholic beverage you pour for that person can be assumed for ritual purposes to fall under the class of "ale," which seems to have been a fairly nebulous term anyway. Also note that it is not necessary to fill the horn to the brim for

the rite to be carried out; a thimbleful may be poured into the holy vessel for greeting a child, for instance.

5. Ash is a masculine tree, elm its feminine correspondent. In the "Mead" greeting, "boar" (ON jófurr) is accounted a name of glory for a warrior, but "sow," although it is a name of Freyja ("Sýr"), does not sound such a compliment. If you wish to make this greeting more like for man and woman, you might choose to use "thou mighty Sýr" for the feminine, which seems a more direct likening of the woman in question to the Frowe.

6. Even if you never drink whole milk (for reasons of health or whatever), you should use it in rituals, because giving skimmed milk to holy beings implies stinginess, which is a very bad thing, much worse than not holding the feast at all.

7. *Snorra Edda*, ch. 44.

8. Newall, *An Egg at Easter*, 115.

9. Marwick, 109.

10. Newall, 253.

11. *Encyclopedia Britannica*, 7:866.

12. Newall, 316.

13. See the recipe under Bread Beasts in chapter XVII: Crafts.

14. Pronounced "sow-un"; means "Summer's End" in Gaelic.

Chapter 17

CRAFTS

 ANY OF THE TOOLS for worship which I have spoken of in this book are not available commercially; and even when they are, it is better for you to make your ritual gear with your own hands, for in so doing you bring yourself closer to the world of your elder kin—even when you use the most modern tools to do it. None of these things you cannot do without at need, but the more you turn towards the ways of your folk, the more likely you are to want them for your blessings and feasts.

THE DRINKING HORN

As well as being the greatest tool of the Teutonic way, the drinking horn is also the most difficult to purchase. Glass ones are occasionally available, but these are usually too small for group rites, and difficult to scribe with runes as well as being fragile and expensive. Otherwise, Renaissance Faires sometimes have booths which sell both drinking and blowing horns. Tourist shops in Norway and Sweden also routinely carry grossly overpriced horns which consist of a metal or glass cup sunk just below the rim of a horn and various degrees of metalwork on the outside. These are basically inferior for every purpose whatsoever. Making your own horn will probably get you the highest quality for the least expense.

Getting the Horn

The basic cattle-horn can probably be purchased at Tandy Leather (a nationwide chain) and probably at similar stores. It comes in two forms, one with a great deal of raw matter on the outside and one roughly sanded. The latter is preferable; there is no advantage to the former, except that it means several hours of work getting it down to the roughly sanded condition.

Cleaning the Horn

Whatever the outside of the horn looks like, the inside is likely to be encrusted with dirt and nameless substances. Begin preparing your horn by washing out all the dead bugs, organic matter, etc. A brass scouring pad may help in loosening ingrained material. A bottle brush is also very good for this, as it is basically the only way to reach the unseen depths of the horn.

When you no longer feel any tatters hanging off the inside of the horn, heat water to a vigorous boil, prop the horn up securely, and fill it with the boiling water. This quite often causes a very nasty smell, which is perfectly natural and does not mean anything is wrong with your horn. Leave the boiling water in the horn to soak until it is cool; empty; scour again, and repeat sterilization. For extra insurance, you can add a couple of Campden tablets (available at any store that sells supplies for home winemaking) to the water. When the water runs absolutely clear, proceed to either paraffining or curing.

Waxing

The advantage of using beeswax or paraffin to seal the horn's interior is the fact that at no time is there any risk of debris, odor, or taste from the horn infiltrating your drink. The disadvantage is that you cannot use hot liquids in it, and if your car has no air conditioner, you cannot leave it in the car or drive long distances in the summer with it. Nevertheless, it is surprisingly durable if not subjected to heat.

Melt half a cake of paraffin or a medium-size beeswax candle in a small pot, preferably a double boiler. *Do not leave the melting wax unattended at any time, as it is exceedingly flammable!* Pour the wax into the horn and swirl it around until the entire inside of the horn is coated fairly evenly, then pour the excess back into the pot—it will stop up a sink.

Curing

Curing is more difficult than paraffining, but also lasts longer and does not disintegrate in the heat. Scrub the clean horn's interior with a mix of three tablespoons dishwashing detergent and boiling water. Let sit until cool. Rinse it out. Refill the horn with boiling water and leave it to sit overnight. The next day, rinse it very thoroughly, wash it with simple dishwashing soap, and rinse it again, scrubbing with a bottle brush if you have one. When it is thoroughly clean, season it by filling it with a strong beer, ale or stout and let it sit for several days before pouring the beer out. This last step is to get rid of the natural flavor of the horn, which really isn't so nice.

Finishing

The rough outside of the sanded horn will need some work to bring it to its best. The first step in finishing the horn is to rub down the outside with a fine steel wool, which will smooth it and bring out the color. For a better polish you can cover a rough cloth with jeweler's rouge (available at any jewelery supply or rock shop) and rub the horn to a high luster.

Decorating

Any sort of decoration can be scribed into the horn—runes, holy signs, or more ambitious artistic projects. For simple designs such as runic inscriptions, a grooved chisel or V-bladed X-Acto knife is probably the best way to carve the horn, if you are careful not to break through its walls. The wider grooves produced can then be dyed or stained in the usual fashion.

More ambitious projects are better achieved through scrimshawing. First draw your design on the rough-sanded horn in pencil. Then follow the lines precisely with the tip of a razor blade or sharp knife. Cover the area with India ink; let it dry, and rub the ink off with steel wool. The lines of your design will be left black against the polished horn.

Scrimshawing is only really effective on white or very light horns. If your horn is a medium to dark color, carved grooves painted red will show up much better.

A woodburning set can also be used and generates surprisingly little odor. You can also use a dremmel tool, but you must be very careful in order not to cut right through the walls of the horn.

Fittings

The simplest fitting possible for a horn is leather. This requires a long strap of leather, two rivets, and epoxy. Measure the circumference of the horn two inches from each end; rivet a corresponding loop in your strap; coat the inner surface of the leather with epoxy. Slip each loop in turn over the small end of the horn, slide them as far up the horn as you can force them to go. Be sure to clean off any epoxy that gets on the surface of the horn before it sets.

A more adventurous craftswo/man may wish to put silver fittings on the horn, binding the rim and/or decorating the tip. The most workable way I have found to do this is to measure the horn rim and purchase a strip of 24- or 25-gauge fine silver (0.99% pure, as opposed to sterling silver which is 0.95%), 1–1¼ inches wide and the length of the rim circumference or just a millimeter shorter, at a jewelery supply house. When ordering your length, remember that it is easier to saw or grind the rim of a horn down to a silver band that is a trifle too small than it is to trim and resolder the silver! I recommend fine silver, rather than sterling, because soldering of sterling creates a shadow called fire scale on the metal, and this is a great trouble to polish off. Fine silver is also softer and easier to manipulate and force into shape around the rim of your horn.

If you want a loop for a strap, you should solder this on while the strip of silver is still flat, then solder the ends of the strip together. Sand the rim of the horn and the inside of the silver to roughen them and coat both with epoxy. Force the ring onto the horn. It should not be polished until the epoxy has dried; polishing it before it is put on the horn will deform the soft silver, whereas afterwards it will help to shape it.

A simple metal tip for the drinking horn can be made thus:

1. Measure distance from half an inch up the horn tip to projected tip of metal cone.
2. Measure widths around tip; it will be easiest to make a paper or thin cardboard template in the shape of the projected cone.
3. Saw or shear your silver, using your template as a guide; 22 gauge fine silver is probably best for the purpose.
4. If loops for a strap are being used, solder the loop on.
5. Solder length sides together. Shape by forcing over horn tip.
6. Saw and file cone tip flat.
7. Remove cone and stand on a piece of flat silver and solder. Saw around the join and polish away edges. Epoxy cone and horn tip; force cone onto horn.

Otherwise a small metal knob, large bead, or like thing can be glued to the horn tip, or you can wrap it with silver or copper wire.

If you want to make your horn into a blowing horn, saw off the pointed end and boil the horn in water for several hours to soften it (this may take longer than you expect—remember that it takes days to boil horn into glue!). When the horn around the cut-off end is softened somewhat, carefully force a trombone mouthpiece (available at any store that sells musical instruments) into the hole, securing it with tight leather wrappings. Once the horn has cooled overnight, it will re-harden, holding the mouthpiece tightly. If the seal around the mouthpiece is not tight, use epoxy at the join. Such a horn is easy to blow and produces a beautiful deep note.

Horns can also be purchased from Gefjon's Ardhr, P.O. Box 85, Silver City, New Mexico 88062—plain, carved, or made to design.

Bronze Age ritual garb

RITUAL GARB

The descriptions of religious ceremonies among the Nordic peoples make it fairly clear that there was no particular ritual garb; given that the blots often involved animal sacrifice and sprinkling of blood, it is probably safe to assume that whatever our ancestors wore to the blessing was fairly plain and easily washed or permanently stained. The only account we have of a "religious specialist" wearing an elaborate costume is that of the spae-woman in *Eiríks saga rauda*; and she was not a godwoman as such, but rather a shamanic seeress.

In Ásatrú today, the use of ritual garb is something left up to the individual. Some groups eschew it altogether, preferring to emphasize by their dress the fact that they are folk of the twentieth century and that the Northern ways are ways for the present as well as the past; and indeed, a simple Hammer, Walknot, Sunwheel

Roman Iron Age ritual garb

or other amulet is token enough to show your troth. Most, however—particularly godwo/men—choose to dress in traditional
garb at blessings and feasts as a reassertion of their heritage, even
as the folk of rural communities throughout the world dress in traditional native costume at community celebrations. This is appropriate because it reminds us that our ways are not confined to the
sphere of worship alone, but involve a whole culture—a way of
being which truly is separate from the Christian/Mediterranean
thrust of much of "mainstream" Western culture.

There are three main periods of clothing style for Teutonic
heathenism. The earliest is the Bronze Age to Early Iron Age (ca.
2000–200 BCE). Clothing from this period has been found in the
mound burials in Scandinavia, where the damp peaty soil preserves organics well, and is also depicted on small bronze figurines. The woman's garb was found in a mound burial in
Denmark and appears on a statuette of Nerthus from the same

period. It consists of a short corded skirt made of twisted wool,[1] a heavy torque (necklace of twisted wire), and a belt with a large round buckle. Women of this era also wore a short-sleeved, midriff-baring blouse and/or a short cape fastened at the neck. Early ritual costume for men consisted of a horned or eagle-headed helmet, as shown on bronze figurines. These men were nude; art of the Vendel period (ca. 600–700 CE) shows men in similar horned helms wearing nothing but a belt and a sword hung from the shoulder. *This was the only context in which horned helmets were ever worn.* These forms of ritual garb will do well for those who are used to working "skyclad," and are particularly appropriate for worship of Nerthus and Ing.

The clothing of the Germanii during the Roman Iron Age has been preserved in bog burials and is also described in the writing of the Romans and depicted in their sculpture. Men's dress was usually a tunic, trousers, and a cloak; the cloak was the most important garment, and usually consisted of a rectangular piece of fabric pinned at the shoulder or a circular cloak of leather and hide. Women wore a tube dress or a skirt and cloak which left the breasts bare. The tube dress is made out of two long rectangular pieces of cloth sewn together at the sides and pinned at the shoulder, leaving a fold at the top; it is worn belted.

The final period in Teutonic clothing is the Viking Age. The best source of illustrations of Viking clothing is Bertil Almgren's *The Viking.* Men's clothing in this period was basically the same as during the Roman Iron Age. Viking men often added various types of hats to this; the floppy-brimmed hat (which Wodan wears over one eye), the "Russian" style fur hat, or a helmet (plain and conical *without* the comic book cow's horns so often incorrectly attributed to the Viking warrior). Women wore a dress that was essentially a floor-legth T-tunic, which could be sleeveless. The dress was worn belted; it was sometimes pleated. Over the dress, the Viking woman wore aprons—long. rectangular pieces of cloth pinned at the shoulder with large oval brooches shaped like tortoise shells, between which hung necklaces of glass, amber, or metal beads. Women might also wear a triangular shawl, pinned at the neck with a third brooch, and sometimes hoods were worn. Men and women alike wore ankle-boots or a moccasin-like shoe, fastened with leather thongs. Tandy Leather sells a pattern for an identical shoe under the name of "Navaho Boot."

Viking Age ritual garb

The changes in clothing from the Bronze Age to the Viking Age reflect the changes in climate as Scandinavia and Northern Europe steadily became colder.

T-Tunics

1. Fold fabric twice (as in drawing—see nest page). Spread out a loosely fitting shirt as shown. Cut around the outside of the shirt, leaving 2-3 inches around the edges. Make body and arms the length desired; the bottom hem should be roughly hip-length for men, ankle-length for women. Additional fabric may be added to make longer sleeves.

2. Make neck-hole large enough for head to pass through. Men's tunics may be slit to form a key-hole opening, or a square

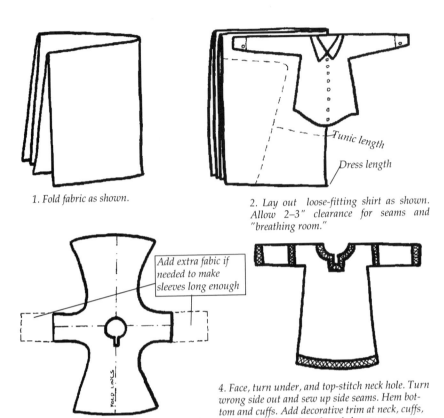

1. *Fold fabric as shown.*

2. *Lay out loose-fitting shirt as shown. Allow 2–3" clearance for seams and "breathing room."*

Add extra fabic if needed to make sleeves long enough

4. *Face, turn under, and top-stitch neck hole. Turn wrong side out and sew up side seams. Hem bottom and cuffs. Add decorative trim at neck, cuffs, and bottom. If you lengthened sleeves, you may want to cover that seam with trim as well.*

3. *Cut neck hole as desired. If sleeves aren't long enough, add extra fabric to lengthen.*

T-tunic construction

neckline may be used. Women's necklines could have a wider opening, or use a key-hole with a loop-and-button closure.

Hem neckline.

3. Turn tunic inside side out and sew up side seams. Turn right side out.

4. Hem bottom and cuffs. Add decorative trim to collar, sleeves, and hemline. Women's dresses were usually not trimmed; decorations were reserved for the aprons which were worn over the dress.

Fabrics, Weave, Color

The most common cloth used in Teutonic clothing was wool. Linen was also used, particularly in women's clothes. If price makes these unavailable, you should try at least to stick to natural fibers if possible. Silk was sometimes imported. Weaves include plain, tabby, twill, and several sorts of tweed; patterns included solid colors, stripes, checks, and plaids. The most favored colors were red and leaf-green; our ancestors were also able to dye cloth in blue, black, brown, grey, various shades of green, ochre, yellow, and white. Since the dyes for the brighter colors were scarcer and more expensive, these hues were worn largely by persons of rank, whereas the poor had to make due with browns, russets, and grays.

The Germanic folk wore a great deal of their mobile wealth on their person, as arm-rings, necklaces, and brooches (and so forth) made out of precious metal. The quantity of large and expensive jewelery worn was in direct proportion to the wealth and rank of the wearer.

The well-dressed Teuton of free birth was almost always armed. Women wore very small daggers hanging from their brooches; men wore a standard size belt dagger. The most usual weapon for men was the spear; axes were only common among the Danes. Swords were very expensive and only possessed by the richest and most noble.

Hairstyles

Unmarried women wore their hair loose, perhaps with a band around the head; married women usually wore it gathered into a knot at the back of the head, often covered by a headdress.

Men wore facial hair most of the time, though shaving was not unknown from the Bronze Age onward. The picture stones show stiffly pointed beards; beards were also braided sometimes. Long hair in men was often associated specifically with holy kingship; even after the conversion of the Franks, a Merovingian king's royal power depended on the length of his hair. Another style was worn by men of the Swabians during the Roman Iron Age; the hair was braided and then tied into a knot on the side of the head.

Rings

The most common article of Germanic jewelery was the ring, which could be sized to fit on finger, arm, or neck. In its simplest form, such a ring is ridiculously easy to make: simply take an appropriate length of copper, silver, or gold wire, file the ends smooth so as not to scratch the wearer, and twist it around your arm or finger in a spiral. An arm-ring should probably be made of 6- to 10-gauge wire; a finger-ring of 12 to 16 gauge. Such rings are fitting gifts to be given to any kindred member or guest who has distinguished him/herself at a feast.

For a more complex ring or a torque to be worn on the neck, buy several strands of wire, clamp the ends in a vise, and twist them together, then bend the length around in a circle of appropriate size. If this ring is to be worn as a simple piece of jewelry, you can finish the ends by twisting them back into loops or soldering some sort of end-pieces on. For an oath-ring, which needs to be unbroken, you should solder the ends of the wires together. If this is not possible, then spiral several feet of 18 gauge silver wire around and around until it has become a visibly seamless whole. An oath ring must have at least an ounce of silver or gold in its composition.

Silver and gold wire can be bought at any jewelery supply house; copper wire can be obtained at most hardware stores.

BREWING MEAD

Although some commercial meads are available, they are usually expensive and not very good (Gibson's Mead is the best of a bad lot). If you are providing mead for more than three people at a time, you will find it infinitely easier and more economical to make your own.

Technically speaking, only a drink brewed exclusively with honey and water can really be called mead. When any sort of fruit is added, it becomes a melomel, while a mead brewed with herbs and spices is known as metheglin. Our ancestors made all of these from a very early time; in my upcoming book, *The Teutonic Magic of Brewing and Herbs*, I shall provide recipes, background, and information on the ritual preparation and use of several of these drinks. The chief honey-drink of the true folk, however, is the unadulterated mead.

To do any sort of home brewing, you need: a white plastic bucket (coloring may leach toxins and/or a bad taste into the drink) capable of holding whatever volume you decide on as your basic batch-size (5 gallons is standard; this weighs 40 lbs., a reasonable weight for most people to move about) plus 2-3 inches at the top to keep it from sloshing over when you move it; a siphon tube, a hydrometer, a 5-gallon glass jar with airlock, and lots of Campden tablets (for sterilization). The more obscure of these items can be found at any shop which sells home-brewing equipment (look in your Yellow Pages under Winemaking), as can the acids, nutrients, etc., for which the recipe calls.

Kveldulf's Basic Mead

(Yields 1 gallon)

3 lbs. honey	¼ oz. malic acid
Water to make up a gallon	Yeast nutrient
Champagne yeast	1 tablespoon strong
¼ oz. tartaric acid	tea (for tannin)
	1 Campden tablet

Sterilize all your equipment with a mixture of one gallon water to two crumbled Campden tablets. You must do this to everything before it comes into contact with your mead, otherwise you risk wild bacteria which will turn the mead into something akin to Nolan's Infamous Weed-Killer (one of the worst meads in history).

Dissolve the honey in about half a gallon of warm water. Add the yeast nutrient, tea, and acids. Fill to one gallon with cool water and crumble one Campden tablet into the mixture. Cover tightly (a clean plastic garbage bag with a rubber band around the rim will do nicely) and leave overnight. Sprinkle in the yeast and cover again. At this time, if you measure with the hydrometer, you will find out how alcoholic you can expect your mead to be if all the sugar ferments out, which, with Champagne yeast, it probably will.

Hopefully within the next three to five days you will get a violently bubbling fermentation (the primary, or aerobic fermentation) which will make your whole kitchen smell like, well, fermenting mead. A head of froth will form and float upon the drink. This is what should happen. If, after two days, your mead just sits there letting out a bubble now and again, either your area is too cold (yeast likes 75–85 degrees Farenheit) or your water lacks the trace components which allow yeast to ferment and thrive. In this case you should buy more yeast nutrients and ask your home-brew shopkeeper about something for reviving a stuck fermentation.

When the primary fermentation stops frothing, measure with the hydrometer again. The sugar content should be down to nearly nothing. If you have no hydrometer, you can make a pretty good guess on this by taste. If the mead is still sweet or the specific gravity too high, your fermentation is stuck, probably for one of the reasons listed above.

Here you come to one of the major grounds for contention among mead-drinkers: dry or sweet. This is solely a matter of individual taste. If you like it dry, transfer it to the glass jar for secondary fermentation and cap the jar with the airlock so that carbon dioxide can escape and no floating bacteria can get in. If, on the other hand, you want sweet mead, add another pound or two of honey per gallon of mead and cover it up again. Repeat this until the mead refuses to ferment any more (which occurs when the alcoholic content becomes high enough to kill all the yeast) and sweeten to taste, then siphon into the jar and close with the airlock. This produces a very strong brew! If you prefer a sweet mead which is not so powerful, use a Sauternes or Madeira yeast instead of Champagne. There is a commercially marketed "mead yeast," but it is not particularly good.

When you have moved your mead to the secondary fermentor, set it in a dark place which is not likely to get too hot or too cold and leave it for six months. At the end of this time, you will have a clear mead with a lot of yeast sediment on the bottom. This sediment is not unhealthy, but it will cloud your mead (causing it to look like swamp water) and is not very attractive. Carefully siphon the mead off the sediment and decant it into sterilized wine bottles or glass gallon jugs. If your mead still contains sediment, refrigeration of the wine bottles or gallon jars of mead will cause the sediment to fall out, then you may siphon the clarified mead off the remaining sediment and re-bottle. Finally, label each bottle with your name, the date on which you started the brewing, and whatever it is that you call your mead. Gunnora Hallakarva adds that keeping a record of each of your brewings in a small notebook is a good idea. When you start a batch, record the ingredients used and the date. Also note any additions of nutrients you must make and the date they were added, the date when secondary fermentation was begun, etc. When the mead is consumed, you can record your impressions on its quality. This record will be very useful when you have produced an outstanding batch of mead, allowing you to re-create a batch with all the excellent qualities of the original.

By six months, your mead should be drinkable, but it will seldom be better than that; it doesn't usually get good till after a year or two. You might start by making two batches, one for immediate consumption and one to put away for aging. Our Kindred normally does its brewing just before each great feast to be sure that there is good mead ready for the same feast next year.

The Yule wreath

THE YULE WREATH

For making a Yule wreath, you will need evergreen branches, four apples (either real ones or small wooden models), several long strips of paper, red ribbons, wire, and a round frame of wood or dried grapevines (available as a wreath base in most craft stores).

Other items such as nuts, mistletoe, boar and goat-shaped cookies, straw animals, etc. may be added as you see fit. When you plan the wreath's size and materials, you should be aware that you will be burning it at sunrise on Twelfth Night, and so you need to scale it to a reasonable size for your fireplace (if burning the wreath is absolutely impossible, for whatever reason, when the time comes you can pull the wishes out and burn them in a bowl with a few of the evergreen needles and a pinch of each apple).

The basic design is that of a sunwheel with an apple at each of the four points. If you are using real apples, thread a ribbon through the body of the apple (you may need to make a "needle" by looping wire to accomplish this) and tie the apple down to the wreath. Use ribbon to tie the evergreen branches down wherever they must be secured; wire only if you must. As you are weaving the wreath, each person present must weave in the strip of paper on which his/her own wish for the new year is written in runes.

THE YULE TREE

The tree which is decorated at Yule would be the house's living Bairn-Stock. This is another way of giving worship to your family line, from the eldest ancestors to the yet unborn. The treasures which you hang on the tree are gifts to and from your own heritage, some of which may have been passed down through the generations and will be for years to come.

If you have no earthly growing tree which is your family's Bairn-Stock, or if you want to have an indoor evergreen as well as a tree outside, this too may serve as an embodiment of your line. A tree which you have bought commercially is likely to have been felled and treated without respect; to make up for this, you should touch three drops of your blood to the place where the tree has been cut from its roots, whispering, "Stretch deep roots to steads long hid / Might flow from memory's depths."

Traditionally such a tree is adorned with little cookies in the shapes of animals and humans, candles, and similar things. Due to the risk of fire, wooden candles (or even electric lights) ought to be substituted for real flames. In Sweden, straw goats and pigs are often used on the Yule tree.

The Yule tree

EOSTRE EGGS

The Eostre eggs can either be blown out for hanging, or hard-boiled and colored. To blow an egg out, make a small hole with a needle at either end, being sure to pierce the yolk. Place your mouth over one end and blow gently until all the contents are out. If this doesn't seem to work, either you're not blowing hard enough, the hole is too small, or you haven't broken the yolk membrane.

When you have done this, take a piece of wire which is an inch or so longer than the egg and make a loop in one end. You can either make a hanger out of the wire itself by twisting the bottom end until it won't pass through the hole in the egg, or else tie a piece of yarn or ribbon to the wire and pull it through the egg, tying it off at the bottom.

Blown eggs are best painted with water-soluble, quick-drying acrylic paints. These give you the brightest colors and allow for a great deal of detail in egg design. First put on a base coat or two in the color you want, then hang the egg up until it is dry. After this, you can paint whatever designs you wish on over it. If you mean to hang your eggs outside, or to keep them for more than one season, you can shellac them with several coats of clear spray-on polyurethane, either matte (for a natural finish) or gloss (for a laquered look). Enough of this will make the eggs not only water-proof, but virtually unbreakable.

Hard-boiled eggs are best dyed with either commercial "Easter egg" dye or food coloring mixed with a little bit of vinegar. If you choose to do this, there are several traditional methods of decorating the egg. The simplest, though it requires a delicate touch, is the scratch-technique: after the egg is dyed, use a steel engraving pen or other sharp tool to carve a pattern of white lines in. The most common method is applique: when the egg is dyed, an item such as a flower, a frond of fern, a piece of lace, or a cut piece of paper is bound onto it, leaving a pattern on the egg. Another, perhaps more accessible, technique, is that of waxing. At its simplest, this merely involves drawing a design on the egg with a wax crayon before dying; afterwards, when the egg is gently heated and the wax wiped off with a warm rag, the design is left in white. The designer must be careful; even if a mistake in wax is removed, it leaves a greasy place where the color will not take. A more ambitious egg-maker can then cover the colored areas with wax and dye the white parts another color, eventually getting as many shades on one egg as he/she has the patience to achieve. If you want a colored design on a white background, dye the egg, wax the design onto it, and then soak it in sauerkraut juice or a vinegar solution, the acid of which will remove the dye everywhere except under the wax. For a relief effect, wax of different colors can be applied to the egg and left on it. Dyed eggs can also be painted with acrylic.

Some natural dyes which have been used for eggs are carrot, red cabbage, and beets (for red); saffron and gorse flowers (yellow to orange or brown, depending on the cooking time); spinach, artichoke leaves, sage, mint (green); beetroot, sunflower seeds, elderberry fruit/bark (purple); gall nuts, oak bark, alder twigs or bark (black). Onion peel can be used to get any color from yellow to red to dark brown. The egg is gently cooked in a strong solution of whatever colorants you have chosen in water with a few drops of vinegar. From my personal experience, I would say try the natural dyes to see how they work out, but have a selection of food colorings and paint ready anyway.

It is traditional to make eggs with inscriptions declaring love or wishes for the coming year. These should be done in runes. Certain members of our Kindred have found that eggs painted with inscriptions aimed towards luck in love are especially effective, as might be expected from the association of the egg with fertility and new life.

Other symbols which are most fitting for an egg are the leek, the sun-wheel or swastika, the ship, the hex-sign (especially when drawn as a flower), the heart (pierced with an arrow or otherwise), and the coiled wyrm. Any images which remind you of spring and rebirth are good to put on the egg. Wodanists may also make spring eggs for *sig* (victory) with eagles, spears, and fitting inscriptions.

A few general inscriptions for eggs might include ᚨᛚᚢ (ALU, "ale/luck"), ᛚᚨᚢᚲᚨᛉ (LAUKAZ, "leek"—for a man), ᛚᛁᚾᚨ (LINA, "flax"—for a woman), ᛋᛁᚷ (SIG, "victory"), ᛗᚨᛏᛏᛦ:ᛟᚲ:ᛗᛖᚷᛁᚾ (MÁTTR OK MEGINN, "might and main"), and ᚹᛖᚨᛚ·ᚹᚨᚲᛋ ("weal wax").

BREAD ANIMALS

The recipe which I have found most effective for making large bread animals for blessings and feasts is actually a biscuit recipe. This is better than a yeast bread because the dough does not swell up so much while rising, and thus there is less distortion of the animal's shape and so more detail is possible.

2 cups sifted all-purpose flour	2 teaspoons sugar
4 teaspoons baking powder	½ cup butter
½ teaspoon salt	⅔ cup milk
½ teaspoon cream of tartar	

Sift together flour, baking powder, salt, cream of tartar, and sugar; cut in butter until mixture resembles coarse crumbs. Add milk; stir until dough follows fork around bowl. Turn out on a lightly floured surface and shape into your beast. The less kneading the dough gets, the lighter and flakier the end product will be. Bake in pre-heated oven at 350 degrees Farenheit until brown.

If you are making a boar, a "bristled" effect can be achieved by making short snips along its back and side with a pair of clean scissors. The same technique can be used for texturing a horse's mane.

A raisin or nut can be stuck into the dough to make the animal's eye.

FEAST BREAD AND OSTARA CAKES

This bread recipe is one which my sister inherited from our maternal grandmother, a Scandinavian matriarch of the old breed. Usually we double the recipe; if there is too much, this bread freezes very well, but it seldom lasts long enough to be put away.

½ cup warm water	1 tablespoon salt
2 packets yeast	3 eggs
¼ cup butter (melted)	1½ cups milk (warmed)
¼ cup sugar	7 cups flour (roughly)

Melt yeast in warm water. Combine mixture with butter, sugar, salt and eggs. Add warmed milk. Mix in flour until dough is kneadable. Let rise until double in bulk. Make loaves by rolling out long ropes of dough and braiding them. Let rise 30 minutes. Bake in pre-heated oven at 350 degrees Farenheit until done (approximately 20 minutes).

For Ostara cakes, finely chop two golden eating apples and hazelnuts (filberts) to taste per recipe. At the stage where the recipe calls for making loaves, flatten the pieces of dough until they are about half an inch thick and roughly as wide as your hand with fingers outspread. Smear each piece with honey, then put apple chunks and nuts on and roll up loaf with the fillings inside. Pinch the dough shut over the seams so that the honey does not leak out in the baking.

HOUSE PILLARS AND WOODEN IMAGES

The earliest god-images used by our folk were simply branches or pieces of driftwood which bore a natural resemblance to the human form, minimally carved with faces or bodily details. To find such a piece, especially if you live in or near a wooded area, you need only keen eyes and luck—or the favor of the god/esses.

If you wish to make house-pillars or images with a clearer pattern, the simplest way is to start with a sanded piece of flat wood, about half an inch thick—a two-by-whatever your ceiling height is for a house pillar, or the largest piece you can conveniently deal with for your image. A small X-Acto set will provide all the sizes and shapes of blade you need for simple carving, or basic woodcarving chisel sets can often be purchased via hardwood suppliers, craft stores, or even the Boy Scouts.

The easiest wood to carve is basswood or linden, which is light, soft, and yet holds fine detail well. This wood may not hold up well enough to make house-pillars or larger pieces, especially if you mean them to be free-standing. Ash is a harder wood, but also carves fairly easily; oak and cherry are more difficult. Ash and oak are the best from a religious point of view, followed closely by woods from fruit- or nut-bearing trees. Apple or cherry wood may be preferred for the house pillars and ash or oak for images or pillars in a hof.

Begin by drawing your design on the wood in pencil, just as you mean it to appear. If you have never carved before, the easiest way to do this is either to take a wood-burning set and burn the lines in or else to cut grooves along the lines so that you end up with your design basically engraved into the wood. Begin by angling your blade at about 65-70 degrees, using your strong hand on the haft for pressure and guiding the blade with the thumb of your weak hand against the dull edge. Always cut with the grain, never against it. When you have cut one side of the groove, turn the wood around and carve along the line at the opposite angle from the other side, so that you are actually cutting out a thin triangle of wood. If the groove looks messy, you can either cut lightly along it again to chip out stray bits of wood, or else fold a little piece of sandpaper and sand down the groove with the folded edge. This is also the easiest technique for cutting runes, especially if the inscription is to be lasting and visible.

For more elaborate and bas-relief carving, use a thicker piece of wood (one to two inches thick). Using a straight wood chisel, start by making a deep, straight cut all around the outer edge of the design. Then carve in from the edge of the wood, cutting away the excess until your basic outline stands up from the new background. Be careful that your downward cuts are straight and that your cross-cuts stop at the edge of the design; avoid undercutting, which will cause your edges to break off. For knotwork or other such geometric designs, you may want to use a curved chisel to round the edges so that they don't stand up so sharply. If you are doing a face, remember that the nose will be the highest point and trace a block in the middle of the face, then cut the rest of the face down halfway to the background and shape it before you begin work on the nose. Remember that extra wood can always be cut away! Should you break a piece off while you're working, or pare part of your design down too far, wood glue can work wonders and will not be visible after you have stained the piece.

When the piece is carved, begin by sanding it with 150-grit sandpaper and work up in fineness as far as you think necessary—600-grit paper will actually put something of a polish on a hard wood such as oak. You can stain the wood, paint over it, or leave it in its natural color. In all cases, you will probably want to apply a clear sealant of some sort to protect it, especially if you mean to leave it outdoors.

NOTES

1. A recent author's identification of the Danish string skirt as dating from 800–1000 AD is in error. In fact, it is from the Bronze Age, ca. 800–1000 BCE.

Appendix I

Course of Study

Daily practice is recommended to carry out this course of study; the process is one not only of growth of the mind, but also of the soul and understanding. The work of coming to know the god/esses and ways of our elder kin is one which must be woven into everyday life. The best way I have found is to set aside half an hour or so before bedtime for reading and meditation on each chapter or poem, and then to think on what you have read throughout the next day, writing down any sudden bursts of understanding or happenings which seem linked to your studies. This course of study is based on the most accessible texts, and is intended only to give a basic understanding of the tales and ways of our folk. For more advanced study, see the texts recommended in the bibliography.

Basic Texts: *Poetic Edda* (Lee Hollander; University of Texas Press, or Patricia Terry's translation); *Edda* (the *Prose Edda)* by Snorri Sturluson, Anthony Faulkes' translation (Everyman Library); *The Norse Myths* by Kevin Crossley-Holland. The latter is not a primary source, but rather a retelling of most of the material in the two others, along with one or two tales from other sources. It is the least necessary of the three, and often will simply repeat what is in the Eddas. However, it is also probably the most readable.

CREATION AND COSMOS

Teutonic Religion: Cosmos and Wyrd
Poetic Edda: "Völuspá" stanzas 1–20, "Váfthrúdhnismál" 1–39.
Prose Edda: pp. 9–15.
Norse Myths: Chapter I.

COSMOS, WYRD, RAGNARÖK

Teutonic Religion: The Shaping of the Worlds and Wyrd, pp. 7–17.
Poetic Edda: finish "Völuspá" and "Váfthrúdhnismál"; read "Grím-nismál."
Prose Edda: pp. 15–21.
Norse Myths: Chapters 3, 32.
Teutonic Magic: Chapter 2 (optional—describes Wyrd in more detail).

GOD/ESSES AND WIGHTS

Teutonic Religion: Knowing the God/esses, pp. 19–29.
Poetic Edda: "Lokasenna."
Prose Edda: pp. 21–6, 66–77, 96–7.
Norse Myths: Chapters 10, 30.

Wodan

Teutonic Religion: Wodan, pp. 31–40.
Poetic Edda: "Hávamál," "Hárbarzljódh."
Prose Edda: pp. 61–64.
Norse Myths: Chapters 4, 6.
Other: *Saga of the Völsungs* (tr. Jesse Byock). This is a rather lengthier work, which at this point of study is needful only to those who feel very strongly called towards Wodan; most will do better to continue the program and come back to this saga later.

Frija

Teutonic Religion: Frija, Berchta/Holda, pp. 40–49.
Poetic Edda: Prologue to "Grímnismál"; "Váfthrúdhnismál" 1–4.

Thunar

Teutonic Religion: Thunar, Sif, pp. 49–57.
Poetic Edda: "Thrymskvidha," "Hymiskvidha," "Alvíssmál."
Prose Edda: pp. 37–47, 77–83.
Norse Myths: Chapters 16, 19.

Fro Ing

Teutonic Religion: Fro Ing, pp. 89–96.
Poetic Edda: "Skírnismál," "Gróttasöngr."
Prose Edda: pp. 31–2, 106–109.

The Frowe

Teutonic Religion: The Frowe, pp. 82–89.
Poetic Edda: "Völuspá" 21–26, "Hyndluljódh."
Norse Myths: Chapters 2, 13.

Heimdallr

Teutonic Religion: Heimdallr, pp. 63–66.
Poetic Edda: "Rígsthula," "Völuspá hin skamma."
Norse Myths: Chapter 5.

Balder

Teutonic Religion: Balder, pp. 60–63.
Poetic Edda: "Baldrs draumar."
Prose Edda: pp. 48–51.
Norse Myths: Chapter 29.

Tiw

Teutonic Religion: Tiw, pp. 57–60.
Prose Edda: pp. 26–29.
Norse Myths: Chapter 7.

Walkyriges

Teutonic Religion: Walkyriges, pp. 97–104.
Poetic Edda: Helgi lays; "Sigrdrífumál."
Other: *Njal's Saga*, Chapter 157.

Other Wights

Teutonic Religion: Idises, Alfs, House-Ghosts, Trolls, pp. 104–117.
Other: *Icelandic Folktales and Legends* (Jacqueline Simpson, University of California Press, 1979); appropriate chapters in Grimm's *Teutonic Mythology*.

SOUL AND AFTERLIFE

Teutonic Religion, pp. 135–150.
Poetic Edda: "Helreid Brynhildar."
Prose Edda: pp. 27, 32–34.
Other: *Eyrbyggja saga*. For more advanced work, read H.R. Ellis' *The Road to Hel*.

TROTH AND CLAN

Teutonic Religion, pp. 151–160.
Other: *Beowulf*, especially lines 2220 to the end; *Egil's Saga*, Chapter 78; "Battle of Maldon"; *Njal's Saga*, especially Chapters 127–129; *Saga of the Völsungs*, Chapter 8.

Appendix II

Runes, Holy Signs, and Other Correspondences

The Runes are the traditional writing of the Germanic people. Discovered by Wodan after his nine nights' ordeal on Yggdrasill, they first began to be used by humans between 200 BCE–50 CE. They were, and are, used firstly for magic and memorial inscriptions, and very seldom for mundane communications.

The magical use of runes is in itself a highly specialized art, which I describe much more fully in my book *Teutonic Magic* (Llewellyn, 1990). It is not necessary to be a skilled rune-master in order to use the runes for religious purposes, though the more knowledge and might you are able to put into the objects you carve with runes, the stronger they will be.

The main reason for using runes on religious tools and such is that words written in runes are burning beacons of the soul which shine through all the worlds, bringing your tools into the sight of the god/esses and wights. The process of risting (carving) and reddening the runes is in itself a hallowing, particularly if you are writing the names of the god/esses or words of holy meaning. When you set memorial stones or want to mark the bounds of an outdoor holy place with carven rocks, you will wish to use the runes for what you write there. Also, some rites involve the writing of a wish on a strip of paper or an egg; this, too, must be done in runes, not only so that the god/esses can read it readily, but, if you are leaving these items where other folk (especially non-heathens) may see them, you will probably want your words to be hidden—and the very meaning of the word "rune" is "secret"!

There are four major runic futharks[1] in use today. The eldest, from which the others all sprang, is called the Elder Futhark. It has twenty-four staves. The Elder Futhark is the system most commonly used for magical purposes, and in my brief runic analyses of the names of the gods and runes corresponding to sundry things, I have used the Elder Futhark names, staves, and symbolism.

The Anglo-Saxon or Anglo-Frisian Futhorc adds several runes to the twenty-four of the Elder Futhark. In *A Book of Troth*, Edred Thorsson suggests that this futhorc be used for more everyday writings, while the Elder Futhark is reserved for magical workings. The advantage of this is that the Anglo-Saxon Futhorc is better phonetically adapted to the English language. Even in the Christian manuscript tradition, however, runes clearly had a "special" significance, and should therefore be used for "mundane" purposes only with great care: they are mighty in and of themselves, a might which is only partially dependent on the worker. Meaning well will not protect you from the dangers of mis-written staves!

The Younger Futhark, a condensed version of the Elder Futhark in which several of the staves can stand for either of two phonetic values, was developed and used by the Scandinavian people after ca. 800 CE. There are several versions of it; I present the most common.

The Armanen Futhark was invented or discovered by the German seer Guido von List at the beginning of the 20th century, as a result of his meditations on the 18 magical songs of "Hávamál" during a period of blindness. It consists of the 16 runes of the Younger Futhark, one stave brought in from the Elder Futhark, and one which von List invented himself. It is primarily used by German magicians today.

ELDER FUTHARK

Stave	Name	Phonetic value
ᚠ	fehu ("fee")	F
ᚢ	uruz ("aurochs")	U
ᚦ	thurisaz ("thurse," a giant)	Th
ᚨ	ansuz ("Ase")	A
ᚱ	raidho ("riding," "wain")	R
ᚲ	kenaz ("torch")	K/hard C
ᚷ	gebo ("gift")	G
ᚹ	wunjo ("joy")	W/V
ᚺ	hagalaz ("hail")	H, Ch
ᚾ	nauthiz ("need")	N
ᛁ	isa ("ice")	I
ᛃ	jera ("year," harvest)	Y, J
ᛇ	eihwaz ("yew")	EI (almost never used)
ᛈ	perthro ("pear" or "lot-box")	P
ᛉ	elhaz ("elk")	Z, final R in Old Norse
ᛊ	sowilo ("sun")	S
ᛏ	tiwaz ("Tiw")	T
ᛒ	berkano ("birch")	B
ᛖ	ehwaz ("horse")	E
ᛗ	mannaz ("man" as human being)	M
ᛚ	laguz ("lake")	L
ᛜ	ingwaz (Ing)	Ng
ᛞ	dagaz ("day")	Dh, D
ᛟ	othala ("udal lands")	O

ANGLO-SAXON FUTHORC

Stave	Name	Sound
ᚠ	feoh	F
ᚢ	ur	U
ᚦ	thorn ("a thorn")	Th
ᚩ	os ("mouth")	short O
ᚱ	rad	R
ᚳ	cen	Ch, soft C
ᚷ	gyfu	soft G, J
ᚹ	wyn	W
ᚻ	haegl	H
ᚾ	nyd	N
ᛁ	is	I
ᛄ	ger	Y, J
ᛇ	eoh	Y (very rare)
ᛈ	peorth	P
ᛉ	eolh-secg ("elk-grass")	X
ᛋ	sigel	S
ᛏ	tir ("glory," a star-name)	T
ᛒ	beorc	B
ᛖ	eh	E
ᛗ	man	M
ᛚ	lagu	L
ᛝ	Ing	Ng
ᛞ	dag	Dh, D
ᛟ	othel	long O
ᚪ	ac ("oak")	A

Stave	Name	Sound
ᚫ	æsc ("ash")	Æ
ᛦ	yr ("yew-bow")	Y
ᛡ	iar ("serpent")	Ia
ᛠ	ear ("earth," "dust")	Ea
ᛢ	quern ("mill")	Q, Qu
ᛣ	calk ("cup")	K, hard C
ᛥ	stan ("stone")	St
ᚸ	gar ("spear")	hard G (as in "get")

YOUNGER FUTHARK

Stave	Name	Sound
ᚡ	fé	F
ᚢ	úr (drizzle)	U, V, W
ᚦ	thurs	Th, Dh
ᚨ	áss	long A, O
ᚱ	reidh	R
ᚴ	kaun ("sore," "boil")	K, C, G
ᚼ	hagall	H
ᚾ	naudh	N
ᛁ	íss	I
ᛆ	ár	A (long or short)
ᛋ	sól	S
ᛏ	Týr	T, D
ᛒ	bjarkan	B, P
ᛘ	madhr	M
ᛚ	lögr	L
ᛣ	ýr ("yew-bow")	final R

To these staves the Armanen Futhark adds:

ᛇ	eh (marriage)	E
ᚷ	gibor (gift)	G

HOLY SIGNS

In addition to the runes, there are a number of holy signs which have religious and magical significance within the Teutonic tradition.

Hex Sign: Warding, holiness, "good luck." This sign shows the true shape of the Nine Worlds; no force of disorder or disruption can withstand it. It is the snowflake-shape of the Younger rune hagall, the "sickness of snakes." This sign is often put on houses.

Sun-Wheel: This sign shows the Sun's might working weal upon the earth. It is a sign fitting for all the Wanic powers, but is tied most closely to Fro Ing and the Light Alfs.

Sun-Ring (ON *sólarhringr):* This sign shows the eight stations of the Sun on her daily circle; it also shows the *ættir* as the eight directions of the compass.

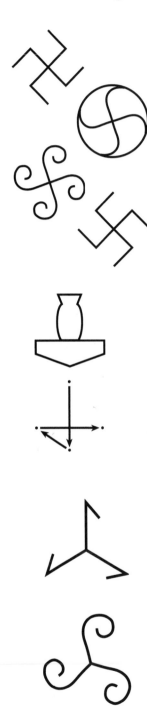

Swastika or **Fylfot:** This is the sign of the Sun's strength as the unstoppable whirling might of Will. It is one of the holiest and oldest signs in the world, known to nearly every tradition. Drawing it widdershins does not pervert its force or make it "evil" in any way. The Germanic peoples used both forms of the symbol. The swastika is also associated with the Hammer of Thunar. A softer swirling form can also be used by those for whom recent associations make the angular form difficult to deal with as a sign of weal.

Thunar's Hammer: The Hammer is the greatest sign of heathen troth. Hammer-amulets are worn by most true folk, whether they are personally close to Thunar or not. The Hammer is also a mighty sign of warding, and is used to hallow objects and persons. See also the illustration of various Hammer-amulets in the section on Thunar in Chapter 3.

Trefot: The trefot (called the triskelion in its swirling form) shows might whirling from the three great realms of being: the Overworld, the Underworld, and the Middle World. It can be put on things in order to fill them with might. The triskelion is the emblem of the Island of Man. In the Celtic tradition, it is associated with Mannanan mac Lir. Because of the similarities between Mannanan mac Lir and Heimdallr, and because of Heimdallr's role as father of the three classes of humankind, the trefot might be used as a sign of Heimdallr, since there is no historical tradition associating any emblem with this god.

Helm of Awe (ON *aegishjálmarr):* This sign strengthens its wearer and causes awe or terror in those who view it. It may be used as a marker at the boundaries of a wih-stead. The rune elhaz (shown below the Helm of Awe) may be used for the same purpose.

World-Tree: This sign shows the tree Yggdrasill with its branches stretching upward and roots stretching downward. It was used on rock carvings from the Bronze Age and on one of the early Gotlandic picture stones (ca. 400–600 CE).

Heart: This sign actually shows the female buttocks and genitals, rather than the heart. It is a sign of the Frowe's might, and used to call upon her as Frowe of Love.

Walknot (ON *valknútr):* "Knot of the Slain." This is the sign of Wodan, showing his craft of binding and loosening and his might over the knots of Wyrd. It is worn only by those who choose to give themselves to Wodan. The Walknot has two forms, the interlocked and the unicursal. The latter is the better when the Walknot is being traced as a holy gesture.

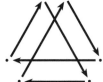

Horn Triskelion: This is the sign of the thule or the Wodanically inspired one. The three horns show the three cauldrons in which the mead Wod-Stirrer is kept. Today, it is also used as the emblem of the Rune-Gild.

Footprint: A sign of fruitfulness, associated with Njordhr/Nerthus. Found in the Bronze Age rock carvings.

Ship: The ship is the emblem both of fruitfulness and of death. In both these aspects, it is associated with the Wans, who rule water and earth; as a sign of faring between the worlds, it is also associated with Wodan.

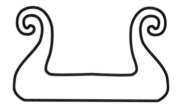

Wain: The Wain is associated with several of the god/esses. Drawn by horses, it is the vehicle of the Sun; by goats, it is the sign of Thunar; by cats, it is the wain of the Frowe.

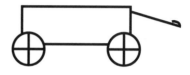

Shield-Knot: a sign of warding. Still used today in Scandinavia to mark off protected sites of archaeological interest and ancient cultural heritage.

Ring: The unbroken ring is the sign of troth; it may also show the sig-blessing of the gods. See "Oath-Ring" in Chapter 11: Tools.

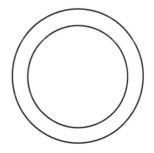

Staring Eyes: Especially associated with Thunar, but also with holiness and great might of soul in general. A hero has eyes "keen as an adder's," and the undead are also said to have huge staring eyes.

Spindle and Distaff: Signs of Frija and Berchta/Holda, also of the Norns and of women in general.

Basket of Fruit: a characteristic attribute of the idises.

Knotwork: used for ornamentation; also may have a warding effect.

ANIMALS

Bears—Thunar, possibly also Wanic.

Bees—Walkyriges, women's magic, healing.

Boar, swine in general—Wanic; however, any hero can be called "boar" as a compliment, and Wodan's warriors in Walhall eat of the boar Saehrimmnir every night.

Bull, cattle in general—Wanic.

Cats—The Frowe.

Eagle—The noblest bird; one of the three Beasts of Battle (the other two are raven and wolf). Wodan. Etins also take the shape of an Eagle often.

Falcon—Frija, the Frowe. Feminine correspondent to the masculine Eagle.

Goats—Thunar.

Horse—Sunna's Wain; faring between worlds; Fro Ing (stallion); Hella (mare); Wodan's horse is the eight-legged gray Sleipnir.

Ram—Heimdallr.

Ravens—Wodan.

Seal—Heimdallr.

Stag—The noblest beast. Fro Ing.

Swan—Walkyriges, Norns.

Wolves—Wodan.

Wyrm (dragon or snake)—A sign of hidden might. The Wanic forces; Wyrd; Wodan; the Middle-Garth's Wyrm is closely bound to Thunar.

COLORS

The three great colors of the Indo-Europeans are white, red, and black.

White—Highest holiness. Heimdallr, Balder.

Red—Life, magic, strength, a fierce mood. Calling someone "the Red" as a by-name is a compliment (cf. "Red Thórr"). Germanic warriors whose hair was not naturally red would often dye it to make themselves look more warlike and manly. Thunar.

Black/Dark Blue—Death, things hidden. Wodan, Njördhr/ Nerthus, Hella.

Yellow—Sunlight, an ordered world, frith. Fro Ing, Light Alfs.

Green—The earth, Wanic might.

Brown—The earth, Swart Alfs. May also be seen as a lesser red.

Purple—A combination of red and dark blue. Among the Anglo-Saxons, red, blue, and purple were the colors of magic.

NUMBERS

Three—The most general number of holiness and magic power. Ritual actions are repeated thrice or nine times; the Nine Worlds are divided into the three realms of the Overworld, the Earth, and the Underworld; each of the god/esses (and most humans) works with the three functions of intellect/soul, strength, and fruitfulness.

Four—Stability; the four cardinal directions of the compass, the solar cross.

Eight—Also stability; the *ættir*, or eight directions of the compass.

Nine—Holiest of numbers.

Twelve—The number of completion. There are 12 gods and 24 goddesses; berserker-bands often come in companies of 12.

PLANTS

Apple—Yule, the Bairn-Stock, life, rebirth, wyrd. Idunn; Wodan.

Ash—Yggdrasill; Wodan. Ash and oak are best for wooden harrows.

Birch—The Frowe; Holda/Berchta; Frija. Birth, death, and cleansing. Birch branches should be used for ritual chastisement, especially those symbolic beatings which increase fruitfulness. Spring festivities.

Elder—The Frowe; Holda/Berchta.

Hazel—The marker of holy boundaries. Fosite; Tiw.

Oak—The holiest tree of the Indo-Europeans. Tiw; Thunar.

Yew—Yggdrasill; Wuldor; Wodan; death; the wih-stead.

SUNDRY CORRESPONDENCES

Drinks—Ale is associated with the Wans and Wyrd; mead with Wodan and his gift of poetry; wine with Wodan. Hard cider is best to drink at Yule, and is holy to all the god/esses.

Weapons—The Sword is the weapon of Fro Ing and sometimes a gift given by Wodan to his heroes; the Spear is the weapon of Wodan; the Bow that of Wuldor and Skadhi; the Hammer and the Axe are weapons of Thunar.

Sacrifice—Hanging is Wodanic, but Wanic sacrifices are also sometimes hanged or strangled. Hanging and stabbing are specifically Wodanic. Drowning and burying an item are Wanic; burning is the best way to sacrifice an item to the Ases. The greatest sacrifices are those which are destroyed in the threefold manner of hanging, stabbing or burning, and drowning simultaneously. In ancient times, our ancestors often sacrificed weapons and other precious items to the god/esses.

Metals—Gold is fire and especially associated with Freyja and the Wanic powers; silver is ice. The word "iron," as Sunwyn Ravenwood has made known to me, first meant "holy metal," which may tell us something about its might as a warder in the soul-realm; it may be most closely tied to Thúnar and the Ases in general.

Amber—The Frowe; Thunar. Warding from all ill; fruitfulness; might.

Bells—Rung at Wanic ceremonies and as part of ritual drama, or whenever noise is needed.

NOTES

1. The runic alphabet is called the "futhark" or "futhorc" from its first six letters: ḟehu, ụruz, ṯhurisaz, ạnsuz (or ọss), ṛaidho, ḵenaz. The principle is the same as the Greek alpha, beta = alphabet.

Appendix III

Names and Kennings

Names which are essentially the same name in various languages will be put in parentheses after the Germanic English form which I have used throughout the book; other names will be listed beneath the primary form. For a further and much more extensive list of kennings and description of the means by which they may be formed, see the "Skaldskaparmal" section of the *Prose Edda*.

WODAN (Ódhinn, Wotan, Woden, Godan)
    Drighten of the Spear, Cargo-God, Sig-Father, All-Father, Wal-Father, Lord of the Gallows, Drighten of Draugs, Hanged, Gallows'-Load, God of the Hanged, Yggr (the Terrifying or Awesome), Gautr, Vidhur, Hel-Blind, High One, Hoar-Beard, Evil-Worker, Gizur, Sigmundr (Victory-Gift), Raven-god, Raven-Tempter, Godhi of the Raven-Blót, Father of Men, Völsi, Gelding, Horse-hair-Bearded, Old Man of the Berg, Vidhrir, Jólnir (from "Yule"), Gan-grádhr, Way-Tame, Eagle-Headed, One-Eyed, Grímnir ("Masked"), Blindi ("Blind"), Tvíblindi ("Double-Blind), Balefire-Eyed, Long-Bearded, Skilfingr, Sváfnir ("Luller to Sleep" or "Slayer"), Galdr-Father, Frigg's Husband, Feng, Fjölnir, Fimbulthulr (Great Thule), Hroptr (The Maligned), Thunderer, Bestla's Son, Gizur the Warrior of the Greutingi, Sig-Deemer, Walhall's Ruler, Irmin, Lord of Hlidhskjalf, Friend of Lódhurr and Lopt.

THUNAR (Thórr, Donar)

Middle-Garth's Warder, Single-Handed Wyrm-Bane, Wih-Stead's Warder, Vingthórr, Módhi/Magni/Thrudhr's Father, Sif's Husband, Son of Earth, Mjöllnir's Wielder, Etins'/Thurses' Bane, Whetstone-Skulled, Owner of the Main-Girdle, Awesome, Helper of Men, Driver-Thunar, Wodan's Helper, Giants' Challenger, Eindridi, Meili's Brother, Wodan's Son, Oppressor of Trolls, Giant of Vimur's Ford, Wigithunar, Thunar Karl (Old Man Thunar), Thunderer, Thunder-God, User of Goats, Drighten of Goats, Fjörgyn's Son.

TIW (Týr)

One-Handed God, Feeder of the Wolf, the Wolf's Leavings.

HEIMDALLR

Son of Nine Mothers, Rigr, Loki's Foe, Warder of the Gods, Golden-Toothed, Hallinskidhi, Whitest Ase, Owner of the Gjallarhorn.

WULDOR (Ullr)

Bow-Ase, Snowshoe-Ase, Hunting-Ase, Shield-Ase.

BALDER

Frija's Son, Wodan's Son, Nanna's Husband, Fosite's Father, Breidhablik's Ruler, Bloodied God, Bright God, the Good.

LOKI

Rede-Bane of Balder, Laufey's Son, Farbauti's Son, Loptr, husband of Sigyn, Thief of Brisingamen, Striver against Heimdallr and Skadhi, Hvedhrungr (the Roarer), Father of Fenrir and the Middle-Garth's Wyrm and Sleipnir, Wodan's Brother, Thief or Harmer of Sif's Hair, Sly God, Slanderer, Crafty One, Bound God.

THE FROWE (Freyja, Freya)

Mardöll, Hörn ("Flax"), Owner of Cats, Wod's Bedfellow or Wife, Fro Ing's Sister, Njördhr's Daughter, Giver, Wanadis, Wan-Bride, Sow, Fair-Tears, Hnoss' Mother, Gullveig, Owner of Brisingamen, Most Famed of Goddesses, Heidh, Gray ("hound").

FRO ING (Freyr, Frey)

God of the World, Ingvi-Freyr, Frodhi (the Fruitful), Beli's Foe,

Njördhr's Son, Most Famed of Gods, Up-Rider, Blessing-God of the Swedes, Husband of Gerdhr, Protector of the Ases, Ruler of the Armies of the Gods, Harvest-God, Wealth-God.

NJÖRDHR

Fro Ing's Father, Skadhi's Husband, Noatun's Ruler.

POETRY

Wod-Stirrer (ON *Odhroerir*), Kvasir's blood, dwarves' ship, dwarves' mead, etins' mead, Svitungs' mead, Wodan's mead, Ases' mead, the cauldrons Wod-Stirrer and Bodhn and Son, cauldron of Hnitbjorg, winning or finding or cargo or gift of Wodan, the cup of Ygg, Vidhur's theft, the feast of Gaut, the holy cup of the Raven-god, the gift of Grimnir, the seed of the eagle's beak, the sea of Wodan's breast. All of these and the many other kennings for poetry derive from the tale of the creation and winning of the mead Wod-Stirrer.

GOLD

Sea-fire, Kraki's seed (or barley), Ottar's weregild, fire of the wyrm's bed, Welsh grains, arm-fire, Frowe's tears, Frodhi's meal, Ægir's fire or light, Holgi's mound-roof.

HUMANS

May be referred to by names for trees (battle-oak, necklace-linden) or god/esses (helm-Odhinn, amber-Freyja, sword-Freyr, linen-Skogul); by function (a ruler is a ring-breaker or gold-giver; a sailor is a sea-steed's rider; a warrior is a helmet-harmer, wolf/raven/eagle-feeder); descent from or friendship with the god/esses (scion of Fro Ing's line, friend of Thorr), or relationship to heroes (kinswo/man of the Volsungs.

Appendix IV

Chronology

PREHISTORIC PERIOD
4000 BCE (BEFORE COMMON ERA)–100 BCE

4000 BCE—The Indo-European migrations begin, starting in the regions around the Caspian Sea or southern steppes or Russia.

1500 BCE—Bronze Age begins in Scandinavia.

1000 BCE—The ancestors of the Germanic peoples, settled in the general area of modern Scandinavia, begin to develop a linguistic/cultural/religious complex separate from that of the general Indo-European stock.

500 BCE—Scandinavian Iron Age begins.

ca. 500–200 BCE—Celtic rule throughout most of continental Europe.

ca. 200 BCE—The East Germanic folks (Goths, Burgundians, and others) migrate down from Scandinavia to Eastern Europe, settling the steppes and the Black Sea area. The West Germanic peoples migrate downwards into the area of modern Germany, displacing the Celts who had previously ruled the region. By this time, the Proto-Germanic language is beginning to divide into North Germanic (Scandinavian languages), West Germanic (continental German and later Anglo-Saxon, eventually German, English, Yiddish, and Dutch), and East Germanic (Gothic; no modern survivors); by 400 CE, these dialects will be mutually incomprehensible.

250 BCE—Also known as 0 RE (Runic Era). According to modern tradition, Wodanaz revealed the runes to humankind in this year. Many Ásatrú groups date from this year rather than using the Christian or Common Era system of dating; simply add 250 to the Common Era date.

ca. 250–100 BCE—The runes are discovered/developed in the human world.

ROMAN PERIOD

ca. 150–100 BCE—The Germans meet the Romans—hate at first sight.

ca. 100 BCE–500 CE The practice of sacrificing/executing people in bogs is carried out in Scandinavia on a fairly regular basis.

9 CE (Common Era)—Hermann ("Arminius") defeats the Romans at the battle of Teutoberger Wald, preventing a Roman conquest of Germania.

ca. 50 CE—The first surviving artifact with runes on it, the Meldorf brooch, is made in Denmark.

98 CE—Tacitus writes the *Germania,* the earliest full account of the culture and religion of the Germanic folk.

MIGRATION AGE (OR "HEROIC AGE")
ROUGHLY 300–700 CE

ca. 325–400—The Goths converted to Arian (as opposed to Catholic) Christianity; Ulfilas writes his translation of the

New Testament, the only surviving work of written Gothic, ca. 350–375.

378—The Goths defeat the Romans in the East, at the battle of Adrianople.

406/7—A coalition of Germanic tribes cross the Roman frontier at the Rhine and take lands on the Roman side.

410—Alaric, king of the Visigoths, conquers Rome.

436/7—The Huns, aided and encouraged by the Roman emperor Aetius, overrun the East Germanic Burgundian kingdom on the Rhine, killing the king Gundahari (Gunther or Gunnar of the later sources) and the rest of the royal family; a major historical source of the *Nibelungenlied/Völsunga saga* story.

449—Hengest and Horsa begin the Anglo-Saxon conquest of Britain.

ca. 450—The West Germanic tribes living around the North Sea (Angles, Saxons, and Frisians) begin to add runes to the Elder Futhark to deal with changes in the sound-system of their own dialect, creating the Anglo-Frisian Futhork.

493–526—The Visigothic hero/king Theodoric the Great rules in Rome until his death.

500–530—Beowulf, Hrothgar, Hrolf Kraki, and the other characters of their cycle live.

638—Approximate date of the Sutton Hoo ship-burial, the richest Germanic burial ever found in Britain; notable particularly for the ship in the cairn and the elaborately worked boar-helmet.

659—Penda, last heathen king of England, dies heroically in battle.

ca. 700—Primitive Norse, or Runic, gives way to Old Norse.

772—Charlemagne begins his genocidal wars against the Saxons, destroying the Irminsul.

VIKING AGE
793–1066

793—The Norse sack the Anglo-Celtic monastery on Lindisfarne.

795—Norse begin raiding Ireland

ca. 800—The Elder Futhark gives way to the Younger (16-rune) Futhark in Scandinavia.

810—Death of Charlemagne.

844/5—Norse raiding Moorish Spain.

852—The Swedish Rus become dominant along the Volga.

860s—Ragnar Loddbrok killed at York; the Rus found Novgorod and Kiev.

870—The settlement of Iceland begins.

878—Alfred the Great of England overcomes Guthrum and forces him and his army to convert to Christianity in return for lands in England. Haraldr Hairfair finishes overcoming and uniting the whole of Norway and the Orkneys; many Norwegians flee to Iceland.

912—Gongu-Hrolf and his men take lands in Normandy as vassals of the French king and become the Normans.

922—Ibn Fadlan, an Arab ambassador to the Scandinavians (Rus) along the Volga, writes his account of their customs, including a full description of a ship/cremation funeral.

930—First Althing held at Thingvellir in Iceland.

965—Haraldr Bluetooth, king of Denmark, converted to Christianity.

982—Eirikr the Red discovers Greenland.

986—Greenland settled.

990—Egill Skallagrimsson, famed skald, warrior, and Odhinsmadhr, dies.

1000—Iceland officially converts to Christianity by decree of the Lawspeaker Thorgeirr; heathen practise is still permitted in private. Olafr Tryggvason killed.

1000–1005—Leifr Eiriksson makes his voyages to Vinland (America); attempts to settle there are made but are unsuccessful.

1016—Brian Boru triumphs over the Norse in Ireland at the battle of Clontarf, in which he and the Jarl Sigurdhr of Orkney are slain.

1030—Olafr the Lawbreaker (St. Olafr) killed.

1066—Haraldr Hardrada, king of Norway, dies fighting against Harold Godwinson, king of England; Harold Godwinson is killed in battle against William the Bastard of Normandy and the Norman Conquest takes place. The practice of "going viking"—Norse sea raids on the southern realms—ends.

ca. 1075—Adam of Bremen writes his description of the great heathen hof at Uppsala.

POST-HEATHEN PERIOD

1100—Christian missionaries destroy the great hof at Old Uppsala, eventually replacing it with a Christian church.

ca. 1175—The original *Nibelungenlied* is written in Germany.

1200–1450—The Icelandic sagas, most of which are based on a corpus of earlier verses, are written.

1220—Snorri Sturluson writes the *Prose Edda.*

ca. 1250–1300—Most of the poems of the *Poetic Edda,* which had previously been circulating orally are collected and written down in the manuscript called Codex Regius, the oldest manuscript containing the Eddic poems.

REBIRTH

ca. 1650–1700—The "Gothic movement" in Sweden, a national/antiquarian movement headed by Johannes Magnus and Johannes Bureus of Sweden, begins. The Dane Ole Worm also carries out a massive body of historical/religious/cultural Scandinavian studies.

1844—Jacob Grimm publishes *Teutonic Mythology*, a massive compendium of Germanic legend, folklore, and linguistic studies.

1876—First performance of Richard Wagner's *Der Ring des Nibelungens*.

Late 19th century—The Boy Guides (English) and Boy Scouts (American) are founded specifically and consciously for the purpose of educating young men in the values of their Anglo-Saxon forebears.

1908—The German Guido von List, inspired by the *Poetic Edda* and his own visions, creates the 18-rune Armanen Futhark and writes "Secret of the Runes."

1973—Stephen MacNallen founds the Ásatú Free Assembly (A.F.A.) in America; Sveinbjorn Beinteinson founds the Ásatrúmenn of Iceland.

1980—Edred Thorsson founds the Rune-Gild.

1987—A.F.A. breaks up; Edred Thorsson founds the Ring of Troth.

1988—Ásatrú Alliance is founded.

Appendix V

Calendar

The Germanic folk never had a single calendar; several sources giving local data do, however, exist. Einhard's *Life of Charlemagne* describes how the Frankish emperor gave the months Frankish names; in *History of the English Church and People,* Bede speaks of the Anglo-Saxon month-names and heathen festivals; the Icelandic month-names survived long enough to be written down. We know that the Icelandic months did not correspond exactly to the Roman months; thus Thorri should properly be January-February, Goi February-March, etc. It is worth remembering that the Germanic folk used both a solar and a lunar calendar—that is, the solstices were held at the proper phases of the solar year, but the "monthly" time-reckoning was probably measured by the phases of the Moon. Thus the first month on this list in all cases would probably properly begin on either the first new or the first full moon within the corresponding Roman month.

Roman	Frankish	Anglo-Saxon	Icelandic
January	Wintermanoth	After-Giuli	Thorri
February	Hornung	Solmonath	Goi
March	Lentzinmanoth	Hredhmonath	Einmánudhr
April	Ostarmanoth	Eostre	Gaukmánudhr/ Sáidtidh

Roman	Frankish	Anglo-Saxon	Icelandic
May	Winnemanoth	Thrimilcmonath	Eggtídh
June	Brachmanoth	Ærre-Lithe (Midsummer's)	Sólmánudhr
July	Hewimanoth	Æfter-Lithe	Heyannír
August	Aranmanoth	Weodmonath	Tvímánudhr
September	Witumanoth	Haligmonath	Hanstmánudhr
October	Windume-manoth	Winterfyllith	Gormánudhr
November	Herbistmanoth	Blotmonath	Frermánudhr
December	Heilagmanoth	Ærre-Giuli (Before-Yule)	Hrútmánudhr

The Frankish names, in order, mean: Winter-Month, Turn of the Year, Lent-Month (obviously a christian replacement of the original), Ostara-Month, Joy-Month, Breaking (ploughing)-Month, Hay-Month, Grain-Ear-Month, Wood-Month, Wine-Harvest-Month, Harvest-Month, and Holy-Month. The Anglo-Saxon are After-Yule, Sun-Month, Glory-Month, Eostre, Three-Milkings-Month, Before-Midsummer's, After-Midsummer's, Weed-Month, Holy-Month, Winter-Full Moon, Blessing-Month, and Before-Yule. The Icelandic are Thorri (?), Goi (?), Single Month, Cuckoo-Month or Seed-Tide, Egg-tide, Sun-Month, Hay-Toil, Double-Month, Harvest-Month, Slaughter-Month, Frost-Month, and Ram-Month.

There is also a set of modern month-names including "Fog-moon," "Wolfmoon," and "Snowmoon." These are 20th-century romantic inventions which have no place in any ancient tradition, Germanic or Celtic.

FESTIVALS

The festivals of the Teutonic year are:

Yule—Twelve nights beginning on December 20 and ending on January 1.

Feast of Thunar—Full or new moon of January.

Charming of the Plough—New moon of February.

Eostre—Sometime near the Spring Equinox; we use the first full moon after the Equinox.

Walpurgisnight—Night of April 30.

May Day—First of May.

Midsummer's—June 20/21.

Loaf-Fest—August 1.

Winternights—Sometime near the Autumnal Equinox, as above.

Other feasts held in modern Ásatrú are the feasts held in remembrance of various heroes, most of whom are described further in the chapter on Heroes in this book.

January 9—**Remembrance for Raud the Strong,** a Norwegian chieftain murdered by Óláfr Tryggvason for keeping the heathen faith. Óláfr slew him by forcing a horn down his throat, then putting an adder into the horn and heating it until the snake escaped into Raud's stomach. On this day, we give worship to all those folk who died rather than giving way to Christianity.

February 9—**Remembrance for Eyvindr Kinnrifi,** a Norwegian Asaman murdered by Óláfr Tryggvason. When bribery failed to convince him to convert, a metal bowl was set on his abdomen and red-hot coals heaped on it to torture him into accepting baptism. In spite of this agony, Eyvindr refused to turn away from the god/esses of his folk, dying at last when his belly burst asunder from the heat.

February 14—**Feast of Váli.** Modern folk etymology has connected Váli with Valentine's Day, though there is actually no evidence for this; the pagan origins of this semi-Christianized feast are derived from the Roman Lupercalia, not from anything Norse. Nevertheless, there is no reason not to hail Váli on this day, and many Ásatrúar do.

March 28—**Ragnar Löddbrok's Day.** A feast in memory of this great Norse hero, who sacked Paris on this day in 845 CE.

Memorial Day—**Einherjar Day,** when we remember the slain heroes who now drink and fight in Wodan's Halls.

June 9—**Remembrance for Sigurdhr the Völsung** (see "Heroes").

July 9—**Remembrance for Unnr the Deep-Minded**, one of the early Icelandic settlers and great Scandinavian matriarchs, who led her clan from Norway to Iceland when they were threatened by the ambitions of King Haraldr Harfagri. Her tale is found in *Laxdæla Saga*.

July 29—**Death of Óláfr the Lawbreaker** (St. Óláfr), a Norwegian king whose sainthood was given to him in recognition of his actions in murdering, maiming, and dispossessing a great many Norwegians who would not submit to Christianity. Óláfr was killed on this day at the Battle of Stikklestad in 1030 CE.

August 9—**Radbod's Day**; a feast to the memory of the Frisian king who held back the tide of Christianity in his lands (see "Heroes").

September 9—**Remembrance for Herman the Cheruscan**, greatest of the chieftains who warded the Germans from the Roman conquest (see "Heroes").

Columbus Day—**Remembrance for Leif Eiríksson Day** (and his sister Freydís—see "Heroes"), when we drink to the earliest European settlers of America.

October 28—**Remembrance for Eiríkr the Red.**

November 9—**Queen Sigrídhr of Sweden Day;** remembrance for the heroic Queen Sigrídhr the Strong-Minded, defender of heathenism.

Thanksgiving—**Weyland Smith Day.** Worship is given to the great smith-hero of our folk. I don't know why Thanksgiving is Weyland's Day, but this is how it's celebrated in modern Ásatrú.

December 9—**Remembrance for Egill Skallagrimsson.**

Appendix VI

Word-Hoard

atheling—noble (can be used either as a noun or an adjective)

bale—poison

bale-fire—funeral pyre

bane—slayer

byrnie—a mail shirt or hauberk

carl—free man

carline—free woman

doom—judgment (verb: to deem), not necessarily in a woeful sense

draugur—walking corpse

drighten—lord (in the sense of leader of a band of thanes)

drightine—fem. of drighten

elder kin, kin who have fared before us, forebears—ancestors

eldest kin—the god/esses

ergi—a perverted/cowardly action; ergish may be used as an adjectival form.

etin—a giant of vast and primeval wisdom

fane—temple

frith—fruitful peace, happiness

fro—lord (in the sense of ruler over lands, administrator, judge)

frowe—fem. of fro

garth—a yard, enclosure, homestead

ghost—spirit or soul (in the sense of a living person's soul as well
as a disembodied personality)

gram—fierce, hostile, angry

hallow—to make holy

hof—temple

holt—forest

howe—burial mound

hyge—thought, intuition

irmin-—great, very large (used as a prefix)

meet—fitting or proper

mickle—great (in the sense of large); mighty

mood—courage, thought, feeling

nithling—a coward and oath-breaker

rede—counsel, advice

rime—ice

ris—a giant

siege—throne, castle

sig—victory

spill—destroy

stead—place

hane—person bound by oath to a drighten/ine, usually an atheling

thrall—slave

thurse—a fierce and not very clever rock- or rime-giant

tir—glory; tir-fast—glorious

trollish—magical (in an ill sense), unnatural

troth—honor, truthfulness

udal—owned by right of inheritance (especially used for lands)

wain—wagon (or car)

wal—slaughter, battle, the slain

ween—to expect

wend—to go

wight—being

wih—holy (used as a prefix).

wit—to know. Also "wot"; "I wit that..." or "I wot that..."

wod—fury, intoxication, inspiration

worship—honor

wreak—to make or do (as: "to wreak vengeance"); "wreaking" is used as a noun for a spell.

wyrm—dragon, serpent

Glossary

ætt, ættir (pl)—The term ætt can be used to describe a kin-group or the eight points of the compass. When a ritual action is done "to the ættir," the word indicates that the eight compass-points should be sprinkled, hallowed, or whatever.

ale—Any malt beverage—beer, ale, stout, or even whisky.

alf, alfs (Old Norse alfr, alfar.)—Elf; sometimes male ancestral spirits. Fully described in Chapter 6: Wights.

alu—Literally "ale"; also means "luck" or "magical might." See the section on the Horn in Chapter 12: Holy Tools.

Ásatrú—"True to the gods"; the name most often used by followers of the Northern ways for both persons and the religion itself.

Ase, Ases (ON Æs, Æsir.)—The race of god/esses which includes Wodan, Frija, Thunar, and all their kin.

Ases' Garth (ON Ásgardhr)—The dwelling of the god/esses.

BCE/CE—Before Common Era/Common Era. The Common Era dates from the height of the Roman Empire in the West—that is to say, BCE/CE dates are identical to BC/AD dates. The Common Era terminology is used by non-Christians and by whomever is sensitive to the problems inherent in forcing a single religion's dating system on a world filled with people of varied faiths.

blessing (ON blót)—The religious portion of a holy feast, at which drink is poured out for the god/esses and a bread-animal may be symbolically "sacrificed."

deosil—In the direction of the sun; that is, clockwise. Used for drawing down heavenly might.

draug (ON draugr)—A walking corpse.

drighten (fem. drightine)—Leader. See Chapter 11: Holy Folk.

East Germanic—The languages deriving from the Germanic dialect spoken by the folk who migrated from Scandinavia to Eastern Europe and the steppes ca. 200 BCE. Gothic is the only recorded East Germanic language; none have survived into the modern period.

einherjar—"Single Combatants"; Wodan's chosen/slain champions who fight in Walhall every day.

Elder Edda—The Old Norse compilation of mythological and heroic poems. All "Eddic poems" or "Eddic lays" are found in this volume.

etin (ON jötunn)—A wise and ancient giant. See Chapter 6.

Etin-Home (ON Jötunheimr)—The eastern world, home of all giants.

fro (fem. frowe)—Lord/lady. See Chapter 11.

garth—Enclosure, homestead.

Germanic—Describes the traditions, heritage, and culture of the various people speaking languages within the Germanic branch of the Indo-European language groups (see North, East, and West Germanic). Identical to "Teutonic." This is *not* a racial term; it describes language and culture.

ghost—A spiritual being; not necessarily the soul of a dead human.

godwo/man (ON godhi/gydhja)—A priest/ess.

hallow—To make holy.

hamingja—"Mana"; magical power. See Chapter 8: Soul and After-life.

harrow—Altar. See Chapter 12: Holy Tools.

hugr—Thought, spirit, heart/mood. See Chapter 8.

idis, idises (ON dís, dísir)—Ancestral female spirits. Fully described in Chapter 6.

Indo-European—Relating to the common cultures, religions, and languages of the folk that migrated to Europe from the Caucasus Mountains. The Indo-European languages/cultures include Greek, Latin, Celtic, Germanic, Slavic, Baltic, Sanskrit, and Iranian. Like "Germanic," this is not a racial term, but rather a linguistic/cultural description.

leek—Any plant of the genus *Allium*—leeks, onions, chives, garlic, shallots, and so forth.

life-age (ON aldr)—Vital essence. See Chapter 8.

main, might—Aspects of psycho-physical strength. See Chapter 8.

mead—An alcoholic drink made from honey. Technically, only a drink made from honey alone is true mead, while the addition of fruit juice makes it a melomel and herbs make it a metheglin. For ritual purposes, however, any drink brewed with honey can be counted as a mead. Directions for brewing are given in Chapter 17: Crafts.

Middle-Garth (ON Midhgardhr)—The world of humankind.

mood (ON mód)—Bravery, soul. See Chapter 8.

Norns—The cosmic embodiments of *ørlog* and causality. See Chapter 2. The term "norn" is also used for female ghosts who embody and shape individual *ørlog*, such as the idises and walkyriges. See Chapters 6 and 8.

North Germanic—The languages deriving from the dialect spoken by the Germanic folk who stayed in Scandinavia. Old Norse/modern Icelandic, Danish, Swedish, and Norwegian are all North Germanic.

Odinism—An alternate name for Ásatrú, so called because Wodan/Ódhinn is the chief of the gods.

ørlög—"Ur-law" or "ur-layer"; destiny. See Chapter 8.

Poetic Edda—See Elder Edda (above).

Prose Edda—A prose compilation of Norse myths and poetic information, written by Snorri Sturluson ca. 1220 CE.

stead—A place.

Swart-Alf (ON Svartálfr)—A dwarf. See Chapter 6.

Teutonic—See Germanic (above).

thule—A ritual/inspired speaker. See Chapter 11.

thurse—A fairly stupid elemental giant. See Chapter 6.

troll—A general term for an ill-willing uncanny wight. See Chapter
   6.

troth—Loyalty; honesty; a pledge or compact; the keeping of same.

ur—A prefix meaning "proto-" or "primal."

völva—A seeress. See Chapter 11.

Walhall (ON Valhöll)—Valhalla, "Hall of the Slain."

walkyrige (ON valkyrja)—A valkyrie. See Chapter 6.

Wan, Wans (ON Vanr, Vanir)—God/esses of earth, water, and hidden wisdom.

warg (ON vargr)—Outlaw, wolf.

West Germanic—The languages spoken by the Germanic folk who
   migrated into the area of contemporary Germany ca. 200 BCE.
   German, Anglo-Saxon, English, Dutch, Frisian, and Yiddish
   (which is derived from Middle German—not to be confused
   with Hebrew, which is a Semitic language), are all West Germanic languages.

widdershins—Against the sun; counterclockwise. Used for drawing up might from the earth.

wight—A being of any sort.

wih- (ON vé)—Holy, in the sense of being filled with such an
   intense might that it is set apart from everyday things.

wod—Fury, inspiration, drunkenness.

Wod-Stirrer (ON Ódhroerir)—The mead of poetry.

Wyrd (ON Urdhr)—"That-which-is"; the Eldest Norn; the word
wyrd is also used for an individual's "fate."

Yggdrasill—"Ygg's Steed"; the World-Tree.

Younger Edda—See *Prose Edda* (above).

Book-Hoard

STUDY BOOKS

For the basic program of learning about the Norse god/esses and lore.

Crossley-Holland, Kevin. *The Norse Myths*. New York: Pantheon, 1980. This is the text to use if you have trouble finding a translation of the *Prose Edda*. Crossley-Holland retells, rather than translating, the myths, but remains fairly true to the originals. Except for his inclusion of the tale of Freyja and the Four Dwarves, this edition is especially suitable for children.

Davidson, H. R. Ellis. *Gods and Myths of Northern Europe*. Baltimore: Harmondsworth, 1964. A basic overview of the Norse mythology, with interpretation which is both wise and inspired. Assume that all books by H. R. Ellis Davidson are very highly recommended, whether they appear in this bibliography or not.

Gamlinginn. *The Ordhasafn of Gamlinginn*. Albuquerque: Hrafnahús, 1981. A dictionary of names, events, items, and generally most everything from Teutonic history, literature, and mythology. Can be ordered through the heathen magazines *Mountain Thunder* and *Idunna* (addresses at back of this book).

Hollander, Lee M. *The Poetic Edda*. University of Texas Press: Austin, 1986. This edition is available in most university bookstores. It is very poetic, but not particularly accurate; the Chisholm translation is much better to study from. However, Hollander's version does contain the heroic poems in addition to the mythological poems, so it is worth having.

Sturluson, Snorri; Anthony Faulkes (tr.; ed.). *Edda*. J. M. Dent & Sons: London, 1987. This is the basic *Prose Edda*. This edition is particularly useful because it includes the entirety of the sections on poetic composition, which many editions leave out.

SAGAS

Fell, Christine (tr.). *Egils saga*. J. M. Dent and Sons: London, 1975. Highly recommended, especially to Wodanists.

Hollander, Lee M. *Saga of the Jómsvíkings*. University of Texas Press: Austin, 1989. Recommended.

Magnusson, Magnus; Herman Pálsson (trs.). *Laxdaela Saga*. Penguin Books: New York, 1981.

Magnusson, Magnus; Herman Pásson (trs.). *Njal's Saga*. Viking Penguin Inc.: New York, 1987. Generally considered to be the best of the sagas.

Pálsson, Hermann; Paul Edwards (trs.). *Eyrbyggja Saga*. Viking Penguin Inc.: New York, 1989. Highly recommended. Contains more information on religious practice and ghosts than any other single saga.

Sturluson, Snorri; Erling Monsen, A. H. Smith (eds., trs.). *Heimskringla*. Dover Publications, Inc.: New York, 1990. The history of the kings of Norway, beginning with Ódhinn. Very highly recommended.

PRACTICAL TEXTS

Fitch, Ed. *The Rites of Odin*. Llewellyn Publications: St. Paul, 1990. This book has good pictures and a fair presentation of the Northern philosophy. Not highly recommended.

Pennick, Nigel. *Practical Magic in the Northern Tradition.* Aquarian Press: Wellingborough, 1989. An excellent compendium of Nordic, German, and British wisdom, with a strong emphasis on the folk tradition. His Germanic materials are better than his Celtic; his one gross error is his insistence on transsexualizing Mani, the male embodiment of the moon, into a "moon goddess," a fault which he also repeats in *Runic Astrology.* Recommended.

Thorsson, Edred. *A Book of Troth.* Llewellyn Publications: St. Paul, 1989. A skeleton outline for the practice of Germanic religion; uses Anglo-Saxon terminology, god-names, and so forth. There is very little detailed information on any subject in *Book of Troth:* it is more an outline for areas of study. It also includes rites for the seasonal blessings. Recommended.

Runic Studies

Many of these books have worthwhile religious material in them, but I have separated them out because their primary emphasis is on the runes.

Aswynn, Freyja. *Leaves of Yggdrasil.* Llewellyn Publications: St. Paul, 1990. A first-class discussion of the runes and runic magic, which is especially notable for the author's feminine perspective. Highly recommended.

Elliott, R. W. V. *Runes.* Manchester University Press: Manchester, 1959. One of the basic scholastic texts on runes.

Flowers, Stephen E. *Runes and Magic.* Peter Lang: New York, 1986. This work is the most important reference any serious runic worker can have, discussing the work of the eldest runemasters and the ways in which they empowered their magical formulae. It is currently out of print, but if letters to Peter Lang Publishing indicate a market, there is a chance that they may republish it. Extremely highly recommended.

Gundarsson, Kveldulf. *Teutonic Magic.* Llewellyn Publications: St. Paul, 1990. Detailed instructions on the use of the runes and on the practice of Germanic magic in general. For me to say more about it would be to brag greatly. Very highly recommended.

Moltke, Erik; Foote, Peter G. (tr.). *Runes and their Origin: Denmark and Elsewhere.* The National Museum of Denmark, 1981. Moltke is a "skeptical" runic scholar, that is, with little belief in the runes as a magical system. The worth of this book is that it is a compendium of runic inscriptions with a great deal of material from which a runic worker can draw much insight.

Thorsson, Edred. *FUTHARK: A Handbook of Rune Magic.* Samuel Weiser, Inc.: York Beach, 1984. Highly recommended.

SCHOLASTIC TEXTS

For intermediate religious study:

Chisholm, James (ed., tr.). *Grove and Gallows.* Rune-Gild: Austin, 1987 (?). In this work, Chisholm has collected every Greek and Latin reference to the religious and magical practices of the Germanic people and translated them. Very highly recommended; absolutely indispensable to any serious student of the Northern ways. At last notice, manuscript copies could still be ordered through the Rune-Gild.

Davidson, H. R. Ellis. *Myths and Symbols in Pagan Europe.* Syracuse University Press: Syracuse, 1988. Discusses Scandinavian and Celtic heathen beliefs. Also recommended by Tadhg Mac-Crossan, well-known Druid and author of *The Sacred Cauldron* (Llewellyn, 1991).

Davidson, H. R. Ellis. *The Road to Hel.* Greenwood Press: Westport, 1977. A detailed discussion of the Norse beliefs concerning the afterlife and the mystical journey down to the underworld. This is the book with which you should begin if you wish to research the path of the soul after death.

Gløb, P. V. *The Bog People.* Faber & Faber: Boston, 1977. Deals with the Iron Age practice of sinking human sacrifices in the bog. Highly recommended to anyone who is working with the cult of the Wans, especially Nerthus.

Grimm, Jacob; James Steven Stallybrass (tr.) *Teutonic Mythology* (4 vols.). Peter Smith: Gloucester, 1976. The best collection of heathen Germanic folklore, literary motifs, and religious practices ever made. An indispensable reference. Very highly recommended.

Grönbeck, Vilhelm. *The Culture of the Teutons.* Oxford University Press: London, 1931. The most beautiful book on the ways of our ancestors yet written, explaining the very roots of our thought and beliefs about worship, the soul, and the ways of the worlds. Very highly recommended.

Keyser, Rudolph. *Religion of the Northmen.* Charles B. Norton: New York, 1854. A useful collection of information on the Old Norse practice of heathen religion. Recommended.

Owen, Gale R. *Rites and Religions of the Anglo-Saxons.* Barnes & Noble: New Jersey, 1981. Discusses the practices of the heathen Anglo-Saxons. Recommended.

Phillpotts, Bertha S. *The Elder Edda and Ancient Scandinavian Drama.* University Press: Cambridge, 1920. An excellent reference if your kindred means to use holy folk-drama as a means of ritual practice and celebration of the great feasts of the year. Phillpotts discusses the ways in which each of the poems shows a dramatic structure and their possible enactments at seasonal/ritual feasts. Highly recommended.

Turville-Petre, E. O. G. *Myth and Religion of the North.* Greenwood Press: Connecticut, 1975. Probably the single most useful source for information about the religion of the North. Very highly recommended.

SCHOLASTIC TEXTS

Advanced study and miscellaneous.

Bauschatz, Paul. *The Well and The Tree.* University of Massachusetts Press: Amherst, 1982. The ultimate book on Wyrd and Germanic space-time concepts. Quite complex and requiring some work to fully understand: but when you have worked through it, you will *know* Wyrd as our ancestors did. Very highly recommended.

Braune, Wilhelm; E.A. Ebbinghaus (eds.). *Althochdeutsches Lesebuch.* Max Niemeyer Verlag: Tübingen, 1979. A collection of everything written in Old High German. Totally inaccessible to anyone who does not read German pretty well.

Chadwick, H. M. *The Cult of Othin*. Cambridge: University Press, 1899. The first major study done on the origins and history of Wodan and the practice of the cult; slightly dated now, but still the basic text. Recommended.

Dumézil, Georges. *Gods of the Ancient Northmen*. University of California Press: Berkeley, 1973. Dumézil discusses his tripartite theory in the Germanic context. This book needs to be read with considerable caution, as Dumézil was a very speculative thinker who often ignored historical and literary facts in favor of his own theories.

Flowers, Stephen E. *Sigurdhr: Rebirth and Initiation*. Rune-Gild: Austin, 1985. This text discusses *Völsunga saga* as a model for Germanic heroic initiatory structure and for the Germanic beliefs concerning rebirth. The best single description of the relationship between ancestry/clan and reincarnation. At last notice, manuscript copies could still be ordered through the Rune- Gild. Highly recommended.

Jung, Erich. *Germanische Götter und Helden in christlicher Zeit*. J.F. Lehmanns Verlag: München & Berlin, 1939. Discusses the survival of Germanic heathen belief through the Middle Ages to modern times. Highly recommended: it's worth slogging through the old Gothic script to read.

Helm, Karl. *Altgermanische Religionsgeschichte*. Carl Winters Universitätsbuchhandlung: Heidelberg, 1953. A compendium of the religious and magical practices of the Germanic folk. Good, although slightly dated. Particularly useful in that Helm separates the lore by the various branches of the Germanic folks, rather than using the Scandinavian material as his primary source and everything else as secondary. Highly recommended.

Marwick, Ernest W. *The Folklore of Orkney and Shetland*. B. T. Batsford Ltd.: London, 1986. Deals with folk-beliefs in an isolated set of islands which were originally settled by the Norse. Recommended.

Neckel, Gustav (ed.). *Edda*. Carl Winters Universitätsbuchhandlung: Heidelberg, 1914. The Old Norse text of the *Poetic Edda*.

Newall, Venetia. *An Egg at Easter*. Indiana University Press: Bloomington, 1971. Everything you ever wanted to know about the folklore and history of the decorated egg, together with really amazing pictures. Really very good.

Nordal, Sigurdur (ed.). Egils saga Skalla-Grímssonar. Hidh islenzka fornritafélag: Reykjavík, 1933. Old Norse text.

Nýlen, Erik; Jan Peder Lamm. *Stones, Ships, and Symbols*. Gidlunds Bokförlag: Stockholm, 1988. Describes the Gotlandic picture stones. Highly recommended.

Polomé, Edgar. *Essays on Germanic Religion*. Institute for the Study of Man: Washington, 1989. A collection of articles containing in-depth discussion of some of the more problematic elements in Norse myth (the Baldr legend, the identity of Ódhinn's brother Lódhurr, and so forth).

Storms, G. *Anglo-Saxon Magic*. Martinus Nijhoff: The Hague, 1948. A full discussion of the Anglo-Saxon charm spells and their magical theory, with the texts in both Old English and translation. Recommended.

Sturluson, Snorri; Finnur Jónsson (ed.). *Edda*. Nordisk Forlag: København, 1931. The text of the Prose Edda in Old Norse.

Wren, C.L.; W.F. Bolton (eds.). *Beowulf* (3rd ed.). Short Run Press Ltd.: Exeter, 1988. Old English text.

RESOURCES

The Ring of Troth is a religious organization which seeks to further the worship of the Northern god/esses and the study of the Germanic culture. It is a non-discriminatory organization which requires that its members affiliate for cultural and religious reasons rather than for racial and/or political reasons.

Membership in the Troth costs $24 a year, which includes a subscription to its quarterly publication, *Idunna*. Write to:

Ring of Troth
PO Box 25637
Tempe AZ 85285-5637

Followers of the Northern ways may also wish to subscribe to the independent Ásatrú publication *Mountain Thunder* ($18 for 5 quarterly issues in the U.S.A., $20 in Canada, and $26 abroad).

Mountain Thunder
1630 30th St. #266
Boulder CO 80303

STAY IN TOUCH

On the following pages you will find listed, with their current prices, some of the books now available on related subjects. Your book dealer stocks most of these and will stock new titles in the Llewellyn series as they become available. We urge your patronage.

To obtain our full catalog, to keep informed about new titles as they are released and to benefit from informative articles and helpful news, you are invited to write for our bi-monthly news magazine/catalog, *Llewellyn's New Worlds of Mind and Spirit*. A sample copy is free, and it will continue coming to you at no cost as long as you are an active mail customer. Or you may subscribe for just $10.00 in U.S.A. and Canada ($20.00 overseas, first class mail). Many bookstores also have *New Worlds* available to their customers. Ask for it.

Stay in touch! In *New Worlds'* pages you will find news and features about new books, tapes and services, announcements of meetings and seminars, articles helpful to our readers, news of authors, products and services, special money-making opportunities, and much more.

Llewellyn's New Worlds of Mind and Spirit
P.O. Box 64383-260, St. Paul, MN 55164-0383, U.S.A.
* * *

TO ORDER BOOKS AND TAPES

If your book dealer does not have the books described on the following pages readily available, you may order them direct from the publisher by sending full price in U.S. funds, plus $3.00 for postage and handling for orders *under* $10.00; $4.00 for orders *over* $10.00. There are no postage and handling charges for orders over $50.00. Postage and handling rates are subject to change. UPS Delivery: We ship UPS whenever possible. Delivery guaranteed. Provide your street address as UPS does not deliver to P.O. Boxes. UPS to Canada requires a $50.00 minimum order. Allow 4-6 weeks for delivery. Orders outside the U.S.A. and Canada: Airmail—add retail price of book; add $5.00 for each non-book item (tapes, etc.); add $1.00 per item for surface mail.

FOR GROUP STUDY AND PURCHASE

Because there is a great deal of interest in group discussion and study of the subject matter of this book, we feel that we should encourage the adoption and use of this particular book by such groups by offering a special quantity price to group leaders or agents.

Our special quantity price for a minimum order of five copies of *Teutonic Religion* is $39.00 cash-with-order. This price includes postage and handling within the United States. Minnesota residents must add 6.5% sales tax. For additional quantities, please order in multiples of five. For Canadian and foreign orders, add postage and handling charges as above. Credit card (VISA, MasterCard, American Express) orders are accepted. Charge card orders only ($15.00 minimum order) may be phoned in free within the U.S.A. or Canada by dialing 1-800-THE-MOON. For customer service, call 1-612-291-1970. Mail orders to:

LLEWELLYN PUBLICATIONS
P.O. Box 64383-260, St. Paul, MN 55164-0383, U.S.A.

Prices subject to change without notice.

TEUTONIC MAGIC
The Magical & Spiritual Practices of the Germanic Peoples
by Kveldulf Gundarsson

The word "Teutonic," once used exclusively to denote a specific German tribe, now encompasses a heritage as large and varied as Northern Europe. In *Teutonic Magic*, Kveldulf Gundarsson presents the theory and practice of Teutonic magic, a style of magic of particular interest to anyone of Northern European descent.

The focus of the book is primarily on the Elder Futhark, the magical rune alphabet. Gundarsson explains runic divination, rune magic, rituals for carving rune-tines and more. There is also a considerable amount of information on Teutonic ritual practice and the Teutonic worlds, gods and spirits.

For a country that almost had German as its official language, the United States has very little literature that preserves the ancient Germanic secrets. This book is perfect for those of Northern European ancestry seeking to recover their heritage. It will also interest those who have studied such subjects as Seax-Wicca, Odinism or Asatru. Written by a member of the Rune Gild and the Ring of Troth, it is entirely factual and full of rich Germanic spirit.

0-87542-291-8, 336 pgs., 6 x 9, illus., softcover   **$12.95**

NORTHERN MAGIC
Mysteries of the Norse, Germans & English
by Edred Thorsson

This in-depth primer of the magic of the Northern Way introduces the major concepts and practices of Gothic or Germanic magic. English, German, Dutch, Icelandic, Danish, Norwegian, and Swedish peoples are all directly descended from this ancient Germanic cultural stock. According to author Edred Thorsson, if you are interested in living a holistic life with unity of body-mind-spirit, a key to knowing your spiritual heritage is found in the heritage of your body—in the natural features which you have inherited from your distant ancestors. Most readers of this book already "speak the language" of the Teutonic tradition.

Northern Magic contains material that has never before been discussed in a practical way. This book outlines the ways of Northern magic and the character of the Northern magician. It explores the theories of traditional Northern psychology (or the lore of the soul) in some depth, as well as the religious tradition of the Troth and the whole Germanic theology. The remaining chapters make up a series of "mini-grimoires" on four basic magical techniques in the Northern Way: Younger Futhark rune magic, Icelandic galdor staves, Pennsylvania hex signs, and "seith" (or shamanism). This is an excellent overview of the Teutonic tradition that will interest neophytes as well as long-time travelers along the Northern Way.

0-87542-782-0, 224 pgs., mass market, illus.   **$4.95**

A BOOK OF TROTH
by Edred Thorsson
One of the most widespread of the ancient pagan revivals is Asatru or Odinism. Its followers seek to rekindle the way of the North, of the ancient Teutonic peoples. Until now, no book has completely expressed the nature and essence of that movement *A Book of Troth* is that book.

This is the most traditional and well-informed general guide to the practice of the elder Germanic folk way. An official document of the organization known as the "Ring of Troth," *A Book of Troth* is not a holy book or bible in the usual sense. Rather, it outlines a code of behavior and a set of actions, not a doctrine or a way of believing.

The first section of the book explores the various themes or teachings of the religion, laying the intellectual groundwork for the practice. The second section is the heart of the book since the Troth is a way of doing, not of believing. Here the reader actually learns how to practice the various religious observances with complete rituals, the tools needed, timing, and proper arrangement of the sacred space. The third part of the book outlines the curriculum and training program for qualifying as a priest, priestess or Elder in the Troth.

0-87542-777-4, 244 pgs., 5-1/4 x 8, illus., softcover   **$9.95**

THE NINE DOORS OF MIDGARD:
A Complete Curriculum of Rune Magic
by Edred Thorsson
The Nine Doors of Midgard are the gateways to self-transformation through the runes. This is the complete course of study and practice which has successfully been in use inside the Rune-Gild for ten years. Now it is being made available to the public for the first time.

The runic tradition represents a whole school of magic with the potential of becoming the equal of the Hermetic or Cabalistic tradition. The runic tradition is the northern or Teutonic equivalent of the Hermetic tradition of the south. *The Nine Doors of Midgard* is the only manual to take a systematic approach to initiation into runic practices.

Through nine lessons or stages in a graded curriculum, the books takes the rune student from a stage in which no previous knowledge of runes or esoteric work is assumed to a fairly advanced stage of initiation. The book also contains a complete reading course in outside material.

0-87542-781-2, 320 pgs., 5 1/4 x 8, illus.   **$12.95**

RUNE MIGHT
Secret Practices of the German Rune Magicians
by Edred Thorsson

Rune Might reveals, for the first time in the English language, the long-hidden secrets of the German rune magicians who practiced their arts in the beginning of the century. By studying the contents of *Rune Might* and working with the exercises, the reader will be introduced to a fascinating world of personalities and the sometimes sinister dark corners of runic history. Beyond this, the reader will be able to experience the direct power of the runes as experienced by the early German rune magicians.

Rune Might takes the best and most powerful of the runic techniques developed in that early phase of the runic revival and offers them as a coherent set of exercises. Experience rune yoga, rune-dance, runic hand gestures (mudras), rune singing (mantras), group rites with runes, runic healing, runic geomancy, and two of the most powerful runic methods of engaging transpersonal powers: the Ritual of the Ninth Night and the Ritual of the Grail Cup.

The exercises represent bold new methods of drawing magical power into your life—regardless of the magical tradition or system with which you normally work. No other system does this in quite the direct and clearly defined ways that rune exercises do.

0-87542-778-2, 176 pgs., 5-1/4 x 8, illus. $7.95

THE BOOK OF OGHAM
The Celtic Tree Oracle
by Edred Thorsson

Drink deeply from the very source of the Druids' traditional lore. The oghamic Celtic tradition represents an important breakthrough in the practical study of Celtic religion and magick. Within the pages of *The Book of Ogham* you will find the *complete and authentic* system of divination based on the letters of the Celtic ogham alphabet (commonly designated by tree names), and a whole world of experiential Celtic spirituality.

Come to understand the Celtic Way to new depths, discover methodological secrets shared by the Druids and Drightens of old, receive complete instructions for the practice of ogham divination, and find objective inner truths concealed deep within yourself.

The true and inner learning of oghams is a pathway to awakening the deeply rooted structural patterns of the Celtic psyche or soul. Read, study and work with the ogham oracle. . . open up the mysterious and hidden world within . . . and become part of the eternal stream of tradition that transcends the individual self. Come, and drink directly from the true cauldron of inspiration: the secret lore and practices of the ancient Celtic Druids.

0-87542-783-9, 224 pgs., 6 x 9, illus., glossary, softcover $12.95

Prices subject to change without notice.

LEAVES OF YGGDRASIL
Runes, Gods, Magic, Feminine Mysteries, Folklore
by Freya Aswynn

Leaves of Yggdrasil is the first book to offer an extensive presentation of Rune concepts, mythology and magical applications inspired by Dutch/Frisian traditional lore.

Author Freya Aswynn, although writing from a historical perspective, offers her own interpretations of this data based on her personal experience with the system. Freya's inborn, native gift of psychism enables her to work as a runic seer and consultant in psychological rune readings, one of which is detailed in a chapter on "Runic Divination."

Leaves of Yggdrasil emphasizes the feminine mysteries and the function of the Northern priestesses. It unveils a complete and personal system of the rune magic that will fascinate students of mythology, spirituality, psychism and Teutonic history, for this is not only a religious autobiography but also a historical account of the ancient Northern European culture.

0-87542-024-9, 288 pgs., 5 1/4 x 8, softcover $12.95

A PRACTICAL GUIDE TO THE RUNES
Their Uses in Divination and Magick
by Lisa Peschel

At last the world has a beginner's book on the Nordic runes that is written in straightforward and clear language. Each of the 25 runes is elucidated through no-nonsense descriptions and clean graphics. A rune's altered meaning in relation to other runes and its reversed position is also included. The construction of runes and accessories covers such factors as the type of wood to be used, the size of the runes, and the coloration, carving and charging of the runes. With this book the runes can be used in magick to effect desired results. Talismans carved with runescripts or bindrunes allow you to carry your magick in a tangible form, providing foci for your will. Four rune layouts complete with diagrams are presented with examples of specific questions to ask when consulting the runes. Rather than simple fortunetelling devices, the runes are oracular, empowered with the forces of Nature. They present information for you to make choices in your life.

0-87542-593-3, 192 pgs., illus., mass market $3.95

RUNE MAGIC
by Donald Tyson

Drawing upon historical records, poetic fragments, and the informed study of scholars, *Rune Magic* resurrects the ancient techniques of this tactile form of magic and integrates those methods with modern occultism so that anyone can use the runes in a personal magical system. For the first time, every known and conjectured meaning of all 33 known runes, including the 24 runes known as "futhark", is available in one volume. In addition, *Rune Magic* covers the use of runes in divination, astral traveling, skrying, and on amulets and talismans. A complete rune ritual is also provided, and 24 rune worlds are outlined. Gods and Goddesses of the runes are discussed, with illustrations from the National Museum of Sweden.

0-87542-826-6, 224 pgs., 6 x 9, photos, softcover   **$9.95**

RUNE MAGIC CARDS
by Donald Tyson

Llewellyn Publications presents, for the first time ever, Rune Magic Cards created by Donald Tyson. This unique divinatory deck consists of 24 strikingly designed cards, boldly portraying a Germanic "futhark" rune on each card. Robin Wood has illuminated each rune card with graphic illustrations done in the ancient Norse tradition. Included on each card are the old English name, its meaning, the phonetic value of the rune, and its number in Roman numerals. Included with this deck is a complete instruction booklet, giving the history and origins, ways of using the cards for divination, and magical workings, sample spreads and a wealth of information culled from years of study.

0-87542-827-4, 24 two-color cards, 48-pg. booklet   **$12.95**

THE THREE BOOKS OF OCCULT PHILOSOPHY
Completely Annotated, with Modern Commentary—The Foundation Book of Western Occultism
by Henry Cornelius Agrippa, edited and annotated by Donald Tyson
Agrippa's Three Books of Occult Philosophy is the single most important text in the history of Western occultism. Occultists have drawn upon it for five centuries, although they rarely give it credit. First published in Latin in 1531 and translated into English in 1651, it has never been reprinted in its entirety since. Photocopies are hard to find and very expensive. Now, for the first time in 500 years, Three Books of Occult Philosophy will be presented as Agrippa intended. There were many errors in the original translation, but occult author Donald Tyson has made the corrections and has clarified the more obscure material with copious notes.

This is a necessary reference tool not only for all magicians, but also for scholars of the Renaissance, Neoplatonism, the Western Kabbalah, the history of ideas and sciences and the occult tradition. It is as practical today as it was 500 years ago.
0-87542-832-0, 1,080 pgs., 7 x 10, softcover $29.95

THE SACRED CAULDRON
Secrets of the Druids
by Tadhg MacCrossan
Here is a comprehensive course in the history and development of Celtic religious lore, the secrets taught by the Druids, and a guide to the modern performance of the rites and ceremonies as practiced by members of the "Druidactos," a spiritual organization devoted to the revival of this ancient way of life.

The Sacred Cauldron evolved out of MacCrossan's extensive research in comparative mythology and Indo-European linguistics, etymology and archaeology. He has gone beyond the stereotypical image of standing stones and white-robed priests to piece together the truth about Druidism.The reader will find detailed interpretations of the words, phrases and titles that are indigenous to this ancient religion. Here also are step-by-step instructions for ceremonial rites for modern-day practice.
0-87542-103-2, 302 pgs., 5.25 x 8, illus., softcover $10.95

Prices subject to change without notice.

FIRE & ICE
Magical Teachings of Germany's Greatest Secret Occult Order
by S. Edred Flowers

The hidden beliefs and practices of German occultism have long held a strong fascination for the poet as well as the historian. The greatest of the modern German secret lodges—the Fraternitas Saturni—revealed neither its membership, its beliefs, nor its rites. Through a chance occurrence, the inner documents of this order were recently published in Germany. Fire & Ice is the first comprehensive study of these documents, and the inner workings of the FS which they reveal, to be published in any language.

This book relates the fascinating histories of the founders and leaders of the Fraternitas Saturni. You will witness the development of its magical beliefs and practices, its banishment by the Nazi government, and its many postwar dissensions and conflicts. The Saturnian path of initiation will be revealed in full detail, and the magical formulas which are included can be used for your own self-development as well as for more practical and concrete goals.

Fire & Ice throws a unique light on one of the world's darkest and most mysterious philosophical corners. No matter what your magical system may be, you will learn much from the adherents of *Fire & Ice!*

0-87542-776-6, 240 pgs., 5 1/4 x 8, illus., softcover $9.95

SECRETS OF THE GERMAN SEX MAGICIANS
A Practical Handbook for Men & Women
by Frater U∴ D∴

Secrets of the German Sex Magicians is an introduction to one of the oldest disciplines of a secret lore. It is a complete system of sex magick, in theory and practice—with exercises to develop related abilities for visualization, concentration, breath control, psychic energy arousal and flow. It discusses the fundamental principles in an open manner and with lack of prejudice. The dangers of sex magic and suitable protection measures are also carefully considered.

General interest in this branch of magic is still increasing, yet this may be the only practical introduction to the subject available. This book also differs from the others because, instead of the traditional male orientation, it regards men and women as having equal rights and status. For the sex magician, the sexual power is first of all a neutral energy, to be directed magically for any purpose. Experience shows that it is very suitable for "success-magic": charging talismans, amulets and sigils, and the achievement of professional, material and psychological advantages.

0-87542-773-1, 240 pgs. 6 x 9, illus., softcover $17.95

THE 21 LESSONS OF MERLYN
A Study in Druid Magic & Lore
by Douglas Monroe
For those with an inner drive to touch genuine Druidism—or who feel that the lore of King Arthur touches them personally—*The 21 Lessons of Merlyn* will come as an engrossing adventure and psychological journey into history and magic. This is a complete introductory course in Celtic Druidism, packaged within the framework of 21 authentic and expanded folk story/ lessons that read like a novel. These lessons, set in late Celtic Britain ca A.D. 500, depict the training and initiation of the real King Arthur at the hands of the real Merlyn-the-Druid: one of the last great champions of Paganism within the dawning age of Christianity. As you follow the boy Arthur's apprenticeship from his first encounter with Merlyn in the woods, you can study your own program of Druid apprentiship with the detailed practical ritual applications that follow each story. The 21 folk tales were collected by the author in Britain and Wales during a ten-year period; the Druidic teachings are based on the actual, never-before-published 16th-century manuscript entitled *The Book of Pheryllt*.
0-87542-496-1, 420 pgs., 6 x 9, illus., photos, softcover   **$12.95**

ANCIENT WAYS
Reclaiming the Pagan Tradition
by Pauline Campanelli, illus. by Dan Campanelli
Ancient Ways is filled with magick and ritual that you can perform every day to capture the spirit of the seasons. It focuses on the celebration of the Sabbats of the Old Religion by giving you practical things to do while anticipating the sabbat rites, and helping you harness the magical energy for weeks afterward. The wealth of seasonal rituals and charms are drawn from ancient sources but are easily performed with materials readily available.

Learn how to look into your previous lives at Yule . . . at Beltane, discover the places where you are most likely to see faeries . . . make special jewelry to wear for your Lammas Celebrations . . . for the special animals in your life, paint a charm of protection at Midsummer.

Most Pagans and Wiccans feel that the Sabbat rituals are all too brief and wish for the magick to linger on. *Ancient Ways* can help you reclaim your own traditions and heighten the feeling of magick.
0-87542-090-7, 256 pgs., 7 x 10, illus., softcover   **$12.95**

THE ANCIENT & SHINING ONES
World Myth, Magic & Religion
by D.J. Conway

The Ancient & Shining Ones is a handy, comprehensive reference guide to the myths and deities from ancient religions around the world. Now you can easily find the information you need to develop your own rituals and worship using the Gods/Goddesses with which you resonate most strongly. More than just a mythological dictionary, The Ancient & Shining Ones explains the magickal aspects of each deity and explores such practices as Witchcraft, Ceremonial Magick, Shamanism and the Qabala. It also discusses the importance of ritual and magick, and what makes magick work.

Most people are too vague in appealing for help from the Cosmic Beings— they either end up contacting the wrong energy source, or they are unable to make any contact at all, and their petitions go unanswered. In order to touch the power of the universe, we must re-educate ourselves about the Ancient Ones. The ancient pools of energy created and fed by centuries of belief and worship in the deities still exist. Today these energies can bring peace of mind, spiritual illumination and contentment. On a very earthy level, they can produce love, good health, money, protection, and success.

0-87542-170-9, 448 pgs., 7 x 10, 400 illus., softcover   **$17.95**

NORSE MAGIC
by D. J. Conway

The Norse: adventurous Viking wanderers, daring warriors, worshippers of the Aesir and the Vanir. Like the Celtic tribes, the Northmen had strong ties with the Earth and Elements, the Gods and the "little people."

Norse Magic is an active magic, only for participants, not bystanders. It is a magic of pride in oneself and the courage to face whatever comes. It interests those who believe in shaping their own future, those who believe that practicing spellwork is preferable to sitting around passively waiting for changes to come.

The book leads the beginner step by step through the spells. The in-depth discussion of Norse deities and the Norse way of life and worship set the intermediate student on the path to developing his or her own active rituals. Norse Magic is a compelling and easy-to-read introduction to the Norse religion and Teutonic mythology. The magical techniques are refreshingly direct and simple, with a strong feminine and goddess orientation.

0-87542-137-7, 240 pgs., mass market, illus.   **$3.95**

Prices subject to change without notice.

THE CRAFTED CUP
Ritual Mysteries of the Goddess and the Grail
by Shadwynn

The Holy Grail—fabled depository of wonder, enchantment and ultimate spiritual fulfillment—is the key by which the wellsprings of a Deeper Life can be tapped for the enhancement of our inner growth. *The Crafted Cup* is a compendium of the teachings and rituals of a distinctly Pagan religious Order—the *Ordo Arcanorum Gradalis*—which incorporates into its spiritual way of worship ritual imagery based upon the Arthurian Grail legends, a reverence towards the mythic Christ, and an appreciation of the core truths and techniques found scattered throughout the New Age movement.

The Crafted Cup is divided into two parts. The first deals specifically with the teachings and general concepts which hold a central place within the philosophy of the *Ordo Arcanorum Gradalis*. The second and larger of the two parts is a complete compilation of the sacramental rites and seasonal rituals which make up the liturgical calendar of the Order. It contains one of the largest collections of Pagan, Grail-oriented rituals yet published.

0-87542-739-1, 420 pgs., 7 X 10, illus., softcover   **$18.00**

THE BOOK OF GODDESSES & HEROINES
by Patricia Monaghan

The Book of Goddesses & Heroines is an historical landmark, a must for everyone interested in Goddesses and Goddess worship. It is not an effort to trivialize the beliefs of matriarchal cultures. It is not a collection of Goddess descriptions penned by biased male historians throughout the ages. It is the complete, non-biased account of Goddesses of every cultural and geographic area, including African, Egyptian, Japanese, Korean, Persian, Australian, Pacific, Latin American, British, Irish, Scottish, Welsh, Chinese, Greek, Icelandic, Italian, Finnish, German, Scandinavian, Indian, Tibetan, Mesopotamian, North American, Semitic and Slavic Goddesses!

Unlike some of the male historians before her, Patricia Monaghan eliminates as much bias as possible from her Goddess stories. Envisioning herself as a woman who might have revered each of these Goddesses, she has done away with language that referred to the deities in relation to their male counterparts, as well as with culturally relative terms such as "married" or "fertility cult." The beliefs of the cultures and the attributes of the Goddesses have been left intact.

Plus, this book has a new, complete index. If you are more concerned about finding a Goddess of war than you are a Goddess of a given country, this index will lead you to the right page. This is especially useful for anyone seeking to do Goddess rituals. Your work will be twice as efficient and effective with this detailed and easy-to-use book.

0-87542-573-9, 456 pgs., 6 x 9, photos, softcover   **$17.95**

Prices subject to change without notice.

GLOBAL RITUALISM
Myth & Magic Around the World
by Denny Sargent
Your mythology helps you fit into the universe. It tells the story, via tales of
gods, spirits and heroes, of who you are, why you came to be and of your role
in the cosmic dance of spiritual evolution. Rituals are sets of actions that
translate these myths into dynamic reality. Tragically, today, our racial,
national and personal mythologies and rituals are breaking down and disap-
pearing; as a result, many people are losing their roots and sense of spiritual
and psychological participation in the unfolding of the world.

What can you do to escape this "mythic alienation?" *Global Ritualism* provides
the resources and guidance so that you can weave and synthesize your *own*
personal mythology from the world's stories. It points out and analyzes the
common themes and components of "higher" ritual from Hati to Egypt so
you can construct your own vibrant living spiritual rituals and mythologies
with full understanding of what you are doing. By managing your own spiritual evolution, you are on your path to a more fulfilling life.
0-87542-700-6, 250 pgs., 7 x 10, 130 photos, 24 color pgs $19.95

EARTH GOD RISING
The Return of the Male Mysteries
by Alan Richardson
Today, in an age that is witnessing the return of the Goddess in all ways and
on all levels, the idea of one more male deity may appear to be a step backward. But along with looking toward the feminine powers as a cure for our
personal and social ills, we must remember to invoke those forgotten and
positive aspects of our most ancient God. The Horned God is just, never cruel;
firm, but not vindictive. The Horned Gods loves women as equals. He provides the balance needed in this New Age, and he must be invoked as clearly
and as ardently as the Goddess to whom he is twin.

The how-to section of this book shows how to make direct contact with your
most ancient potentials, as exemplified by the Goddess and the Horned God.
Using the simplest of techniques, available to everyone in any circumstance,
Earth God Rising shows how we can create our own mystery and bring about
real magical transformations without the need for groups, gurus, or elaborate
ceremonies.
0-87542-672-7, 224 pgs., 5 1/4 x 8, illus., softcover $9.95